THE ENGLISH PRIMERS
(1529-1545)

ā al this lande of the whiche I haue
spoke so ofte to yow shal I gyue to
yowr seaders & ye shall possesse it a
longe tyme. Ā fyrt this prayr y lor
de was peased so y he powered not
forth his wrath vpō his people as
he sayde y he wolde haue done.
Consideringe therfor prayr to be of
sich efficacy & vertue / & y Christe
hīselfe cōmāded vs to praie also i
theis perellous daies: me thinketh
it necessary y y laye people shulde
haue y prayers moste cōueniēt for
this tyme / which prayers at y psa.
& y in Englishe y their faithe mi
ght y more encrese & their deuotiō
also by whose prayers y wrath of
god mought be peased & we myght
be restored into his fauour & grace
whiche graunte vs ower father by
his sōne Iesu Christe. AMEN.

Lorde
opene
thow
my li
ppes: & then shal
my mouthe she
w forthe thy pr
ayse.

O god bende thi
selfe into my hel
pe: lorde haste y to helpe me. O lory
be to y fath / to the sonne / and to the
holi goste. Ā sit was in the begin
ninge: as it is now & ev shalbe amē
¶ Prayse ye the lorde.
¶ Inuitatoriū. Mathei. 11.
Come vnto me all ye that labour ād
are laden: and I shall refreshe yowe.
Ome and let vs ioyfully ge
ue thankes vnto y lorde: let
vs reioyse in god ower saviour / let
E

JOYE'S *ORTULUS ANIME* OF 1530

The Earliest Extant Printed English Primer
(Showing the beginning of Matins)

*(Reproduced from the unique copy in the
British Museum by permission of the Trustees)*

THE
ENGLISH PRIMERS
(1529-1545)

Their Publication and Connection with the
English Bible and the
Reformation in England

by

CHARLES C. BUTTERWORTH

Philadelphia
UNIVERSITY OF PENNSYLVANIA PRESS
1953

Preface

COMPARATIVELY few people have even a little knowledge of the English Primers which are the subject of this book. This poses a problem for the writer; for while the hardier sort of readers will see a challenge in the prospect, others may perhaps be frightened off. Moreover, to invite the casual inquirer to take up the study of a topic about which he knows so little is not only to involve him in a web of continual explanation; it is also to arouse his natural skepticism and lead him to ask, "To what end?—why seek to rescue these Primers from the repose of that oblivion, perhaps deserved, which has been slowly gathering upon them? And why obtrude them at this late hour upon our notice?"

It is a legitimate question. Who will be interested in these Primers? Well, some fifteen years ago the writer was not so much as aware of their existence, and *he* has found them interesting! To the bookseller and librarian they are reckoned as scarce and valued treasures. To the educator they are of importance as manuals in the rudimentary art of learning to read; to the churchman they are significant as formative experiments in the liturgy of the Church of England; to the historian they mirror the cross-currents of religious controversy that troubled the reign of Henry VIII. Finally, to the general student of literature they are not only books that were widely and popularly read in the second quarter of the sixteenth century, but they also constitute a little-known chapter in the early development of the English Bible.

While it is hoped that these several phases of interest will each be reflected in the present volume, it was specially for the reason that the Primers were connected with the history of the English Bible that I first came to investigate them, and it may be said that their connection with the Scriptures emerges as the dominant theme of this work. When I wrote

The Literary Lineage of the King James Bible (1941), I decided that the Primers ought to be accorded their rightful
place in the story of the English versions; and it was while
contemplating a revision of that book that I discovered how
very little was actually known of the first printed English
Primers, and withal how inaccurate were some of the things
I had set down in print about them. In the meanwhile, also,
the rise of the use of microfilm as an instrument of scholarly
research has made it feasible to consult the extant Primers
themselves as by a sort of proxy.

The earliest of the printed English Primers thus constitute
a territory largely unexplored. Till now only a few books have
been published dealing with the materials treated in this work.
The pioneering was done by Edward Burton, who in 1834
published at Oxford a book called *Three Primers Put Forth
in the Reign of Henry VIII.*[1] Burton's first edition included
a preface of more than sixty pages reviewing the history of the
Primers. While not by any means free of errors, it marked,
for its day, a brave beginning. Later, in 1901, Edgar Hoskins
published a monumental catalogue covering the entire field
from 1478 to 1867, nearly four centuries. This catalogue, elab-
orately indexed, was called *Horae Beatae Mariae Virginis or
Sarum and York Primers with Kindred Books,* and embodied
nearly all the statistical information then available. Needless
to say, anyone who now delves into this field is under very
great obligation to the labors of these two men.[2]

For there is little else to consult save the Primers themselves. Quite recently there has appeared a book by Miss Helen
C. White, of the University of Wisconsin, called *The Tudor
Books of Private Devotion* (1951), which allots several chapters to the Primers, especially to those editions represented in
the collection of the Huntington Library in California. Another work, still awaiting publication, has been compiled by

---

[1] These three, which Burton reprinted in full or in synopsis, are discussed in
Chapters X, XV, and XIX of this present work.

[2] Mention should also be made of the careful investigation by William Maskell in
volume III of his *Monumenta Ritualia Ecclesiae Anglicanae* (1882), though he deals
almost entirely with the earlier history of the Primer, i.e., before the introduction
of the printing press.

Edwyn C. Birchenough, Esq., giving bibliographical details of "The Prymer in English." I am indebted to him for graciously affording me opportunity of going over with him the typescript of his bibliography. Some years ago Mr. Birchenough also contributed to *The Library* a useful and helpful article on the Primers.[3]

Beside these, there have been published a few specialized studies, such as *Martin Bucer and the English Reformation,* by Constantin Hopf, or *William Shakspere's Petty School,* by T. W. Baldwin, in which certain of the Primers are singled out for specific attention. But in the more general histories of the period the Primers are either tacitly ignored or dismissed with a few casual observations, sometimes incorrect.

Since some of those who have thus taken cognizance of their existence were Anglican clergymen, it is only natural that they should have treated the Primers in relation to the advent of the Book of Common Prayer, laying emphasis on the liturgical element. In this work, however, as was said, the accent is rather on the contents of the Primers and their relation to the English Bible. We shall also chronicle the circumstances of their publication: for not only did the Primers serve as active agencies in disseminating the "New Learning" of the Reformation; they were in turn also affected by the ebb and flow of its fortunes under the English King. Our story starts from obscure beginnings, with unique or little-known early printings, and records the rise of a multiplicity of texts and editions. The whole story covers little more than twenty years and culminates in the publication of an authorized Primer put forth in 1545, which was a direct forerunner of the Book of Common Prayer.

From 1530 to 1540, and particularly in the middle years of that decade, momentous changes were taking place in the realm of England, full of meaning both for the subsequent history of the nation and for the formation of an English Bible. Concerning any distant time, the more we can learn about it, and the more exact our knowledge in any particular field of

[3] See section C of the Bibliography at the end of this volume.

its activity, the more certainly will the seemingly unrelated bits of information we have gleaned be found to fit together into a satisfying picture of what really went on in those days. So may this book bring some measure of enlightenment to bear upon the age of Tyndale and More, of Cranmer and Coverdale, of Luther and Henry VIII, and of the establishing of the English Bible.

C. C. B.

Mount Airy, Philadelphia
October, 1952.

Acknowledgments

A BOOK such as this is not written without friendly assistance from many people, which it is a pleasure to acknowledge. Most of the research was carried on in libraries; and let it be said that no class of persons known to the writer is marked by a higher degree of professional zeal to render unselfish service than is the staff of a well-equipped library: they willingly go to great lengths to be of help and to answer questions, and every aid is placed at one's disposal.

I deeply appreciate the generous coöperation of friends at home and of correspondents abroad. Among the latter I am specially indebted to Rev. J. F. Mozley, our leading authority on William Tyndale, who was kind enough to bring to my notice the recent discovery of the *Hortulus Animae* of 1530, and who has unstintingly supplied much valuable information concerning that period. I am also thankful for the loyal collaboration of Miss Sylvia L. England, who undertook research on my behalf in the British Museum and elsewhere in London. Mr. William A. Jackson, of Harvard University, and Mr. F. S. Ferguson, formerly of Quaritch's, have been longsuffering in the answering of difficult queries. Other valuable bits of knowledge have come through the kindness of Professor Edward C. Ratcliff, of St. John's College, Cambridge, and Rev. Constantin Hope, of Oxford.

Nearer home, I have often had the privilege of consulting with Mr. Rudolf Hirsch at the library of the University of Pennsylvania, where much of the exploration was conducted. And for much kindly and intelligent assistance, both in personal conference and in the criticism of the manuscript, I am most grateful to Dr. Allan G. Chester, of the English Department of the University. Will the many others who rendered services not mentioned here, please accept the writer's grateful acknowledgment?   C. C. B.

Contents

Chapter		Page
I.	The Primer and the Book of Hours (1494-1527)	1
II.	The First Printed English Primer (1529-1531)	11
III.	George Joye and the *Hortulus Animae* (1530-1533)	18
IV.	Contents of the English Hortulus (1530)	28
V.	An English Primer Is Printed in London (1530-1534)	47
VI.	Special Features of the Marshall Primer (1534)	59
VII.	Thomas Godfray's Primer (1534-1535)	70
VIII.	Robert Redman's *Prayers of the Byble* (1535)	79
IX.	Redman's Primer After the Use of Sarum (1535)	87
X.	William Marshall's *Goodly Primer* (1535)	104
XI.	The Composite Primer of John Gough (1536)	118
XII.	The Rouen Edition in English and Latin (1536)	131
XIII.	Primers with Liturgical Epistles and Gospels (1537)	140
XIV.	The Effect of the Injunctions and the Royal Proclamation (1538)	162
XV.	Bishop Hilsey's *Manual of Prayers* (1539)	181
XVI.	Editorial Enigmas (1540)	200
XVII.	Stress and Counter Stress (1541-1542)	221
XVIII.	Steps Towards Uniformity (1543-1545)	237
XIX.	The Authorized Primer of Henry VIII (1545)	256

Appendices

I

	Page
(A) Martin Luther and the Marshall Primers	279
(B) The Two Issues of Mayler's Primer of 1540	286

II

Synopsis of Scriptural Passages in the Primers   288

III

Specimens of Variant Readings: 291
    1. Psalm 51:1-12   293
    2. The Lord's Prayer (Matt. 6:9-13)   301

Bibliography

A. Primers, Books of Hours, Etc.   305

B. Kindred Books Belonging to the Period:
    1. Bibles, Testaments, Psalters, Etc.   310
    2. Prayers, Devotions, Commentaries, Etc.   313
    3. Proclamations, Statutes, and Books Issued by
        Authority   316
    4. Miscellaneous   318

C. Books Touching on the History of the Primers   319

D. Books on Related Subjects   322

Indexes

I. Index of Scriptural Citations   327

II. General Index   329

List of Illustrations

I. THE *Ortulus Anime* OF 1530, showing the beginning
of Matins   *Frontispiece*

II. THE *Ortulus Anime* OF 1530, showing a hymn and
the eighth Psalm   41

III. THE GRAFTON-WHITCHURCH PRIMER OF 1540   210

IV. THE AUTHORIZED PRIMER OF HENRY VIII (May 29, 1545)   264

xiii

THE ENGLISH PRIMERS
(1529-1545)

Chapter I

The Primer and the Book of Hours
(1494-1527)

THE story of the English Primers bears directly on the history of the English Bible at a time when the task of translating the Scriptures was still in a formative stage. The Primers also afford a fascinating field for study in themselves. They played a vital part in the instruction of children and of others. They illustrate how the English tongue at length supplanted the Latin, not only in the classroom but in the services of the Church as well. They reflect, at times with vivid detail, the changing pressure of stress and strain that marked the political and ecclesiastical history of England in the second quarter of the sixteenth century, a period of great reforms and controversies.

At the same time they throw fresh light on the current practice of that generation of printers who carried forward the pioneering work of William Caxton and Wynkyn de Worde. We can see, through these little books, what sort of problems the publishers were then confronted with and how they sought to overcome them. For the Primers enjoyed an extensive popularity: more than 180 editions of them appeared during the crucial years from 1525 to 1560—some in Latin, some in English together with the Latin, and many in English alone. No wonder the printers took an interest in a product that could absorb an average of five new editions a year!

The Primers contained, along with other devotional matter, a significant amount of Scripture—from forty to sixty Psalms in their entirety as well as familiar passages from the New Testament and occasional excerpts from the Old. When it is realized that several of the English Primers preceded the

1

first printing of a complete English Bible—the Coverdale Bible (October 4, 1535)—and when it is borne in mind that the selections in the Primers were among the best-known and best-loved portions of the Bible, it will be seen how these Primers had their part in shaping the English text. In certain passages they gave entirely independent renderings of Scripture, a few of which enjoyed a continuous identity and welcome as late as 1550.

After the Church of England was separately established and had issued its own Book of Common Prayer (1549), the function of the Primer was gradually superseded. Yet it is significant that during the reign of Queen Mary (1553-58) the Primer was one of the few books allowed to circulate in England containing portions of the Scriptures in the English tongue.

What, then, were these Primers? The name itself was given by the people of England, as early as the fourteenth century, to what was known in Latin as the Book of Hours of the Blessed Virgin Mary. Compiled from materials used in church and monastery, the Primer was intended specially for the laity, to guide the devout layman in his private daily devotions or to help him bear his part in the services of the Church.

In the medieval Church certain prayers and devotions were assigned to certain portions of the day, and these 'Hours'—consisting mainly of prayers, psalms, hymns, and adorations of the Virgin or of the Cross—were as follows: *Matins* and *Lauds* were said at dawn; *Evensong* (or Vespers) and *Compline* were said in the evening; while during the day, which began at six in the morning according to biblical reckoning, there were four designated hours—*Prime, Terce, Sext,* and *None*—observed at six and nine A.M., noon and three P.M., respectively. The last three of these were usually called simply Third, Sixth, and Ninth Hours.

Moreover, in various parts of Western Christendom the more prominent religious centers developed their own usages in observing the canonical Hours. In England the form of service that gained the widest acceptance was the usage of

Salisbury, generally known as the 'use of Sarum' after the ancient name of that town. Thus Caxton, the first English printer, is known to have published Books of Hours in Latin, or *Horae ad usum Sarum*.

The Primer was thus a religious handbook; though not an official ecclesiastical publication, it was based on the usage of the Church. There appears to have been originally little or no strict regulation of its exact contents. It was from the beginning a compilation, but it always centered about the Book of Hours. It generally included an almanac or table to find the date of Easter, and a calendar of saints' days; it often gave the Paternoster, Creed, and Ten Commandments, and sometimes included brief expositions on such themes; it might contain one or several edifying treatises, and any number of approved special prayers and graces, as well as some form for the confession of sins; but its essential features were the regular observances or offices of the Church, given in shortened form for the use of laymen and comprising the canonical Hours, the Litany, the Dirge, the Seven Penitential Psalms, and so on.

It is supposed by some that the name *Primer* was derived from *Prime*, the first of the Hours. But most authorities believe that from the start the name was applied to what was naturally regarded in many households as their first book (*liber primarius*), either because it was in such constant service or, more likely, because it was useful in learning to read, especially in Latin. No evidence at hand is of sufficient antiquity to settle the question.

Sometimes, if the Primer was intended particularly for the use of children, the alphabet would be included to assist them in their reading. Chaucer, in his Prioress's Tale (lines 1688-91, 1706-33), tells of the legendary counterpart of Hugh of Lincoln, going as a small child to school—

> That lerned in that scole yeer by yere
> Swiche manere doctrine as men used there,
> That is to seyn, to syngen and to rede,
> As smale children doon in hir childhede. . . .

This litel child, his litel book lernynge,
As he sat in the scole at his prymer,
He *Alma redemptoris* herde synge
As children lerned hir antiphoner;
And, as he dorste, he drough hym ner and ner,
And herkned ay the wordes and the noote,
Til he the firste vers koude al by rote.

Noght wiste he what this Latyn was to seye,
For he so yong and tendre was of age,
But on a day his felawe gan he preye
Texpounden hym this song in his langage, . . .

"Now certes I wol do my diligence
To konne it al, er Cristemasse is went,
Though that I for my prymer shal be shent
And shal be beten thries in an houre,
I wol it konne, our lady for to honoure."

Chaucer does not tell us whether this "prymer" would have been in Latin or in English, but it must have been a very elementary textbook since the child was of tender years, unable to comprehend the Latin words of the hymn. It would have been in manuscript of course, but it may not have been, properly speaking, a Book of Hours; rather perhaps some simple manual of instruction in the rudiments of religion, beginning with an alphabet.[1]

Yet we do find as early as the time of Chaucer and Wycliffe —that is, in the latter half of the fourteenth century—regular Books of Hours in manuscript form translated into the English vernacular. Several of these have been edited and made available in print to modern readers.[2] They were full-scale Primers after the use of Sarum. So far as one can judge, they were not

[1] Such an elementary textbook is reproduced in photograph in G. A. Plimpton's *The Education of Chaucer, Illustrated from the Schoolbooks in Use in his Time* (New York, 1935).

[2] For example, William Maskell included "the Prymer in English" in his *Monumenta Ritualia Ecclesiae Anglicanae* (vol. III, second edition, Oxford, 1882), and Henry Littlehales edited two such manuscripts, the first entitled *The Prymer, or Prayer-Book of the Lay People in the Middle Ages, in English dating about 1400 A.D.* (London, 1891), and the other for the Early English Text Society (Orig. series, 105, 109) with a similar title though the Primer is a different one, *The Prymer or Lay Folks Prayer Book* (London, 1895-97).

specially designed for the instruction of children. They included the Hours of the Virgin from Matins to Compline, as well as the Litany and Dirge with other supplementary material as described above. Though crude in their wording, they were the legitimate forerunners of later Primers printed in English after the use of Sarum.

As was natural, the vernacular version given in these manuscripts, embracing selections from the Psalms or other portions of the Scripture, showed the influence of the Wycliffite translation of the Bible. Nevertheless, in a manuscript of about 1400, edited by Littlehales in 1891, the Bible passages show many independent and interesting turns of speech, as we shall have occasion to observe later on.

Soon after the time of Wycliffe, and as a result of the stir aroused by his insistence that the Bible be put into the hands of English readers, the Church authorities imposed a series of severe and suppressive restrictions on the English translation of the Scriptures. A council or convocation, convened at Oxford under Archbishop Arundel, decreed in the so-called 'Constitutions of Clarendon' (1408) that "no one shall in future translate on his own authority any text of holy scripture into the English tongue" under penalty of excommunication.[3] And this prohibition continued in effect for over a hundred years. Indeed, not until William Tyndale departed from his native land for the sake of circumventing this ecclesiastical veto did any avowed portions of the Scripture appear in English. Consequently, after the introduction of printing, from 1490 to about 1523 the text of the Psalms and of other biblical passages included in the Primers was printed exclusively in Latin.

This did not prevent the early printers from making use of the English tongue for such features of their Primers as were not scriptural. It was customary, for example, to print English rubrics over the Latin prayers. Certain other non-

[3] The most careful treatment of this subject is that by Margaret Deanesly in *The Lollard Bible* (Cambridge, Eng., 1920); see especially pp. 295, 296.

scriptural items might be printed in English altogether. According to Hoskins,[4] a Primer published by Caxton's successor, Wynkyn de Worde, about 1494 contained an English rendition of "The Fifteen O's," a popular series of supplications ascribed to St. Bridget, which Caxton had previously published in separate form; and this same Primer also gives some half-dozen other "devout prayers" in their English dress.[5]

In this way, more and more as the years passed, the natural demand of English readers emboldened the publishers to increase the Engish content of their Latin Primers. For example, in a Primer which he printed in 1513 (*S.T.C.* 15914), Wynkyn de Worde introduced a paraphrase of the Ten Commandments versified in English rhymes. In the next year, in a Primer published by Richard Pynson (*S.T.C.* 15917), though the title of the book is still in Latin, we find on the title-page this quaint little English prayer, which is sometimes sung as a hymn even at the present day:

> God be in my heed [i.e., *head*]
> And in myn vnderstandynge
> God be in myn eyen
> And in my lokynge
> God be in my mouthe
> And in my spekynge
> God be in my herte
> And in my thynkynge
> God be at myn ende
> And my departynge.

In the same year, 1514, we have also a Primer published at Paris particularly for the use of children (*S.T.C.* 15916) and so designated in the Latin title, which begins: "Hore b*e*ate marie vi*r*ginis ad vsu*m* Saru*m* pro pueris." This is one of the first Primers in print to contain the alphabet, which was pre-

---

[4] *Horae Beatae Mariae Virginis or Sarum and York Primers with Kindred Books and Primers of the Reformed and Roman Use together with An Introduction* (London, 1901), by Edgar Hoskins, is the most thorough study of the Primers that has been made hitherto.

[5] This Primer is No. 7 in Hoskins' list. It is No. 15875 in *A Short-title Catalogue of Books Printed in England, Scotland, & Ireland And of English Books Printed Abroad 1475-1640,* by Pollard and Redgrave (London, 1926), hereinafter referred to as *S.T.C.*

ceded, as was customary, by the sign of the cross (✠) known as Christ-cross or criss-cross.

How useful and suitable the Primers were for the education of children will become clearer if we recall certain facts. Books were still comparatively scarce in those days, and many people were illiterate. The materials used in teaching children how to read were prescribed by the usages of the Church, and the immediate goal of all formal education was to fit the scholar to master his Latin grammar.[6] Consider, for example, the educational program devised by John Colet, the illustrious Dean of St. Paul's and the friend of Erasmus and Thomas More.

About 1509, Colet, one of the most advanced thinkers of his day, founded the present St. Paul's School and set up rules and standards for its government. He appointed as headmaster William Lily, whose Latin Grammar was famous all through the sixteenth century. In a manuscript of the *Statuta*[7] he wrote for the school in 1511, Colet says:

> . . . for my entent is by thys scole specially to increase knowlege and worshipping of god and our lorde Crist Jesu and good Cristen lyff and maners in the Children And for that entent I will the Chyldren lerne ffirst aboue all the Cathechyzon in Englysh and after [i.e., *afterward*] the accidence that I made or sum other yf eny be better to the purpose to induce chyldren more spedely to laten spech And thanne Institutum Christiani hominis which that lernyd Erasmus made at my request and the boke called Copia of the same Erasmus . . .

What exactly Colet meant by this Catechism in English, which was to be taught first of all, we can only conjecture. It seems to have been a booklet containing a synopsis of the Creed and a few other rudiments of Christian doctrine.[8] Similarly, the *Institutum* of Erasmus, to which Colet refers, was a series of Latin stanzas composed on the Creed, the Sacraments, and

[6] For detailed discussion of primary education in the middle part of the sixteenth century, see T. W. Baldwin, *William Shakspere's Petty School* (Urbana, Illinois, 1943).

[7] Printed in R. B. Gardiner, *The Admission Registers of St. Paul's School* (London, 1884), p. 382.

[8] What purports to be the text of a 'Catechyzon' by Colet is given in an article by M. Reu entitled "Religious Instruction of the Young in the Sixteenth Century" published in *Lutheran Church Review*, vol. 34, p. 577 (1915).

so on; it survives in an early edition printed by Wynkyn de Worde in 1510 (*S.T.C.* 5162). But of Colet's own *Accidence* (or handbook of Latin inflections) there is no earlier imprint now remaining than an edition published in 1527—eight years after his death—in which it was coupled with materials taken from Lily's Latin Grammar.[9]

This little volume of 1527 is interesting on account of the preliminary material that Colet provided for it, showing what he deemed suitable for elementary instruction; such as "The artycles of the Faith," "The seuen sacramentes," "Preceptes of lyuynge," etc., all in English. We observe, however, that the Lord's Prayer and the Ave Maria are given only in Latin. Colet also wrote what he called "A lytell proheme to the boke," which concludes rather sweetly:

Wherfore I praye you al lytel babys, al lytel chyldren, lerne gladly this lytel treatyse, and commende it dylygently vnto your memoryes. Trustynge of this begynnynge that ye shal procede and growe to parfyt lyterature, and come at the last to be grete clarkes. And lyfte vp your lytel whyte handes for me, whiche prayeth for you to god. To whom be al honour and imperyal maieste and glory. Amen.

It is significant that as late as 1527 the Lord's Prayer was not printed in this schoolbook in its English form. This makes even more remarkable the fact that in November 1523 Wynkyn de Worde dared to publish in London a Primer which contained not only the Creed and a form of confession in English, but also "the Pater noster in englysshe." At about the same time a Dutch bookseller living in London, Pieter Kaetz, imported another Primer which was probably printed in Antwerp, also containing an English version of the Lord's Prayer.[10]

These two are probably the earliest printings of the Lord's Prayer in English. They are notable in that they anticipate by nearly two full years Tyndale's first attempt to publish the Gospel of Matthew in English. The version in de Worde's

[9] *S.T.C.* 5542. The full title of the book is *Ioannis Coleti Theologi, Olim decani diui Pauli, aeditio, una cum quibusdam G. Lilij Grammatices rudimentis.* The text of it has been reprinted in *Shakespeare Jahrbuch*, vol. 44, p. 65.

[10] See Hoskins, Nos. 62, 63; *S.T.C.* 15934, 15935; see also below, Appendix III.

Primer shows some similarity to the wording given in the older manuscript Primers of Wycliffe's time; it reads:

Our fader that arte in heuen sanctyfyed be thy name. Thy kyngdome come to vs. Thy wyll be done in erth as in heuen. Our dayly breed gyue vs to daye & forgyue vs our dettys as we forgiue our detters. And lede vs not into temptacyon. But delyuer vs from euyll. Amen.

The version in the Kaetz Primer is not quite the same and betrays the influence of a foreign printer's hand in its spellings:

⫷ The pater noster in Engelys.
Owre father that art in heuen holy bemade thy name thy kyngdome muste come tho vs/ thy wyl be done in erthe as in heuen/ our dayly brede gyue vs to daye and forgyue vs our synnes/ as we forgyue other/ and suffer nat vs tho be tempted/ but delyuer vs from all euyll. Amen.

Thus the English tongue began to make its way into the Latin Primers.

Finally, we come upon what appears to have been the first printed Book of Hours to have an English title and to be designated as a Primer, even though the bulk of its contents was still in Latin. According to the *Short-title Catalogue,* this volume was put forth in Paris on December 13, 1527, by the French publisher, François Regnault (*S.T.C.* 15955). It was several times reprinted. It featured particularly a great many woodcuts, under most of which were supplied four-line jingles in English expounding the artist's subject. The title also stresses the point that the Latin prayers and devotions are printed out at length instead of being cited merely by their familiar opening words. It reads:

⫷ This prymer of Salysbury vse is set out a long without ony serchyng/ with many prayers/ and goodly pyctures in the kalender/ in the matyns of our lady/ in the houres of the crosse/ in the .vii. psalmes/ and in the dyryge [i.e., *dirge*]. And be newly enprynted at Paris. 1527.

On this same title-page appears also the little prayer beginning:

God be in my hede
And in myn vnderstandynge.

These, be it borne in mind, were all Roman Catholic Primers and almost entirely in Latin. But by this time the leaven of the Protestant Reformation was at work; Tyndale's New Testament in English had been published on the continent in 1526, and the importation of Lutheran and 'heretical' books was flooding into England from the Low Countries, to the distress of the clergy.

Chapter II

The First Printed English Primer
(1529-1531)

IT IS in connection with the suppression of heresy that we
first hear of a printed English Primer. Such a Primer was
said to have been in the possession of Sir Thomas Hitton,
whose shadowy figure comes to life in the pages of Tyndale
and Thomas More and in the somber annals of John Foxe. In
the first edition of Foxe's *Actes and Monuments of these latter
and perillous dayes* (1563) we read on page 460:

> Nowe the memoriall of Thomas Hytten calleth me backe again out
> of Skotlande into England, of whome there remaineth nothing in
> wryting but only his name, but that William Tindall in his Apologye
> againste More, and also in another booke entituled the practice of
> prelates, dooth once or twyse make mention of him by way of digression.

In the "Kalender" in the front of his book, under March 9,
Foxe assigns Hitton's martyrdom to the year 1530.

In the latter part of that same year Tyndale's *The practyse
of Prelates* was published, probably by Johannes Hoochstraten
in Antwerp, to become part of the long, hard-fought controversy between More and Tyndale. In this work (fol. R6)
Tyndale writes:

> And More amonge his other blasphemies in his Dialoge sayth that
> none of vs dare abyde by our fayth vnto the deeth: but shortlye ther-
> after/ god to proue More/ that he hath euer bene/ euen a false lyare/
> gaue strength vnto his servaunte syr Thomas Hitton/ to confesse and
> that vnto the deeth the fayth of his holie sonne Iesus/ whiche Thomas
> the bisshopes of Caunterburye & of Rochester/ after they had dieted
> and tormented him secretlye murthered at Maydstone most cruellye.

As Foxe recorded, Tyndale also included a similar but shorter
allusion to Hitton in *An answere vnto Sir Thomas Mores*

11

dialoge (fol. I5), which was printed at about the same time.[1]

More was not loth to take up Tyndale's challenge, and in *The confutacyon of Tyndales answere* (1532) he refers slightingly to Hitton as a doubtful-looking character who, while trying to flee the country, had been apprehended by the authorities on the suspicion that he was a thief, only to be turned over to the archbishop as a heretic.

By the time Foxe brought out his final edition of the *Actes and Monuments,* with the title changed meanwhile to *The Ecclesiasticall Historie* (1583), he had procured from somewhere additional information about Thomas Hitton which he submits in an appendix (p. 2136) under the heading: "The trouble and examination of Thomas Hitton Martyr, with his examinations, answers, condemnation and Martyrdome, An. Dom. 1529. the 20. of February." In the course of this summary he says of Hitton:

[The Archbishop] demanded of him from whence he came, and whether he intended to haue gone, if he had not bene intercepted. . . . Then the Bishop asked him if he had euer bene beyond the seas before, and what bookes he had brought ouer. He answered, that he had bene once beyonde the seas before, and had brought certaine bookes with hym from thence, namely, two new Testaments, and one Primer in English.

Recollecting that it was often the practice in those days to date the new year from Lady Day, March 25, then by this reckoning Hitton's martyrdom occurred about February 20, 1530, according to our calendar. This not only accords with Foxe's previous entry in his 1563 edition, but it also coincides with Tyndale's statement that Hitton was apprehended shortly after More had published his *Dialogue*. This volume was

---

[1] Hitton is mentioned also in the foreword of two other works edited by Tyndale. One is *The examinacion of Master William Thorpe* (S.T.C. 24045), in which it is said of Hitton that he "was brente/ now thys yere/ at maydstone yn Kent." The printer was probably Hoochstraten and the publication, though undated, belongs to 1530. The other is *The prayer and complaynt of the Ploweman vnto Christ* (S.T.C. 20036) which has a foreword headed "w. T, to the reder." In this foreword, which is dated "The last daye of February. An. M.ccccc,xxxi," Tyndale refers to the early Christian martyrs and then to "that innocent man of god/ Thomas Hytton/ whom wyllyam werham/ bysshoppe of Canturbury/ & Iohan Fyssher/ bysshoppe of Rochester murthered at Maydeston in Kente. Anno. M.d.xxx. for the same trouth."

dated by its printer as having appeared in June 1529. If from all this we conclude that Hitton was put to death in the early part of 1530, and that he had previously been across the Channel and had brought home an English Primer, it is reasonable to reckon that the first Primer in English must have been printed on the Continent before 1530, probably not long before but in the year 1529. No known copy of this edition has survived.

This conclusion is borne out by the earliest official citation of an English Primer.

On May 24, 1530, at the instance of King Henry VIII, an assembly of prominent churchmen was held for the purpose of combating and suppressing heretical books. In charge of the meeting were William Warham, Archbishop of Canterbury, and Cuthbert Tunstall, recently appointed Bishop of Durham, who was officiating in Wolsey's stead, since the Cardinal had come to grief in the preceding autumn. In attendance were many dignitaries, including Sir Thomas More, the Lord Chancellor.

A "Publick Instrument" drawn up by this assembly cited specific errors and heresies from seven different books including a Primer.[2] Aside from the Primer, whose date has not been ascertained, the other volumes can all be identified as having been published from 1527 to 1529. It is likely that the complaints were prepared by Thomas More, who had been granted special permission to keep and read forbidden books for the sake of refuting them.

Against the Primer it was charged specifically (fol. 190^v) that in "the kalender of the prymar" it is said that "God toke Enoche away (that is to say) he departed owt of this worlde like other men." To this, objection is raised (in Latin): "primo male vertit, nam scriptura dicit, transtulit, non abstulit"; in

---

2 Preserved in the register of Archbishop Warham in the library at Lambeth Palace (fol. 188), this document has been printed in Wilkins' *Concilia Magnae Britanniae et Hiberniae* (edition of 1737, vol. III, p. 727). Besides the Primer, the books cited were: *The Parable of the Wicked Mammon* and *The Obedience of a Christian Man*, by Tyndale; *The Revelation of Antichrist*, by John Frith; *The Sum of the Holy Scripture* and *A Supplication for the Beggars*, by Simon Fish; and *An Exposition on the Seventh Chapter of First Corinthians*, perhaps by William Roy.

other words, that the Scripture is poorly translated, for the word is not *abstulit* ("took away") but *transtulit* (or "translated"). Since the complaint calls attention to a faulty rendering, it was certainly an English Primer that was being criticized. Another fault cited from "the kalender" had to do with David and Nathan; while against the Primer itself it was objected: "He puttith in the boke of the vii. Psalmes, but he leveth owt the whole latanye [i.e., *litany*] / by which apperith his erronyous opynyon agenst praying to saint*es*."

Such a Primer must therefore have been known in England early in 1530. Indeed, it is not beyond belief that the very copy that Thomas Hitton had brought into the country might have been confiscated among his effects and turned over to More for examination and rebuttal. But assuming that such a Primer had appeared in 1529, there were probably other copies of it smuggled into England by the time the assembly met in May 1530. For any Primer in English printed at that early date would certainly have been suspected as 'heretical.'

In June a royal proclamation was issued forbidding the possession of the forementioned books "and diuers other bokes made in the englisshe tonge, and imprinted beyonde the see." Confiscated books were burned, and persecution of offenders went forward with some severity. Foxe, in his edition of 1563, recounts the accusation, trial, and execution of several martyrs who refused to recant. Among the more prominent was Richard Bayfield, at whose hearing on November 20, 1531, the Bishop of London, John Stokesley, presided. The charges against Bayfield included his having read a veritable library of forbidden books both in Latin and in English, all carefully listed. An excerpt from the list as enumerated by Foxe (p. 483) shows:

The new testament in english *with* an introduction to the Romains. The parable of the wicked Mammon. Thobedience of a christen man. A.B.C. of Thorpes. The sum of scripture. The primer in English. The Psalter in English. A dialoge betwixt the gentleman & the plowman.

In his "Newly recognised and inlarged" edition of 1570, Foxe mentions many lesser persons who decided to abjure their heretical opinions rather than suffer death by fire. At least two of these were charged with having owned an English Primer (see vol. II, pp. 1188, 1191). One was Walter Kiry, servant:

Hys Article: That hee, after the kynges proclamation, had and vsed these bookes: the Testament in Englishe, the Some of Scripture, a Primer and Psalter in Englishe hydden in hys beadstraw at Worcester.

This was in 1531. Another, in the following year, was John Wyly the elder:

Item, the foresayd *Iohn Wyly* the elder, had a Primmer in English in hys house, and other bookes.

Also, he had a younge daughter of x. yeres olde, which could render by hart ye most parte of ye 24. chap. of S. Mathewe: . . .

Pursuant to several proclamations on the subject of heresy, the bishops were authorized to denounce certain books by name and forbid the reading of them by all persons in their diocese. Several lists of such books still remain, but it is difficult to determine their exact dates.[3] Time and strife have blurred the historical details, and standard authorities are not in agreement over them. Foxe, for instance (*ibid.*, vol. II, p. 1159), prints "A Proclamation for resistyng and withstandyng of most dampnable heresies" which he assigns to the year 1529. Wilkins in his *Concilia* (vol. III, p. 757) dates the same proclamation 1530. The *Short-title Catalogue* (No. 7772) says that it was printed by Pynson in 1528; and Robert Steele in *Tudor and Stuart Proclamations* (p. 13) concludes that it was issued prior to March 6, 1529.

After giving the text of this proclamation, Foxe remarks that books forbidden in general terms by the edict itself were afterward specified by name in the registers of the bishops. He thereupon appends a list of such books as were in English,

[3] For example, Wilkins in his *Concilia* (vol. III, p. 717) prints a list several columns long which he took from a manuscript in the British Museum (Ms. Cott. Cleop. F.ii, fol. 54). He admits the manuscript is undated but confidently assigns it to 1529. Actually, certain of the books on the list were not published till at least 1530. Robert Steele in *Transactions of the Bibliographical Society* (vol. XI, p. 214) assigns the list to a Provincial Council held in 1532. One item near the end of the list is "Hortulus Animae, in sermone Anglicano" (compare the list of Bishop Stokesley cited below).

amounting to sixteen in all, which he says was copied from the register of the Bishop of London. Now in 1529 the Bishop would have been Cuthbert Tunstall; but Tunstall was transferred to the see of Durham in February 1530. Again, some of these sixteen books (so far as we know) did not appear in print until 1530; so the list is certainly not as early as the proclamation. Yet it is a comparatively early list and contains at least three items of special interest, which Foxe records as follows: (1) "Mattens and Euensong, vij. Psalmes, and other heaue*n*ly Psalmes, with the commendations, in Englishe"; (2) "Dauides Psalter in Englishe"; (3) "Hotlulus animae in Englishe"—the last being a misprint for *Hortulus Animae* or "Garden of the Soul."

A fuller and somewhat later list of prohibited books was promulgated by John Stokesley, who succeeded Tunstall as Bishop of London in July 1530. On the first Sunday in December,1531, he authorized the preacher at Paul's Cross, in London, to denounce certain books publicly by name. The list comprises thirty items; among them many that Stokesley had just previously cited against Richard Bayfield at the latter's trial for heresy. Along with works by Tyndale, Frith, Roy, and Fish, we come upon "Ortulus anime, in Englissh," "The Prymer in Englissh," and "the Psalter in Englissh."[4]

If we compare Foxe's list, dating from about 1530, with the corresponding entries on Bishop Stokesley's list in the following year, we can see at once that, for two of the three items we are considering, the listings are identical—that is, for the Psalter and the *Hortulus Animae*. What of the other item, which Stokesley calls the Primer in English but which Foxe lists as "Mattens and Euensong, vij. Psalmes, and other heaue*n*ly Psalmes, with the commendations, in Englishe"? Are

---

4 Stokesley's list is preserved in manuscript in the Lambeth Palace library (Ms. 306, fol. 65). It was printed in a miscellany edited by F. J. Furnivall for the Early English Text Society, entitled *Political, Religious, and Love Poems* (Orig. Series, no. 15, edition of 1903, p. 62). It is reprinted with modern spelling in *Letters and Papers, Foreign and Domestic, of the Reign of Henry VIII* (vol. V, Appendix, p. 768, no. 18) and is given in a different arrangement in Anderson's *Annals of the English Bible* (edition of 1845, vol. I, pp. 305, 306). Anderson's list says that the Psalter in English is by Joye, but in the original manuscript the author is not named.

these two different books, or two different entries for the same book?

We know that an English Primer was outlawed by the ecclesiastical commission of 1530; and we may be quite sure that any Primer in English at that time would have been considered suspect by the authorities. Had there been *two* such publications current, in addition to the Hortulus, surely both would have been entered on Bishop Stokesley's list. It is therefore virtually certain that both the entries listed above refer to the same book, the lost edition of the Primer of 1529. Indeed, it is possible that Foxe may have been citing the actual synopsis of the contents as it would have appeared on the title-page of the book itself; for it was a usual custom to print underneath the title "The contentes of this boke." And in view of what Sir Thomas More had alleged before the assembly of bishops, it may also be significant that Foxe's descriptive entry should include no mention of either Litany or Dirge.

Having said these things, we have said all that is known at the present time about the first printing of the English Primer, a copy of which Sir Thomas Hitton confessed he had brought over with him from "beyonde the seas."

Chapter III

George Joye and the *Hortulus Animae*
(1530-1533)

THE Psalter which Foxe listed as "Dauides Psalter in Englishe" and which the Bishop of London proscribed as a forbidden book is undoubtedly to be identified with a small volume published on January 16, 1530, bearing the title:

> The Psalter of Dauid in Englishe purely and faithfully translated aftir the texte of Feline: euery Psalme hauynge his argument before/ declarynge brefly thentente & substance of the wholl Psalme.

Only three copies are known to remain. Since this was the first English Psalter to appear in print (*S.T.C.* 2370) and since it figures prominently in the history of our subject, some brief account of it is in order.

According to its colophon, it issued from the press of Francis Foxe in "Argentine," which was the printers' quarter in the city of Strassburg:

> Emprinted at Argentine in the yeare of oure lorde 1530. the .16. daye of Ianuary by me Francis foxe.

But scholars have now ascertained that some of the colophons in proscribed books of that period were fictitious, designed to throw heretic-hunters off the scent. On the following day, for instance, William Tyndale issued his first edition of the Book of Genesis ostensibly from the press of Hans Luft in Marburg; but modern research attributes these "Marburg" imprints to the press of Johannes Hoochstraten in Antwerp.[1] Likewise with the Psalter of 1530; it is now ascribed to the press of Marten de Keyser, also of Antwerp.

[1] See "Notes on English Printing in the Low Countries (Early Sixteenth Century)" by M. E. Kronenberg, in *The Library* (Series IV, vol. 9, p. 139).

It can now be set down as certain that the English version printed in this Psalter was the work of George Joye.[2] Joye, a graduate of Peterhouse, had been one of the group of reformers that met at the White Horse tavern in Cambridge. Near the end of 1527, when he was in danger of apprehension by agents of Cardinal Wolsey, he decided it would be prudent to flee from England. Later he appears to have been associated with Tyndale for several years in Antwerp as a rather intractable collaborator. He was active both as a controversialist and as a translator of Scripture, particularly of those books of the Old Testament, from Psalms to Lamentations, on which Tyndale himself was not at work.

It should be observed that Joye's translation in the Psalter of 1530 is said to have been based upon the text of Feline, that is, of "Aretius Felinus," a pseudonym used by the German scholar Martin Bucer. The latter had composed a new Latin version of the Hebrew Psalter, along with a commentary, which had just been published in Strassburg in September 1529. It is typical of Joye that his free-handed translation of Bucer's Latin Psalms should have been got ready by the following January.[3]

Concerning the *Hortulus Animae* in English—likewise listed by Stokesley and Foxe as among the books proscribed—it was long assumed that no copy of it had survived. Aside from a few contemporary references, such as the one by Foxe, no mention of it as actually existing is to be found in any subsequent history of that period. Perhaps the book was involved in further obscurity through some confusion that arose over the terms *Hortulus* and *Primer:* sometimes they were used in contrast; sometimes they were regarded as virtually the same.

2 About 1531 Joye published a reply to *The letters which Iohan Ashwel . . . sente secretely to the Bishope of Lyncolne (S.T.C.* 845), in which he wrote as follows [fol. B3]: "Vvherfore the scripture comenly ioyneth these two wordes/ mercie & Truthe or faithfulnes togither especially in the Psalmes as I noted in the argument of the .89. Psalme/" etc. The "argument" prefixed to this Psalm in the Psalter of 1530 bears out Joye's assertion. For further discussion of this Psalter and its authorship, see Butterworth, *The Literary Lineage of the King James Bible 1340-1611* (Philadelphia, 1941), pp. 64-67.

3 For an account of the Latin Psalter of Bucer, or "Aretius Felinus," see C. Hopf, *Martin Bucer and the English Reformation,* chapter VI (Oxford, 1946).

The traditional Hortulus was a compilation or anthology of miscellaneous prayers, strongly imbued with Catholic dogma. It was current especially in Germany, where the followers of Luther repudiated it as superstitious. The earliest such specimens to be printed belonged to the fifteenth century. At Augsburg they went under the German name of *Seelenwurzgarten;* at Strassburg under the Latin name of *Ortulus anime.*[4] Afterward a few editions embodying the use of Sarum were printed for the English trade. As late as June 1531 the *Short-title Catalogue* (No. 15972) records such an edition printed at Paris. This was an extensive anthology including certain features of the Primer, with an elaborate title announcing that it contained the Hours of the Virgin, the Seven Psalms, and the Dirge.[5] Now it is clear that so orthodox a Bishop of London as John Stokesley was in 1531 would not have objected to a Hortulus such as this; what he would then have denounced as heretical must have been a Protestant edition in the English tongue. But, as was said, no such edition was known to have survived.

It was consequently an event wholly unlooked-for when, in February 1949, a unique copy of the Hortulus in English was offered for sale in London and promptly purchased by the British Museum. It is quite a small volume of 144 leaves (or 288 pages), similar in size and in style of type to the Psalter of 1530.[6] Coming from a private library in Cornwall, the owner

---

[4] See Hain, *Repertorium Bibliographicum* (1826), Nos. 8936 and 14584-87. Later editions appeared at Leyden and Antwerp. The University Library at Cambridge has a Latin edition according to Sarum usage, *Hortulus anime ad vsum insignis ecclesie Sarum,* published at Antwerp in 1524. The next year a Dutch edition was put forth at Antwerp, *Ortulus anime in duytsche vol schone oracien* (see Nijhoff and Kronenberg, *Nederlandsche Bibliographie van 1500 tot 1540,* No. 1138).

[5] Listed also in Hoskins' catalogue as No. 86, its title runs: ¶ *Hortulus anime recenter diuersis/ ac odoriferis flosculis decoratus: cum additionibus varijs . . . adiectis* secundum *vsum Sarum. horis beate Marie virginis/ septem psalmis atque vigilijs.* [Etc.] Hoskins, mistakenly assigning it to the year 1528, gives a synopsis of such of its contents as were not usually contained in the Primers (*op. cit.,* pp. 33, 135-47). An incomplete copy is preserved in the Lambeth Palace library, and a still less perfect one at Cambridge University.

[6] Collation: Signatures A-S in eights (excepting J, of course, which was not in use). In this unique copy one leaf (fol. B3) is missing from the calendar of saints. The work is unrecorded in the 1926 edition of *S.T.C.* Very recently a comprehensive bibliographical note on "The *Hortulus Animae* in English, 1530" was contributed by Mr. L. A. Sheppard to *The Library* (Series V, vol. VI, p. 109); it appeared while the present chapter was in the publisher's hands.

of which prefers not to disclose his name, this Hortulus was at one time, near the end of the seventeenth century, in the choice collection of Narcissus Luttrell and bears the stamp of his monogram. Its colophon, which resembles that of the English Psalter, reads:

⟨ Emprinted at Argentine in the yeare of ower lorde .1530. by me Francis Foxe Praise ye the lorde.

Like the Psalter, it was really printed in Antwerp by Marten de Keyser, and it is undoubtedly identical with the Hortulus prohibited by Stokesley in December 1531.

Of this book, the earliest extant English Primer in print, it can be asserted that it too was the work of George Joye. Its title, in a style typical of Joye, reads as follows:

⟨ Ortulus anime. The garden of the soule: or the englisshe primers (the which a certaine print*er* lately corrupted/ & made false to the grete sclaunder of thauthor & greter desayte [i.e., *deceit*] of as many as boughte and red the*m*) newe corrected and augmented.

From this curious title we are warranted in drawing certain definite inferences. Some other printer than de Keyser (perhaps Hoochstraten, or Christopher van Endhoven) had "lately" put forth a previous edition by the same author— probably toward the end of 1529, as was surmised in our last chapter. Though the new publication, therefore, was plainly a revised edition, it is by no means certain that the printing which preceded it was likewise entitled *Ortulus anime;* for Joye delighted in variety. The earlier edition may simply have been called *The Primer in English,* or conceivably its title-page may have been worded as Foxe recorded: "Mattens and Euensong, vij. Psalmes, and other heauenly Psalmes, with the commendations, in Englishe."

Apparently Joye made no distinction in his own thought between a Primer and a Hortulus. His use of the plural term on the new title-page—"the englisshe primers"—might simply import that he was thinking of the books themselves which had been "boughte and red" in their "corrupted" state.

What the faults were, in the earlier edition, which Joye

deemed prejudicial to his reputation we have no way of knowing; but his temperament was apt to be touchy, and it looks as
if he had heard that the Lord Chancellor ("to the grete
sclaunder of thauthor") had singled out certain heretical
errors in the "kalender of the prymar" of 1529. He could easily
have been informed of what took place through one of his
Cambridge associates, Hugh Latimer, who was present at the
assembly of 1530. Nor would it have been incompatible with
his disposition to try to pass off upon his printer whatever
faults might have been discovered. At any rate, in the new
edition of the Hortulus the calendar has been revised and is
free of those defects of which Sir Thomas More complained.

Below the title comes a partial summary of the contents of
the Hortulus, and from it we can gain some notion of how the
new edition was "corrected and augmented." It reads:

> Firste there is a newe kalendarie
> The passion of owre saviowre Christe: orderly with the con-
> cordance of the fower euangelistes
> A fruteful instruction for children
> A christen dialoge ful of lerning
> A general confession before god
> Ther is a psalm. added to the euensong & Iudica me to the
> complene with Salue re. and a colete [i.e., *collect*] therto.
> The seuen psalmes.
> The psalmes of the passion.
> The commendacions.
> Al the psalmes newe corrected

If the changes in the "newe kalendarie" were made out of
sensitiveness to the censures of More, then it is logical to date
the new Hortulus as belonging to the latter half of 1530, or
at least later than May, when the "Publick Instrument" was
drawn up condemning heretical books. We can imagine Joye's
further discomfiture, when he came to inspect this revised
edition, on finding that the Psalms of the Passion,[7] announced

---

[7] Secular folk may need to be informed that the Psalms of the Passion commenced
with Ps. 22 and ended with Ps. 31:5. The Seven Penitential Psalms were Ps. 6, 32, 38,
51, 102, 130, 143. Primers strictly in accordance with the use of Sarum (which Joye's
were not) would also include the Fifteen Psalms (Ps. 120-134). "Commendations"
consisted of Ps. 119 in full, sometimes with the addition of Ps. 139. See below,
Appendix II.

on the title-page, were left out of the new volume entirely.

Before discussing in detail the contents of this Hortulus, we should first review the evidence connecting the name of George Joye with the authorship of these earliest printed English Primers.

In 1532 Thomas More, carrying forward his controversy with Tyndale, published *The confutacyon of Tyndales answere,* in the preface to which he alludes to the English Primer. His remarks recall the complaints he had laid before the assembled clergy in 1530. After dealing with the writings and activities of Robert Barnes, a prominent heretic who had recanted, More continues:

> Then haue we ferther yet besyde Barns boke, the a b c for chyldren. And bycause there is no grace therin/ lest we shold lakke prayours, we haue the prymer, and the ploughmans prayour, and a boke of other small deuocyons, and then the hole psalter to. . . . For the Prymer and Psalter, prayours & all/ were translated and made in this maner, by none other but heretykes.
>
> The Psalter was translated by George Iay [i.e., *Joye*] the preste, yt [i.e., *that*] is wedded now/ and I here say the Primer to, wherein the seuen psalmes be set in wythout the lateny, leste folke shold pray to sayntes. And ye Dirige is lefte out clene/ lest a man myght happe to pray theron for hys fathers soule.

This is the earliest coupling of Joye's name with the English Primer.

Proceeding further, More takes up the case of Thomas Hitton, who (it will be remembered) suffered martyrdom in the early part of 1530:

> In theyr calendar before theyr deuout prayers, they haue sette vs a new saynt/ syr Thomas Hitton the heretyke that was burned in Kent, of whom I shall tell you more after. Hym haue they set in on saynt Mathy is euen [i.e., *St. Matthias' eve*], be the name of saynt Thomas the martyr.

A page or two farther on, More repeats this:

> . . . they haue as I sayde sette his name in the calendar byfore a boke of theyr englyshe prayours, by the name of saynt Thomas the martyr, in the vigyle of the blessed apostle saynte mathye, the xxiii. daye of February/ . . .

In the light of More's observation, it is a point of uncommon interest to discover that in the 1530 Hortulus, alone of all surviving books of the period, the calendar of saints' days reads for the 23rd of February: "Sei*n*te Thomas mar." The inclusion of Thomas Hitton among the saints and martyrs is typical of the boldness, or rashness, that characterized the publications of both Joye and Tyndale in the year 1530. It is true, of course, that More does not here refer to the book as a Primer; he calls it first "theyr deuout prayers" and second "a boke of theyr englyshe prayours": but these descriptions would not be out of place for a little book that More may have known only as a Hortulus. Indeed, it might also have been the Hortulus to which More was referring, a couple of pages earlier, as "a boke of other small deuocyons." Nevertheless it is barely possible that "Saint Thomas" [Hitton] may likewise have been inserted in the calendar of some other little volume, now lost, such as the one listed by Foxe as "Godly prayers" or *"Piae precationes."*[8]

But Joye's connection with the translation of the Primer does not rest entirely on More's hearsay. In the Hortulus of 1530 occurs a group of four prayers taken from the Bible, the first of which comprises the last five verses of chapter 63 and all of chapter 64 of Isaiah. This is provided with an elaborate title (fol. I8ᵛ) in Joye's best manner:

(Here foloweth an effectuous prayer very nedefull for theis laste and perellous dayes to be saide withe teares and depe sighes frome the botome of ower harte, the prayer of the Prophete Esaye in the .lxiij. and .lxiiij. Chapiters of his prophesyes for the restoringe of Christes poore Chirche scaterde abrode withe persecution, forsaken and brente.

Whether or not the 1529 edition of the Primer also contained this prayer of Isaiah we cannot tell. Since it was not featured among the contents printed on the title-page of the revised edition, we may surmise that the prayer was not a novelty when it appeared in the Hortulus.

---

[8] It seems more likely, however, that this refers to some edition of Luther's *Betbüchlein*, which was known in Latin as *Enchiridion piarum precationum* (see below, in Appendix I).

In the following year, May 10, 1531, Joye published a translation of the entire Book of Isaiah (*S.T.C.* 2777), but this time under his own name and entitled simply: "The Prophete Isaye/ translated into englysshe/ by George Ioye." The colophon, which is fictitious, ascribes the printing to Balthassar Beckenth (a mouth-filling name!) supposedly of Strassburg; but modern scholars assign the publication to the press of de Keyser in Antwerp. In this volume we find that the prayer of Isaiah, described above, is given a different rendering from that in the Hortulus; yet the style of both is characteristic of Joye and there are many resemblances between the two versions, as may be seen in the opening verses of chapter 64:

(H30)—I wolde thou woldist alto breke   hevens & come downe
(GJI) —I wolde thow woldest cleve insondre heaue*n* and come downe

wons y*t* theis hyllis might   melte awaye at thy presens   as in y*e*
        that the hylles mought melte awaye at thy presens even as agenst

brenynnge of a consuminge fyer/   where even water
an hotte fyer a*n*d that the violent tyra*n*ts mought be set a fyer as is water

boyllethe oute   fyer: that thi name might   be knowne to   thyne
inflammedde with fyer: that thy name mought be knowne vnto thy

enymes/ & theis vngodly might   be shamed and troubled at thi
enymes/ a*n*d these haithen mought   tremble at thy

presens.
presens.

Next in the chain of evidence are two letters dated April 29, 1533, which speak of this particular prayer of Isaiah and the diversity of its rendering. The first letter was written by Joye to Hugh Latimer, who had recently been summoned before the Bishop of London on account of his unorthodox views; the other, which is addressed to "Brother Will*i*am," is signed by John Coke, an English merchant residing in Antwerp. Nevertheless, I believe the second letter was originally penned by Joye.[9]

9 Preserved in the Public Record Office, the contents of these two letters are reported in *Letters and Papers of the Reign of Henry VIII* (vol. VI, nos. 402 and

In the letter to Latimer, Joye writes:

... William Tindall receyvyd a letter frome John ffrythe wherin John ffrythe is somewhat offendyd for that I wrote secretly a letter to one that askyd me a questione as concernyng why I translatyd the prayer of Esaie not all alyke in the hortulus and in the prophete wherin incidently I shew by the diuersitie of translacions what profytt may come therof/ ... this letter of myne I desyre youe to see/ for it is so paynefull to me to wryte that I coulde not leve any copye with me/ ye shall haue yt among the bretherne I cannot tell his name that askyd me the questione and vnto whome I sent the letter. but I sent itt by one William hill Mr. Cosens servaunt. I beseche youe gett itt and rede ytt and send me your Iudgement and mynd in the matter/ for ffrythe wrytythe that it is lyke to gendre dissensione. ... this berer shall gett yt youe callyd henry smythe. I wolde wryte vnto youe more but this berer goethe hastely hense and may not tarye me/ ... god preserue youe/ the 29 daye of apryll

Yours as he was wont   george Joye

The portions omitted here would show that the "secret" letter contained a statement of Joye's views on the Resurrection, which were at variance with those of Tyndale and Frith.
    The second letter reads as follows:

Brother William I hartely commend me vnto youe/ I was not content that ye breake so sodenly awaye and tooke not wythe youe my letters as ye promised me. Syr I sent a letter as concernyng the answer to him that wolde know why the prayer of Esaie so varyed in the primer and the prophete and left my self no copye of whiche letter it is thought that dissensions among the wyse bretherne begynne to growe. I pray youe in any wyse monyshe him vnto whome ye delyveryd ytt of this folye/ and byd him in any wyse to send me the letter agayne or els a copie therof/ and byd him as ever I shall do for him to take hede howe they expounde and descant apon so playne a matter—and byd him send

---

402-II). The second of them is printed in full in J. F. Mozley's *William Tyndale* (London, 1937), p. 272.
    The letters present difficulties. Gairdner, editor of the *Letters and Papers*, assumes that they are in Joye's handwriting and that the second is addressed to William Tyndale. Mozley concludes that the second is a copy of a letter sent to Tyndale by Coke. I can make but little sense of it on such a hypothesis. I think it likely that the original letters were intercepted and copied by one of Cromwell's agents and that these are the copies preserved; also that Joye wrote both of the original letters. Whoever copied them may have mistaken the signature on the second, or it is even possible that Joye used Coke's name as an alias in writing the second letter. In such a case, the second letter was certainly not to Tyndale, but perhaps to the "William hill" mentioned in the first letter. The wording given herewith was transcribed from the documents themselves.

Mr. latymer a copye therof. Remember my woode and my chese &c.
God preserue youe. the 29 daye of Apryll.

Your John Coke.

Even if this letter was not written by Joye but was in fact composed by the John Coke whose signature appears at the bottom, it is still apparent that both the letters were referring to
the same topic and to the same query.[10]

It is not evident that any special distinction was intended
in these letters between the Hortulus mentioned in the first
and the Primer mentioned in the second. Furthermore, the
two versions of the prayer are compared in the same sequence
in both letters: one says, "in the hortulus and in the prophete,"
and the other, "in the primer and the prophete." This suggests
that "the prophete" was the later publication; and in fact it
did not appear until 1531.

In 1548, while Joye was still alive, John Bale published the
first edition of his *Illustrium Majoris Britanniae Scriptorum
Summarium,* in which he lists twenty separate titles as the output of Joye's labors up to that time. Among those that Joye
translated from the Bible or from 'other works by Christian
authors' (fol. 239ᵛ) Bale lists the item, *Hortulum animae.*

Taking all the evidence together, it seems undeniable that
George Joye, the avowed author of *The Prophete Isaye* in
1531, was also the translator of the newly found Hortulus of
1530 and, by inference, of an earlier Primer that appeared
about 1529. While it is not certain that the Primer to which
the bishops raised objection in 1530 was the same as Joye's
earlier edition, it is more than likely that it was. As for the
possibility that there might have been an orthodox or Sarum
Primer printed in the English tongue at so early a date, we are
to recall the pronouncement of Sir Thomas More: "For the
Prymer and Psalter, prayours & all/ were translated and made
in this maner, by none other but heretykes."

---

10 In Joye's *Apologye* (1535) the matter of the secret letter is brought up again,
and the person who had raised the question about the prayer of Isaiah is referred
to as "the yonge man." But by this time Joye says he has with him "the copye of my
letters sent vnto this man." See Arber's reprint of the *Apologye* (Westminster, 1895),
p. 32.

Chapter IV

Contents of the English Hortulus
(1530)

O N ACCOUNT of its rarity as well as its priority, the contents of the 1530 Hortulus will now be passed in review, whereby the reader may also get some clearer idea of what these Primers were like, as first printed in English.

On the reverse side of the title-page was an almanac or table setting forth the dates of Easter from 1530 to 1547. The next pages were devoted to a calendar of saints' days and holy days, including also the 'golden numbers' and the 'dominical letters' that were used in determining the date of Easter, from which so much of the calendar was reckoned. In Joye's *Ortulus anime,* unlike the Sarum Primers, the calendar presented a mixture of martyrology and propaganda: the names of saints and holidays, printed in red ink, were fewer than usual, while the intervening spaces were occupied with theological comment, markedly Protestant in tone.[1] At times this comment is not too enlightening, as for example in the passage beginning February 23, referred to in the last chapter, which appears in this form (fol. A3ᵛ):

ix	e	Sei*n*te Thomas mar.	23
	f	Matthye Apo. Acto. 1.	24
xvii	g	Mathias before his e-	25
vi	A	leccio*n* was one of the.	26
	b	lxx. disciples whiche	27
xiiii	c	euer abode with their	28

master Christe from their first cal-
linge/ and slipte not from him nev*er*
to come ageine as some men dreame

---

[1] In Burton's *Three Primers Put Forth in the Reign of Henry VIII,* the preface to the first edition (1834) reprints the entire calendar (pp. xvii-xxxi) as contained in the Marshall Primer of 1534. Marshall copied it from the Joye Hortulus with a number of small modifications, and from this Primer we can reconstruct the probable wording of the missing leaf in the calendar of the Hortulus.

In July the feast of St. Thomas of Canterbury was celebrated, and Joye has this to say about the following Sabbath,
known as Relic Sunday, evidently aiming to offset the veneration of the relics of saints by bringing in a new interpretation:

> The sondaye after the feste of Saynte Thomas is ever Relique Son-
> daye. If ye childrene of Israel were as many in nowmbre as the sandes
> of the see: yet shall there be saued but theire reliquyes that is to saye
> but very fewe esaye in the tenthe chapter and alledged of Paule in ye
> nyenthe to the Rhomans.

The so-called 'Decollation' of John the Baptist, celebrated
on August 29, is seized upon by Joye as an opening for warning his readers of the impending wrath of God upon those who
discredit His prophets and preachers. This congenial theme
occupies the remainder of the free space in the calendar clear
to the end of the year. For example, opposite October 28 we
read:

> There was never siche plente of prophetes/ of teachinge/ of exhor-
> tynge to penance & rebukynge &c of synne: as was emonge the people
> of Israell and Iuda when their miserable captiuite and so soden de-
> struccion hanged over their heades.

At last his admonition reaches its peroration, from December
8 to 31 (with names of saints and holidays duly interspersed),
and closes thus:

> And thinke ye not yt [i.e., *that*] nowe in this laste vpsprynginge of
> Christes gospell with so many writers & prechers ther of there is lyke
> trouble and calamite abydinge vs? ye hanginge over owre heades? are we
> not yet Israel? haue we not dayly/ Noah/ Moses/ Aharon with the
> Prophetes? ye & Christe hym selve withe his Apostles monishinge and
> warnynge vs of theys plages to be at hande? Other [i.e., *Either*] cometh
> he shortly to iugement: or els loke for a meruelouse soden change Lyfte
> vp yower heades to god. Repente ye & turne ye to hym.

After the calendar comes "❡ The Passion of our sauiowre
Christe" (fol. B7). This is a lengthy account pieced together
out of the four Gospels and interlarded with moralizing com-
ments by the compiler. It is in ten parts or sections and is introduced with a brief foreword. As it stands, it is undoubtedly
the work of Joye himself, but it did not originate with him.

It has now been shown to be a translation, just as the Psalter was, of a work by Martin Bucer. In its original Latin form it was called *Historia Svpplicii Domini Iesu* and was published in 1528 as part of Bucer's *Enarratio* on the Gospel of John.[2] As a harmony or "concordance" (as Joye calls it) of those portions of the Gospels dealing with the Passion, it is a conscientious and intelligent piece of work. Joye's rendition of it shows by its turns of speech that he was familiar with Tyndale's phraseology in the first printed New Testament of 1526. The following brief excerpts will sufficiently illustrate Joye's idiomatic style and the viewpoint of his comment.

The foreword begins by referring to Jesus' discourse to his disciples before he was betrayed, and then goes on:

... whiche heavenly wordes/ only sainte Iohan dide write shewinge yt he dide not sleape and laye his head vppon his master Christes breste in vayne. This sermone beginneth at the .xiiii. chapiter of Iohan and continueth vnto the xviii. cap. where beginneth the historye of his Passion/ whiche here foloweth orderly as he suffred/ every Euangelists name/ setto their owne sainges.

The "third part" of the Passion ends with mention of the "certain young man" spoken of by Mark (14:51),[3] although Mark's name is omitted at this place:

Then the sergeaunts/ the officers and servants of the Iues toke Iesus and bounde hym/ and led hym firste vnto Annas/ for he was father in law to Caiaphas which was byshope for that yeare/ and Caiaphas was he that counselde the Iues sayinge/ it is expedient yt one man dye for the people. .... Also there was then a certaine yonge springolde that foloued Christe decked vppon his bare with fyne clothe of raynes/ whiche yonge ladde/ ye wother boyes that came with them begane to set holde vppon/ but he fled awaye naked from them/ his clothe of raynes lefte behynde him.

[2] For this information I am indebted to an article by Constantin Hope in the *Journal of Theological Studies* (Oxford, April 1951) entitled "The Story of the Passion and Resurrection in the English Primer" (New series, vol. II, pt. I, p. 68). Hoskins (*op. cit.*, p. 197, note) cites a Latin volume in the Lambeth Palace library as a source for this Passion, but I am informed that this work does not correspond to the version used by Joye. Bale, in his *Illustrium Scriptorum Summarium* (fol. 239v), lists a *Compendium passionis Christi* among Joye's compositions in English.

[3] As a standard of reference, all citations of chapter and verse in this book are given according to the text of the King James version. Actually, verse-divisions were not introduced into English Scripture until 1557.

In this passage Tyndale had said "high priest" instead of "bishop"; "young man" instead of "springold"; and "linen" instead of "cloth of Rennes." The old expression "upon the bare" is likewise found in Tyndale. Joye was often partial to the form "wother" for "other."

In the fifth section, the priests' disposal of the silver money deposited with them by Judas moves the author to an outbreak of scorn:

> Then toke the chefe preestes ye money sayinge/ it is not lawful to put this money into owre offeringe boxe for bloude was bought & sollde therwith. Here was a mervelose religion. They shamed not ne feared to shed thinnocent bloude/ but ye pryce therof derste they not mingle withe their wother money yt was offred to them: thus do hypocrites strayne oute a gnatte and swelowe over a camel. Wherfore these vntowerde and overwharte Religious men caste their frowerde heades to gither and boughte a felde of a potter with the money to burie yn strangers.

Tyndale was responsible for the reading "strain out a gnat," but Joye inserted the word "over" after "swallow," perhaps on the analogy of "to gloss over." The unusual form "over-wharte" was a variant spelling of "overthwart," meaning contrary or perverse.

The ninth part of the Passion commences thus:

> Then theis vilens [i.e., *villains*] when they had crucified Iesus/ fower of them toke his clothes makinge fower partes of them/ yt eche of them myght haue a pese/ and as fore his knytte cote whiche was with oute seme/ because it coulde not well be kutte they casted dyse for it/ that ye .22. psal. myght be fulfilled. They deuyded my clothes to them selves and vppon my tother garmente they thrwe dyse/ And all this dyd the vilene souldiers whiche sote there and kepte Iesus.

It is interesting to find that the little Psalter of 1530 had used the words, "and for my tother cote they casted dyse." Tyndale had said "cast lots."

The account of the Passion closes with the placing of a guard of soldiers at the sepulchre to keep it secure till the third day be past. There is also a concluding collect and a quotation from the fifth chapter of Romans (verses 8 and 9). The latter

is partly based on Tyndale, but not entirely, and ends as follows:

... for seynge y*t* whyles we were yet synners Christe dyed for vs: miche
more then nowe (seinge that we are iustified in his bloude) shalwe be
preserved from damnacion thorow hym   Rhoma.5.

The next portion of the Hortulus is devoted to the religious
education of children. Since it furnished no alphabet, Joye
seems not to have intended his Hortulus primarily for children, but their interests were not to be neglected. So (beginning on fol. H1) we have "❡ A fruteful & a Very Christene
Instruccion fore childrene"; and (on fol. H6) "❡ A Dialoge
VVheryn the Childe asked certayne questions/ answerth to
the same." The former of these consists chiefly of prayers to be
said morning and evening, and of graces before and after
meals. The latter "Dialoge" is an early form of catechism covering the Creed and the Ten Commandments.

The "Fruitful Instruction" bids the child upon arising in
the morning rehearse his Creed, Paternoster, and Ave Maria;
which are given—in English of course. The translation of the
Lord's Prayer is of particular interest.[4] After going through
many subsequent modifications it ultimately formed the basis
of the wording adopted by the Church of England in its Book
of Common Prayer. A comparison of the reading in the Hortulus with the text in Tyndale's first New Testament shows
that the phraseology of the Prayer was not yet fixed at that
period. In the Hortulus (fol. H1ᵛ) we read:

Owre father whiche arte in hevene/ halowed be thy name. Let thy
kyngdome come over vs. Thy will be fullfilled as well in erthe as it is in
heaven. Geve vs this daye owre sufficiente fode. And forgeve vs ower
trespases as we forgeve them that trespas ageinste vs. And lede vs not
into temptacion/ but delyvre vs frome thevel spirit. Amen.

When the Prayer occurs again in Matins (fol. L6), it is given
in the same wording. In the fragmentary Testament of 1525
Tyndale had written:

❡ O oure father/ which art in heven halowed be thy name. Let thy

4 See also below, Appendix III.

kyngdom come. Thy wyll be fulfilled/ aswell in erth/ as hit ys in heven. Geve vs this daye oure dayly breade. And forgeve vs oure treaspases/ even as we forgeve them whych treaspas vs. Lede vs nott in to temptacion. but delyvre vs from yvell/ Amen.

The other prayers and graces are not without interest also. The morning prayer and the graces before and after dinner are derived from Lutheran sources,[5] but there are additional graces for which no source has been found. The prayer to be said in the morning concludes as follows in the Hortulus (fol. H2ᵛ):

... Thy holy Angell be with me/ leste the devel my adversary have eny power over me. Amen.
    Thus thou armed with goddis helpe spede the forthe to schole/ orto thy krafte/ & to thy callynge.

This is followed by a grace:

(The Grace or blessinge of the table to be sayed of chyldrene standinge before it, their handes eleuated and ioyned togither sayinge thus deuoutly and sadly,
    The eyes of all thinges loke vp and waite vppon the (O lorde): and thou geuest them meate in due tyme. When thou geueste it them: then they gather it: when thou openest thy hande then ar they well satisfyed. Thou openeste thy hande and replenyshest all thinges lyvinge with thy blessynge. Ower father &c.

In spite of its Lutheran background, this grace proved to be very popular in England, made up, as it was, of verses from the Psalms. It is instructive to notice that in these graces, though adopting the wording given in his Psalter of 1530, Joye freely amends it to suit his taste. For instance, in the grace after dinner, the Hortulus reads in part (fol. H3) :

... He geueth catell their foode/ and feadethe the ravens byrdes yt call vpon him   He delyghteth not in stronge stedes: nether standeth his plesure in the trompets of men. But he is wel pleased with them that feare hym and trustye [sic] in his mercye.

5 Two Latin editions of Luther's *Betbüchlein* and his *Kleiner Katechismus* were put out in 1529; one entitled *Enchiridion piarum precationum* and the other *Parvus Catechismus pro pueris in schola*. While both contained the same graces, it seems likely that Joye borrowed his from the latter. See also below, in Appendix I.

In the Psalter of 1530 the corresponding passage (147: 9-11) read:

> Which geveth catall their foode: & meate also to the ravens chekens callynge for it.
>
> He delighteth not in stoughte and stronge stedes: nether hath he plesure in the trompetes of men.
>
> But his plesure is in them that feare hym: and truste vpon his mercy.

In both places Joye translates the Latin word *tibia* as "trumpets," confusing it with *tuba*. This also demonstrates that he was using a Latin rather than a German source; for Luther's word was "beynen," and Coverdale renders the passage, "nether delyteth he in eny mans legges."

Among the special graces is one called "The Grace for fisshe dayes." This cites the words of Jesus about those things which defile a man, namely, "evel thoughtes"; and these are specified in the same terms that Tyndale used in his New Testament (Matthew 15:19).

The "Fruitful Instruction" ends with a prayer "when thou shalte go to bed," the concluding words of which are:

> . . . that thou woldeste wete salve [i.e., *vouchsafe*] of thy gracyouse goodnes to kepe me this nighte: for I committe my selve both bodye and soule and all myne into thy handes. Thy holy Angel be with me/ leste my dedely aduersarye haue entrese into me. Amen.

Inasmuch as they bore upon the education of children, these particular pages of the Hortulus came in for momentary mention in the religious controversy raging at that time. Sir Thomas More in his *Apologye,* published in 1533, defending himself against the charge of cruelty, explains why he had one of the lads in his service thrashed for spreading heresy in his household. He describes the boy (fol. 196ᵛ) as—

> . . . a chylde and a seruaunt of myne in myne own house, whome hys father hadde ere euer he came with me, nowseled vp [i.e., *nurtured*] in suche maters, and had sette hym to attende vpon George Iaye or Gee otherwyse called Clerke, whych is a preste, and is now for all yt wedded in Antwarpe/ . . . Thys George Iay dyd teche thys chylde hys vngra-cyouse heresye agaynst the blessed sacrament of the aulter/ whych

heresye thys chyld afterward beynge in seruyce wyth me, began to teche another chyld in my howse, whyche vttered hys counsayle.

The boy's name was Dick Purser, and the following year Joye published *The Subuersion of Moris false foundacion,* in which he refers to More's statement "that I taught pursers sonne attending vpon me at London .viij or .ix. dayes/ my vngracious heresyes agenst the sacrament of the auter." To this Joye replies (fol. G3ᵛ):

And as for dicke purser/ verely the chylde laye withe me that lytell whyle and fetched me meat/ whome I taught to saye by herte his Pater Noster/Aue. And Credo yn Englysshe/ withe the two Prayers folowynge in the Ortulus Anime/ to say them in the morninge and euenynge/ and this/ yn good faith/ was all the Heresye that I tawght him.

If Joye was actually lodging in London when Dick Purser waited upon him, as he says, this would have been about 1527, before the Hortulus was first printed in English. Hence Joye's identification of "the two Prayers" as those contained in the *Ortulus Anime* is an extra bit of evidence connecting the Hortulus with his name.

The "Fruitful Instruction" is followed in the Hortulus by a "Dialoge" or catechism (fol. H6), and this also contains its quota of interesting material. It starts out thus:

The question.
Speke my deare Chylde/ what arte thou?
The answer.
As concerninge my firste byrthe/ I am a creature of god endued withe witte and reason/ the sonne of Adam: and as touchinge my newe and seconde byrthe I knowledge my selve to be a Christiane.

Later the child is asked to repeat the Ten Commandments and is questioned upon them:

The question.
Why? What are his commaundementes?
The answere.
These are his commaundementes. firste. Thus saythe god. Exod. 20 I am the lorde/ thy god. Thou shalte have no nother goddes in my syghte.

It turns out that the Commandments are worded as in Tyndale's Pentateuch, which had appeared in January 1530, except for an occasional alteration, as when Joye says, "For the lorde wyl not reken hym gyltlesse that taketh his name in vayne," where Tyndale had written, "wil not holde him giltlesse."

In matters of doctrine Joye's Lutheran leanings may be seen from the following excerpt (fol. 12ᵛ):

The question.
For as myche then as god is the spirite and maye not be ymagined of ower wittes: howe shall we knowe hym?
The answere.
Faithe and truste fynde hym when we are in perel and shewe hym vnto vs/ and yet this faythe to fynde hym must he geve vs: for if we gete vs a faithe of owre owne fasshoninge wherby we beleve and truste in eny wother thinge then god, then make we vs an idole: for it is the faithe and truste only in owre hartes that maketh other [i.e., *either*] god or ydole: . . .

The Dialogue ends on a typical theme:

❡ The question asker concludethe.
Then are we all sinners and have broken all goddis commaundementes
The answerer.
We ar all synners and have nede of the mercy of god: . . .

Next in the Hortulus, logically enough, comes a General Confession (fol. 15ᵛ) which is headed:

❡ Here foloweth A generall confession fore every synner broughte into the knowledge of his synnes, to confesse hym selve with penetent harte before God at all tymes.

This is an abject recital of shortcomings, the catalogue of which extends through several pages and ends as follows:

. . . Thus grevously have I synned levynge the commaundementes (Oh father) to do deades of my nowne imaginacion. Wherfore I krye the mercy/ my god/ my father/ desyeringe forgevenes in ye bloude and for the dethes sake of thy sonne my sauioure Iesus Christe/ to whom wt the be glory worlde with oute ende Amen. Then saye the one and fiftye Psalme/ called .Miserere mei deus the fowerth emonge the .vii. Psalmes.

Following the Confession, we have a group of four prayers selected from the Old Testament. The first is the prayer from Isaiah,[6] which was discussed in our last chapter. As was pointed out, it is possible that these prayers were also included in the earlier lost edition of Joye's Primer. But, historically at least, this portion of the Hortulus is one of the most significant because, being composed of excerpts taken neither from the Pentateuch nor from the Psalms, it represents the earliest printing we have in an English version of these particular passages from the Bible.

The prayer of Jonah when he was "deliured oute of the whales belye" (fol. K6ᵛ) was often reproduced in later Primers. It reflects certain of Joye's characteristic traits as a translator, his fervor, his extravagant mode of expression, and withal the fresh effect of his unstudied and offhand approach; for example, in the following verses (Jonah 2:3,5,6):

. . . for thou haddest throne me forthe into the middes of the depeste of the see And ye waters closed me aboute/ all thy grete waues and flowdes wente over me. . . . for waters haue compassed me yn/ even vp vnto my soule. The derke depeth closed me yn and the fowle stinkinge wedes of the see covred my hed. I sanke downe vnder the foundacions of the hilles/ so that the waters barred me oute from therthe for ever. But thou madest my lyfe to aryse frome dethe (O lorde my god) .

In the spring of 1531, when Tyndale published his version of "The prophete Ionas," he rendered the latter verses more capably, thus:

The water compassed me euen vn to the very soule of me: the depe laye aboute me: and the wedes were wrappte aboude myne heed. And I went downe vn to the botome of the hylles/ & was barredin with erth on euery syde for euer. And yet thou lorde my God broughtest vp my life agayne out of corrupcion.

It happens that all four of the prayers selected by Joye were included, along with many others, in a collection of prayers compiled from the Latin Bible by Otto Brunfels in September 1528 under the title, Precationes Biblicae; and it

6 Beside this one, the group comprises: I Samuel 2:1-10; Daniel 9:4-19; and Jonah 2:1-10.

is quite possible that Joye took note of them in that volume. Brunfels, who was a follower of Luther, had published his compilation early enough for Joye to have made use of it, even for the first edition of his Primer. Some color is lent to this assumption by another point of resemblance between the Hortulus and the *Precationes*. There is a short admonition or exhortation printed in the Hortulus (fol. K7ᵛ) under the heading "Prayer peaseth Goddis wrathe," which commences:

> For as miche as we have nowe grevously offended ower Lorde God/ and the dayes nowe beginne to apere of the whiche Christe and his Apostles prophecyed saynge there shulde come perellous tymes syche adfliccion and persecution as haue not be sene frome the beginninge of the worlde: I cannot se howe we myghte eny other wise pease goddis wrathe then by continual fervent prayer. What thinge is it/ but the importune pray*er* of faithful men hathe obtained it of god at the laste?

This is unmistakably an echo of the first part of the foreword to all the faithful, which Brunfels printed in his *Precationes*.[7]

Near the end of his exhortation Joye brings in a timely observation of his own. Having shown the efficacy and virtue of prayer, he goes on:

> . . . me thinketh it necessary y*t* y*e* laye people shulde haue y*e* prayers moste co*n*uenie*n*t for this tyme/ which prayers ar y*e* psa. & y*t* in Englishe y*t* their faithe might y*e* more encrese . . .

It would be enlightening to be able to know whether Joye added this remark about the need for English Psalms *before* or *after* he brought forth his edition of the Psalter of David; that is, whether this passage was also in the first edition of his Primer. It rather sounds as though it might have been written while he was still at work on the translation of the Psalter.

Finally, after nearly eighty leaves of preliminary material, we come to the main body of the Hortulus (so to speak) with Matins. The opening lines with their familiar words, "O

---

[7] Under the heading "Fidelibus Omnibus in Christo Iesu" Brunfels' foreword commences thus: "Quando tam multis hodie malis obnoxii sumus, et ea incipiunt apparere tempora, de quibus praedixerunt Christus et Apostoli, quae erunt periculosa, et afflictio tanta, qualis ab initio mundi non fuit, usque ad tempus hoc: non videbam quomodo aliter occurreremus vindictae irae Dei, quam si indefinenter et sedulo oremus. Quid enim non impetrat sedula, humilis et importuna oratio?" For a rendering of this in 1535, see below, p. 80.

Lorde opene thow my lippes," are embellished by a small ad-
joining woodcut of the Annunciation, the only one in the
entire volume (fol. L1) . These Matins, Hours, Evensong, etc.,
are not altogether like those of Sarum use. While the general
outline is similar, and most of the Psalms correspond to those
in Sarum Primers, there are many variations in other respects.
There are different responses, hymns, collects, etc., beside the
introduction of scriptural 'lessons' in the Matins and the omission of prayers addressed to the Virgin. For instance, the traditional 'invitatory' Psalm in the Sarum Primers called for the
use of "Hail Mary, full of grace: the Lord is with thee";
whereas Joye used this verse from the Gospel of Matthew:
"Come vnto me all ye that labour and are laden: and I shall
refreshe you."[8]

In all, the Joye Hortulus included the text of thirty-nine different Psalms.[9] These naturally appear, for the most part, in
the same version that he had published in January 1530, albeit
with a good many emendations. It will be recalled that he said
on the title-page of the Hortulus that all the Psalms were
"newe corrected." This poses a nice dilemma: Does it mean
that he revised the wording as compared with his Psalter of
David, or as compared with his earlier edition of the English
Primer? And did this earlier edition appear *before* or *after* the
16th of January, 1530, the date when the Psalter was published? If before, then what translation of the Psalms would it
have used?—for the Bucer version did not appear until September 1529. And if it were later than the Psalter, would there
have been time for Sir Thomas Hitton to have gone across the
Channel and brought a copy home before he was apprehended
in February 1530? Perhaps Joye translated first those Psalms he
needed for the Primer and then went on to finish the whole
Psalter, and later on revised certain ones for his Hortulus.

Actually, only a few Psalms in the Hortulus show any con-

8 It may be worth recording here that in the first edition of the Book of Common
Prayer (1549) Cranmer included the following in the Communion Service: "Come
vnto me all that trauell and bee heauy laden, and I shall refreshe you." "Traueilen"
was a Wycliffite word but "refreshe" seems to have come through the Primers.
"Heauy" was Cranmer's own contribution, and very effective.
9 See the table in Appendix II, below.

siderable revision as compared with the *Psalter of Dauid in Englishe,* and these occur chiefly at the beginning of Matins, as though Joye had started out to revise his translation and then had given it over. Neither is much light shed on the question by those Psalms that were specially mentioned on the title-page as being new additions: "Ther is a psalm added to the euensong & Iudica me to the complene." For the first of these (Ps. 115) is rendered alike in both the Hortulus and the Psalter, while the second (Ps. 43, "Judica me" in Latin) has been amended at the outset so as to read more smoothly in the Hortulus; hence the evidence is inconclusive.

The opening Psalm of Matins (Ps. 95) shows the greatest variation from the text of the 1530 Psalter, being practically a new translation. For example, the latter portion of this Psalm had read as follows in the Psalter:

Se that ye harden not yowre hartes as they dyde in the deserte of Meribah in the tyme of temptacion.

When yowre fathers tempted and prouoked me: and yet thei se my workes.

Fortty yeares I chide with yt nacion: and I sayd/ this people errethe in their hartes/ they alowe not my wayes.

Vnto whom I swore in myn Angre: they shall never entre in to the lande of my reste.

In the Hortulus (fol. L2) it reads:

. . . se yt ye harden not yower hartes/ as they did in the place of temptacion in wildernes bitterly murmuringe and spekinge ageinst god/ where yower fathers tempted me and prouoked me to anger ye althoghe they se my myracles. . . .

Forty yearis was I at debate chydinge with yt generation. Wherfore I sayd ever/ theyr hartes are gone fro me/ they knowe not my waies: to whome I swore in my grete anger that they shulde not enter in to the lande of my reste/ . . .

It may be that these changes were introduced to make the rendition of this Psalm conformable with the text of the Latin Primers rather than with Bucer's version. At any rate, the Hortulus wording of this Psalm persisted for over twenty-five years.

nowe and ever fhalbe. A ME N.

¶The hymne.

P Rayfed be god ower father/for he hathe geuē vs his fōne to be ower fauioure.

W e ar fynners, vnrightwife, folyfhe and flefhly.

C hrifte is owre mercy ftole: owr rightwifnes, and ower wifdome verely

W e are vnclene, holden vnder y̆ danger of dethe and fynne.

C hrifte is ower holynes, ower lyfe ower fatiffaccion, and redemption.

G lory be to the, o lorde, borne of the vyrgyn Marye, glory to the father, ¶ to the holy gofte. euer. AM EN.

Lorde/ye ower lorde/ howe woundrefull reuerente and cleare is thy name over all the erthe: which hafte lyfted vp thy highe ma-

gnificence above the hevens.

De and that by the mouthes of the foukynge babes that cānot yet fpeke hafte thoufet vp y̆ prayfe of thy myghte ageinfte thy enymes: to cō founde thy aduerfary that will avenge hym felfe.

I fhall therfore lokevp ꝗ woundre at thy hevens: fo / theis are the workes of thy fyngere / the mone and ftarres/thou hafte fet them fo goodly.

But lo/what thinge is man mortall that thou thus remembrefte hym: what is the fonne of Adamy thou regardeft hym fo gretly?

Þou hafte made hym not myche inferior then Angefe: withe fo grete dignite and glory hafte thou endued hym.

Þou hafte made hym lorde of thy

THE *ORTULUS ANIME* OF 1530

Showing Joye's version of the eighth Psalm
and the hymn, "Praised be God"

(Reproduced by permission of the Trustees of the British Museum)

The several Psalms that follow this one (Ps. 8, 19, 93) show what might be called a maximum of emendation, resulting generally in improved renditions; yet certainly the Psalms of the Hortulus taken as a whole are simply a reprint of the text of the 1530 Psalter. They are not so crude as to be without value, and there is a distinct probability that they were consulted by Coverdale, in the Psalter if not in the Hortulus, when he came to translate the Bible in 1535.[10] Joye's workmanship—slipshod rather than scholarly, uneven rather than temperate, yet generally fresh and racy—may be seen to good advantage in his version of Psalm 8 as given in the Matins of the Hortulus (fol. L2ᵛ) :

Lorde/ ye ower lorde/ howe woundrefull reverente and cleare is thy name over all the erthe: which haste lyfted vp thy highe magnificence above the hevens.

Ye and that by the mouthes of the soukynge babes that cannot yet speke haste thou set vp ye prayse of thy myghte ageinste thy enymes: to confounde thy aduersary that will avenge hym selfe.

I shall therfore loke vp & woundre at thy hevens: lo/ theis are the workes of thy fyngers/ the mone and starres/ thou haste set them so goodly.

But lo/ what thinge is man mortall that thou thus remembreste hym? what is the sonne of Adam yt thou regardest hym so gretly?

Thou haste made hym not myche inferior then Angels: withe so grete dignite and glory haste thou endued hym.

Thou hast made hym lorde of thy handy workis: thou haste caste all thinges vnder hys fete.

As flockes of shepe all herdes of neate: and also the wylde beastis.

Foules of the ayer and fysshes of the see: and what so ever swimmeth in the water.

Lorde/ ye owre lorde: howe woundrefull reverente and cleare is thy name over all therthe?

The second verse above had stood in need of improvement in the *Psalter of Dauid,* wherein the Psalm began:

Lorde/ ye/ ower lorde/ howe woundrefull reverent is thy name in every lande? which haste lyft vp thy highe magnificense above the hevens.

10 E.g., for Coverdale's use of "bugges" in Ps. 91 and of "staffe and shepehoke" in Ps. 23, see Butterworth, *Literary Lineage of the King James Bible,* pp. 78 and 286.

Ye and that of the mouthes of ye lytel souklinges haste thou stab-
lesshed thy myghty prayse ageinste thy enymes: to smytdowne aduer-
sary/ & hym that will avenge hym selfe.

Among the scriptural 'lessons' which Joye injected into his
Matins, two are from the New Testament, slightly modified
from the Tyndale version. The third, being from the Apocrypha (Wisdom 5: 2-7; 6: 4-6), had not been previously
printed in English. The version is Joye's own though not in
his best vein, and is deficient in punctuation even for the
printing of that time. It commences (fol. L8ʳ):

In the laste iugemente when theis vngodly shall beholde ye rightwismen they shalbe troubled with horrible feare and shall meruell at
their so soden helthe vnlokedfor wailinge for the sorowfull anguysshe
of their mynde sainge with in them selve beyinge heuy & moorninge
for the anguishe of their mynde. Theis are they whome we had som-
tyme in derision/ and into lyklyhode of opprobrious laughter: but we
ower selve beynge then with out ower wittes had wende yt their lyfe
had bene but madnes: and so their ende to haue bene withe oute honour. But nowe se howe they are counted emonge the childrene of god/
and their heretage is emonge the saintes.

In verse 7 there is a hint of his happier style:

... we were weried and tyerde in the waye of wikednes and perdicion:
we walked harde and wery wayes/ for the waye of the Lorde we
knewe not.

Special interest attaches to this 'lesson' because Joye himself utilized it later on. Thus it furnishes still another bit of
evidence, if more were needed, linking the name of Joye with
the Hortulus of 1530. For after Tyndale had brought out a
revised New Testament, in November 1534, which included
a section of so-called 'epistles' from the Old Testament, Joye
too brought out an edition of the Testament containing these
same 'epistles.' This was in January 1535 (S.T.C. 2827).
Now the epistle for "saynt Philip and Iacobs daye" was taken
from the Wisdom of Solomon (5: 1-5), and when Joye came
to this, he adapted the opening verse from Tyndale's translation, but the rest of it he copied from his own Hortulus, making only a few alterations. "Rightwismen" becomes "the

ryghtwyse" and "lyklyhod of opprobrious laughter" becomes "the lykenes of an obprobriouse laughter"; and so on.

Among the curious features of the Hortulus are the hymns that Joye devised in crude English verse. Altogether eight of them occur, one at the beginning of each of the four canonical Hours, and one each in Matins, Lauds, Evensong, and Compline. No doubt they were translated from Latin, perhaps from a Lutheran source. Their Latin ancestry is attested by the following quatrain (fol. N5):

> Ower nature is sore vitiate.
> And nedeth regeneration.
> Lighten ower myndes execate [i.e., *blinded*].
> O lorde ower consolation.

Perhaps the most appealing of the lot is the one which introduces the Nunc Dimittis in Compline (fol. Q2) :

> ⟨ The hymne.
> Worshipe we the spirit pureli.
> Whiche moued Simeon the sage.
> In his armes to take reuerently
> Ower sauiour yet tender of age.
> When his father and his mother
> Presented theyr yonge chylde Iesus.
> Simeon emonge all wother
> Praysed the lorde sayinge thus.

Nowe letest thou thy seruant departe/ o lorde/ accordinge to thy promyse/ in peace.

For myn eyes haue sene the saviour: sente from the.

Whom thou hast set forthe in the presens of all people.

To be a lyght/ lyghteninge ye gentils & to be ye glory of thy people Israel.

The passage just quoted (Luke 2: 29-32) illustrates Joye's method of dealing with material taken from the New Testament. As a rule he used the Tyndale version of 1526 for a basis but altered it freely to suit his own fancy. In the Benedictus, for example, the version in the Hortulus (fol. N2) diverges frequently from the wording of Tyndale. The opening verses (Luke 1: 68-71) will suffice for a comparison:

(T26)—Blessed be the lorde   god of israhel/ for he hath
(H30)—Praysed be the lorde/ God of Israel: for he hath graciously

visited   and redemed his people. And hath reysed vppe the   horne off
visited/ and redemed his people. He hath   set vp   ower myghty

health vnto vs/ in the housse of his servaunt David. Even as
helthe: in ye house of Dauid his servante Accordynge to

he promised by the mougth of his holy prophetes which were sens
his promyses/by ye   mouthes of his holy prophetes of a longe tyme

the worlde began. That we shulde be saued   from   oure
paste.   Promysinge yt we shulde be preseruede frome ower

enimys/ And from the hondis of all   that hate vs: . . .
enymes: and frome the handes of all them that hate vs.

Likewise in the Magnificat, the rendering given in the
Hortulus follows Tyndale quite closely at first but departs
strikingly in the latter portion. For instance, where Tyndale
had said (Luke 1: 51-53):

He hath shewed strengthe with his arme/ he hath scattered them
that are proude in the ymmaginacion of their hertes.
He hath putt Downe the myghty from their seates/ and hath exalted
them of lowe degre.
He hath filled the hongry with goode thinges: And hath sent awaye
the ryche empty. . . .

Joye launches into his own mode of expression (fol. P6):

He hath declared his myghte by his power: he hath dispersed ye
proude men by the vayne study of their owne hartes.
He hath plucked downe men of power from their seates: and hath
lyfted vp the poore lowlyons [i.e., *lowly ones*].
The hongry men he hath satisfyed with goodnes: and them that
appered riche he hath lefte voyde.

Being a zealous reformer, Joye eliminated from his Hortulus
all the elaborate prayers and devotions addressed to the Virgin
under poetic names. He retained the simple form of the Ave
Maria, but deleted the "Salve Regina," which the Protestants
generally frowned upon. Instead of the latter, Joye inserted at

the end of Compline an alternative devotion, favored by the reformers and known as "Salve Rex." This was not in the earlier edition, for the title-page of the Hortulus reminds us that Compline has been amplified "with Salue re. and a colete therto." This is presumably its earliest appearance in English.[11] It is in the mood of tearful contrition of which the early Protestants seem to have been especially fond. The opening lines are:

Hayle (Iesu christe) kinge of mercye ower lyfe/ ower swetnes/ and ower hope/ We salute the: vnto the we krye whiche are ye banneshed chylderne of Eue: vnto the we syghe/ sobbinge and wepinge in this vale of wretchednes: haste ye therfor ower mediator: turne vnto vs those thy mercyfull eyes.

With the conclusion of Compline we come to the end of the canonical Hours. There is, as More complained, neither Litany nor Dirge in the 1530 Hortulus. The remainder of the volume—some twenty leaves—is given over to the Seven Penitential Psalms and the "Commendations." Of the Seven Psalms—"❡ Here beginne the seuen Psalmes in Englysshe" (fol. Q4) —two may be considered of special interest—the 51st and the 130th—on account of their multiple occurrence in subsequent Primers, especially those of Sarum use. All that need be said of them at present is that the version in the Hortulus follows that in the Psalter of 1530, except at the beginning of Psalm 51 which, instead of reading, "Have mercy vpon me (god) for thy ientlenes [i.e., *gentleness'*] sake," as in the Psalter, is here given as "Haue mercy vpon me (God) for thy fauourable goodnes."[12] Concerning the Commendations, which here consists of the entire 119th Psalm, it is enough to say that once more Joye copied the wording out of his *Psalter of Dauid,* including even the 'argument' prefixed at the head of the Psalm. As was mentioned earlier, the Hortulus failed to include the Psalms of the Passion, although

[11] A slightly different version, under the heading "❡ The true Salue Regina, grounded vpon the scripture," was published in 1538 by James Nicolson along with the Magnificat, Benedictus, etc. (*S.T.C.* 17536). In the Hortulus the running head on fol. Q3 is "Salue re" as on the title-page, but on the reverse of Q3 it is "Salue rex."

[12] For variant readings in this Psalm, see below in Appendix III.

these were noted among the contents listed on the title-page.

Just above the colophon of this unique little volume (fol. S8ᵛ) Joye printed a motto from the beginning of chapter 59 of Isaiah, evidently as a sort of *envoi*. It is phrased differently from the corresponding verse in his *Prophete Isaye* of 1531, and reads thus:

Lo, the lorde is yet alyue, whose power is not so minisshed but he maie vs yet saue, nether are his eares so stopped but he will vs yet heare.

How typical this is of Joye's peculiar style may perhaps be felt by comparing it with the rendering of the same verse in the Coverdale Bible of 1535:

Beholde, the Lordes honde is not so shortened y*t* it can not helpe, nether is his eare so stopped y*t* it may not heare.

Chapter V

An English Primer Is Printed in London
(1530-1534)

THE Joye Hortulus appeared at a time when great political, as well as religious, issues were seething in England, and during the next few years events drew steadily to a climax. On November 30, 1530, the death of Cardinal Wolsey while on his way to answer to charges of treason closed one chapter and opened another in Henry's reign. Not long before this, Tyndale had published his controversial treatise called *The practyse of Prelates,* to which we have had occasion to refer in connection with Sir Thomas Hitton. After the usage of the time, the word 'practice' in this title signified artifice, strategy, or chicanery. The book itself was of no great consequence, but it had a significant sub-title: "❡ Whether the Kinges grace maye be separated from hys quene/ because she was his brothers wyfe."

Tyndale, taking counsel of the Scripture rather than of his own prejudices, concluded that there were no sufficient grounds for setting aside the King's marriage. This must have been highly displeasing to the King, for ever since 1527 Henry had been scheming how he might divorce his Queen, Catherine of Aragon, so that he could marry Anne Boleyn. During 1531 two competent men came into prominence because of their fitness and willingness to assist the King in this project: one was Thomas Cranmer, whose sphere was religion; the other, Thomas Cromwell, whose field was politics. While Cranmer was upholding the validity of the King's contemplated divorce, Cromwell embarked on a program aimed at alienating the clergy from their allegiance to the Pope and making them subordinate to the power of the Crown. Seeing what was coming, Sir Thomas More resigned as Lord Chancellor in 1532, being replaced the next year by Thomas Audley.

After the death of the aged Archbishop of Canterbury, William Warham, in August 1532, Henry adopted franker and bolder measures to usher Anne into public notice as his future Queen. In September she was made Marchioness of Pembroke, and a month later she accompanied the King on a royal visit to France. In January 1533, Henry and Anne were privately married; in March, Cranmer was installed as Archbishop of Canterbury; and in May, Henry's marriage to Catherine was declared annulled. The new Queen had her coronation on the first day of June.

Though favoring Catherine's cause, the Pope had hesitated to make any final pronouncement on the subject till his authority was called into question by Henry's insistent course. At length, in July, he reached the decision that the marriage to Catherine was still valid; but this decision was not formally announced nor was it publicly known in England until March of the following year, when it was accompanied by a threat of excommunication to Henry.

The momentous year of 1534 began with the reassembling of Parliament on January 15. Before it was prorogued at the end of March, Parliament had enacted the Act of Succession acknowledging Anne as the rightful Queen of England. At the same time, under Cranmer's primacy, Convocation passed the famous resolution declaring that the Bishop of Rome—in other words, the Pope—had no more authority in the Church of England than any other foreign bishop. In April, Sir Thomas More and John Fisher, Bishop of Rochester, were imprisoned because they refused to take the oath of allegiance required by the recent Act of Succession. Later in the year, in November, Parliament enacted a bill declaring Henry to be Supreme Head of the English Church.

Thomas Cromwell by his ability and diligence, along with his unscrupulous statecraft, had made himself of great value to the King during these developments and was duly rewarded with various posts of preferment. He became Chancellor of the Exchequer, then Secretary of State and Master of the Rolls, and early in 1535 was made Vicar-General to the King. The more his policy veered away from subservience to the Papacy, the more it was inclined to conciliate the Lutheran party. While Henry did not object to this on political grounds, it is doubtful if he ever really sympathized with any Lutheran alliance, for he was not forgetful of the title bestowed on him by the Pope, some dozen years before, of "Defender of the Faith." Cromwell, however, had no such scruples; and Archbishop Cranmer, by education and by disposition, was friendly to the Reformation so far as this was expedient. Luther's completed German version of the Bible was published in 1534; and both Cromwell and Cranmer, though perhaps for different reasons, were in favor of a wider circulation of the English Scriptures. At length in December, Convocation was induced to petition the King for an English translation of the Bible.

At some time between March and December, then, it had become clear that the publication of the Scriptures in English would no longer be officially frowned upon since it had the tacit approval of both Cranmer and Cromwell. Exactly when this came about we do not know, but the printers and booksellers of Antwerp had been waiting for this very change, and thousands of volumes containing portions of the Scripture in English began to be imported into England. When George Joye, for example, published his version of *Ieremy the Prophete* in May, he dared to put his own name on the title-page. In August he published also a fresh translation of the Psalms over his own name, besides an anonymous and pirated edition of Tyndale's New Testament which was the source of a famous quarrel between the two men. Tyndale too was not idle; he put out a revised edition of his "Genesis" (this time with his initials on the title-page), and in November he brought out his first revision of his own New Testament. Not only did he give his full name in the title of this latter volume, but he also made bold to present a specially bound copy of it to Queen Anne herself—though not in person.

No wonder, then, that Joye, writing in his *Apologye,* which was dated February 27, 1535, should say concerning that summer of 1534 (fol. C4ʳ):

... for now was ther geue*n* tha*n*ked be god a lytel space to breath & reste vnto christis chirche aftir so lo*n*ge and greuouse pe*r*secucion for reading the bokes ...

Finally, and more to our purpose, it was in 1534—probably in that same summer—that the first English Primer was published in the city of London itself.

But before turning to this Primer we must first take notice of yet another mention of the *Ortulus anime*—a very puzzling allusion contained in a letter written by Cuthbert Tunstall, Bishop of Durham. The letter concerns an *Ortulus anime* in English, to which Tunstall took great exception because of something said in the 'gloss' which accompanied the calendar.[1] Presumably, the letter was written to Cromwell, who is spoken of as "Your Mastership," but there is no name given. Neither is the year specified, unfortunately, the letter being dated simply "the vijᵗʰ day of Julye."

The relevant portion of the Bishop's letter reads:

... ther is conuey to my handes a litill booke printed in englysshe callyd Ortulus anime whiche was brought in by some folkes of the newe castell and as I am enformyd ther be verey many late brought into the realme of them chefely into London and into other haven townes. Whiche bookes if they be suffered to goo abrode be like to do great harme emonge the people, for ther is in them a manyfest declaracyon agaynst the effecte of the acte of pa*r*lement late made for the establysshement of the Kinges highnes succession, as ye shall pe*r*ceyue mor playnly in redinge the place yo*ur* self. which declaracion is made in the Kalender of the said booke abowte thend of the monyth of August opon the day of the decollation of saynt Joha*n* Baptyst, to shewe the cause whye he was behedyd.

Now this is very strange. Apparently the letter belongs to

---

1 For fuller discussion see the writer's article, "Bishop Tunstall and the English *Hortulus"* in the *Library Chronicle* of the University of Pennsylvania for Summer, 1950 (vol. XVI, p. 37). The original letter is preserved in the British Museum (Ms. Cleop. E.v.388). The full text is given in modern spelling in Strype's *Ecclesiastical Memorials* (edition of 1822, vol. I, part 2, p. 274) and an abstract is printed in *Letters and Papers of Henry VIII* (vol. VIII; no. 1005).

the year 1534, considering the recent importation of books and the Act of Succession passed by Parliament in March. But the only English Hortulus known is the recently discovered edition of 1530, and there seems to have been nothing offensive in the calendar of that edition at the particular point mentioned, the end of August. The matter is further complicated by the fact that the very leaf disclosing what it was that John the Baptist said to Herod is the only leaf missing in the one extant copy. But here the English Primer printed in London in 1534, mentioned above, comes to our rescue; for it reprints the entire calendar of the 1530 Hortulus with very few alterations. In this Primer, then, the corresponding passage in the calendar reads:

The cause wherfore Iohan the Baptiste was prysoned & headyd foloweth, he monysshed Herode louyngly and tolde hym charytably, supposnyg to haue wonne hym saieng/ syr it is not lawful for you to haue your brothers wyfe.

In the Joye Hortulus the wording is interrupted by the missing leaf after the words, "he monished Herod."

If we suppose that Tunstall was referring to the Act of Succession of 1534, there is no apparent reason why this passage should have been deemed at variance with the interests of Queen Anne; rather it would militate against the claims of Catherine. Or if we suppose that he was referring to a later Act passed in favor of Jane Seymour in 1536, there is still nothing in the wording of the Hortulus hostile to the interests of Jane. Later than July 1536, Cromwell would have been addressed as "Your Lordship" instead of "Your Mastership," as in this letter.

Assuming, then, that the letter was written on July 7, 1534, there would seem to be only two tenable hypotheses to account for Tunstall's agitation or reconcile it with the known facts. If, on the one hand, he was referring to the Hortulus of 1530, then we must assume that unsold copies of this were being imported from Antwerp by way of Newcastle during the summer of 1534, and, further, that Tunstall must have been overly sensitive to any contemporaneous allusion to John the

Baptist, either because Bishop Fisher (then in prison) was known to have compared himself to John in his stand against the King's marriage with Anne, or because embarrassing implications might be drawn from Henry's alleged illicit relations with Anne's older sister. Yet in either case Tunstall was taking counsel of his fears and indulging in gross exaggeration by terming the wording of the calendar a "manyfest declaracyon" against the recent Act of Succession.

If, on the other hand, he was referring to some other edition of the Hortulus in English, no longer known to have existed, then we must suppose that, with the fresh influx of imported books into England, either Joye or someone else was prompted to bring out a new edition of the *Ortulus anime* with a revised calendar, in which some damaging reference to Queen Anne had unluckily been inserted. Neither of these hypotheses is in any sense really satisfactory, and the mystery remains.

Turning now to the English Primer of 1534 (*S.T.C.* 15986), we are struck by the probability that it was the first book to be printed in England containing entire Psalms and other avowed portions of the Scripture in the English tongue.[2] We naturally should like to know just when it appeared, but this must be gathered by conjecture.

Only two copies of this most interesting little volume are known, one in the Bodleian Library, the other in the Boston Public Library. The copy preserved at the Bodleian lacks only one leaf of being complete. It is entitled:

¶ A Prymer in Englyshe, with certeyn prayers & godly meditations, very necessary for all people that vnderstonde not the Latyne tongue.

Printed by Byddell, its publication was sponsored by William Marshall, as may be gathered from the colophon:

¶ Thus endeth the prymer in Englysshe with many goodly and godly prayers. Imprented at London in Fletestrete by Iohan Byddell.

---

2 Caxton's *Golden Legend* (1483) contained many consecutive passages from the Pentateuch but they were not distinguished as such. See Butterworth, *Literary Lineage of the King James Bible*, pp. 52-54; also, "How Early Could English Scripture Be Printed in England?" in the *Library Chronicle* of the University of Pennsylvania (October 1947, vol. XIV, no. 2).

Dwellyng next to Flete Brydge at the signe of our Lady of pytye/ for Wyllyam Marshall.

Bound together with this Primer is an English translation of an Exposition by Savonarola on the 51st Psalm, likewise printed "at the sygne of our lady of pytye."

Now Byddell moved from this address to another shop (at the sign of the Sun) in the spring of 1535. Moreover, the almanac at the beginning of this Primer giving the dates for Easter commences with the year 1534. Such bits of evidence, corroborated by others of similar import, point to the publication of the book (which is undated) as belonging to the summer of 1534. Also, though it proves nothing, the fact that Marshall did not make use of the new version of the Psalter which Joye issued in August of that year would suggest that the Primer was compiled not later than September.

Underneath the title we come upon these rather surprising words on the title-page, "Cum priuilegio Regali"; and below these is a large cut of the royal coat-of-arms. We need not conclude from this that the King gave his personal sanction to the publication of this Primer. The royal "privilege" was a formal permit issued to the printer confirming his right to produce the book; it did not apparently license the contents of the book itself nor sanction the reading of it by the populace. On the other hand, it did mean that the work was not issued surreptitiously but was duly known to the authorities.

In some quarters the scope of this privilege seems to have been misunderstood even at that period. There is a quaint record of a complaint made by some of the congregation in the village church of Langham in Essex,[3] protesting that the churchwarden's assistant, one John Vigorous, would not allow them "to reade privyledgede bokes" including an English

---

3 Preserved in the Public Record Office, Records of the Exchequer, Miscellaneous Books, Treasury of Receipt, vol. 120, p. 117. The complaint is briefly noted in *Letters and Papers of Henry VIII*, vol. VII, no. 145. It is mentioned specifically in "The Regulation of the Book Trade Before the Proclamation of 1538" by A. W. Reed in *Transactions of the Bibliographical Society* (vol. XV, pp. 176, 177); see also Reed's *Early Tudor Drama* (London, 1926), pp. 160 ff. The assigned date in the *Letters and Papers* is 1534; this Reed accepts, but it seems too early by at least a year.

Primer,—"so that we can not lyue by hym peasably as god wolde & the kynge." The complaint begins by lauding the King for—

> ... puttynge forth certeyne bokes printede & openly soulde *with* in the same realme *with* his ryght royall privyledge sett un to the same/ to thentente truly (as we do take it) that no man shulde feare but rather be encoragede to occupye them.

One item of the complaint runs:

> Apon the ascensyon day laste paste, didde ij maydens sytte in theyr pue or stole [i.e., *stool*] in the churche/ as all honeste & virtuous people use to do at matyns tyme sayyng theyr matens together apon an englisshe primer. Vigorous this seing was sore angry/ insomoche that therfor & for no other thing elles/ he didde bydde the maydens to auoyde out of churche . . .

The document itself is undated but has been assigned (mistakenly, it seems to me) to the year 1534. If this date should prove correct, and if the privileged Primer was the one issued for William Marshall, then the date of its publication would have to be set considerably earlier, for Ascension Day fell on the fifteenth of May in 1534.

Further evidence has come to light confirming the likelihood that the Marshall Primer was in circulation by the end of the summer of 1534. This occurs in a manuscript recently acquired by the Bodleian Library (Ms. Don. c. 42) which is a sketch of Anne Boleyn's career written by William Latimer the younger, who served for a time as chaplain to Queen Elizabeth.[4] Writing some thirty or forty years after the event, Latimer speaks about Anne Boleyn "being in progresse at Wynchecome" and having visited Hailes Abbey nearby, and proceeds to describe a visit which she paid to the nuns of Sion Middlesex, a convent at Isleworth, near Richmond. The relevant portion of the manuscript (fol. 31) reads:

> Likewyse in the ende of that same progresse her Ma*iestie* lyeing then at Richemonde vowchsaved in her owne persone to visite the Noones of Syon, whoo beinge at their common prayer in their close Quyre (as their manner was) denyed her highnes entrye into the same . . . The

---

4 See Cooper's *Athenae Cantabrigienses* (Cambridge, 1858), vol. I, p. 481.

Quene her highnes persisted earnestly in her requeste, and so at the laste with fayer and swete wordes haith optayned free ingresse with her trayne, where she fownde them all prostrate and grovelinge with their faces downewarde to the grownde vnto whome she made a breife exhortacione . . . and disswading them from their dissimuled holynes and ygnorante praying vpon their Laten prymars gave them prayer bookes in Englishe to exercise them selves with all, that they might both vnderstande, what they did praye for, and therby be stired to more devocion: which they refusinge for a tyme (as profane) not to be admitted in their professione, at the last received them notwithstanding moste humblye with faythfull promisse to performe her graces desire.

Now, biographers of Anne report that the King and Queen were on progress during the summer of 1534. Friedmann says, "The rest of the summer Henry and Anne employed in a progress through the midland counties; and both did their utmost to win the hearts of those whom they met."[5] And it is known specifically that on the 22nd of October, 1534, Anne "attended by many ladies and gentlemen" went to see her infant daughter Elizabeth, who was then being kept at Richmond.

According to Latimer's account, therefore, "the ende of that same progresse," when her Majesty was staying at Richmond, would have been either in September or October of 1534, at which time Anne promised to give the nuns of Sion "prayer bookes in Englishe." These must have been the newly printed Primers of William Marshall. Such a conclusion is reinforced by a report, current at that time, that Queen Anne had been enlisted as one of Marshall's supporters.

Concerning William Marshall himself little is known. Some have confused him with others by the name of Marshall; some have concluded that there was no such person. But on the basis of a few letters preserved in the Public Record Office,[6]

[5] P. Friedmann, *Anne Boleyn: A Chapter of English History 1527-1536* (London, 1884), vol. II, p. 12. Similarly, perhaps in echo of Friedmann, P. W. Sergeant, *The Life of Anne Boleyn* (New York, 1924, p. 218) writes: "During the summer Henry and Anne went on another of their progresses in the Midlands, and we do not hear much of them until nearly the end of September."

[6] See *Letters and Papers of the Reign of Henry VIII*, vols. VI, no. 752; VII, nos. 308, 422, 423, 722; IX, nos. 345, 523. See also Dibdin's *Typographical Antiquities* (edition of 1809-19), vol. III, p. 417.

the *Dictionary of National Biography* credibly reports that William Marshall served as one of Cromwell's confidential agents, employed in the regulation of the monasteries, particularly of Charterhouse. He was of course a zealous partisan of the Reformation and he seems to have been in Cromwell's confidence as early as 1533. Judging by inference from what is said in the letters, he was probably a lawyer of sufficient learning to be conversant with what went on in the two Universities. He was anxious to have such books published as would advance the Protestant cause and he looked to Cromwell for financial aid in this enterprise. He is referred to in 1534 as a gentleman learned in the temporal law and often in attendance upon Cromwell ("much waiting upon your mastership"). The tone of his two extant letters to his patron suggests that he was no mere sycophant; rather his attitude towards Cromwell implies that they had been acquainted before the latter's rapid rise to power, perhaps in the days when Wolsey still had command.

In particular, Marshall sponsored the publication of a number of books, in which activity he is supposed to have had the encouragement of Queen Anne; at least it is to her that he dedicates the preface of one of them (*S.T.C.* 26119), signing it "your dayly Oratour and moste bounden bedeman Wylliam Marshall." Beside the Primers that bear his name, there were some dozen other books with which he was associated either as publisher or as translator.[7] It is pretty certain that he actually translated many of these, though as a rule there is no direct statement to this effect in the books themselves. He speaks, for instance, of a work called "The Gift of Constantine" and of a treatise by Erasmus on the Creed (*S.T.C.* 5641, 10504) and says in a letter to Cromwell, "I trust you wolle lyke the translation of the saide two bokes, they have cost me bothe labor & money & that largely." This seems to imply that he himself was the translator. In another letter he refers to some delay in the printing of a work called *The defence of peace* (*S.T.C.* 17817), "which," he says, "has been translated

---

[7] E.g., *S.T.C.* 5641, 10498, 10504, 16963, 17817, 21795, 24238/9, 25127, 26119.

this twelvemonth." This too in all probability means that it was Marshall who translated the work from the Latin of Marsilius of Padua; but in the book itself all that is said is: "nowe fyrste Imprynted and publysshed or sent forth abrode in the englysshe tonge by Wyllyam Marshall" (fol. A1ᵛ).

From a survey of the volumes connected with his name we can attempt a few hazardous guesses at his literary style. The indications are that it was labored and involved, full of parenthetical interruptions and legalistic pairs of synonyms. The simplest terms are apt to be twice "nominated in the bond" (to borrow Shylock's phrase). The treatises themselves make dreary reading; yet even the title-pages disclose some of his literary characteristics. One of his earliest titles (*S.T.C.* 5641) starts off as follows:

⟨ A treatyse of the donation or gyfte and endowment of possessyons/ gyuen and presented vnto Syluester pope of Rome by Constantyne emperour of Rome . . .

Another (*S.T.C.* 24239), which quite fills the title-page and is fairly typical, is here given at full length:

⟨ A treatise declaryng & shewing dyuers causes taken out of the holy scriptures/ of the sentences of holy faders, & of the decrees of deuout Emperours, that pyctures & ymages which were wont to be worshypped/ ar in no wise to be suffred in the temples or churches of Christen men. By the whiche treatise the reder that is indifferent [i.e., *impartial*], shall se and perceyue, how good and godly a dede it was of the Senatoures of Argentine [i.e., *Strassburg*], that of late daies they caused all the ymages with their auters [i.e., *altars*] to be cleane taken out of their churches.

⟨ The authours of this litle treatise ar the open preachers of Argentyne.

I dout nat but some popish doctor or peuish proctor wyl grunt at this treatise/ but yet fyrst rede and then iuge.

His final fling, at the bottom of the page, betrays Marshall's ardent Protestantism, shared also by Joye and others of that period. Indeed, it may be suspected that this very vehemence was what made Marshall useful to Cromwell at a time when the King was working to undermine the influence of the Pope in England. Yet it is small wonder that another of Cromwell's agents, reporting to his chief on September 11, 1535,[8] could say:

William Marshall, whom you know, has printed a book against the worship of images . . . and especially against the Mass. The people greatly murmur at it. I therefore thought it my duty to send you the same, for ye know what Marshall is.

But the pioneers of any reform are seldom popular. Devoted to the advancement of their cause, they manifest no tender regard for the cherished opinions of others. William Marshall was apparently such a person; yet it was he (so far as we know) who first ventured to bring out in the city of London a volume containing avowed portions of the Bible in the English tongue, thus certifying that the restrictive influence of the so-called 'Constitutions of Clarendon' was at an end.

[8] *Letters and Papers,* vol. IX, no. 345.

Chapter VI

Special Features of the Marshall Primer
(1534)

MARSHALL gave the printing of his Primer into the hands of John Byddell, one of the most intrepid and capable printers then in London. Byddell, who had been trained in the printing house of Wynkyn de Worde, seems to have started out for himself about 1533. For the first year or so he arranged to have his printing done by others, and there are several books extant that were printed for him by de Worde. But during 1534 he issued a few books over his own imprint from his shop at the sign of "Our Lady of Pity"—an address that had formerly been used by de Worde. Beside the Primer, William Marshall was apparently involved also in the publication of another of these imprints, "Of ye olde god & the newe" (*S.T.C.* 25127), which was dated June 15, 1534.[1] Upon the death of de Worde in January 1535, Byddell was named one of the executors under his will, and later moved into his master's more commodious quarters at the sign of the Sun.

The first edition of the Marshall Primer betokened a rapid and radical change in the attitude of officialdom toward the English Scriptures and toward such books as had been suspected of heresy. For upon examination we discover that fully three-fifths of this Primer was reprinted from the Joye Hortulus of 1530. In fact, virtually the entire contents of the Hortulus is reproduced in Marshall's Primer, though in somewhat altered sequence. Not only so, but the remainder of the Primer is largely drawn from the writings of Luther, without acknowledgment of course; while the Psalms of the Passion are taken from the Joye Psalter of 1530. In other words, texts that

[1] See *Letters and Papers of Henry VIII*, vol. VII, no. 423.

were prohibited as heretical near the end of 1531, together with borrowings from Luther himself, could now be published in London with official recognition, especially if the source material was not disclosed.

Like the Hortulus, the Marshall Primer of 1534 contained 144 leaves, but these were a little larger and averaged 29 lines to a full page.[2] This Primer, which boasted no table of contents, might be roughly described as made up of the following ingredients: A calendar, confession, and preface; a series of religious commentaries; the Matins, Hours, etc., down through Compline; the Seven Psalms, Commendations, and the Psalms of the Passion; and a catechism and a group of prayers. Like the Hortulus, it had neither Litany nor Dirge.[3] Its editor, William Marshall, was satisfied to act mainly as a compiler, though he was probably the translator of such materials as he took from Lutheran sources. At certain places he made slight editorial revisions, but only one item, a special prayer which will be noticed in its turn, has not been traced to some earlier publication.

Reviewing now those features that are of special interest, we note first that the calendar of the Primer is taken over from the Joye Hortulus with a few alterations. For example, the name of "Seinte Thomas mar." on February 23, referring to Sir Thomas Hitton, is omitted. Again, opposite July 26 (St. Anne's Day), Joye had made no mention of the Virgin's mother but referred instead to Anna, the daughter of Phanuel (Luke 2:36). Marshall rather neatly saved the situation by inserting editorially the words "but not this":

Saynt Anne. Ther was one Anna but not this whiche cam into the temple whan Christe was presented & she preched hym to all that loked for his redemption in Ierusalem. Luke the .ij. chapitour.

---

[2] Collation of the volume:—✠8 A4 B-I8 K-R8 S4; 2A-D8. The Bodleian copy lacks fol. E4. An imperfect copy in the Boston Public Library contains the following leaves: B-I8 K4,K5, R2-7, S4; 2A-B8, 2C1-3,6-8. The colophon of the Primer is on fol. S4, the reverse side of which is a full-page cut of the printer's device of Our Lady of Pity. The colophon of the Exposition on Psalm 51 is on fol. 2D8, and is similar to the one in the Primer.

[3] This statement corrects an error in the author's *Literary Lineage of the King James Bible* (p. 104). Since that work was published, the useful and valuable services of University Microfilms, Inc., have made possible a more detailed study of rare volumes housed in European libraries.

We have already pointed out that, at the end of August, this Primer supplied the words of rebuke spoken to Herod by John the Baptist, where they were missing in the extant Hortulus. Finally, because the pages of the Primer were larger, the printer, John Byddell, found he had more space in this calendar than he had copy; so he equalized the difference by filling in nearly all the space between September 8 and October 8 with patterns of asterisks. This idiosyncrasy would have been unexplained had it not been for the discovery of the Joye Hortulus.

After the calendar comes a form of General Confession, which is closely copied from the Hortulus, save that near the end, where Joye had written, "Thus grevously have I synned levynge the commaundementes (Oh father) to do deades of my nowne imaginacion," Marshall altered these last words, doubtless under the influence of Luther, so as to read (fol. A4ʳ): ". . . leuyng thy commaundementes (o father) to fulfyll the desyre of my flesshe, the word,[4] and the deuyll."

One of the most characteristic features of this Primer is "The preface/ to the reader" which comes next (fol. B1). This is an adaptation of Luther's preface to his *Betbüchlein* (1522). Its tone of militant reform carries the war to the enemy in its very first sentences:

Among other innumerable pestilent infections of bokes & learnynges/ with the which christen people haue bene pytyously seduced and deceyued (brought vp in dyuers kyndes of dyffydence & false hope) I may iudge and that chiefly/ those to be pernicyous/ on whom they be wont in euery place to pray/ and haue also learned by herte/ both curyously & with great scrupulosite to make rehersal of theyr sinnes. These bokes (though they abounded in euery place with infynyte errours/ and taught praiers, made with wycked folishnes/ both to god and also to the sayntes) yet by cause thei were garnished with gloryous tytles and with redde letters promysyng moch grace and pardon (though it were but vanite) haue sore deceiued the vnlearned multy-tude/ one is called ye gardeyn of the soule/ another the paradyse of the soule/ & by cause I wyll be short loke thou thy selfe/ what dyuerse and glorious names be gyuen vnto them/ wherfore here nedeth sharpe reformation/ yea and many of them be worthy to be vtterly destroied.

4 *Sic;* misprint for "world" of course.

Here it is to be noticed that the "Garden of the Soul" (in other words, *Hortulus Animae*) is frowned upon with disapproval.[5] This also was a Lutheran touch and refers, of course, to Roman Catholic editions of the Hortulus such as were current in Germany at the time. After proceeding further in the same vein, the preface alludes briefly to the subsequent content of Marshall's Primer:

> . . . I wyll declare after a symple & playne maner (by the which euen as by a glasse thou shalt knowe) what ye knowledge of sinne is, and how we ought trulye to pray folowyng the rehersal of the commaundementes and of the Pater noster.

Lastly, emphasizing that prayer should be from the heart rather than the lips, and extolling the virtue of the Lord's Prayer, the preface closes in a milder strain:

> . . . for a good prayer stondeth not nether consysteth in the multytude of wordes as Christe sayeth in the syxte of Mathew. But here stondeth the pythe that thou syghe to god often from the botom of thyn harte, for to haue strenght to do his wyll, to fulfyll his commaundementes, and this syghe ought to endure contynually. Therfore I desyre al persones that fromhensforth they forget suche prayers as be saynte Brigittes and other lyke, whiche greate promyses and perdons haue falsely aduaunced. And you shal retorne vnto this symple prayer nedeful for euery Christen, whose comen vse doeth yet perseuer amonge all men, yf they dyd vnderstonde it, and applyed theyre myndes to it. Suche vertue hathe the Pater noster, that the longer and the more thou vse it, the swetter and more accepable it is, whiche I desyre that the master of this prayer conferme Iesus Christe whiche is blessed eternally. So be it.

It was probably Marshall himself who Englished this preface. Some years later, in 1542, Bishop Bonner drew up another list of forbidden books which included "The Preface made in the English Prymmers, by Marshall."[6] But no matter who fashioned its phraseology, the significant fact is that this preface is simply a free translation of material originally set down by Martin Luther. The steps by which this was appropriated

---

[5] The "Paradise of the Soul" is still another compilation, of which the earliest printing is said to have been an *Orationale Paradisus Anime Nuncupatum* published at Basle by Pfortzheim in 1498 (Hain, No. 12028).

[6] See Burnet's *History of the Reformation of the Church of England* (edition of 1865), vol. IV, p. 518.

to the use of the Primer are still somewhat obscure, nor was any acknowledgment made of its Lutheran paternity.[7]

Having promised in the preface to set forth "what ye knowledge of sinne is, and how we ought trulye to pray folowyng the rehersal of the commaundementes and of the Pater noster," the Marshall Primer proceeds at once to consider these topics in a series of expositions. This portion of the Primer is furnished with an introduction of its own, which is subjoined to the general preface described above. This introduction begins (fol. B2):

It was neuer ordeyned withoute ye synguler prouidence of god that the multitude of Christen people shuld learne by herte the tenne commaundementes, the Crede, and the Pater noster, for truely he that vnderstondeth these hath the pythe of al those thynges, which holy scripture dothe conteyne . . .

The Ten Commandments are taken up individually, and the discussion brings out what is involved in the transgression or the fulfilment of each one. The Commandments are cited briefly, not at full length, and they are divided according to the older scheme whereby the first two are counted as one, and the tenth is subdivided into two. The articles of the Creed are next discussed under three headings, corresponding to the Persons of the Trinity. The Lord's Prayer comes next, and is accorded both a brief "goodly interpretation" and a more careful exposition—the latter dealing with the "seven petitions" embodied in the Prayer. Then follows a brief discussion of the Ave Maria—"the salutation of our most blyssed lady"—setting forth the Protestant view of Mary's place in Christian worship. But again it is to be noted that the entire section—introduction, Commandments, Creed, Paternoster, and Ave—is but the translation of material derived from the *Betbüchlein* of Luther.[8]

The next portion of the Marshall Primer is derived partly from Luther, partly from Joye. First we have, from one of Luther's early sermons, here rendered in English (fol. E5),

[7] For fuller discussion see below, in Appendix I.
[8] See below, Appendix I.

"An oration or sermon/ howe and in what maner/ we oughte to pray to almyghty God." Next we have (fol. F2) the story of the Passion, in ten parts as Joye had arranged it, the whole copied closely from the Hortulus of 1530. This in turn is followed by "A deuoute frutfull & godly remembraunce of the passion" (fol. I3ᵛ), which is taken from another of Luther's sermons.[9] Then comes (fol. K6ᵛ) "A fruetfull and a very Christen instruction for Chyldren." This, though drawn mostly from the corresponding portion of the Hortulus, both introduces a few new prayers and graces and also leaves out certain graces used by Joye such as the one "for fysshe days." It is perhaps worth noting that where the Lord's Prayer occurs, both in this "Christian Instruction," and earlier in the "goodly interpretation," Marshall models his wording on that of Tyndale in preference to that of Joye.

At length, after some ninety leaves of preliminary edification, we come to the body of the Primer itself (fol. L3ᵛ), the beginning of Matins with its customary Psalms and devotions. And so on through the Hours, Evensong, and Compline. All this portion of the Primer follows closely the text of the Joye Hortulus. Where the Lord's Prayer occurs in Matins, it is Joye's wording that is used. Such editorial revisions as Marshall made in this portion of the Primer are found chiefly in the hymns; for Joye's versification was sometimes slipshod, and Marshall sought to make it more regular.

Next (fol. O6ᵛ) come the traditional groups of Psalms: The Seven Psalms, the Commendations, and the Psalms of the Passion. All but the last of these were taken word for word from the Hortulus; even the verse from Isaiah 59 (see above, p. 46), with which Joye had concluded his Hortulus, appears here at the close of Commendations. As for the Psalms of the Passion, which Joye had inadvertently omitted, they are here reprinted from the Psalter of 1530. The first edition of the Marshall Primer thus includes forty-eight Psalms in all,[10] besides a portion of Psalm 31.

---

[9] For further details of these sermons, see below, Appendix I.
[10] See below, Appendix II.

Following the Psalms, Marshall printed the prayer of Jonah, which is given in Joye's version, and the catechism which Joye had used, "A Dialoge wherin the Chylde asked certayne Questions, answereth to the same" (fol. R1). This is printed without any paragraphing, the headings being incorporated in the solid text, but it follows the wording in the Hortulus exactly. Lastly, Marshall has a section of prayers (fol. R4^v), of which all but the first had appeared in the Hortulus, and which include the prayers of Isaiah, Hannah, and Daniel, and the prayer to appease God's wrath, with which the Primer ends.

The new prayer which Marshall introduced at the beginning of this final group is entitled "(A prayer for the molifieng and suplyeng [i.e., *suppling*] of our harde hertes, the lyghtnynge of our blynde hertes and the true conuertyng of our impenitente hertes." It embodies numerous texts from the Bible, and one of these is developed in an interesting way; especially if we bear in mind that this Primer probably appeared well in advance of the session of Convocation in which the King was petitioned for an English text of the Bible. This portion of the prayer reads (fol. R5^v):

. . . prouer. xxj. The kynges hert is in thyne handes (Oh lorde) that where thou wylte thou mayest inclyne it, for soo sayeth thy scrypture. Inclyne his herte to this purpose (oh father) that it wyl please hym to commaunde his prelates of his realme no lenger to kepe from his people: his louynge subiectes the lyght of thy worde, the lyght of holy scrypture, the lyght of the testament of thy deare sonne our sauyour Iesu christ, the lyght wherin he yt walketh erreth not neyther stumbleth at ony [i.e., *any*] stone   put it in his mynde lorde to commaunde that lyke as thrugh thy secrete inspyration other nations alredy haue: so his people also by his commaundement maye haue in to theyr tonge truely translated thy holy scrypture wherin they may learne & perfytely know thy godly wyll & pleasure . . .

The implication in this passage, that the King was the champion of the rights of the people against the conservative mistrust of the prelates or bishops, is wholly in keeping with the ardor of English reformers at that time. There seems good reason to suppose that this prayer for the mollifying of hard hearts was written by William Marshall himself.

Savonarola's Exposition on the 51st Psalm, which (as was said) follows immediately after the first edition of Marshall's Primer and was bound with it, includes a complete text of the Psalm, sentence by sentence, interspersed with a lengthy meditation both contrite and lugubrious, of the sort that seemed to appeal especially to many of the early Protestants. Since it is the earliest known printing of this treatise in the English tongue,[11] and since it was often reprinted in later Primers, some description of it is warranted here.

The title at the head of the first page reads:

⟨ An exposition after the maner of a contemplacyon vpon ye .li. psalme/ called Miserere mei Deus.

The colophon is almost identical with that in the Primer, with which it was undoubtedly contemporary:

⟨ Here endeth the exposition vpon the li. Psalme/ called Miserere mei deus. Imprented at London in Flete strete by Iohan Byddell/ dwellynge next to Flete brydge at the sygne of our lady of pytye/ for wyllyam Marshall.

The original author was the famous Italian reformer, Girolamo Savonarola, a native of Ferrara, who was executed as a martyr at Florence in 1498, but his name is not mentioned in this particular edition.[12] Neither is the name of the translator divulged. It would throw further light on the history of these early Primers if we could tell for certain whose English version this was. Judging simply by the style, I somehow doubt that it was by Coverdale or Joye. Other translators were in the field, of course, lesser-known men such as Leonard Cox and Thomas Swinnerton and William Turner, whose work was being put through Byddell's press at this same pe-

11 It is separately listed in *S.T.C.* as No. 21795, but the date there assigned to it (1540?) is obviously too late by at least five or six years. See also the footnote on p. 74 below.

12 Savonarola's expositions on Psalms 31, 51, and 80 were printed at Venice in 1505 under the title, *Fratris hieronymi Ferrariensis Expositiones in psalmos*. He also expounded Psalm 5, published separately.

riod.[13] All in all, it seems most likely that we have here more of Marshall's own work. For Marshall was clearly a staunch Lutheran, and in 1523 Savonarola's expositions on Psalms 51 and 31 had been published at Wittenberg along with a letter of recommendation written in Latin by Luther himself.[14]

The Exposition on Psalm 51 begins as follows in English:

Alas wretche y*t* I am/ confortlesse & forsaken of all men/ which haue offended both heuen & earth. whether shall I go? or whether shall I turne me? To who*m* shall I flye for socoure? Who shall haue pytye or *com*passion on me?

Later, commenting on the words of the Psalm "Cast me not away from thy face," we come upon this passage (fol. B7ᵛ) which may stand as a sample of the composition:

The woman of canane folowed the/ she cried and made piteous noyse she moued the dyscyples vnto *com*passyon/ and thou heldest thy peace/ . . . vnto whose importunyte (Lorde) thou answeredst/ it is not good to take the chyldrens breede and caste it to houndes as thoughe thou sholdest haue geue*n* her a full answere and sayd departe from me/ you Canaanites ar dogges/ . . . What shalt thou now do thou woman of Canaan? thou mayste nowe be a shamed and gette the away/ for the lorde is angry not with the alone/ but also thy hole nacyon. Oh lorde god/ who wolde not haue bene *con*founde & haue pyked hym away [i.e., *taken himself off*] at these thy wordes? who wolde not haue mum-bled and grudged agaynst the? who wolde not haue iudged the to be cruell? And yet did this woman contynue styll in prayer. She cast not away hir confydence/ she toke not these harde wordes heuelye [i.e., *heavily*]/ she was not angry/ but she hu*m*bled hir self the more and abode styll in hir petycyon and sayde with good fyaunce: It is truthe lorde that thou sayest/ . . .

Special interest attaches to the version of the Psalm itself, which is presented piecemeal. We may suppose that whoever made this translation was acquainted with the rendering in the Psalter of 1530, which was also printed in the body of the Primer itself among the Seven Psalms. Very likely the trans-lator had before him this version of 1530 (which was based on the Latin of "Feline") and the ordinary Latin text of the

---

13 Cf. *S.T.C.* 10503, 23552, and 25127.
14 See the Weimar edition of Luther's *Werke*, vol. XII, pp. 245-248.

Vulgate Bible, and he reconciled the one to the other as best he could. This would account for the fact that in some verses the two translations run nearly parallel, while in others they diverge surprisingly. Here is a comparison (verses 7-12):

(P30)—Sprinkle me   with hyssope and so shall I be clene: thou
(Sav)—Sprynkle me Lorde with ysope and so shall I be clene/ thou

shalt wasshe me/   & then shall I be whighter then snowe.
shalt washe me/ and then shall I be whytter then snowe. . . . Vnto my

        Powre vppon me   ioye and gladnes: make my bones to
hearynge shalte thou   geue ioye and gladnes/ &   my brosed bones

reioyse which thou hast smyten. Turne thy face fro   my sinnes: &
shall be refreshed. . . .   Turne thy face from of my synnes and

wype awaye all my wikednes.   A pure harte create in me (Oh lorde):
wype awaye all my wyckednes. . . . A pure herte create in me oh god

and a stedfaste right spyrit make a newe withyn me.   Caste me not
& an vpryghte   spiryte make a newe within me. . . . Caste me not

awaye: and thy holy ghoste take not fro   me.   Make
away from thy face/ and thy holy ghost take not from me. . . . Make

me ageine to reioyse whyls thou bryngest me thy savynge helthe: and
me agayne to reioyse   in   thy sauynge healthe/ and

let thy chefe governynge fre spyrit strengthen and lede me.
strengthen me with a pryncypall spirite.

The 51st Psalm (the 50th in the Latin Psalter)[15] was probably printed more often than any other portion of the Old Testament, except the Ten Commandments. Its historic connection with the story of David and Bath-sheba invested it with a special poignancy for the medieval worshipper, and many a Psalter and Primer of the first half of the sixteenth century was enlivened with a woodcut, crude perhaps but as unmis-

---

[15] The Hebrew and Latin Psalters were numbered alike for Psalms 1-8 and 148-50. In Latin, Psalm 9 embraces 9 and 10 in Hebrew; hence the Latin numbering is one less until Psalm 113. Psalms 114-16 are divided differently in Latin. Then from 117 to 146, the Latin number is again one less than in Hebrew; but Psalm 147 in Hebrew embraces 146 and 147 in Latin. See below, Appendix II.

takable as a merchant's shop-sign, showing King David watching from his balcony while his messenger approaches the modest Bath-sheba at her ablutions.

At the conclusion of the Savonarola treatise the editor tells us:

〔 To fyll vp the lefe we haue touched certeyne places which we thought most necessary to edefye the congregacion of Christ.

Then follow four paragraphs, each of Lutheran extraction, on Faith, The Power of Faith, The Work of Faith, and Good Works. At the end of these comes the colophon.

Chapter VII

Thomas Godfray's Primer
(1534-1535)

Duʀɪɴɢ the latter part of 1534 the Convocation of Canterbury held several sessions. Much of their discussion turned upon 'suspected' books. On December 11, an abbot from Northampton drew their attention to a certain book commonly known as a Primer, in which there were questionable rubrics at the head of certain prayers. It is not stated positively that it was an English Primer; simply that it was 'popularly called a Prymer.'[1]

Now this abbot may well have been John Dassett, in charge of the abbey of St. James, near Northampton. Dassett had formally acknowledged the King as Supreme Head of the Church on August 17, 1534, and his monastery was later given a favorable report by George Gifford, who paid it an official visit in 1536 as part of Cromwell's program for the suppression of the monasteries.[2] Not knowing clearly to which party the abbot belonged, whether orthodox or liberal, we cannot tell for certain what sort of Primer he would have raised objection to. It has always been assumed that it was a 'reformed' English Primer. But if so—if Convocation was being invited to scrutinize a copy of the recent Marshall Primer, for instance—the only headings in this that might have been deemed at

---

[1] The Latin minute for December 11, as recorded in Wilkins' *Concilia* (vol. III, p. 769), reads: "abbas monasterii de Northampton. exhibuit quendam librum 'a Prymer' vulgo dictum, cum quibusdam rubricis sive rubricellis praecedentibus quasdam orationes et precationes ejusdem libri, quae reverendissimo et confratribus suis videbantur suspectae, et non ibidem inferendae, eo quod non consonant determinationi S. matris ecclesiae; ideo decretum fuit, quod populus non deberet exinde instrui, ne crederent contentis in dictis rubricis, aut aliquam spem ponerent in ijsdem."

[2] See *Letters and Papers of Henry VIII*, vols. V, no. 1139(23); VII, 1121(28); X, 916, 917, 1166; XI, 87.

variance with official pronouncements of Holy Church would
be the captions over the prayers of Isaiah and Daniel, both of
which (as taken over from the Joye Hortulus) refer to the
sorry condition of Christ's Church "in these laste and perylous
dayes." Yet, as a matter of fact, the Marshall Primer, which
was published "cum privilegio regali," was allowed to circulate for quite a few years.

Rather, the whole tenor of the action as reported suggests
that it was some Latin orthodox Book of Hours that was being
questioned. We recall that Luther had already warned his
followers not to put their trust in extravagant promises of
grace and pardon, such as the rubrics in older Primers often
contained, though "garnished with gloryous tytles and with
redde letters," as the Marshall Primer phrased it.

There was, for example, a volume published by Regnault
in Paris this very same year (1534) under the title, *Hore
Beatissime virginis marie ad legitimum Sarisburiensis Ecclesie
ritum* (*S.T.C.* 15984), which would have been popularly
known as a Primer; and this included a number of Latin
prayers headed with English rubrics. These were simply reprinted from older editions of the Primer as far back as 1511.
Typical of such rubrics is one that reads (fol. 51ᵛ) :

《 Our holy father Sixtus the .iiij. pope hath graunted to all them
that deuoutly say this prayer before the ymage of our lady the somme
of .xj.M. yeres of pardon.

People were now to be warned not to put their hope *("aliquam
spem ponerent")* in such promises. Another rubric, much
more elaborate though in dubious English, runs (fol. 54):

《 Our holy father the pope Sixtus hath graunted at the instaunce of
the hyghe moost and excellent princesse elizabeth late qwene of eng-
londe and wyf to our souerayne lyege lorde kynge henri the teuenth
[*sic*], . . . that euery day in the mornynge after thre tollynges of the aue
bell say .iij. times the hoole salutacyon of our lady . . . for euery tyme
so doynge is graunted of the spirituall tresour of holy chyrche .iij. C
dayes of pardon . . . And also our holy father the archebysshop of
cantorbery and yorke wit[h] other .ix. bysshoppes of this reame haue
graunted .iij. times in the day .xl. dayes of pardon to all them that be

in the state of grate [*sic*] able to receue pardon/ the whyche begonne
the .xxvj. daye of marche Anno .M.cccc.xcij. . . .

In view of the determined stand taken by Convocation in the
spring of the year, it would not seem surprising if the present
'reverendissimus' (Cranmer) and his confreres should deem
this sort of thing objectionable; and in fact, in the British
Museum copy of this Primer, these particular rubrics have
been deleted with rough cross-hatchings.

Be this as it may—whichever sort of Primer it was, orthodox
or reformed, that was viewed with suspicion—Convocation
adopted a resolution on December 19 that owners of all such
suspected books should be obliged to declare and show which
books they owned, in the presence of some competent authority. But the books seem never to have been listed and no system
of enforcement was set up; so it is doubtful if the measure ever
became effective.

Of much greater importance, Convocation at the same time
petitioned the King to allow the Bible to be translated into
English. While this action failed to enlist enough support to
insure the production of an authorized version of the Bible
at once, it did nevertheless have certain definite results. It
stimulated fresh publication of English New Testaments in
the neighborhood of Antwerp. At least three new editions were
brought out early in 1535. One of these was a reprint of Tyndale's Testament of November 1534, this time evidently set
up by a Flemish compositor whose ignorance of English frequently disfigured the current spellings (*S.T.C.* 2828). Another was Joye's second issue of the edition which he had
brought out surreptitiously in the preceding August. The
new volume, dated January 9 (*S.T.C.* 2827), contained a section of 'epistles' taken from the Old Testament, to match those
that Tyndale had included in his November edition. Joye
seems to have drawn upon Tyndale's wording for these, except
that wherever there was a passage which he himself had translated, he made use of his own in preference to Tyndale's
rendering.[3] The third New Testament was Tyndale's final

[3] E.g., see above, p. 42.

revision of his own work, the last he was destined to publish. Printed for Godfried van der Haghen (*S.T.C.* 2830), this revision became the basis of the text of the New Testament in the Matthew and Great Bibles.

Meanwhile, in London, the Marshall Primer was evidently meeting with immediate success. Enterprising publishers saw that the time was now ripe to venture on the printing of books which embodied portions of Scripture translated into the English tongue. Beside John Byddell, who printed the Marshall Primer, there were two others who promptly took advantage of the new field thus opened to them; these were Thomas Godfray and Robert Redman, each of whom had already been instrumental in publishing at least one book for William Marshall.[4]

Concerning Thomas Godfray not much is known. His most famous product was an edition of Chaucer dated 1532; but he seldom dated what he published and his colophons are unrevealing, to say the least. He is thought to have brought out some thirty or more books between 1530 and 1536, but his craftsmanship was not always of the best, and of his personal career he seems to have left no record.

Sometime during 1535, or the latter part of 1534, Godfray put forth several volumes of great rarity today, and one of these was an English Primer.[5] Its title, which stands above a table of contents, reads: "A Prymer in Englysshe/ with dyuers prayers & godly meditations." The colophon, like that in most of his publications, merely discloses, "Printed at London by Thomas Godfray. Cum priuilegio Rygali." The almanac at the beginning of the Primer, giving the dates for Easter, commences with the year 1535—the only positive clue to the date of publication, though not by any means infallible. Godfray may also have coupled with his Primer, as Marshall did, the Savonarola Exposition on the 51st Psalm; for there is a copy

4 Namely, *S.T.C.* 5641 and 10504, assigned to the years 1534 and 1533 respectively.
5 The Primer is *S.T.C.* 15988a. The others include (but who can tell in what sequence?): *The Psalter of Dauid in Englysshe* (*S.T.C.* 2371), a reprint of the 1530 Psalter; *The Fountayne or well of lyfe* (*S.T.C.* 11211) noted below; and *The proverbes of Solomon newly translated into Englyshe*, together with *The boke of Solomon called Ecclesiastes* (*S.T.C.* 2752), in a version by George Joye.

of this work in the Bodleian Library which issued from his press at about this time, a reprint of the Exposition as Byddell had published it for Marshall.[6]

Though the wording of the title of Godfray's Primer suggests that it was modeled on the Marshall Primer of 1534, the text itself turns out to be derived directly from the Joye Hortulus of 1530, with certain modifications and with some additional material, as will now be explained. In the first place, Godfray not only uses the older orthodox form of calendar, devoid of all comment or gloss, but he prints it in Latin instead of English, a month to a page. Perhaps he had got word of Bishop Tunstall's complaint about the gloss. As for Marshall's uncompromising preface to the reader, Godfray decided it would be prudent to omit this altogether.

Instead he begins with "A christenmans lernyng deuyded in thre partes" (fol. A8). These, as usual, deal with the Commandments, the Creed, and the Paternoster. Although this covers the same ground as in the Marshall Primer, it is for the most part an independent treatment. It will be recalled that Marshall's introduction began, "It was neuer ordeyned withoute ye synguler prouidence of god" etc. (see above, page 63); whereas in the Godfray Primer the prologue commences:

Ye haue desyred me oft and many tymes/ dere brother and frende/ truely and faithfully to write vnto you/ the some & effecte of a Christenmans lernynge/ that is to say/ the princypall thyng that a christen man is bounde to know/ wherby I perceyue that ye are a thurste and hungre after ye knowlege of god/ . . .

This is hardly distinguished writing and the author of it, as usual, is unnamed. At times it has a homely, salty flavor (fol. B3):

These are the thre thynges wherin is hole and full contayned the learnynge of a Christen man/ . . . Therfore I wyll declare them vnto you/ trustyng that ye wyll . . . earnestly regarde them/ and be glad to talke vpon them/ nat only that/ but be dilygent to teche them youre

[6] This Godfray item is unrecorded in *S.T.C.*; for further discussion see the writer's article, "Savonarola's Expositions on the Fifty-first and Thirty-first Psalms," in *The Library* (Series V, vol. VI, p. 162). The Godfray Primer itself is preserved in the Cambridge University Library; its collation is: A-Q8 R7 (135 leaves).

chyldren & housholde/ as ye be straytly bou*n*de by goddes commaunde-
mente/ for to that occupacyon is euery man prentyse. And dout ye nat/
but they that sette so moche by a tale of Robyn hode/ and count these
commaundementes of god but for a flyrynge [i.e., *fleering*] mater/ shall
answere to it. And verily it is a shame to se so many prentyses so well
learned in Robyn hode & noughty tryfels/ and so fewe that knowe the
co*m*maundementes of god/ their belefe/ nor their Pater noster.

The comparison of the popularity of Scripture and of Robin
Hood was often in the mouths of the reformers. It occurs as
far back as *Piers Plowman,*[7] wherein Sloth declares:

> I can noughte perfitly my pater-noster, as the prest it syngeth;
> But I can rymes of Robyn Hood and Randolf erle of Chestre.

Godfray's entire treatise has, no doubt, a Lutheran background, but it does not follow the Marshall text till it reaches
the "fifth petition" of the Lord's Prayer, whereupon the comment suddenly becomes virtually a paraphrase of the Marshall
treatise for the remainder of the Prayer. Marshall's phrasing
is apt to be more elaborate, but the parallel is unmistakable.
In the "seventh petition," for instance, which according to
Marshall asks deliverance from all "euylles of paynes and
punyshmentes as doth the Chyrche in the Letany," the 1534
Primer had said (fol. E3):

Delyuer vs from sodeyne deathe. Kepe vs from the vyolence of water
and fyre, from thundre lyghtenyng and hayle/ kepe vs from hunger
and dearthe, keps [*sic*] vs from warre, and manslaughter, kepe vs from
thy moste greuous strokes, the pestilence, frenshe pockes, fallynge
syknes, and suche other diseases, kepe vs from all euyll and peryll*es* of
the bodye, . . .

In the Godfray Primer (fol. C8ᵛ) we have:

Delyuer vs from sodayn dethe. Kepe vs fro*m* hungre & derth. Kepe vs
fro*m* batayle & shedi*n*g of blode. Kepe vs from gret plages/ fro*m* the
pestilence/ Fre*n*che pockes/ & other sore sycknesses. Kepe vs fro*m* all
euyll both bodily & ghostly/ . . .

[7] From Passus V of the B-text, lines 401-402. Tyndale in the prologue to his
Prophete Ionas says (fol. A3), "And the liues stories and gestes of men which are
contayned in the bible/ they reade as thi*n*ges no moare perteyni*n*ge vn to the*m*/
then a take of Robin hode." Hugh Latimer has an amusing reference to Robin
Hood's Day in his sermon before King Edward on April 12, 1549.

At the conclusion of the commentary on the Lord's Prayer, Godfray prints "An exhortation for them that receyueth the blessed sacrament of the auter." This distinctive item, which Marshall does not give, is likewise Lutheran in tone; near the end of it there is a suggestion of German idiom in the rendering of the Lord's behest concerning the cup (fol. D2) : "Also drynke therout euery one/ and remembre me."

The next features of the Godfray Primer are copied from the Joye Hortulus of 1530: first the "Christen instruction for chyldre," then the catechism and the general confession. In the heading of the catechism (fol. D4ᵛ) Godfray runs afoul of Joye's unusual grammatical construction: Joye had said, "VVheryn the Childe asked certayne questions/ answerth to the same," but Godfray copied it thus: "⟨ A dialogue wherin the childe asketh certayn questions answerynge to the same." But the text is just like Joye's, in which the questions are asked of the child.

With the beginning of Matins (fol. E3), as if to accentuate the devotional features of the Primer, Godfray employs a different font of type, a larger and heavier *Textura*. The wording, however, is Joye's without alteration. At the end of Matins, where Godfray introduces Joye's account of the Passion of Christ (fol. G4), he again reverts to the smaller type. But here Godfray is able to extend the account of the Passion by the use of fresh material.

He calls attention to this feature on the title-page of his Primer; there in the synopsis of contents we read:

⟨ The Passion of our sauiour Christ,
⟨ Ths [sic] Resurrection. Thapparitions
  of Christ to his discyples,
⟨ The ascencion.
⟨ The receyuynge of the holyghost.

Joye's account, in ten parts, had stopped with the soldiers sitting at the tomb; but in the Godfray Primer (fol. K4) we are told:

⟨ Thus endeth the passyon of our sauyour Christ/ & here foloweth the Resurrection. &c.

This brings up the interesting possibility that Godfray may have prevailed on Joye to go on and finish the account; otherwise someone else must have volunteered to do it. In the matter of English style the additions are not specially suggestive of Joye.[8]

Next (fol. L2) come Prime, Hours, Evensong, and Compline, all in larger type again, and all according to the wording of the Hortulus. Then (fol. N7) a section of prayers, in smaller type, copied from the corresponding material in the Hortulus—the prayer of Isaiah, of Hannah, etc., ending with "Prayer peaseth Gods wrathe." Finally, resuming with the larger font of type, Godfray gives us the Seven Psalms, Commendations, and Psalms of the Passion.

In the Commendations (Psalm 119) the dependence of Godfray on the Hortulus of 1530 rather than on the Marshall Primer is evident from verse 64. This verse had somehow been overlooked in the Psalter of 1530 and in the Hortulus; but, whereas Marshall remedied the defect by supplying the words, "The erth is full of thy goodnes lord, nurture me in thy ceremonyes," Godfray omitted the verse just as Joye had done.

The Psalms of the Passion, on the other hand, which inadvertently had been left out of the Hortulus of 1530, are now present and seem to have been copied from those in the Marshall Primer; at least they resemble Marshall's treatment of them in that they are furnished with a preliminary 'argument' pertaining to Psalm 22 (as printed in the Psalter of 1530) but are not supplied with 'arguments' for any of the other Psalms in the series. At the end of them Godfray fills up his page (fol. R7ᵛ) by repeating the words of the hymn near the close of Matins, "Praise ye the Lord omnipotent"; below which comes the brief colophon mentioned above.

One typographical curiosity in the Godfray Primer is worth mentioning: in the calendar the numeral 4 is printed uniformly in reverse position, thus— ᚨ . The same peculiarity is

---

8 The text of the account of the Resurrection in the Godfray Primer, as well as Bucer's original Latin, is reprinted in the article by Constantin Hope in *Journal of Theological Studies* (New series, vol. II, part I, p. 68). Compare footnote on p. 30, above.

observable also in certain other of Godfray's publications;[9] noticeably, for example, in *The Fountayne or well of lyfe/ ... Translated out of latyn in to Englysshe*. This was an early, undated, well-chosen anthology of texts and excerpts from the Scriptures, presented anonymously and without comment save for a brief foreword. Its source is undoubtedly the *Fons Vitae,* a Latin compilation which de Keyser printed in Antwerp in September 1533. Aside from occasional use of Tyndale's phraseology, the English rendering of Bible passages in this volume of Godfray's is unique and full of interest. On the evidence of the reversed 4, it is altogether likely that Godfray published his Primer and *The Fountayne* at about the same time.

[9] It occurs in the "Treatise on the Astrolabe" in Godfray's edition of Chaucer's Works published in 1532 (*S.T.C.* 5068), and in the so-called "Gift of Constantine" published about March 1534 (*S.T.C.* 5641). Likewise it is to be found in the "Treatise on Pictures and Images" (*S.T.C.* 24238/9) published for William Marshall and mentioned in Chapter V above (see p. 57). Though this latter work contains neither date nor printer's name, it appeared about 1535, and the evidence of this reversed 4 would connect it with Godfray's press.

Chapter VIII

Robert Redman's *Prayers of the Byble*
(1535)

ESIDES John Byddell and Thomas Godfray, the third London printer who stood ready to enter upon the lucrative
trade of scriptural publications in the English tongue was
Robert Redman. Redman was an active publisher from 1525
to 1540, whose output was largely made up of books on religion and the law. He had connections with Richard Pynson,
one of the best known of the early London printers, and
occupied his quarters after Pynson's death. His first venture
into the field of English Scripture seems to have been a small
thick volume called *Prayers of the Byble,* issued near the beginning of 1535.[1] Though not itself a Primer, this scarce and
curious little book figures in the subsequent history of our
subject.

It contained a rather crude translation, by whom unknown,
of a Latin compilation of prayers taken from the Vulgate Bible
and first published at Strassburg in 1528 under the title *Precationes Biblicae Sanctorum Patrum.* This was compiled by
Otto Brunfels, a follower of Luther, distinguished as an early
pioneer in the science of botany. Three years later Marten de
Keyser of Antwerp brought out another edition with a similar
title, with its contents expanded to include a good deal of other
material besides Brunfels' *Precationes.* The additional material was drawn from various sources: quite a little came from

[1] Redman also published, probably in 1534, the *Common Places* of Patrick
Hamilton as translated by John Frith, under the title, "Dyuers frutful gatherynges
of scripture" (*S.T.C.* 12733). While this contained a table of the Ten Commandments, most of the text of the work was intermingled with argument. What seems
to be a reprint of a still earlier edition (*S.T.C.* 12732) contains a foreword by Frith
and was apparently first issued before his martyrdom in July 1533; but no printer's
name is given. See below, p. 127.

Luther's *Enchiridion;*[2] there was a treatise by Erasmus on the Lord's Prayer, and one by Cornelius Crocus on the Passion; also two expositions by Savonarola on the 51st and 31st Psalms. It was this particular edition of 1531 on which Redman based his new publication. He did not try to use all of de Keyser's material, but added other selections of his own.

As published in 1535 Redman's volume comprised, in addition to the *Prayers,* five other sections, each with its own signatures and colophon but all in uniform size and style of type. There was a general title-page, printed in red and black, worded as follows:

❡ Prayers of the Byble take*n* out of the olde testament and the newe, as olde holy fathers bothe men and women were wont to pray in tyme of tribulation/ deuyded in vi. partes.

❡ An exposicyo*n* vpo*n* the psalme of Miserere/ and vpon the Psalme of In te domine speraui/ made by freer Hierom Sauonarole of Ferrarie/ with dyuers other good meditations very necessarie for al good true christen people.

❡ Cum preuilegio Regali.

The only complete copy is in the Pierpont Morgan Library in New York City, wherein the two expositions by Savonarola, announced in the title, occupy the last two sections of the volume.[3]

The first of the six sections is devoted to Brunfels' *Prayers,* which are themselves divided into six parts as noted in the title. There is a foreword "To the trewe beleuers in Christe Iesu," which commences:

For asmoche as at this daye we are entangled w*ith* many imcommodites [sic], and the same tymes begyn to drawe on, wherof our maister Christe and his Apostles gaue vs warnyng that shulde be so daungerous and so ful of trouble and afflictio*n* that the lyke hath nat ben sene from the begynnyng of the worlde vnto this present day. I coulde se none other waye, for to auoyde the vengeaunce of goddes wrathe hangyng ouer our heades, otherwyse than to praye continually

2 See below, Appendix I.

3 The work is unrecorded in *S.T.C.* Another copy, lacking one section, is in the library of Lambeth Palace, London, and a third, consisting of only four sections separately bound, is in the Chapin Library at Williams College, Massachusetts. For further discussion, see the writer's article, "Robert Redman's *Prayers of the Byble*" in *The Library* (Series V, vol. 3, p. 279).

and nat to ceasse, for what thyng is it that we may nat obtayne by instau*n*t humble and importune prayour?

This is but an English rendering of the words of the compiler, Brunfels.[4] Further on the foreword states, according to the translator:

This study haue we vndertake*n* vpon this entent (as god be mercyful to vs) nat to gather to gether any other but onely out of holy scripture, that euery trewe christen myght purely make his prayer after the ensample of holy fathers.

It is perhaps significant that in this passage the translator has deserted the Brunfels' wording, which in its Latin form contained an uncomplimentary reference to the *Hortulus Animae* to this effect:

My desire and intention (else may I forfeit the favour of Christ) was not to compile again some new Hortulus or any other old rubbish of the sort.[5]

No doubt Brunfels was thinking of the traditional Hortulus in Latin; but it is conceivable that Redman's editor amended the passage out of consideration for Joye's use of the term in the title of his Primer.

The foreword is followed by "The testament of Moyses. Deuteronomii the xxxii. chapitre"; after which come the six groups of prayers. These are made up entirely of excerpts from the Bible without comment, save for the title of each prayer which also cites the chapter whence it was taken. The fifth group is composed wholly of Psalms, each one complete, thirty-eight in all. It is noteworthy that, whereas the rest of the *Prayers* are presented in a unique English version, these thirty-eight Psalms are identical with the version issued by Joye in Antwerp, August 1534. This proves incidentally that Joye's second Psalter (*S.T.C.* 2372) was known in London within a few months of its appearance.

---

4 See above, p. 38, footnote.

5 For this rendering of the passage as it stood in the *Precationes* I am indebted to Rev. J. F. Mozley, who made it at my request. Brunfels' Latin reads here as follows: "Id nobis studiu*m* fuit, ea intentio aut no*n* sit nobis Christus propitius, no*n* ut rursum nouos hortulos moliremur, & si quid fuit aliud veteru*m* neniarum."

The colophon to this first section[6] reads simply: "❧ Imprynted at London in Fletestrete by me Robert Redman. Cum gratia et priuilegio Regali." The book is undated, but the ancient (perhaps original) binding of the Morgan copy has the figures 1535 stenciled at the base of its spine. This in itself establishes little, but it is borne out by other facts, as will be seen.

The second section of the volume[7] starts off with the words, "In the name of the Father/ of the Sonne/ and of the holy Ghoste." Then comes "The pater noster in Englyshe" in a version that resembles Tyndale's. This is followed by a treatise on "The Crede by the olde lawe and by the newe"; this in turn by the Ten Commandments and an exposition upon them. This material was not in the de Keyser edition of 1531, neither does it correspond with the treatises in the Marshall or Godfray Primers. At the end of the exposition on the Creed we are told:

❧ Neuertheles yf any man can fynde in this Crede any erroure or heresie & grounde hym in holy writ: I wyll mekely reuoke it and lerne to beleue better.

The section concludes with a series of inventories of traditional items such as the ten plagues of Egypt, the seven deadly sins, the five bodily and five ghostly wits, the seven principal virtues, etc.

Some of these religious categories are also to be found in older manuscript Primers of the fourteenth and fifteenth centuries. There is a striking similarity between certain of Redman's phrases and those used in a children's Primer dating from the early fifteenth century.[8] In this interesting old manuscript, "The vij dedly sinnes" are listed thus:

Pride wrathe & enuy ben synnes of the fend [i.e., *fiend*]. Couetice and auarice ben synnes of the world. Gloteny slowthe & lecheri ben synnes

---

[6] The first section is made up thus: Title and foreword occupy two preliminary leaves; Deuteronomy 32 commences on fol. A1. Signatures A to H have eight leaves each; final signature (I) has only four; colophon is on I4v.

[7] Known also in separate form, this section is separately listed in *S.T.C.* as No. 16815, where it is mistakenly assigned to the year 1538.

[8] See G. A. Plimpton's *The Education of Chaucer* (Plate IX, 3).

of the flessh. & thes ben the large weyes to helle & many passen therbi to helle for thei will not bysi them to knowe god*des* commaunde-me*ntes*.

In Redman's book, the paragraph headed "Here ensueth the .vii. deedly synnes" (fol. ²D5) makes use of the same wording exactly, except at two points: "therbi" becomes "by them"; and "to knowe" is enlarged to "knowe & kepe." Again, in the Beatitudes—"the .viii. blessynges of our lorde Iesu Christe"— Redman reproduces the text of the older manuscript with its Wycliffite flavor, except for a few modernizations. May this not suggest that Redman or his editor made use of Lollard sources for this section of his book?

The third section, a short one, contains expositions on the "Crede or Beleue," the Paternoster, and the Ave Maria. Not only is it of Lutheran origin, but it is reprinted, word for word, from the corresponding portion of the Marshall Primer of 1534. The only difference I detect is that Redman omits what Marshall called the "brief interpretation" of the Lord's Prayer and contents himself with giving only the longer one containing the "seven petitions" (see above, p. 63).

The fourth section is entitled "A consolation for troubled Consciences." It comprises a mediocre translation of Luther's "Fourteen Consolations."[9] This treatise was an elaborate dissertation cast in the form of successive 'images' of good and evil. It was not represented in the 1531 edition of Brunfels' *Precationes,* and this translation of it may well have been the first to be published in English.

In the Morgan Library copy of *Prayers of the Byble* the last two sections are devoted to the Savonarola treatises already mentioned.[10] For the Exposition on the 51st Psalm, Redman made use of the very same translation that Byddell had used, which we described in connection with the Marshall Primer. He also reprinted the additional paragraphs on Faith and Good Works (see above, p. 69) and added still another on

[9] Originally published by Luther in 1520 as *Tessaradecas Consolatoria pro laborantibus & oneratis* (see Weimar edition of his *Werke,* vol. VI, p. 106).

[10] See also the article on the Savonarola expositions, cited above, in *The Library* (Series V, vol. VI, p. 162).

Persecution. It is difficult to tell with certainty which publisher borrowed from the other, but there is reason to suppose that Byddell's printing was the earlier. In the Redman volume, this fifth section closes with an unusually full colophon, occupying all the reverse side of fol. ⁵D8 and reading:

Imprynted at London in Fletestrete/ by me Robert Redman/ dwellyng at the sygne of the George/ nexte to Saynt Dunstones church. ❴ Cum priuilegio Regalj,

The final section presents Savonarola's uncompleted Meditation on the 31st Psalm. This is the earliest printing of it known in English and it bears the title:

❴ A meditation of the same Ierom/ vpon the Psalme of In te domine speraui whiche preuented by death he coulde nat fynyshe.

The translation is by an unknown hand, perhaps the same that had translated the *Prayers;* it commences:

Heuynes [i.e., *heaviness*] hath besyged me with a great & stronge oost [i.e., *host*] she hath enclosed me, she hath oppressed my hert with clamours & ceaseth nat with weapons nyght and day to fyghte agaynste me.

The Meditation breaks off after only three verses of the Psalm have been considered. Its closing words happen to be a very unusual rendition of the beginning of Psalm 27:

The lorde is my enlyghtenyng and my helth, whome shall I feare? The lorde is the protectour of my lyfe, of whome shall I be abashed.

On the reverse side of the last leaf (fol.⁶B10) is a full-page cut of the printer's device that had once belonged to Richard Pynson, from among whose effects it was taken over by Redman when he succeeded to Pynson's trade.

Before taking leave of this obscure little volume we should offer some samples of its prayers to show the stamp of its style, which was not without effect upon subsequent Primers. It should be repeated that the *Prayers,* except for the fifth group which was taken from Joye's Psalter, are in a unique English version of unknown authorship. This translation bears such frequent resemblance to the Wycliffite version of the Bible

that the similarity can hardly be accidental.[11] The workmanship does not evince a thorough grasp of the Latin original,
and the result is often tentative and stiff; sometimes refresh-
ing because so unadorned.

When speaking of the Hortulus of 1530 we noticed the
prayer of Isaiah, about which Joye had been questioned, and
cited the opening verses of chapter 64 (see above, p. 25).
This same prayer occurs also in Redman's book, in the second
group—"prayers in tyme of affliction." The version given
herein, which may be compared with Joye's translations, reads
as follows in verses 1-4 of the 64th chapter (fol. C2) :

... wolde god thou woldest braste [i.e., *burst*] out of heuen and come
downe and the hylles might flowe away from thy syght and consume
lyke fyer, & that the waters myght brenne with fyer, that thy name
myght be knowen to thy ennemyes and the gentyls myght be turbled
away from thy syght whan thou shalt do wonders, we shall nat abyde
them. Thou dedyst descende and from thy syght the mountaynes
flowed. Syth the worlde began they neuer herde of such thynges nor
with theyr eares perceyued. No yie hath sene (o lorde god) besydes the
tho thynges which thou hast prepared to them that loke after the.

Another sample, taken from the first group of prayers, is
drawn from the Apocryphal book called the Wisdom of Solomon. It comprises the first three verses of chapter 15, and
Redman prints it as follows:

Thou our god art gentell and trewe, pacient and with mercy
orderyng all thynges. For yf we synne, we be thyne knowyng thy
greatnes, & yf we synne nat we knowe that with the we be rekened.
For to know the, is a perfyte and consumate ryghtwysnes, and to knowe
thy iustice & vertue is the rote of immortalitie.

Now this little prayer achieved a comparatively smooth rendering; but elsewhere, in the fourth group—headed "Fourthly
prayers for subsidies of lyfe, wysedome," etc.—is another excerpt from the Wisdom of Solomon translated much less in-
telligibly. Taken from the ninth chapter it reads in part
(verses 4-6):

[11] See the article, "Robert Redman's *Prayers of the Byble*" in *The Library*, cited
above.

. . . gyue me the assystent wysedome of thy seates and reproue me nat from thy chyldren. For thy seruaunt am I and the sonne of thy hande-mayde, a man weake and of lytle tyme and moche lesse to the vnder-standyng of thy iudgement and lawes. And if any shalbe of moste per-fyte wysedome amongest the sons of men, yf thy wysedome ones flee from hym, he shalbe counted and regarded at naught.

This sort of thing Coverdale could do much better. How natural and easy, by comparison, is the version that appeared the following October in the Coverdale Bible:

. . . geue me wyszdome, which is euer aboute yi [i.e., *thy*] seate. & put me not out from amonge yi children: for I thy seruaunt & sonne of yi handmayden, am a feble personne, of a shorte tyme, and to yonge to the vnderstandinge of iudgment and ye lawes. And though a man be neuer so parfecte amonge the children of men, yet yf thy wyszdome be not with him, he shal be nothinge regarded.

Finally, from the same group of prayers comes a curious ex-ample taken from the thirtieth chapter of Proverbs (verses 7-9). As printed in the *Prayers of the Byble* (fol. D8) it reads:

Two thynges I demaunded that thou woldest nat denye me vntyll that I dye. Vanitie and wordes of lesynge [i.e., *lying*] make farre from me. Beggerlynes and ryches gyue me nat. Onely gyue that is necessary for my lyuyng [i.e., *living*], lest perchaunce beynge in ful abundaunce I myght be prouoked to denye the and say who is lorde? Or compelled by necessitie, I myght be wode and forswere the name of my god. Amen.

The most remarkable part of this is the last sentence, where the translator was confused by the Latin text. The original reading in Brunfels (as in the Vulgate) was *Aut egestate compulsus furer,* which could be rendered literally, "Or by penury compelled I might steal." The version given in the Redman volume implies that this word *furer* (steal) had been mistaken for *furor* (madness) ; for the now obsolete expres-sion, "I might be wood," signified to be mad or beside oneself. In any case, the error was of short duration. In his next scrip-tural publication, which was a Primer, Redman took special pains to insert a correction of it.

Chapter IX

Redman's Primer After the Use of Sarum
(1535)

IN PARIS in the Bibliothèque Nationale is preserved the only surviving copy of the Primer that Redman printed in the spring of 1535. It is of peculiar interest for a number of reasons: It is virtually unknown;[1] it is the first printing in English of a Primer strictly according to the 'use of Salisbury,' the Latin text also being printed down the margin of each page; its English rendering is drawn from a great variety of sources; it forms a definite connecting link between the early manuscript Primers of Wycliffe's day and the printed ones with which we are dealing; and lastly, this Redman Primer is the sire of a numerous progeny. It deserves to be considered in some detail.

Fortunately, this Primer is well printed and is right well preserved. It contains, in all, 186 leaves in small octavo size.[2]

The title-page commences:

❡ This prymer of Salysbery vse/ bothe in Englyshe & in Laten, is set out a longe without any serchyng.

Directly beneath comes "❡ The contentes of this boke."[3] At

---

1 Though not listed in either Hoskins or *S.T.C.*, it is item No. 546 in Lacombe's *Livres d'Heures Imprimés Au XVe et Au XVIe Siècle* (Paris, 1907), and is alluded to in "The Prymer in English," by E. C. Birchenough, in *The Library* for September 1937 (Series IV, vol. 18, p. 185).

2 Collation:—Title, almanac, and calendar occupy four preliminary leaves without signature; then: A8, B6, ✠4, 2A-B8, C-I8, K-T8, V8, X4. Beginning with Matins (fol. 2A1) each leaf is numbered at the top, but the numbering runs into error after fol. 84, as it often did with these early printers.

3 Though fairly complete, the table given on the title-page does not entirely correspond with the actual sequence followed in the book itself. The table reads thus: "❡ Fyrste an Almanacke for .xx. yeres. A calender. ❡ The foure Gospels of ye foure Euangelystes. ❡ The passyon of our Lorde, Egressus Iesus. ❡ The Pater noster, & the Aue, both in Englyshe and in Laten. ❡ The .xii. articles of the faythe. ❡ The .x.

the bottom of the page is "⟨ Cum gratia et Priuilegio Regali." The almanac on the reverse side of the leaf commences with the year 1535.

At the end of the volume the colophon reads:

⟨ Imprynted at London, in Fletestrete *in* saynt Dunstones parysshe at the sygne of the George by me Robert Redman.

Above the colophon (fol. X4^v) occurs the prayer from the thirtieth chapter of Proverbs which was mentioned before. It is the only one of Redman's *Prayers of the Byble* to be printed in this Primer, and it now appears thus:

Two thynges (Lorde) I demaunded that thou woldest nat denye me vntyll I dye. Vanytie and wordes of lesyng make farre from me. Pouertye or ryches gyue me nat. Onely gyue that is necessary for my lyuyng, lest beyng in full abundaunce I myght be prouoked to denye the and say who is lorde? Or compellyd by necessytie, I myght steale and forswere the name of my god. So be it.

A comparison of this with the text in *Prayers of the Byble* (see above, p. 86) would, I think, convince anyone that the wording in the Primer is later—a revision of the other. Besides the use of "steale" in place of "be wode," note also the change from "Beggerlynes and ryches" to "Pouertye or ryches."

The calendar of saints' days, printed two months to a page in double column, is in English but adheres to the style of the Latin calendars carried in Sarum Primers; it has no running comment such as Joye essayed. For example, at the end of August it reads:

> xix c Decolla. of s. Iohan
>   d s. Febix [*sic*] & audacte
> viii e s. Cuthberte virgyne

This last entry is intended for St. Cuthburga, a saint of the old West Saxons; "Febix" is a misprint for Felix.

---

commaundementes. ⁋ Matyns. ⁋ Euynsong. ⁋ Coumplen. ⁋ Salue Regina. ⁋ Gaude Virgo. ⁋ Gaude Flore. ⁋ The .xv. Oes. ⁋ The vii. Psalmes with the Lateny/ Dyrige with the commendacyons. ⁋ The Psalmes of the passyon. ⁋ Saynt Hieroms Psalter. ⁋ A prayer whan thou shalt resceyue ye sacrament. ⁋ A prayer whan yu haste resceyued hit. ⁋ O bone Iesu bothe Englyshe and Laten. ⁋ A prayer of the .vii. wordes that our lorde spake on the crosse at his passyon. ⁋ The prayer of Salomon for a competent lyuyng. Prouerbes the .xxx."

After the calendar come four traditional selections from the four Evangelists, part of a chapter from each. The English rendering of these is taken, for the most part, from the revised New Testament that Tyndale put out in November 1534; but the editor of this English-Latin Primer preferred at times to retain the unrevised wording of the 1526 Testament, and once or twice dared to depart from Tyndale altogether, presumably to bring the English reading into closer accord with the Latin text in the margin.

The next few leaves contain miscellaneous items: A brief prayer in English rhyme commencing, "O lorde of thy great mercy and grace"; followed by a short paraphrase of the Lord's Prayer "by Iohan Colet Deane of Poules," paragraphed in "seven petitions." This item seems to have been copied from an earlier Latin Primer of 1532 (*S.T.C.* 15978) in which the very same English rendering also appeared. Next come the Ave Maria and the twelve articles of the Creed, in Latin and English, without comment; and then the Ten Commandments, the Latin text of which is given according to the fifth chapter of Deuteronomy. The English version of the Commandments is not in prose but in rhyme and is taken (so far as has been ascertained) from the Kaetz edition of the Primer of 1523 (*S.T.C.* 15935), in which edition it began as follows:

> One god onely thou shalt loue/ & worshype perfytely.
> God *in* vayn*e* thou shalt not swere nor by that he made truly.

The rhyme involves merely a series of words ending in -*ly*. Another metrical version of the Commandments had been printed by Wynkyn de Worde in his Primer of that same year (*S.T.C.* 15934) with a somewhat different wording.[4] Such devices were not only to aid the memory, but they were also

---

4 The rhyming version used by de Worde came from an earlier publication of his entitled *The floure of the commaundementes of god* (*S.T.C.* 23876) printed in 1510. Appearing on the title-page of that book, the Commandments begin:

> ¶ Thou shalt worship one god onely.
> And loue hym with thy herte perfytely
> ¶ God in vayne swere not wylfully . . .

and they end thus:

> ¶ Other mennes godes coueyt not lightly
> Nor holde from them vnryghtfully.

This same version appears also in de Worde's Primer of 1513 (*S.T.C.* 15914).

employed to evade the restriction formerly in effect against publishing the plain text of the Scripture in English.

Next (fol. A7) comes "A prayer concernyng the .vii. peticyons yt the synner prayeth to god, for the .vii. tymes that Christe spake on the crosse." This is followed by St. John's account of the Passion, comprising the 18th and 19th chapters of his Gospel. This, again, was taken almost word for word from the Tyndale Testament of November 1534. One curious variation—a printer's error—was copied verbatim in many Primers published afterwards. Concerning the Master's seamless robe, Tyndale had originally written in his edition of 1526 (John 19:23): "The coote was with out seme woven vppon thorowe and thorowe." In 1534 Tyndale revised this to read: "The coote was with out seme/ wrought vpon thorowe out." In copying this the Redman Primer printed it: "The cote was without seme/ wrought open thorowe out."

At length, after the Passion, we come to the preface—"⁋ A preface aduertisynge the Reder of certayne thynges conteyned in this boke folowynge." The tone of this preface is much milder than the tone of the Marshall Primer, though it is still plainly tinged with a Protestant approach. It is anonymous, moderate, generally clear, and remarkably well written. It begins:

> Our mayster Chryste in his holy gospel teacheth a certayne forme of praynge, which in it selfe I dare wel say conteyneth al peticyons necessary for mans saluacyon/ & that is the Pater noster. Howe be it we haue many devoute prayers of holy fathers bothe in the olde and the newe testament/ by the whych, bycause chrysten people may be mouyd vnto vertue & deuocyon they are not to be reiectyd, but to be had in great pryce & estymacyon.

After this veiled allusion to Redman's *Prayers of the Byble* there are a few words about true worship and a right attitude toward saints and temporal rulers, whereupon the writer continues:

> Yet am I not ignoraunt that some people haue ben greatly deludyd of longe tyme about the veneracyon of Sayntes and suche lyke thinges/ partely by ignoraunce/ and partely thorowe impure persuasyons of

false prechors. For the reformacyon whereof almyghty god of hys eterne prouidence hathe put in the myndes of his electe princes, and true pastours of his flocke to purge the fylthynes of false doctryne out of the hartes of them that haue ben seducyd by blinde guydes/ so that noman shal haue cause to erre, but only those whiche are at a poynte to stoppe theyr eares at the trouthe.

He next refers to the fact that the authorities have permitted the Marshall Primer, and now this one, to be circulated in the English tongue:

And for the more increase of vertue and auauncement of true doctryne they haue nowe permyttyd and admytted suche prayours and suffrages as were wonte to be sayde and pronouncyd only in laten (which heretofore none dyd vnderstande but only those yt had the knowlege of the same tonge) to be translatyd into englyshe. And of theyr blessyd zeale vnto the increase of vertue and deuocyon amonge people, where as heretofore none of the Prymars yet emprynted in englyshe hathe ben accordynge in al thinges vnto the comon vsage (to the entent that no man shuld be ignoraunt what he hathe said before time in laten) haue sufferyd the same to goo abrode, not omyttynge any parte of the ordynary seruyce that hath byne vsyd to be sayd. In the settinge forth wherof, albehit yt nether the translator nether the Pryntour haue done theyr parte so wel as myghte haue ben, yf lerned men had taken the matter in hande: yet they most intyerly desyre the reders to be contentyd with theyr good purpose & endeuour, which herein haue regarded nothyng so moche as the honour and glory of god, and edefyeng of the reders.

This is the only allusion to the translator, who was probably also the author of this preface. It is conceivable, too, that he was the same person who had produced the English version of Brunfels' *Prayers of the Byble*. Though no great Latin scholar himself, his apology to more "lerned men" may be set aside as modest deprecation; for the style in which this preface is written gives evidence of considerable literary skill.

In a noteworthy passage he next calls the reader's attention to the discrepancy between the Latin text of the Psalms and their English version, which he says is based on the text of Felinus, *alias* Martin Bucer. Actually, the Psalms in the new Primer were drawn from several publications, but Joye's two Psalters of 1530 and 1534 were the ultimate sources, as we shall note. The preface puts the matter thus:

And where perauenture some persons hauynge no more but ye bare knowledge of their Grammer may be offendid, whan they se the laten & englishe set togyther & not to agre euery where worde for worde but to vary in sentence also? It may please them to be admonyshyd yt all the psalmes are translatyd after the texte of Feline/ which tournid the same out of the pure fountayne of Hebrewe into latyn. And therfore it is no meruayl [i.e., *marvel*] though it vary somedele from the laten texte, consyderyng that the Hebrewe tonge hathe in it so many equyuocacyons (that is to wyte) so many sygnyfycacions for one worde, that yf .xx. lernyd men shuld vndertake to translate one matter out of ye same tong/ yet shulde they all dysagree/ not only in wordes, but many tymes also in sentence/ which is perceyuyd clerely ynough by them that haue any experience in translacyons out of that tonge.

There follow a couple of pages giving instances of false interpretations and of right and wrong methods of prayer. Among other things the reader is cautioned against misuse of the adoration known as *Salve Regina,* which occurs in the course of the Primer itself. Attention is also called to the usage in the Litany wherein a distinction was made in the antiphonal responses: addresses to Deity were answered, "Have mercy on us"; those to the saints, "Pray for us." The preface concludes with these words:

In consyderacyon wherof most benygne reders I thought it ryght expedient to gyue you admonicyon and warnyng before of al suche thinges that myght cause you to be offendyd in the redyng of this boke/ whiche howe necessarie it is to them that haue mynde to be occupied in godly meditacyon/ I wyll nat speake any further at this tyme, leste I shulde seme to be a boster of myne owne workes. And if there be any like faultes in this worke escapyd ether by neglygence or by ignoraunce, wherof I haue gyuen no warnyng. I humbly beseche you (most benygne readers) charitably to reforme them after the rule which I haue shewyd you before/ wherby ye maye meryte hyghly in Christe, who preserue you. Amen.

The reverse side of the leaf on which the preface ends contains a full-page well-executed woodcut of the Annunciation: "⟨ The salutacyon of the aungell Gabriell." This ushers in the beginning of Matins.

As was becoming to a Sarum Primer, the Latin text in the margins of Redman's book proves quite orthodox. Starting

with Matins it reiterates all the traditional features of the
Book of Hours as noted on the title-page, including Litany
and Dirge. Much of this material, particularly in the Hours
and "Suffragia" (or prayers), is liturgical rather than scriptural. Although our main interest will center in the scriptural
passages, it is worth noting that we have in this Primer, apparently for the first time in print, the English rendering of a
number of collects and addresses to the Virgin, some of which,
though spurned by Joye and Marshall, have persisted in use
until the present day.

For example, among the prayers following the Litany is one
familiar to all who know the Book of Common Prayer. As
printed in 1535 it read (fol. M3):

> O God, from whom al holy desyres, al good counselles and al iuste
> workes, do procede gyue vnto vs the same peace whiche the worlde can
> nat gyue that our hertes beyng obedient to thy commaundementes
> (& the fear of our enemyes taken away) our tyme may be peasyble
> thorugh thy proteccyon.

In Latin form this is found in the earliest Books of Hours;
indeed it was translated into English in certain manuscript
Primers of the early fifteenth century. In one of these[5] it read:

> God of wham been holy desyres; rightful conceyles. and iuste dedis.
> gif to thi seruawntes that pees; that the world may nought geue. so
> that oure hertes be geuen to kepe thyn hestes. and drede of oure
> enemyes be taken from us. so that oure tymes be pesible by thi
> protection.

The medieval tone of certain addresses to the Virgin may be
sufficiently exemplified by "A prayer to our blessyd lady for
the pestilence" (fol. H4) . In the Book of Hours this started
off with a Latin hymn, "Stella celi extirpavit." Redman's translator, mistaking this for the more familiar "Stella maris,"
began his versification of it thus:

> The sterre of the see, whiche lorde fosteryd.
> The mortall pestilence, frome vs hathe banyshed . . . .

---

[5] Ms. G-24 the library of St. John's College, Cambridge, edited by Henry
Littlehales in 1891; see below, p. 100, note.

The error was corrected in later editions. Next came the prayer
itself, typical of many. Note, incidentally, the use of curves for
direct quotation:

> O God mercyfull. pytefull, and sufferable, whiche hauyng remorse
> on the afflicyon of thy seruauntes saydest vnto thy aungell whan he
> strake thy people (it is ynoughe.) Nowe holde thy hande ouer vs for
> the loue of the same glorious sterre whose blessyd brestes thou dedyst
> ryght swetely suck against the poyson of our synfulnes . . . .

This prayer was followed by Psalm 130. In traditional material
such as this are many ancient echoes. In the subsequent prayer
for the dead, for instance (fol. H6) , we come upon the words,
"God haue mercy of all christen soules," which immediately
bring to mind the mad Ophelia's ditty with its pious coda.

The scriptural portions of this Primer give evidence of an
unusual eclecticism, the English version having been drawn
from more than half a dozen different sources, none of which
is acknowledged save for the mention of "Feline" in the
preface.

In Matins and Lauds it is generally the Marshall Primer
which is drawn upon wherever its materials coincided with the
use of Sarum. The opening Psalm, for example—the 95th—
is taken almost without change from Marshall, except in the
'responses.' For these Marshall—and Joye before him—had
used "Come vnto me all ye that labour," balanced with "And
I shall refreshe you"; but Redman reverted to the traditional
responses called for by the Latin, "Hayle Mary full of grace"
and "The lord is with the." Since the Psalms in the Marshall
Primer were taken from Joye's Hortulus, and these in turn
from the Psalter of 1530, it was true to say of these that they
were based on the text of Felinus.

That the Redman Primer did introduce an occasional alteration, the beginning of Psalm 93, in the Lauds, will illustrate. In the Psalter of 1530 it had commenced thus:

> The lorde is kinge/ his maieste is gloriously dekte; the lorde hath
> done vpon hym selve strengthe/ and hath gyrte hym selve myghtely.

The Joye Hortulus took over the first member of this just as
it was, but altered the second to read, "the lorde hath armed

hym selfe with strengthe." The improvement was adopted in the Marshall Primer and likewise by Redman, who also changed the first part so that it now read: "hys maiestye is gloryously arayed: the lorde hathe armed hym selfe," etc.

Where Marshall had departed entirely from the Sarum text, Redman had recourse to some hasty innovations. Two of these may be of special interest:

(1) Sarum Primers called for the use of Psalm 51 as an alternative to the *Te Deum* during Lent, and it was inserted between Matins and Lauds. But Joye and Marshall had transferred the use of it to the conclusion of their "General Confession." Redman, therefore, not finding the Psalm in its customary place in Marshall, turned to the version of it that was scattered through the Exposition by Savonarola, and pieced this together for his rendering of the 51st Psalm. He may, of course, have taken this from his own printing of the Exposition in his *Prayers of the Byble.*

(2) As translated in the Joye Hortulus, Psalm 67 (in the Lauds) repeats the phrase "the people mought magnifye the" several times. Led astray by this repetition, Byddell, the printer for Marshall, omitted two entire verses of the Psalm where it appeared in the Primer of 1534 (fol. M3^v). Confronted with this lapse, the Redman editor, to satisfy the Latin in his margin, patched together a new rendering of the whole Psalm.

In the Godfray Primer, on the other hand, this Psalm appeared complete as it was in the Hortulus; from which we may deduce that Redman did not avail himself of direct access to the Hortulus as Godfray had done. Redman's improvised version reads as follows (fol. ^{2}B4):

God haue mercy vpon vs: & blesse vs/ let hym shewe hys face vnto vs/ & haue mercy vpon vs.

That thy way may be knowen euery where in the erthe: and thy sauynge helthe also vnto all nacyons.

Let al peple make knowleg to god: let al nacyons confesse the.

Ioyfull & glad be all folke for thou rulest people with equite and orderest all folkes in erthe.

Peple knowledge the to be god let al nacions confesse to the y*t* the erthe may yelde forth her frute.

Blesse vs our god: & all y*t* inhabite the erth that the [*sic*] vttermost partes thereof y*u* mayst be feryd.

This last verse was garbled by the omission of a preposition. In the Dirge (fol. P6ᵛ), where the same Psalm is printed correctly, it reads, "y*t* in the vtter moste partes thereof thou mayst be fearyd." Redman's rendering of the Psalm has a mixed pedigree: the second and last verses resemble the text of Marshall; the remaining verses might have been put together haphazardly, with a hint or two from Joye. Incidentally, in the Dirge Redman furnishes no heading for this 67th Psalm; it is printed right after Psalm 63 without any break to show where it starts.

Beginning with the portion of the Primer known as the Hours and continuing into the Dirge, the Redman editor forsakes the Marshall Primer as the source of his Psalms and borrows instead from the Psalter that Joye issued in 1534. Now it is by no means true that this Psalter was based on "Feline";[6] but because Joye's name appeared on it, Redman may possibly have assumed that it was. Be this as it may, the 1534 Psalter was the latest available in English, and Redman made good use of it, not only in his *Prayers of the Byble,* but also in his Primer.

The 126th Psalm, which occurs three times in the same rendering (in Hours, Evensong, and Fifteen Psalms), will illustrate how the Redman Primer dealt with the Psalter of 1534. In Joye's version this Psalm had read:

When the Lorde retourned the captiuite of zion: we were restored vnto reste.

Then were oure mouthes filled with laughter/ and oure tongues with ioye.

Then was it reported euen emonge the gentils/ The lorde hath done meruelous grete actis for these men.

---

[6] Rev. J. F. Mozley tells me that the Psalter of 1534 is based on a Latin edition by Zwingli. An earlier theory was that it derived from the Latin of Felix Pratensis; see Lewis, *Complete History of the Several Translations of the Holy Bible* (edition of 1739, pp. 87 ff.). The *Dictionary of National Biography* (under Joye) assumes that the Psalters of 1530 and 1534 were both based on Feline; and therefore, since they varied so much, the earlier one could not have been by Joye; but this may be dismissed as mere assumption, less applicable to Joye than to most translators.

And in very dede the lorde wrought meruelous grete thinges with vs/ which gretely deliteth vs.

Thou hast tourned (oh lorde) our captiuite/ no nother wyse then as at the southe wynde the ryuers encrease.

They that had sowen with teres haue reped with ioye.

He that sometyme went his waye spedely/ and wepinge toke vp his sead to cast it forthe/ retourneth nowe merelye and iocounde [i.e., *jocund*] bringinge home his handes full off corne.

All of this the editor of the Primer approved except for the last verse, which now appeared as follows (fol. E8ᵛ):

[W]han they went forthe to sowe they wente wepynge takynge with them theyr seade koddes.

But whan they shal cum agayn they shal cum *with* great joy bringyng theyr handes full of corne.

And where was this from? It turns out to be the reading in the Marshall Primer.

For the 23rd Psalm, which occurs both in the Dirge and in the Psalms of the Passion, the version in the Psalter of 1534 is used almost throughout, but is freely amended. Where Joye had "The Lorde fedeth me" as the opening words of the Psalm, the Primer has "The Lorde reulyth me"—evidently out of deference to the Latin text in the margin, "Dominus regit me."

In the Commendations, Redman included both Psalm 119 and Psalm 139; Marshall had given only the former. Accordingly, the editor of the Redman Primer took the 139th Psalm from the Joye Psalter of 1534 but preferred the Marshall text for Psalm 119. Where the Psalter of 1530 and the Hortulus both had inadvertently omitted the 64th verse of this Psalm, the Marshall Primer (as noted before) supplied the deficiency with these words: "The erth is full of thy goodnes lord, nurture me in thy ceremonyes." The same words are found in Redman also. Incidentally, it is only in this verse that the word "ceremonies" is used through the entire Psalm instead of "testimonies, law, ordinance," etc., showing that this was Marshall's choice rather than Joye's.

In the Redman Primer, Psalm 51 fared strangely. It occurs four times: in the end of Matins, in the Seven Psalms, in the

Dirge, and in the so-called Psalter of St. Jerome. This last was simply an anthology of selected verses from the Book of Psalms, yet it contained the whole 51st Psalm intact. In Matins (as was mentioned) Redman chose the rendering of the Psalm which had accompanied Savonarola's Exposition, wherein it began:

Haue mercy vpon me (oh god) accordynge to thy greate mercye. And accordinge to the multitude of thy compassions wype awaye myne iniquite.

In the Seven Psalms and the Dirge, Redman again made use of the Savonarola version, but with a different rendering of the opening verse, which now reads (Primer, fol. 18) :

Haue mercy vpon me (oh god) accordyng vnto thy goodnes. For thy gret infinite mercyes do awaye myne iniquite.

This happens to be the same as the wording in the Joye Psalter of 1534, except that Joye had ended the verse thus: "for thy grete infinite mercyes do awaye my transgressions." Finally, where the Psalm occurred in the so-called Psalter of St. Jerome, Redman went all the way back to the original wording in the Psalter of 1530, which had begun as follows:

Have mercy vpon me (god) for thy ientlenes sake for thy grete mercyes sake wype awaye my sinnes.

In the Hortulus and likewise in the Marshall Primer, these opening words had been amended to read, "Haue mercy vpon me (God) for thy fauourable goodnes:" etc., but Redman disregarded this variation. In other words, in the four places where the 51st Psalm occurs in the Redman Primer the opening verse appears in three different forms.[7]

These minor differences are accentuated here for the sake of bringing out that the compilers of these Primers felt perfectly free to range over the field before them and choose their readings from any source available to them. Thus we can realize how fluid and unfixed was the state of Bible translation during those formative years.

[7] See below, Appendix III.

Turning now from the Psalms to other scriptural selections included in the Redman Primer, let us look especially at the Dirge, which had no counterpart in the Hortulus of 1530 or in the first edition of the Marshall Primer. Here we find a number of interesting observations.

The Benedictus (Luke 1: 68-79), given in the Dirge as well as earlier in Lauds, is rendered virtually the same in both places and follows the version in the Marshall Primer, which in turn was taken from the Hortulus. Concerning the Magnificat, it will be recalled that the translation given in the Evensong of the Hortulus started out like that in Tyndale's first New Testament of 1526 but diverged from it definitely in the later verses (see above, p. 44). Marshall made use of this, but Redman, both in Evensong and Dirge, forsook these novelties and followed the Tyndale text throughout, with only a single variation. Tyndale had begun: "My soule magnifieth the lorde. And my sprete reioyseth in god my savioure"; Redman changed "reioyseth" to "reioysed."

One regular feature of the Dirge was the prayer of Hezekiah as found in the Book of Isaiah (38: 10-20). This, of course, was omitted from the earlier Marshall Primer; so it is of interest to discover that Redman went for his version of this prayer to *The Prophete Isaye* by George Joye (1531). Here again the editor introduces modifications, and two of these (verses 14 and 16) are particularly intriguing. As they stood in Joye's translation of 1531, the verses had read:

I moorned lyke a doue/ lyftinge vp my eyes vnto ye hyghe god saynge. Lorde I am sore handled/ . . . For I knowe verely (lorde) yt this lyfe is saufsed [i.e., *sauced*] with galle/ and that my lyfe is subiecte to all bitter myserye.

In the Redman Primer (fol. P7ᵛ) they appear:

I moornyd lyke a Doue. Myne yies daselyd [i.e., *dazzled*] with lokyng vp vnto the hyghe god sayeng. Lorde I am sore handelyd/ . . . For I knowe verely (Lorde) yt this lyfe is sausyd with galle and that my lyfe is subiecte to bytter mysery.

Upon investigation this curious phrase, "Mine eyes dazzled with looking up," is found to be imported from the 119th

Psalm where it occurs several times in the Psalter of 1530. It is likewise to be found, of course, in the Commendations in both the Marshall and the Redman Primers. For the remainder of the passage, in spite of the omission of the word "all," there is no question of the direct indebtedness of Redman to Joye's *Prophete Isaye.*

Finally, the Dirge included several 'lessons' taken from the Book of Job. So far as we know, Job had not yet been published in English. Consequently here the compiler of the Primer was on untrodden ground. What did he do? Perhaps he was shy of producing a version of his own, preferring to be able to point to some prior use of what he was printing, in case he should be called to account under the old ruling that the Bible was not to be translated into English. Perhaps he mistrusted—as well he might—his own skill in the Latin tongue. At any rate, he got hold of an early manuscript of the English Primer, dating from about 1400, modernized its language, and thus obtained a rendering of these particular passages from Job.

Perhaps, too, the old Lollard versions were more in favor with some of the reformers than we now realize. We should recollect that Redman's translator of his *Prayers of the Byble* did not disdain to consult some Wycliffite manuscript in preparing his text of certain biblical prayers, or of the Seven Deadly Sins. Apparently he now adopts a similar course with the Primer.

Happily, this older version of the Primer is known in several manuscripts, one of which was issued in printed form by Littlehales as recently as 1891.[8] Careful comparison shows beyond doubt that it was to one of these manuscripts that Redman or his editor had recourse. It is certainly significant, in these pas-

---

[8] See above, p. 5. Littlehales, in *The Prymer, or Prayer-Book of the Lay People in the Middle Ages* (1891), enumerates some dozen manuscripts, identifying the one he reprints as No. G-24, St. John's College, Cambridge. The text of this Ms. agrees pretty closely with British Museum Additional Ms. No. 27592, excerpts of which appear in the footnotes to Maskell's *Monumenta Ritualia* (vol. III). The text that Littlehales reprinted in 1895 for the Early English Text Society (Cambridge Univ. Ms. Dd.11.82) adheres more closely to the Wycliffite version, as does also the text presented by Maskell (Brit. Mus. Add. Ms., No. 17010).

sages from Job, that where the version in the manuscript Primer diverges from the Wycliffite Bible, it is the reading in the Primer as edited by Littlehales in 1891 that Redman is apt to follow.

In the seventh chapter of Job, for instance, this is how verses 17, 18, and 21 appeared in the Purvey revision of the Wycliffite Bible:

What is a man, for thou magnifiest hym? ether what settist thou thin herte toward hym? Thou visitist hym eerly, and sudeynli thou preuest hym . . . Lo, now Y schal slepe in dust, and if thou sekist me eerli, Y schal not abide.

In the Littlehales edition of the Primer these verses read:

What is man that thou makest gret. or wer to settest thou thyn herte toward hym. Thou uisitest hym in the dawynge: and sodeynliche thou prouest hym . . . . Lo now y slepe in poudre: and yif thou seche me erly; y schal nought withstonde.

And in the Dirge of the Redman Primer (fol. N7) we have:

What is man yt yu [i.e., *that thou*] magnyfyest hym: or wherto settyst yu thy hert against hym? Thou vysytest hym in the dawnyng/ and sodeynly thou prouest hym. . . . Lo nowe I slepe in pourde [*sic;* for *powder*], and yf thou seke me erly I shall nat withstande.

The importance of this resemblance is that it demonstrates a continuity between the manuscript Primers and their printed successors. Considering that the English Primer had been outlawed during the fifteenth century, and considering the stretch of time involved—some hundred and twenty-five years, from 1535 back to about 1410—it is remarkable, to say the least, that we can thus pick up the trail of the English versions in recognizable form.

At the risk of over-elaboration, two further examples are offered, the first from the nineteenth chapter of Job (verses 23-26):

(LhP)—Ho schal geue to me that my wordes   be wryten; Ho
(R35)—Who can cause   that my wordes maye be written. Who

schal geue to me   that they be eered   in a book with a poyntel of
can   graunt me yt they may be wrytten in a boke with a poyntell of

yren and in a plate of leed; other   that they be graue in a flynt   of a
yron, or in a plate of led, or that they may be grauen with a chysell in

chesel;   I wot forsothe that my agenbiere[9] lyueth; and in the laste
ye flynt stone. For I knowe that my redemer   lyueth, & that I shal

day   y schal ryse of the erthe.   and eft y schal be lapped
ryse out of the erthe in the last daye, and that I shalbe compassed

in my skyn;   and   in my   flesch y schal se
agayne with myne owne skynne And that in myn owne fleshe I shall se

god my saueour.
god my sauiour. . .

The last example is from the tenth chapter (verses 8-12)
and this time the Wycliffite version according to the Purvey
revision is presented first, for the sake of comparison with the
Littlehales' Primer and Redman's:

(WPv)—Thin hondis han   maad me, and han formed me al in
(LhP) —Thyn handes   maade me   and schoop me: al in
(R35) —Thyne handes (lorde) made me,   and formed me al in

cumpas; and thou castist me doun so sodeynli.   Y preye, haue thou
compaas and so sodeynliche thou castest me down. Haue mynde y
compas: and doste thou so sodenly caste me downe? Haue mynde I

mynde,   that thou madist me as clay,   and schalt brynge me
beseche thee that as fen thou hast maad me: and in to poudre thou
beseche the that of cley thou haste made me: & into pouder thou

agen in to dust.   Whether thou hast not mylkid me as mylk, and
schalt agen   lede   me.   Ne hast thou soofted me as melk. and
shalte agayne tourne me. Haste thou nat softed me as mylke: and

hast cruddid me togidere as cheese? Thou clothidist me with skyn and
      croddedest me   as cheese: With skyn and fleschsches thou cloth-
      cruddyste me   as chese? With skynne and fleshe thou couer-

fleisch; thou hast ioyned me togidere with boonys and senewis.   Thou
edest me: with boones and synewes thou maadest me to gedere. Lyf
edist me, with bones and synewys   ioynedest me together. Lyfe

hast goue lijf and mercy to me, and thi visiting hath kept my spirit.
and mercy thou gaf to me: and thi vysitacion hath kept my goost.
and mercy thou gaue me,   & thy visitacyon hath kepte my soule.

9 That is, "again-buyer."

After Dirge and Commendations came the Psalms of the Passion, which were drawn from the Joye Psalter of 1534 with emendations; and then came the so-called Psalter of St. Jerome. This was taken largely from the 1534 Psalter also, though the 51st Psalm came from the earlier Psalter of 1530, as noted above.

Finally, the Primer included a brief section of prayers comprising the two to be said before and after receiving the sacrament and "a deuout prayer of saynt Bernarde" ("sancti Bernardini" in the Latin). This prayer, known as "O bone Iesu," was often to be found in the Primers, and this appears to have been the first English rendering of it in print. It commences (fol. X3):

O bountyful Iesu, o swete Iesu, O Iesu the sonne of the pure virgyne Mary/ full of mercy & trouth. O swete Iesu/ after thy great mercye haue pyte vpon me. . . .

The volume is concluded with the prayer of Solomon "For a competency of lyuyng" which was cited at the beginning of this chapter.

Such were the multifarious materials out of which was fashioned the first Primer "of Salysbery vse" to be published in English for the edification of the King's subjects in the reign of Henry VIII.

Chapter X

William Marshall's *Goodly Primer*
(1535)

WE HAVE already noted the outspoken zeal of William Marshall as a partisan of the Reformation. The publishing of orthodox Primers after the use of Salisbury would not have appealed especially to him. But he seems to have been irked by complaints that his Primer had neither Litany nor Dirge. Moreover he probably had one eye on the market and the activity of his competitors. For in June 1535 he brought out a revised edition of his Primer, and it was a thoroughgoing revision (*S.T.C.* 15988). Byddell printed it at his new shop, according to the colophon:

⟨ Imprynted at London in Fletestrete by Iohan Byddell/ dwellynge at the signe of the Sonne/ next to the cundite [i.e., *conduit*]/ for wylliam Marshall/ the yere of our lorde god M.D.xxxv. the xvi. day of Iune.

The specific date in the colophon is of the greatest assistance in fixing the approximate time of publication for other Primers we have been considering.

The title-page is similar in design to that of the 1534 edition, but is somewhat more elaborate:

⟨ A goodly prymer in englyshe, newly corrected and printed, with certeyne godly meditations and prayers added to the same, very necessarie & profitable for all them that ryghte assuredly vnderstande not ye latine & greke tongues.

Above the upper corners of the royal coat-of-arms are two initials, H and A (for the King and Queen), and at the bottom of the page is a notice: "⟨ With the kynges most gracious priuilege for .vj. yeres." The mention of the Greek tongue,

by the way, shows how the leaven of the Revival of Learning
was at work, thanks to Tyndale and Erasmus.

The reverse of the title-page is occupied by a large crude
woodcut of "Truthe, the doughter of tyme," showing Truth
in a plump personification being liberated from a cave or
sepulchre, under the encouraging influence of a winged Father
Time ("Tyme reueleth all thynges") who hovers near, with
long beard and feathered heels; while overhead a winged
demon, labeled "Hipocrisy," pours down a spiteful shower.

It is obvious that Marshall had friends at court. The
"priuilege for .vj. yeres" proclaimed on the title-page refers
to a sort of patent that Marshall was able to procure for the
new publication. Byddell prints it in full on the last page,
in an hour-glass pattern above the colophon, where it reads:

(Be it knowen to all men by these presentes, that it is prohibited
by our soueraigne lorde the kynge, by his letters patentes, to all printers,
boke sellers, and marchauntes, & all others that (without licence had
of hym, that at his costes and charges printed this boke) they in no
wyse do printe, or vtter in sale, or otherwyse, at any place within our
sayde soueraigne lordes dominions, this booke, entitled and called
thenglyshe primer, at any tyme within six yeres nexte after the
printynge hereof, as they wyll answere at theyr perylles, and auoyde
the penalties mentioned in the priuilege hereunto graunted.

Evidently Marshall hoped to forestall Redman, Godfray, and
other competitors from reprinting this *Goodly Primer*. Indeed
it is just possible that Godfray's Primer may have been issued
a little bit later, and that Godfray modeled his Primer on the
Joye Hortulus because he felt debarred by this patent from
using the Byddell editions. In any case, the patent seems
to have been effective. In the six years that followed, other
English Primers were put forth, as we shall find out, but the
Goodly Primer continued to be John Byddell's own preserve.[1]

The granting of a royal patent takes on an extra weight

1 Among Byddell's reprints of his own Primer may be cited *S.T.C.* 15998 and
15999. See also Hoskins' list. It should be recorded that in reality *S.T.C.* 15990
(Hoskins 120) is identical with *S.T.C.* 15999 (Hoskins 130). Also there appears to be
no point of difference between *S.T.C.* 15989 (Hoskins 119) and the *Goodly Primer*.
Hoskins cites the titles as showing a capital *K* and a small *k* in the word "kynge*s*"
but actually the *k* is the same in both imprints.

of meaning when we look at the preface to the new volume. It is now headed, "Admonition to the reder," and is printed at the very threshold of the book, before the almanac and calendar.[2] Its tone is even more contentious than in the earlier Marshall Primer, and the language is less restrained—in fact, it has been deliberately heightened—as may be seen by comparing the two editions. Where the former had said (see above, p. 61):

These bokes (though they abounded in euery place with infynyte errours/ and taught praiers, made with wycked folishnes/ both to god and also to the sayntes) yet by cause thei were garnished with gloryous tytles and with redde letters promysyng moch grace and pardon (though it were but vanite) haue sore deceiued the vnlearned multytude/ . . .

the revised preface, after first crying out upon "pestilent and infectious bookes," proceeds:

For these bokes ouer & besydes that that they habounded in euery place with infinite errours, and peryllous prayers, sclaunderous both to god, and to all his holy sayntes, were also garnyshed with glorious titles, and with redde letters, promysyng moche grace, and many yeres, dayes, and lentes of pardon, whiche they coulde neuer in dede perfourme, to ye great decepte of the people, and the vtter destruction of theyr soules.

And whereas the earlier edition had been content to decry the use of saints' lives and legends and "soche prayers as be saynte Brigittes and other lyke, whiche greate promyses and perdons haue falsely aduaunced"; the revised preface launches forth with "As for an example" and follows with five whole pages of denunciation of "false" prayers, citing more than a dozen, including the *Salve Regina* and the "Fifteen O's." The Church of England had broken away from the Church of Rome only the year before, and it is apparent that in the revision of his preface Marshall gives vent to emotions generated by this change.

[2] The *Goodly Primer* is a small quarto of 169 leaves. The title-page is a preliminary leaf unsigned; the "Admonition" begins on fol. A1. Signatures are lettered from A to F, and then the series is repeated, in a different style of capitals, from A to R, and again from A to T, the colophon occurring on T4v. The collation of the volume may be described thus: [1], A-F4, 2A-F4, G-R4, 3A-F4, 2G-R4, S-T4. The text of the *Goodly Primer* has been reprinted with modernized spelling in *Three Primers Put Forth in the Reign of Henry VIII,* by E. Burton (Oxford, 1834; 2nd ed., 1848).

The "Admonition to the reder" was followed by the almanac and calendar. The latter, though in English, was cast into the traditional form, unlike the one in Marshall's earlier Primer. Rather, it was based on the one that Redman had printed; but, whereas Redman had listed the beatified pontiffs of Rome as "popes" (*e.g.*, on December 31, "s. Syluester pope"), Marshall heeded the ruling recently enacted by Parliament and styled them all "bishops" (*e.g.*, "s. Siluester byshop of Rome").

Apart from the calendar all the distinctive features of Marshall's 1534 edition were reproduced in his *Goodly Primer*—Psalms, prayers, meditations, expositions, as well as the body of the Primer (Matins, Hours, etc.) —but they do not occur in the same sequence as before. The phraseology also has been reëdited in many places, though generally the bulk of it is kept intact. Special care was given to the wording of the hymns. Compared with the Joye Hortulus, for example, the first hymn in Matins underwent quite a transformation.

In 1530 it had read (fol. L2ᵛ):

¶ The hymne.
Praysed be god ower father/ for he hath geue*n* vs his so*n*ne to be ower sauiowre.
We ar synners, vnrightwise, folyshe and fleshly.
Christe is owre mercy stole: ow*er* rightwisnes, and ower wisdome verely
We are vnclene, holden vnder y*e* daunger of dethe and synne
Christe is ower holynes, ower lyfe ower satisfaccion, and redemption.
Glory be to the, o lorde, borne of the vyrgyn Marye, glory to the father, & to the holy goste. euer. Amen.

In the first edition of Marshall's Primer (fol. L4) this was revamped to improve the prosody (Joye was no poet!) and read as follows:

Praysed be god for his exceadynge fauour, which hathe geuen vs his sone to be oure sauyour.
We are synners, vnryghtwyse, folyshe & flesshlye.
Christe is our mercy stole: ryghtwysenes, and wysdome verely.
We are vnclene, holden vnder the daunger of deathe and synne.
Chryste is our holynes, our lyfe, our redemption, and satysfaccion.

Glorye be to the, o lorde, borne of the indefyled virgyn,
glorye to the father, and to the holy Ghoste our soules surgeon.
Ame*n*.

The *Goodly Primer* (fol. ²El^v) was not satisfied with this; the fifth line of the hymn is now made to read, "We are vnclene/ holden vnder the daunger of dethe/ and synnes exaction," to polish off the rhyme. "Indefyled" becomes "vndefiled"; and "So be it" is substituted for "Amen," as it was elsewhere throughout the new edition.

Moreover, in the *Goodly Primer* are important material additions. Both Litany and Dirge are now included, and a table of contents is provided at the end of the volume. Two popular prayers have been added, the "O bone Jesu" and another commencing "Conditor coeli," both given in English, with the former in the same version that Redman had used in his Primer. From Redman also—from the fifth component section of his *Prayers of the Byble*—Marshall now borrows the paragraph on Persecution, beginning (fol. ²D4^v):

After these & suche other workes/ let euery man bolden & conforte his brethern to suffre ye crosse that god wyl lay on them, to proue them, whether they wyll abyde in his worde, or flee backe agayn. And let all men cast theyr penyworthes before. And euery day that they are not vexed, let them counte yt wonne/ and loke euery houre whan ye crosse shall come. . . .

The allusion in "cast theyr penyworthes before" is to the Master's warning (Luke 14:28) that men should count the cost of what they are to build.

The preceding leaf (²D3) contains another new item that is of interest for its connection with the work of Tyndale. This is called "⁋Thoffice of all estates" (that is, the duties enjoined in Scripture upon various classes of society). It is a series of short excerpts from the Bible applicable to different groups of people—bishops, rulers, the commons, husbands, wives, children, etc. Tyndale apparently got the idea of it from Luther and included the 'office' among the preliminary materials in his latest revision of the New Testament;[3] and Marshall borrowed it thence.

A few of these passages seem to have been Tyndale's own contribution, as, for instance, the admonitions to Rulers and to the Commons. The latter, taken from the nineteenth chapter of Leviticus, appears thus in the *Goodly Primer:*

⁋ The comens.

Ye shall not deceyue your brethern, neyther with weight nor measure: but shall haue true balaunces, and true weyghtes, for I am the lorde, your god.

Marshall copied Tyndale's wording closely, save for an occasional rephrasing which he deemed an improvement. For the guidance of Rulers, Tyndale cited these words from Leviticus, using the version in his own Pentateuch of 1530:

. . . Thou shalt not fauoure the poore ner honoure the myghty/ but shalt iudge thy neybour ryghteouslye.

This Marshall amended to read:

. . . Thou shalte not haue respecte to the persone of the poore/ nor honour thou the countenaunce of the ryche, but iudge thy neyghbour ryghtwysely.

The Authorized Version (Leviticus 19:15) has "Thou shalt not respect the person of the poor, nor honour the person of the mighty."

Though his Primer now included both Litany and Dirge, Marshall seems to have made no further effort to conform his new edition to the use of Sarum. Various unorthodox items from his earlier Primer, which had no counterpart in the Sarum Primers, are duly reprinted; for example, the scriptural 'lessons' that were interpolated in Matins. One singular 'anthem' in the Sixth Hour is a fragment from Isaiah (57:20, 21) combined with an interpretative gloss. First printed in the Joye Hortulus, it was taken over by Marshall

---

3 That is, the so-called "G-H" edition of 1535 (see Fry's *Bibliographical Description* of the Tyndale Testaments, Plate No. 5). Tyndale adapted his material from the "Haustafel" which Luther introduced near the end of his Shorter Catechism, or *Enchiridion,* of 1529 (see below, Appendix I).

word for word, and now appears thus in the *Goodly Primer* (fol. H3ʳ) :

The vngodly men are lyke a fearse swellyng see, whiche can not rest, but yᵉ waues of it rebou*n*de with violence, castynge out stynke and fylthynes: the dyuylyshe [i.e., *devilish*] vngodly shall haue no reste (sayth the lorde) but here they shall be euer vexinge the ryghtwyse, and after this, they shall haue a perpetuall gnawynge in theyr conscience.

Chief among the new features of the *Goodly Primer* are the Litany and Dirge. Marshall inserted them grudgingly and furnished each with a short foreword of its own. That for the Litany, which occurs after the Seven Psalms, begins in this vein (fol. L2ʳ) :

Forasmoche good christen reder, as I am certeynly perswaded, that diuerse pe*r*sones of small judgme*n*t and knowlege in holy scripture haue ben offended, for that y*t* in the englyshe prymer, whiche I lately set forthe, I dyd omitte & leaue out the letany, whiche I take God to witnes, I dyd not of any pe*r*uerse mynde or opinion, thynkyng that our blessed lady, and holy sayntes, myghte in no wyse be prayed vnto, but rather bicause I was not ignoraunte of the wycked opinion, and vayne superstitious maner, that dyuerse and many pe*r*sones haue not only vsed in worshyppyng of them: but also thynkyng that god by Christ wolde none otherwyse gladly here and accepte theyr petitio*n*s and prayers, but by his blessed mother, and sayntes, amo*n*ges other carnall & worldly perswasions alledgyng this. That [etc., etc.] . . .

It is logical to suppose that this was written by Marshall himself, since it speaks of "the englyshe prymer, whiche I lately set forthe"; and if this be granted, it affords us some additional evidence of his literary style.

As it had been rendered in the Redman Primer, the Litany was a simple translation of the ancient Latin text given in the margin. Since Redman's was apparently the earliest printing of it in English, Marshall did not ignore this; instead he freely adapted it and amplified it according to his own ends and predilections. It will not be amiss to present here a specimen of these two renderings, for they entered to some extent into the familiar wording which Cranmer later prepared for the Litany of the English Church.

In the Redman Primer each supplication had for its response "lorde deliuer vs" or "we pray the to hear vs." The latter of these Marshall retained, but transposed the former into "delyuer vs lorde." Here, omitting the responses, is a snatch from the Litany of the Redman Primer (fol. L7ᵛ):

From all euyll, . . . From the waytyng of the dyuel, . . . From endeles dampnacion . . . From the immynent peryl of our synnes, . . . From the assaultes of dyuells, . . . From ye spirite of fornicacyon . . . From desyryng of vayne glory . . . From all vnclennes of bodye and soule, . . . From wrathe and hate and all euyll wyll . . . From vnclene thoughtes . . . From blyndenes of herte . . . From lyghtnyng and tempest . . . From sodeyn and vnprouyded deth lorde delyuer vs.

In the *Goodly Primer* (fol. L8ᵛ) the corresponding portion reads:

From all yuell, . . . From ye crafty traynes of ye deuyll, . . . From the imminent peryll of synne, . . . From the possession of deuyls, . . . From the spirite of fornication, . . . From the desyre of vayne glory, . . . From ye vnclennes of mynde & body, . . . From vnclene thoughtes, . . . From the blyndnes of the herte, . . . From sodeyn & vnprouided dethe, . . . From pestilence and famyne, . . . From all mortall warre, . . . From lyghtnynge and tempestious wethers, . . . From seditions and scismies, . . . From euerlastyng dethe. Delyuer vs lorde.

After the Litany comes the Exposition by Savonarola on the 51st Psalm—printed this time right in the midst of the book—and this is followed by the several treatises on the Passion, all copied from the 1534 edition with a few modifications. Then comes the portion dealing with the instruction of children. The Dialogue, or catechism, now appears under a new title (fol. ²H3): "⟨ A dialogue betwene the father and the sonne/ askyng certayne questions/ and the father answerynge." By some strange twist the roles are now reversed, and it is the child who asks the questions, the headings being altered accordingly; but the questions and answers are the same as before.

Edward Burton, in the preface to his *Three Primers Put Forth in the Reign of Henry VIII* (first edition, 1834), not unnaturally supposed that this dialogue might be the same as that which appeared on early lists of heretical books as "A disputation betwene the father and the sonne"; but careful research would have shown that these were not identical.[4]

Turning next to the Dirge, we find it given at full length in the *Goodly Primer* with all its traditional ingredients, including more than twenty Psalms as well as excerpts from Job and the Prayer of Hezekiah from Isaiah.[5] In his preliminary statement about the Dirge (fol. ²K4) Marshall says among other things:

(For a more manifest and clere sight whereof, as touchynge the psalmes, bicause fyrste yu shalte not be ignoraunt of the effecte of the mater conteyned in them, I haue put a lytle shorte argument before euery psalme. . . . And as for the .ix. lessons in the sayde Dirige, taken out of the prophete Iob, I wondre sore of what entente they were ordeyned to be songe or sayde for the soules of the deade. . . . Iob spake these wordes (as I haue sayde before) than beinge in lyue [i.e., *alive*], and in the great rage of his intollerable affliction, And must they now serue for the soules that be departed, and in the paynes of I can not tell what? Finally, there is nothynge in the Dirige taken out of scripture, that maketh any more mention of the soules departed, than dothe the tale of Robyn Hoode.

Marshall's declaration that he was supplying a short 'argument' before each Psalm in the Dirge was a little less than candid, since we find that both the 'arguments' and text of these Psalms were copied directly from the Joye Psalter of 1530—either from the original volume or from Godfray's reprint of it (*S.T.C.* 2371). Marshall paid no heed whatever to Joye's later Psalter of 1534, which Redman had used for his Primer; nor did he consult the rendering of any of these particular Psalms wherever they had already occurred in the

---

[4] The correct title of the earlier and forbidden work was "A Brefe Dialoge/ bitwene a Christen Father and his stobborne Sonne." It was translated by William Roy from a Latin source. The original English edition, printed at Strassburg in 1527, is preserved in Vienna, where it was reprinted by Adolf Wolf in 1874. The text also appeared under a different title in 1550 (*S.T.C.* 14576). See E. G. Rupp, *Studies in the Making of the English Protestant Tradition* (Cambridge, Eng., 1949), p. 53; and R. Steele's "Notes on English Books Printed Abroad, 1525-48" in *Transactions of the Bibliographical Society* (vol. XI, p. 195).

[5] One curious exception is that Marshall omits Psalm 67. This may have been due to the fact that in the Dirge of Redman's Primer this Psalm was printed without heading or other distinction.

forepart of the *Goodly Primer* itself. For instance, in the Seven
Psalms (fol. K4) the 51st Psalm is worded as it was in the
Hortulus and in Marshall's first edition, but in the Dirge (fol.
²O4) it conforms exactly to the wording given in the Psalter
of 1530 (see above, p. 98). Moreover, in the Commendations
which follow the Dirge, the text of the 119th Psalm also reverts
to the wording of the 1530 Psalter rather than to the text of the
Hortulus or the Marshall Primer of 1534, as is indicated by
a number of variant readings.

As to the Dirge, interesting parallels open up between the
Goodly Primer and the Redman Primer, in which (so far as
we have record) the Dirge appeared for the first time printed
in English. For those passages where the English version is
similar in both Primers it is important to determine which of
the two should be accorded priority. Fortunately, Byddell's
printing shows enough margin of differentiation to decide the
question.

It will be recalled that in the prayer of Hezekiah (Isaiah 38)
the Redman Primer departed from the text of Joye's *Prophete
Isaye* in verses 14 and 16. In the former verse Redman had:

I moornyd lyke a Doue. Myne yies daselyd *with* lokyng vp vnto the
hyghe god . . .

Now this is also the wording in the *Goodly Primer*. Neither
Marshall nor Redman could have found such a rendering in
the *Isaye* of 1531; so one of them must have borrowed from
the other.

In verse 16, the three read much alike—Joye and Redman
and Marshall—but with significant variations:

(GJI) —For I knowe verely (lorde)   y*t* this lyfe is saufsed with galle/
(R35) —For I knowe verely (Lorde)   y*t* this lyfe is sausyd with galle
(M35)—For I knowe   (lorde) that this lyfe is saused *with* galle,

and that my lyfe is subiecte to all bitter myserye.
and that my lyfe is subiecte to   bytter mysery.
and that my lyfe is subiecte to   bytter miserie.

Note that the *Goodly Primer* (M35) not only omits the word
"all" as does the Redman Primer, but it also omits the word

"verely." If Redman had been copying from Marshall, he too would have left out the "verely." Furthermore, in verse 12, the Redman Primer follows the phrasing in Joye's Isaiah and reads: "My dayes are folden vp and taken away fro me/ lyke an herdemannes tente"; whereas the *Goodly Primer* transposes the verbs and reads: "My dayes are taken vp and folden away from me" (fol. ²P2ᵛ) .

The evidence indicates, therefore, that the Redman Primer was not dependent on the *Goodly Primer* for its rendering; otherwise it too would have departed from the text of Joye's Isaiah in these instances. Consequently the indebtedness must have been the other way round; Marshall must have borrowed from Redman. This establishes that the Redman Primer was issued some time before June 1535, the date of the *Goodly Primer;* and this in turn makes the date of Redman's *Prayers of the Byble* still earlier, since this book preceded his own Primer according to the evidence of the prayer of Solomon for "a competency of lyuyng."

Similar testimony is supplied by the Benedictus and the Magnificat. Each occurs in the Dirge of the *Goodly Primer* and once besides. For its Benedictus the Redman Primer had gone to the Marshall edition of 1534, in which the passage was given but once, in the Hours. There a portion of it had read (Luke 1: 73, 74):

And also to performe his othe which he swore to Abraham oure father: and promysed hym selfe to gyue it vs.

So that without feare, we delyuerd from the handes of our enemyes: myght serue and honoure hym.

In his Hours Redman copied this correctly, but in the Dirge the unnatural construction of the latter sentence became distorted. Similarly in the *Goodly Primer,* the earlier Marshall text is given correctly in the Hours, but in the Dirge the false reading in Redman's Primer is reproduced as follows (fol. ²P4): "So that *with*out feare, we be delyuered from y*e* handes of our enemies, myghte serue and honour hym."

For its reading of the Magnificat we mentioned that the Redman Primer went back to Tyndale's earliest New Testament and did not follow the rendering in the Primer of 1534.

But in the *Goodly Primer* the revising editor did pretty much as he pleased, after the uncritical method then in use; for where the Magnificat occurs in Evensong, he followed the reading in the Marshall Primer of 1534 except for one verse (Luke 1:51) which he took from Tyndale's revised New Testament of November in that year; but where the Magnificat occurs in the Dirge, he followed the reading in the Redman Primer, based on Tyndale's unrevised edition.

We conclude, then, that in preparing his *Goodly Primer* Marshall took the Dirge of the Redman Primer for his model, except in the Psalms. But we must also make an exception in the 'lessons' from the Book of Job, of which Marshall speaks in his foreword; for here also he parted company from Redman. Perhaps he felt that Redman's version was too old-fashioned and savored too much of its antique source in the manuscript Primers. But, whatever the reason, here the *Goodly Primer* breaks into new ground. The result, while full of interest, is little more satisfactory than Redman's hasty expedient. We cite here for comparison's sake the same passages that were cited above (see pp. 101-2), which now appear in the *Goodly Primer* in this style:

[Job 19: 23-26; fol.²O3]
O wolde god my wordes were wryten in iyerne, or els were grauen in leade or flynte. For I beleue surely I knowe *with*out doubte, that my redemer lyueth euer. And as he is immortall, so shal I ryse agayne out of the earthe, cladde with my flesshe & skyn at the laste day, and lyue with god that is my sauiour, in his syght foreuer.

[Job 10: 8-12; fol. ²M4ᵛ]
Thy handes hath formed me, & by thy power euery parte of me is fasshioned, And wylte thou nowe thus sodeynly destroye thy creature? Remembre, o lorde, I beseche the, that thou haste made me, euyn as the potter his vessell of claye. And wylte thou nowe knocke me agayne all in peces? Haste not thou wroughte me in my mothers wombe, & there gathered me, euyn as curd*es* of mylke? It is thou, o lorde, that hath cladde me with skyn and fleshe, and made me stronge with senowes and bones. Thou haste by thy mercye gyuen me lyfe and lymme, and it is thy goodnes and confort that kepeth me nowe in lyue [i.e., *alive*].

Once again the question arises, Whose work was this? At first sight it seems to be much of a piece with those translations that made their appearance in the Hortulus of 1530, such as the prayers of Jonah and Isaiah. We note the same colloquial touches, the same free-handed expenditure of words, the same zeal both in and out of season. Where Redman had been content to record, "For I knowe that my redemer lyueth" (the very words of the King James Bible, by the way), this translator will assert, "For I beleue surely I knowe *with*out doubte, that my redemer lyueth euer." Where Redman had mildly complained "that of cley thou haste made me: & into pouder thou shalte agayne tourne me"; this writer must fling down a gauntlet of challenge: "And wylte thou nowe knocke me agayne all in peces?"

Are these the earmarks of the work of George Joye? But Joye is not known to have translated any of the Book of Job. Are we to suppose that William Marshall was just such another, and that his style resembled Joye's? Was it possible that Joye could have supplied materials to Marshall for the *Goodly Primer?* Were restrictions so relaxed as to permit of correspondence between the two and thus of possible collaboration in the publication? These, of course, are mere speculations. I can record only my own opinion, which is that whereas the prayers in the Hortulus were undoubtedly the work of Joye, these excerpts from Job in the *Goodly Primer* were probably of Marshall's own translation.

So far as we know, Joye was still abroad. On February 27, 1535, he had put forth his *Apologye* in his own defense in the well-known quarrel with Tyndale over the New Testaments, but it is not quite certain where the book was published. The *Short-title Catalogue* (No. 14820) ascribes it doubtfully to London, to the very press of John Byddell which produced the two Marshall Primers.[6] If this suggestion were to be con-

---

[6] This ascription of Joye's *Apologye* to Byddell's press is due to its having been bound with another of Byddell's publications, namely, *A worke entytled of ye olde god & the newe* (S.T.C. 25127). Sayle, in *Early English Printed Books in the University Library Cambridge* (1903), says of the *Apologye*, "This book is bound with the preceding and is in the same type" (vol. I, p. 112). This opinion, however, is open to serious question, other investigators believing that the *Apologye* was printed abroad, probably at Antwerp. Comparison shows that the type used in the two books is very similar, but there is an observable difference between the capital D's and G's used in each.

firmed it would reinforce the likelihood of some collaboration between Marshall and Joye. Against it is the fact that Joye published the second edition of his so-called "corrected" New Testament in Antwerp on January 9, 1535, and it is natural to conclude that he was there at that time.

As a matter of fact, there is extant a letter from Edward Fox, later Bishop of Hereford, dated June 4, 1535, in which he states that George Joye is lodging in the same house with him at Calais.[7] Antwerp was by then a dangerous place; Tyndale had been betrayed and turned over to the Inquisition less than two weeks before, and Joye was doubtless glad to leave there. The letter from Fox intimates that a way was to be opened whereby Joye could be permitted to return to England before long. Presumably he came back to his native land during that summer.

Before the year was over, one of the great events in the history of that period took place: the first complete English Bible was printed in a translation by Myles Coverdale. It appeared on October 4, 1535, but even yet the exact place of its publication has not been ascertained.[8] Although it was not printed in England, it was certainly circulated there within a short time of its completion.

[7] See *Letters and Papers of the Reign of Henry VIII,* vol. VIII, no. 823; also J. F. Mozley's *William Tyndale* (1937), p. 308, footnote.

[8] See the article by L. A. Sheppard, "The Printers of the Coverdale Bible, 1535," in *The Library* (Series IV, vol. 16, p. 280).

Chapter XI

The Composite Primer of John Gough
(1536)

COVERDALE had been encouraged in his work on the English Bible by the support of that astute politician, Thomas Cromwell. In the summer of 1535 Sir Thomas More and Bishop John Fisher, two staunch champions of the older order, had been executed as traitors after having been in confinement for over a year. Once they were out of the way, Cromwell initiated his program of sending visitors to inspect the monasteries of the realm, which eventually led to their spoliation and suppression. Later in the year the King, trying to strengthen his position in the sphere of European politics, made overtures of *rapprochement* to the Protestant Princes of Germany. He even sought to induce Philip Melanchthon to pay a visit to England to discuss theology and the vexed question of the King's divorce. But nothing came of the negotiations, which dragged on till the following spring, since Henry was not minded to assent to Lutheran doctrines.

Early in 1536 the former Queen, Catherine of Aragon, passed away, her end hastened no doubt by the wrongs put upon her. But before the year had gone far, her successor also found herself fallen from the royal favor and was suspected and accused of infidelity to the King. Though she protested her innocence to the end, and though the evidence against her was by no means conclusive, Anne Boleyn was convicted of treason and was beheaded on May 19, leaving behind her a small daughter, the future Queen Elizabeth. By May 30, the King had married his new Queen, Jane Seymour.

Meanwhile the publication of English Scripture went forward. Editions of the Tyndale New Testament began to be multiplied, one of which (*S.T.C.* 2831) was certainly produced in England. In July, after debate in Convocation, the so-called Ten Articles were promulgated under the title, "Articles deuised by the Kynges maiestie, to establyshe christen quietnes and vnitie amonge vs." The next month injunctions were issued to the clergy (*S.T.C.* 10085) looking toward increased use of the English language in the services of the Church. These provided among other things that children were to be taught "euen from theyr infancy, theyr Pater noster, tharticles of our fayth, and the tenne commandementes in theyr mother tonge."

Over on the Continent, William Tyndale's time was running short: in August he was condemned as a heretic, and on October 6 he was strangled and burnt at the town of Vilvorde, a suburb of Brussels. In England, the desired effect of the Ten Articles was offset by a militant uprising of Catholic sentiment in the northern counties, known as the Pilgrimage of Grace, which threatened to assume serious proportions.

In this same troublous year, according to the date in their colophons, at least two new English Primers were published.[1] Like the Redman Primer of 1535 on which they were modeled, they gave the Latin text also in the margins. The most curious of these, though perhaps not the most important, was a conglomerate Primer published in London by John Gough (*S.T.C.* 15992). Gough was more of a bookseller than a printer, and it is likely that his Primer was not really printed in London but merely sold there. Present opinion regards it as having come from the vicinity of Antwerp, probably from the press of the widow of Christopher of Endhoven; but if so, it was commissioned by Gough.

We first hear of Gough in 1525 when he is said to have trans-

---

[1] Hoskins (*op. cit.,* pp. 93, 213) mentions still another Primer without title-page or date, which he says resembles the Gough Primer. He lists it as No. 117* (not to be confused with 117). It is not recorded in *S.T.C.* and seems to have disappeared from view. From what Hoskins says, it was not identical with either *S.T.C.* 15992 or 15993 or any other Primer we have discussed. It was last heard of in 1918 when Sotheby & Co. sold it to a purchaser named Hirst whom they cannot now identify. In *Book Prices Current* (1919, p. 559) the sale was mistakenly recorded as of the Gough Primer. If the volume could be brought to light it might prove an interesting companion to the Primers mentioned.

lated a book for Wynkyn de Worde entitled "The ymage of Loue" (*S.T.C.* 21473), which was called in question by the authorities. Next year, in October, the Bishop of London, then Cuthbert Tunstall, voiced a warning to some thirty printers and booksellers in his diocese against the dissemination of Lutheran books, and Gough's name is listed as among those present, along with de Worde and Redman and the rest.[2] In March of 1528, Tunstall writes to Cardinal Wolsey that he has just examined several men implicated in the circulation of forbidden books, one of whom was John Gough, "bokeseller and stationer dwelling in Flete Strete." He reports Gough as saying that "he hath not kept any shop of his own past 2 yeres, and before he was servaunt to anodyr." He concludes that Gough has been mistaken for someone else.[3]

It is noteworthy that Gough's name was known so early to the authorities as one who favored the cause of reform. He is known to have occupied premises belonging to John Rastell at the sign of the Mermaid in Cheapside. In the very year 1536, Rastell, who may formerly have been Gough's employer, was cast into prison for his outspoken religious views, and died there. In 1541, Gough himself was arrested for selling seditious books, but he was active again in 1542. All told, up till 1543, the year of his death, he had been associated with the publication of three dozen or more books. Nothing further is known of him aside from the mention of his name in a couple of wills and in a lawsuit involving other printers.[4]

---

[2] Other names on this list that we meet in our survey are: Richard Pynson, John Rastell, Thomas Berthelet, Robert Copland, Robert Wyer, Thomas Petyt, Richard Bankes, and William Bonham. See A. W. Reed, *Early Tudor Drama* (London, 1926), pp. 160-86.

[3] See Foxe's *Acts and Monuments* (Pratt's edition, 1877), vol. V, p. [879].

[4] See E. G. Duff, *A Century of the English Book Trade* (1905; reprinted 1948), p. 58; and his *Printers, Stationers and Bookbinders of Westminster and London* (Cambridge, 1906), pp. 139, 203; also F. S. Isaac, *English and Scottish Printing Types, 1535-1558* (London, 1932), *sub* Gough in the Appendix. See also below, p. 223. For Gough's publications, see *S.T.C.* 1713-76 *passim*, and 656, 3033, 4047, 4350, 5098, 5892, 10507, 11499, 14640, 15285, 15453, 16999, 17982, 18813, 18849, 18878, 19187. Dibdin, in his *Typographical Antiquities* (vol. III, pp. 207, 402), mentions two other books which may be no longer extant, namely, *A profitable treatyce . . . of the famouse reconyng* and *The Ordre or Trayne of Warre*.

For the variety of information it imparts, the title of the Gough Primer is worth reproducing at full length:

⁋ This prymer of Salysbery vse/ bothe in Englyshe and in Laten is set out a longe without any serchyng. And dyuerse expedient holsome exortatyons of crysten lyuynge The matyns. Pryme and houres/ the.vij/ salmes the lateny the salmys of the passion with the salme Beati immaculati/ and saynt Ieroms sauter/ And a confession general Also here vnto Annexed a fruyt ful werck called (the paradyse of the soull) with dyuerce deuote meditations and prayers therin/ whiche hath not ben . vsyal sayd nor redde a fore & al in englyshe. Also with Ihesus matyns with pryme/ and houres and euynsonge. & cetera.

⁋ Cum gratia et priuelegio Regali.

⁋ God saue our most noble kynge the .viij. Henry with his gratious quene Anne and all theyr progeny.

Iohn Gowghe the prynter.

The mention of Queen Anne implies that the book was published before May. The colophon, which occurs at the end of the Paradise of the Soul (fol. CC8), reads:

⁋ Here endeth this prymer with The paradyse of the soule. Imprynted by Iohan Gowhe dwellynge in London in chepsyd [i.e., *Cheapside*] next Paulys gate. 1536.

The reverse of this leaf has a large cut of the royal arms with Gough's name printed beneath.

Only three copies of the book are known: two in the Bodleian Library and an imperfect one at Cambridge University. One of the Bodleian copies[5] has bound with it the two expositions by Savonarola on the 51st and 31st Psalms; the Cambridge copy has only the one on Psalm 31.

The Gough Primer is an interesting, almost surprising, conglomeration of borrowed materials interspersed with a few other items here appearing for the first time, such as the English rendering of Jesus' Matins (so-called) and of certain prayers in the "Paradise of the Soul," as proclaimed on the title-page. The printing is slovenly and the queer spellings attest the likelihood that the volume was printed abroad, in spite of the statement in the colophon. The main sources from

[5] The collation of this copy (Douce B. 238) is: A8, 2A8, B-Z8, AA-CC8; 3A8, 2B-D8; ✠8, ✠✠8. Probably printed by the widow of Christopher of Endhoven.

which the Gough Primer was compiled were the Redman Primer, the Godfray Primer, and the *Goodly Primer* of William Marshall. It contained no preface to the reader, however, nor did it include the Dirge.

Its distinctive features may be singled out without attempting to review the entire contents. The calendar of saints' days is copied word for word, errors and all, from the Redman Primer. Then at the top of fol. ²A1 (which is numbered "Fo.i") comes an alphabet preceded by the customary Christ-cross (✠). This is the first printed Primer in English to contain an alphabet. In accord with the usage of the time, the alphabet has neither *j* nor *w*, but gives two forms each for *r* and *s*, and after *z* it adds two of the commonest abbreviations, namely, the "ampersand" (&) standing for *et* or *and,* and the "semicolon" shaped like a tall narrow *z* and used for the endings of words such as plural forms in *-es.*[6]

The Lord's Prayer is given in Latin and in the English paraphrase by John Colet, as it was in the Redman Primer. Next comes "A Dialoge of crysten lyuinge wherin the Childe asketh certayne questyons/ & answereth to the same." The wording of this heading shows it to have been copied from the Godfray Primer, but the entire dialogue is not used. Instead of rehearsing the Ten Commandments, the text suddenly shifts to a new sub-heading: "Then when the chyld is come to dysscretyon let hym be In duced to know what god is" (fol. ²A4). The next two paragraphs dealing with God and man are traceable to a Primer put forth in Latin by Robert Wyer in 1533 (*S.T.C.* 15983) where they constitute part of "A lessyon for chyldren." But a third paragraph on obedience which Wyer printed, the Gough Primer omits. Instead Gough gives us a few graces for use at mealtimes, unlike any given in the earlier Primers. The section ends (fol. ²A5) with a rhymed grace:

⁋ *Grase.*
Good lord for thy grace mekly we cal
Blesse vs & our meatys & drinckys with al

---

[6] The abbreviation *viz.* for *videlicet* preserves this ancient scriptorial form.

In nomine patris et filij.&c. ⟨[*After grace.*
Blesse we our lord which of his grace
Hath sent vs our food good time and space
And blessed be the name of our lord
Now and euer thorow al the world
And god saue our kinge with his quene anne
with the catholyk churche and send vs peace
And bringe vs al to his blesse that is endlesse
   Al crysten soulys rest in peas. Amen.

This is followed by "The .x. commaundementis. of the old and newe lawe," which turns out to be still another and different discussion of the Commandments and of those who break them. After it comes "An introduction to al persons to fulfyl the commandementes to theyr power" (fol. B2) and then "The confortable wordys and sayenges of cryst at the hye day of iugement" based on the parable in the 25th chapter of Matthew. Gough appends a warning which closes on this forthright note:

. . . and we leue the werkes vndon which: he straytly commandeth vs to do vpon payne of eternall dampnacyon (bere that well in mynd.)

The Gough Primer reverts from time to time to this favorite theme of a wholesome respect for everlasting punishment.

The treatise on the Lord's Prayer and its seven petitions is copied from the Godfray Primer. The "Hayle Mary" and the Office of All Estates and the General Confession are all taken from Marshall's *Goodly Primer*. The Gospel chapters and the account of the Passion according to St. John, as well as "the prayer that the synner prayeth," are transferred from the Redman Primer. But in this preliminary section of the Gough Primer there is also an independent treatment of the Seven Deadly Sins, perhaps of Lollard ancestry, which is headed thus (fol. D2^v): "Yf thou haue grase of the holy ghost in the thou shalt not ned to dred ony peryll of these synnys folowynge."

Starting with Matins (fol. E3^v) the Latin text is printed in the margin. The English version is composed of a combination of the Redman and Godfray Primers. Indeed, one has the feeling that Gough wished to include as much as he could in his Primer so as to please readers of all tastes. In general, wherever the Latin text is given, it is the Redman version that is used; and where there is no corresponding Latin, the wording is that of the Joye Hortulus as reprinted in the Godfray Primer. The specific dependence of Gough upon the Redman Primer is illustrated by a small omission occurring in the Seven Psalms. In the Redman Primer of 1535 the second clause of the 51st Psalm was printed: "For thy gret infinite mercyes do awaye myne iniquite," but the printing was so divided between two pages that the word "do" did not appear in the body of the text but only as a catchword at the inside corner of the bottom of the page. In copying this the Gough editor overlooked the catchword, and thus the sentence was reprinted minus its verb (fol. L7ᵛ).

Gough's treatment of the Litany was most unusual: no Latin text was given, and in place of a register of the saints with the customary invocations there is a long preliminary devotion entitled "Here folowyth the lateny of Iesus Crystys actys and mercy for all synners cordially of hym axynge" (fol. M4ᵛ). It includes a résumé of the Saviour's life with an appropriate petition for each event, thus:

Iesu that wast layed on a hard crybbe Gyue vs patiens in paynes and aduersyte.
Iesu that wast wrapped in symple pore clothes Suffre vs not to syn in excerse of clothynge. . . .
Iesu yt in the temple was dysputynge wt doctors of the law Preserue vs in thy euangelycal law & defende vs from antecrist errors. . . .
Iesu whych raysed dyuerce deed bodyes Arayse vs lord yt layeth sluggynge in deedly synne . . .

And so on for several pages. This was followed by the usual supplications and their responses, according to the version in the *Goodly Primer*.

The Latin text is resumed in the margin (fol. N4ᵛ) with the so-called Athanasian Creed, beginning "Quicunque vult." This is inserted in the Primer without preliminary notice of any kind, though the translation which accompanies it would appear to be among the earliest printings of this Creed in the English tongue. It commences thus in the Primer:

Who so euer wylleth to be saued it is expedyent before al thyngis That he abyde fast in the catholyke fayth.
Except euery person wyll kepe it hole & inuyolat With out dout he shall peryshe eternally.
The catholyke fayth of trewth thys it is That we worshyp one God in trynyte And trynyte in vnyte. . . .

At the end of the Primer proper, it is interesting to come upon the prayer of Solomon "For a competency of lyuyng," taken word for word from the Redman Primer. It is the only one of the *Prayers of the Byble* that Gough uses.

The reverse side of the same leaf (S4) shows a large woodcut of the infant Jesus. Framed within an architectural niche, the babe is seen standing on a flat pedestal and holding in one hand the symbolic orb. At the bottom of the page we read: "Here foloweth the matyns in the honor of the blessed name of Iesu." Concerning these so-called Matins themselves not much need be said. They could be described as an adaptation of the regular Hours, with the use of different hymns and responses and with selected Bible passages appropriately concerning the name of the Lord. In their Latin form they had been known as an adjunct of the Book of Hours as early as 1503 (see *S.T.C.* 15899). Now, in this their first English rendering, they were carelessly edited, poorly printed, and the Latin text was omitted.

The scriptural selections in Jesus' Matins were mostly excerpts from the Psalms, and some of these were duplicates of material already used in the regular Matins. In such instances the Gough Primer used the version available in the Redman Primer. But in four passages there were no previous parallels.[7] The wording of three of these was obviously based on the Psalter of 1530, albeit in a corrupted form. For example, where the Psalter (111: 10) had said:

The beginninge of wysdome is ye feare of the lorde: they savore

7 Ps. 66:1-4; 86:9-12; 111:9,10; and 143:8-12.

rightly that geve dilygence to do hys commaundementes/ the praise of theis men continuethe everlastinge: . . .

the Gough Primer (fol. T5ᵛ) printed this:

. . . The begynnyng of wysdome is the feare of the lord.
They vnderstand and sauore ryghtly is that gyueth dylygens to his commandementys the prayse of these men contynew for euer.

Such a passage is strong argument for the printing of this Primer on foreign soil,—"& al in englyshe" as the title-page says!

For the other one of these four Psalms (66: 1-4) I have found no previous translation even resembling the version that Gough gives, which I here submit as a curiosity (fol. S6) :

Shew some tokens of myrth vnto goddys honorable name al ye that dwell vppon erth.
Synge ye of the maieste of his name declare we openly how gret prayse he is worthy.
Speke ye of god how gretly art thou to be worshypped/ for thy werkys through the gretnesse of thy power.
Thy ennemyes shal be knowen openly to have ben lyers such as ascribeth not diuinite to the.
All the erthe shal worshyp the and shall synge salmys to thy prayse and they shall magnyfye thy namys with songys.

The interpolation of the words "such as ascribeth not diuinite to the" suggests that the origin of this version might be found in some obscure fifteenth-century Psalter. At any rate, the added words are not in Wycliffe or Joye or Coverdale.

After the so-called Hours of the name of Jesus we read (fol. T8): "Here foloweth deuote meditations and prayers with contemplacions called the paradyse of the soule." This miscellaneous collection in English alone, and occupying the last 57 leaves of the Primer, is adequately summarized by Hoskins in his *Horae Beatae Mariae Virginis* (p. 220). The first portion of it is mostly made up of traditional material and, curiously enough, a few of the prayers are repetitions of those already given in the main body of the Primer. A fresh item of interest is a series of seven prayers, one allotted to each day of the week (fol. V6). Also the "Paradise" contains a rendering of the Fifteen O's ascribed to St. Bridget, which Gough had omitted from the body of his Primer. This particular translation he may have made for himself, as it is quite unlike the Caxton version which Redman had included in his Primer of 1535.

The latter portion of Gough's "Paradise of the Soul" is a signal example of the current practice of publishers as regards plagiarism. The concept of property rights in literary production either was undeveloped or was generally ignored; for free-handed borrowing, imitation, and adaptation were common, with no vestige of acknowledgment.

At the close of the Fifteen O's, for instance (fol. CC1), we come upon this heading without further preliminary: "⟨ The nosegay or posee of lyght to lede and comfort al synner [sic] that walke in darknesse gadred out of the new testament." Commencing with an appropriate motto ("Qui ambulat in tenebris," etc.) given in both Latin and English, it launches forthwith into a discussion of the law of God: "The lawe of god is a doctrine that biddeth good & forbiddeth euil..." Afterward it branches into a commentary on faith and charity and good works, extending to more than a dozen pages.

Thus unannounced does Gough adapt, or rather preëmpt, the text of a well-known work by Patrick Hamilton which had been translated into English a few years before by the celebrated John Frith. First published (one infers) while Frith was yet alive, it was later reissued by an unknown printer under the title: "⟨ Dyuers frutful gatheringes of scrypture concetnyng [sic] fayth and workes" (S.T.C. 12732).[8] Then about 1534 Redman reprinted the work under a somewhat similar title, and from this edition Gough now incorporates it in his Primer under a new and different heading.

Had he seen fit to label the material with the names of its author and translator, he would have stirred up smoldering emotions hardly cooled. For Hamilton, a young Scotch abbot

---

[8] The reissue is ascribed to the press of William Copland about the year 1549 (see McKerrow and Ferguson, Title-page Borders, p. 22). But the state of the text itself seems to be earlier than in Redman's edition.

of noble birth, had compiled his *Loci Communes* (or Common Places) after he had espoused with fervent zeal the doctrines of Martin Luther, and in 1528 he became one of the Reformation's first martyrs in Scotland, where he suffered death at the command of Cardinal Beaton. The translator, John Frith, was the promising young man, acquainted with Tyndale and the Cambridge reformers, who had just undergone martyrdom in London as recently as 1533, having been led from the Tower to the fires at Smithfield.

One special bit from Frith's translation was picked up out of Gough's "Paradise" for use in later Primers. In what seems to have been the original text (*S.T.C.* 12732) the passage read (fol. B4ᵛ):

> Of cherite
>
> Cherite is the loue of thy neighboure The rule of cheryte is this, Do as thou woldest be doune to for chryste holdeth all alyke the ruche the poore the frend and the foo ye thankefull and vnthankeful ye kinseman and straunger A comparison betwene faith hope and cherite. Fayth cometh of the word of god hope commeth of health & cherite springeth of them both.

In the Redman edition the middle of the second line read, "For charyte holdeth all a lyke" etc.; and in Gough's "Paradise of the Soul" (fol. CC5ᵛ) the sentence was shortened to read: "For charite holdeth all a like the rich and the poore: the frende & the foo." These later editions also had ". . . hope cometh of fayth," instead of "cometh of health."

Finally, when Gough was getting near the end of his last signature, he unceremoniously forsook the Frith and Redman text and embarked on some paragraphs concerning the passion of Christ. These were lifted from the latter part of the "Fruitful Remembrance of Christ's Passion" which Marshall had translated from Luther for his Primer of 1534. In the Marshall Primer the borrowed portion began as follows:

> ❡ Whan thou arte dyseased wyth any sorowe or malady/ then thynke howe small the payne is/ yf thou shuldest compare it wyth Chrystes crowne of thorne . . .

But Gough's foreign-born compositor came forth with this reading (fol. CC3ʳ) : "When thou art dyspleased with ony sorow or malady/ . . ."

What he borrowed from Marshall's "Fruitful Remembrance" Gough tailored to fit the space he had left so as to fill out his final page. Here, just above the colophon, we read the concluding sentences, noticing how different the strain of Marshall's Lutheranism is from that of Hamilton and Frith:

> How be it the maner of this remembraunce is very rare & out of vse\ now a dayes. And we haue chaunged it al together in to an outwarde apperaunce and haue thought it sufficient to beholde ye story of ye passion painted vpon ye walles. But there are very fewe (yea almoste none) yt call it to theyr remembraunce for thentent to knowe theyr sinnes by it\ or to quyet theyr tremblynge consciences\ or to ordre & compare theyr lyfe to this ensample.

Incidentally, it is instructive to note the number of contractions that Gough's printer used in these last lines in order to make them come out even on the page.

The two expositions by Savonarola, bound with the Bodleian copy of the Gough Primer (Douce B.238), have their own quiring and may also have been published and sold separately. But apparently they were printed at the same time as the Primer, that is, in the early part of 1536.[9] The Exposition on the 51st Psalm follows the text of the Marshall edition of 1534, except that to fill out the leaves of signature D, it incorporates "A deuout short prayer to Iesus" (in verse-form) and "The Pater noster/ spoken of the Synner\ God answerynge hym at euery peticyon"; also "A prayer for the Kynge, and the quene," neither of whom is mentioned by name. Now the last two of these three items were also printed by Godfray

---

[9] See the article on these expositions cited above (p. 74n.). Gough's edition of the Exposition on Ps. 51 is identical with *S.T.C.* 21795a and 14503; it is also listed in Nijhoff and Kronenberg, *Nederlandsche Bibliographie 1500-1540*, as No. 3851. Miss Kronenberg ascribes the printing to Godfrid van der Haghen, but Mr. F. S. Ferguson maintains it was printed by the widow of Christopher of Endhoven. The Meditation on Ps. 31 is also listed separately (*S.T.C.* 21799). Both items are set in the same style of type as the Primer, and were probably intended to accompany it.

without date (*S.T.C.* 16818), and it is likely that Gough borrowed them from Godfray's little booklet.

The Meditation of Savonarola on Psalm 31, which comes at the end of the Bodleian copy, seems to have been drawn from the final section of Redman's *Prayers of the Byble*. In the colophon of this treatise Gough refers to Savonarola as "Hierom of Ferrarie," while in the title of it he uses the Latin form of his name and calls him "Ierom de fararia." The Latin text, however, does not accompany either of these expositions in the Gough edition.

Chapter XII

The English-Latin Primer of Rouen
(1536)

THE other Primer to be published in 1536 was a very carefully, indeed handsomely, printed volume emanating
from Rouen without any printer's name attached (*S.T.C.*
15993). It was quite conservative in tone, compared with the
Gough Primer. Nor can we be altogether certain which of
these two Primers was the earlier; but since Gough's was
issued before the month of May we have spoken of it first.
Each seems to have been put forth entirely independently
of the other, though each was called into being by the success
of the Redman Primer of the preceding year.

The Rouen Primer was in effect a revision of Redman's.
It faithfully conformed to the use of Sarum, giving the text
in both English and Latin. The publisher was probably François Regnault, printer to the University of Paris, or else it
might have been his agent at Rouen, Nicholas LeRoux. The
title, which stood at the head of a table of contents, was simply
worded:

⟨ Thys prymer in Englyshe and in Laten is newly translatyd after
the Laten texte.

The colophon was equally brief and direct: "⟨ Imprynted in
Rowen the yere of our Lorde 1 5 3 6." A complete copy in the
Bodleian Library (Douce BB. 231) has bound with it the two
expositions of Savonarola, in both Latin and English, with
another colophon at the end of them just like the one in the
Primer.[1] An imperfect copy of the Primer portion is in the
Cambridge University Library.

1 Collation: ✠8, A-I8, K-V8, x8, y6; a-c8, 2D-G8, 2H5.

131

As first issued, the Rouen Primer must have been an attractive publication—a good-sized octavo of 182 numbered leaves (plus another 61 for the Savonarola section) . The volume was enriched with several well-designed woodcuts. The English text was printed in a large comely black-letter, well spaced on the page, with the Latin in smaller type down the margin.

As to its contents, the Rouen Primer introduced only a few new features. The calendar of saints' days was reprinted from Redman's Primer, two months to a page, except that names of Popes were now entered as "by. of Ro." (for "bishop of Rome") instead of as "pope." This, of course, was in recognition of the stand taken by Convocation two years before.

The Ten Commandments were presented twice; first in a numbered table beginning:

   i. Thou shalt nat haue straung goddes in my syght.
   ii. Thou shalte nat vsurpe the name of thy god in vayne. [etc.]

This was followed by "The .x. commaundementes, in metre" taken from the Redman Primer. Two other new items appear in these preliminary pages: "A lytle metre conteynynge the duety of a chrysten man" and "An Inuocacyon vnto the holy Trinyte, to be sayde in the mornynge, whan thou shalt ryse vp."

Further along (fol. E6) we come upon another new feature, a metrical explanation preceding the commencement of Hours, "Howe the sayenge of houres fyrst began, & why they are socalled." This reads as follows:

¶ At certayne houres, vnto god for to praye.
Was fyrst begonne, by the prophete Daniell.
Whiche knelynge on his knees thre tymes euery day.
Dyd inuocate god/ and as the Actes do tell.
Saynte Peter the apostell of a customable vse
Prayed vnto god certayne houres of the day
Which thing doutles dyd fyrst induce
The seruyce of these houres that dayly saye.
And by that example/ as wryteth .S. Cypriane.
Suche prayenge was receyued in the churche chrystian.

On the other hand, in a section of Prayers at the end of

the Primer we find several items of borrowed material: there is the "Conditor coeli" reprinted from the *Goodly Primer;* the prayer of Solomon (Proverbs 30) copied from the Redman Primer; and also two other prayers (Wisdom 9: 1-11 and I Kings 3: 6-9) both drawn from Redman's *Prayers of the Byble.*

All in all, the claim advanced on the title-page of this Primer that it was newly translated is found to be somewhat exaggerated. In its liturgical features, as distinct from the scriptural portions, it retains the renderings used in Redman's Primer. Hymns, collects, addresses to the Virgin, and so on, all recur here in the same wording as before. For instance, the well-known Latin hymn, *Veni Creator Spiritus,* commences as follows in the Rouen Primer (fol. E7):

> Cum holy ghoste, O creatour eternall.
> In our myndes, to make visitacion
> And fulfyll w*t* grace supernall
> Our hertes y*t* be of thy creacyon.

This accords verbally with Redman, except that the earlier printing, adhering to the meter, read more correctly in the third line, "And fulfyll y*u,* w*t* grace supernall." Even at that, the verse is wooden; and it is small wonder that Cranmer undertook to reform it in later years. In the new *Ordinal* of 1549 (*S.T.C.* 16462), Cranmer's attempt to improve on these particular lines read:

> Come holy ghost eternall god procedyng from aboue,
> Bothe from the father and the sonne, the God of peace & loue,
> Visite our myndes, and into vs, thy heauenly grace inspire,
> That in all truthe and Godlinesse, we maie haue true desire.

Where the Rouen Primer did break into new ground—and it was an important departure—was in the translation of Scripture, especially of the Psalms. The real point of the new title was to call attention to the fact that this Primer was translated "after the Laten texte." We may recollect that Redman had relied for his version of the Psalms on the Marshall Primer and the Joye Psalter of 1534, and had announced in his preface that they were Englished according to the version of Felinus.

It was now felt, evidently, that the discrepancies were too noticeable between the Vulgate text in the margin of the Primer and the informal translations of George Joye. Accordingly, the Rouen Primer, while it printed practically all the rest of Redman's preface, deleted the portion about the text of Felinus, and actually introduced a new translation of nearly all the Psalms it used. Thus the Rouen Primer cut loose from the tradition of Joye and Marshall, and based its version, with conservative fidelity, on the accompanying Latin text in its margin.

We have recorded above (see p. 96) how the Redman Primer dealt with Psalm 126. Let us present for comparison the same Psalm as printed among the Fifteen Psalms of the Rouen Primer (fol. M3ʳ):

Whan the lorde tourned the captiuite of Syon: we were made gladde.
Then was our mouth ful of myrthe: and our tongue of wylfulnes.
Then shall they say amonge the gentyls: the lorde hathe magnifyed to do with them.
The lorde hath magnyfyed to do with vs: we are made ioyfull.
Lorde conuerte our captiuyte: as a ryuer in the southe.
They that sowe with teares: shall reape with gladnes.
They goynge forthe, wente and wepte: castynge theyr sedys.
But commynge agayne they shall cum with ioye: bearynge theyr handes full of corne.

How thorough this revision was, can be illustrated from another Psalm (27: 1-3). First we show the text of Joye's Psalter (1534), which was reprinted in the Dirge of the Redman Primer almost without change. Notice how similar in some points, how unlike in others, is the version now given in the Rouen Primer (fol. V3) :

(GJP)—The Lorde is my light & my helthe: whom then shal I feare?
(R36)—The lorde is my lyght & my helth: whom   shal I feare?

the lorde is the strength of my lyfe/ of whom then shal I be afrayde?
The lorde is the defender of my lyfe: at whom   shall I quake.

Whyle ther comeforth agenst me the maligne myscheuouse/ and euen
Whylste euyll doers approche vnto me for to deuoure my flesshe.

my enemyes to deuower me hole/   lo thei fal downe   al to smiten
Myne enemyes whiche trouble me/   they were made weake and fell downe.

When their tentis ar pitched agenst me/   yet I fere not: when thei
If   they   pytche   pauilyons   againste me/   my herte shall nat feare.

be incensed to batail agenst me/ then am I most suer.
If a battayle ryse agaynste me/ I shall truste in it.

Occasionally, however, a few of the Psalms in this Primer
were not set forth in a new version but were copied instead
from Redman, sometimes with but slight alteration. Where
Redman's version had departed from the text of Felinus, the
Rouen editor felt justified in retaining it; but his editorial
practice seems not too consistent in this. It will be remembered
that the opening Psalm of Matins (Ps. 95) had been rendered
afresh by Joye for his 1530 Hortulus and that Marshall and
Redman had used Joye's rendering in their Primers; also that
in the Redman Primer the 51st Psalm had been drawn from
the wording in the Savonarola exposition. Since neither of
these was based directly on the Latin of Felinus, the editor
of the Rouen Primer was content to leave them alone. But in
the so-called Psalter of St. Jerome, Redman took his wording
of the 51st Psalm from the Psalter of 1530, and in this context
the Rouen editor offered a new translation of the Psalm, quite
different from what he uses in other parts of the volume, e.g.,
in the Seven Psalms.[2]

Among the Seven Penitential Psalms five were newly translated, but both the 51st and the 130th were left as Redman
published them. Concerning the latter Psalm ("De pro-
fundis"), one would have expected a new version of it and
no special reason appears for leaving the old one intact. The
Psalm occurs four times in these Sarum Primers, and each time
the Rouen edition kept to Redman's wording of it, drawn
from George Joye's Psalter of 1534 and beginning in his
typical vein, "Out of the botomles pytte of my heuy trouble,"
etc.

2 See below, Appendix III.

A singular case-history of what went on in these revisions is offered by the 67th Psalm. In the Psalter of 1530 it had started off:

God mought favoure and have mercy vpon vs: he mought lighten vs with his presens. Salah.

In the earlier Marshall Primer this reading was followed, but without the "Salah." But Byddell inadvertently omitted the whole of verses four and five, and this posed an editorial problem (see above, p. 95). In his *Goodly Primer,* Marshall supplied the missing lines from the 1530 Psalter, but he also observed that in the Psalter of 1534 Joye had inserted a note about 'Selah' in the margin to the effect that it could be read, "So he mought"; and the Goodly Primer reads accordingly, "He mought lyghten vs with his presence, so he mought."

As was mentioned above, when Redman's editor noticed the missing verses in the first Marshall Primer, he decided to recast the entire Psalm, but ran into trouble through a misprinting of the final clause. Whereupon the Rouen editor, while adopting Redman's wording as a basis, brought in a couple of variations of his own.

The ending of the Psalm (verses 4-7) will illustrate what took place. The reading of the 1530 Psalter was undeniably cumbrous:

The haithen mought ioye and triumphe: in yt thou doste righte vnto the people/ and directest the nacions vpon therthe. Selah. The people mought sprede thy name (oh God): ye all people mought magnifie the. The erthe also mought give ageine hyr encrese: and god which is ower god mought do vs good. God mought blesse vs: and all that inhabit the erthe evene vnto the vttermoste partes therof mought feare hym.

Redman's attempted simplification was drastic (fol. B4):

Ioyfull & glad be all folke for thou rulest people with equite and orderest all folkes in erthe.

Peple knowlege the to be god let al nacions confesse to the yt the erthe may yelde forth her frute.

Blesse vs our god: & all yt inhabite the erth that [in] the vttermost partes therof yu mayst be feryd.

So the Rouen Primer (fol. D1) amended the latter portion
to read:

People knowledge the to be god let all nacyons confesse to the: for
the earth hath yolden forth her frute.
Blesse vs our god: & all that inhabyte the earth, that all the partes
therof may feare the.

In passages from the New Testament little or no alteration
was made; but in the Dirge the prayer of Hezekiah from
Isaiah 38 was now deemed unsatisfactory, presumably because
the rendering that Redman had used was copied from Joye's
Prophete Isaye. Here again the Rouen Primer tried to pattern
the English more closely after the Latin, as may be judged
from these few verses (14-17). In the Redman Primer (fol.
P7ᵛ) they had appeared:

Myne yies daselyd wt lokyng vp vnto the hyghe god sayeng.
Lorde I am sore handelyd/ delyuer me vpon thy worde: what myght
I thinke or what might I say/ that he wolde thus moch for me?
That I mought yet peruse al my dayes/ ye althoughe it be to my
bytter payne.
For I knowe verely (Lorde) yt this lyfe is sausyd with galle and that
my lyfe is subiecte to bytter mysery.

In the Rouen Primer (fol. R4ᵛ) these lines read:

Myne eyen daselyd with lokynge on hyghe.
Lord I am enforcyd, aunswere for me what I shall saye: or what he
shall aunswere me syns I haue done it.
I shall reuolue all myne yeres vnto the with greate bytternes of herte.
Lorde if they lyue thus & the lyfe of my spiryte be in suche thynges:
yu shalt correrte [sic; for *correct*] me & quicken me: lo in peace my
sorewe is most bytterest.

These various new translations which occurred all through
the Rouen Primer—what we may call the Rouen version—
embraced over fifty of the Psalms. The author of them is
entirely unknown. It is conceivable that he was the same person who had compiled the Redman edition of the Primer
and of the *Prayers of the Byble*. His translations are certainly
not remarkable and sometimes are inaccurate, but at least they

are direct and for the most part obediently faithful to the Latin, even when the result is not too intelligible. Comparison of the wording does not disclose that any special use was made of the recently published Coverdale translation of the Bible; it rather appears that older Wycliffite versions may have been consulted. But this inference is hard to establish; for it is always difficult to judge whether an apparent similarity to the Wycliffite wording may not be the mere natural outcome of diligent adherence to the Latin Vulgate text on the part of both translators, working independently. On the other hand, one feels a certain kinship in style between the new renditions in the Rouen Primer and the translation of Brunfels' selections as given in Redman's *Prayers of the Byble;* the same workman might have produced both. No direct comparison is available, however, for the reason that the selections from the Old Testament comprised in Redman's *Prayers* were not the same as those included in the Rouen Primer, except the three at the end of the Primer, which were undoubtedly copied directly from the *Prayers* themselves. Likewise, the Psalms afford no basis for comparison, since Redman had used no new translation of these in his *Prayers,* but had taken over his version from Joye's Psalter.

In still another respect, the Rouen Primer could properly claim to be "newly translatyd." This was in the 'lessons' of the Dirge, selected from the Book of Job. The Rouen translator was evidently dissatisfied with the tentative version used in the Redman Primer, as well as with the more elaborate one in the *Goodly Primer* of Marshall. At any rate he reverted to the antiquated practice of rendering these lessons into English verse—a sort of doggerel paraphrase. Indeed, the Rouen Primer evinces a certain fondness for such versifications. The result is not always happy, but it proved to be acceptable to the changing religious sentiment that marked the later years of Henry's reign. We have already cited part of the lesson from the nineteenth chapter of Job as printed in the Redman and Goodly Primers (see above, pp. 101 and 115); let us look now at the same passage as versified in the Rouen Primer (fol. Q6^r):

Who shall warrante me that my dedes shal be wrytten
Or who can promyse me other y*t* they shall
Be regysteryd so, they shal nat be forgetten
In yron, lede, or in the stony wall
But one thing I knowe that fyrst is of all
That my redemer shall euer lyue this I knowe for trewe
And in the laste daye that I shall ryse a newe
And with this skynne agayne than I shall be clad
And *in* my flesshe I shall playnly se
My sauyour and my god, whyche hathe me wrought and made.

Because of its greater fidelity to the Latin in its prose passages—if not in its verse—the Rouen Primer promptly superseded Redman's Primer as the accepted standard for the 'use of Sarum.' Though the Marshall Primers also persisted for a while, they were never accepted by the more conservative readers; but the Rouen Primer fitted in with the spirit of the time. It underwent numerous modifications in successive editions, as we shall see; but even as late as Mary's reign, when Catholic influence was paramount, it was the version in the Rouen Primer that provided the publishers with an approved vehicle for supplying to ordinary English readers the more familiar passages of Scripture at a time when the English Bible was forbidden to circulate.

Chapter XIII

Primers with Liturgical Epistles and Gospels (1537)

DURING 1537 the strong-handed policies of Thomas Cromwell began to prevail more and more. With the increase of oppression and the consequent mounting of resentment, vigorous counter stresses made themselves apparent in the reactions of the people. These in turn gave rise to such constant shifts of royal policy as to confound all later historians of that period. The Catholic uprising known as the Pilgrimage of Grace was put down with stern measures in February of this year, and by means of false promises its leader, Robert Aske, was taken into custody and afterwards executed in July. In the latter month also, Archbishop Cranmer, together with Edward Fox and a committee of other prelates, issued a current statement of orthodoxy as approved by the Church of England, published under the title, "The Institution of a Christen man" (*S.T.C.* 5163).[1]

The political leanings of Cromwell toward the Protestant party ensured an open door for the further circulation of the Scriptures. In 1537 the first English Bible to be printed in England was published by James Nicolson, being a corrected edition of the Coverdale Bible. More momentous was the importation into England during this summer of the so-called Matthew Bible, which under the editorship of John Rogers combined the fruits of the labors of both Tyndale and Coverdale, thus becoming the fountainhead of all subsequent Eng-

---

[1] In the preface to his book, *Three Primers Put Forth in the Reign of Henry VIII* (edition of 1834, pp. xlvi-l), Edward Burton has demonstrated that Cranmer and Fox made use of phraseology found in the *Goodly Primer* of Marshall and borrowed many of its terms for "The Institution of a Christian Man." The latter is sometimes referred to as the "Bishops' Book."

lish Bibles. It was published "with the Kinges most gracyous lycence," having secured the cordial approbation of Cromwell and Cranmer.

On October 12, the whole nation congratulated itself on the birth of a Prince, the future Edward VI, Henry's only son; but in the midst of the general rejoicing the Queen, Jane Seymour, passed quietly away less than two weeks after her son was born.

Although no English Primers are known bearing the date 1537 on their title-pages or in their colophons, there are at least two that can be safely assigned to this year. One, a revision of the Rouen Primer of the year before, was published by Redman in London; and the other, a revision of Marshall's *Goodly Primer,* by Byddell. Each carried the Latin text in its margins and, more important, each was supplemented with a separate section of scriptural passages appointed to be read in church on every Sunday and holiday of the year. These were known as 'Epistles and Gospels'; attention has already been drawn to a similar collection of 'Epistles' drawn from the Old Testament and appended to the New Testaments of Tyndale and of Joye.

The new Redman Primer (*S.T.C.* 15997), which appears to be the earlier of the two, bore its title—"Thys prymer in Englyshe and in Laten is newly translated after the Laten texte"—printed above a table of contents.[2] It represents a fairly conscientious reworking of the Rouen Primer of 1536, with a few extra items inserted, not to speak of the supplementary 'Epistles and Gospels.' After the almanac and calendar comes a set of doggerel rhymes on the days of the week. This item seems to have been introduced for the first time in a Latin Primer published early in 1531 by the same Christopher of Endhoven who formerly printed certain lost editions of the Tyndale New Testament. As given in the Endhoven Primer (*S.T.C.* 15966) under the heading of "The dayes of the weke moralysed" the rhyme for Sunday ran as follows:

2 The collation of the entire volume is: [*]4, ✠6, A-I4, K-T4, V4, X-Z4, AA-II4; 2A-I4, 2K-L4; 3A-I4, 3K-L4; 2M-R4; 250 leaves in all.

I am sonday honourable
The heed [i.e., *head*] of all the weke dayes
That day all thyng labourable
Ought to rest/ & gyue lawde and prayse
To our creatour/ that alwayes
Vvolde haue vs rest after trauayle
Man/ seruaunt/ and thy beest he sayes
And the other to thyn auayle

And this wording is copied almost without change in the Redman Primer.

Thereupon Redman sets forth (fol. ✠1ᵛ) still another treatise on the Ten Commandments, this one headed:

《 The commaundementes of god gyuen by Moses/ and expounded by Christe/ in our mother tongue/ very necessary and expedient for youthe and all other to learne and knowe.

The exposition of the Commandments in this case is restricted to citations from the Scripture, chiefly from the words of Jesus and the epistles of Paul. The version given of these excerpts is based on the first of the Tyndale New Testaments; but we observe here what we have noted before in other Primers, that the wording has been edited in places and does not follow Tyndale exactly.

Indeed it seems likely that this entire feature was borrowed from a little booklet published by John Byddell in 1537 (*S.T.C.* 16820); at least the same errors of citation are common to both. But whereas, in Mark 4:19, the Byddell imprint reads correctly, "for the care of this worlde and the disceitfulnes of ryches, choke the worde," and in Matthew 5:34 reads, "swere not at all"; the Redman Primer has "choke the worlde" and "sweare nat all." The title of this handbook of Byddell's ran:

《 The Pater noster. yͤ Crede. & the commaundementes of god in englysh, with many other godly lessons/ ryght necessary for youth & al other to lerne & knowe: accordyng to the commaundement & Iniunctions gyuen by thauctorite of the kynges hyghnes through this his realme.

The reference, of course, is to the injunctions of 1536 (*S.T.C.* 10085). Despite some cloud of doubt still resting on these injunctions, how far they were actually put into effect, this little *Pater noster* of Byddell's (which he dated) is evidence that he accepted them as valid in 1537. One item of the injunctions might even be interpreted to imply that some agreement had been reached between Cromwell and the printers for the issuance of just such booklets; for in one place they provide that

> . . . the sayde curates shal in theyr sermons deliberately and plainly recite of the said pater noster, articles or commandementes, one clause or artycle one daye, and an other an other daye, tyll the hole be taught and lerned by lyttell and lyttell. And shall delyuer the same in writinge, or shewe where printed bokes conteyninge the same be to be solde, to them that can reede, or wyll desyre the same.[3]

Moreover, Byddell printed at the end of his booklet three other items that reflected official pronouncements: (1) "Thabolysshynge of the bysshop of Romes pretensed & vsurped power & iurisdiction within this Realme," the phrasing of which was based on the first article in the forementioned injunctions. (2) "An order and forme of byddynge of the bedys, by the kynges commaundement," derived from an enactment of 1535 which specified that worshippers should pray for the King and Queen as well as for "the hole congregacion of Chrystes churche." As recorded in Wilkins's *Concilia* (vol. III, p. 783) this 'form' had mentioned both Queen Anne and the Princess Elizabeth; but in Byddell's printing of it (fol. K 2) we are exhorted to pray for the King "& the moost noble & vertuous lady quene Iane, his moost laufull wyfe." This argues that Byddell printed his booklet comparatively early in 1537.[4] (3) "A copy of thacte made for thabrogacion of certayne

---

[3] These "printed bokes" might, of course, have been English Primers. Another item of the same injunctions stipulated that each parish church was to be provided with "a boke of the hole Byble, bothe in Latin, and also in Englyshe"; but the only English Bible available in 1536 would have been the Coverdale translation, unless we assume that the injunctions anticipated a new English version such as Convocation had already petitioned for on June 9, 1536, which turned out to be the so-called Matthew Bible. See also W. H. Frere and W. M. Kennedy, *Visitation Articles and Injunctions of the Period of the Reformation* (London, 1910), vol. II, pp. 1-11.

[4] He brought out another edition of "The Pater noster, the crede, and the commaundementes" apparently in 1538, though undated (*S.T.C.* 16821), in which Jane's name is omitted and instead we have: "and also for oure mooste noble Prynce Edward." At length, in 1539, Redman also put forth "The Pater noster/ the Aue/

holydayes," which reproduced the act passed by Convocation in the summer of 1536.

Returning now to the Redman Primer of 1537, after the section on the Commandments we come upon the Athanasian Creed, in both Latin and English, the latter exhibiting some revision as compared with the crude translation in the Gough Primer mentioned in a preceding chapter. This is followed by "The office of all estates," taken directly from the wording of the *Goodly Primer*.

Next (fol. A1) there is a lengthy preface to the reader based upon the one in the Rouen Primer, which in turn was drawn from Redman's Primer of 1535. In this 1537 edition the preface gives evidence of careful rewriting. Besides occasional amendment of a word or phrase, there are three new considerable interpolations, moderate in tone like the rest of the preface, but quite definite. Of this fresh material the following is perhaps the most interesting:

For euyn as it is a poynte of christian prudence and circumspeccyon nat to receyue any thynge for certayne and vndoubted, whiche is nat expressyd in manyfest scripture, so contrary wyse is it a poynt of presumptuos peruersite and arrogance proudly to reiecte that thing which the religious contemplacion of good and godly men haue eyther taughte . . . or lefte to the instruccion of the vnlerned multitude/ of which sorte [are] al these prescripte fourmes of prayours, worshyppynges of sayntes and such lyke, whiche (as me semeth) ought mekely to be receiued as mennys tradicyons, so longe as they varie nat from that only and synguler precedent (after whiche all thynges ought & muste be fashyoned) I meane the worde of god. . . . Is it not merueyl [i.e., *marvel*] that many be so ferre from all indifferency of iudgement frowably [*sic*] to refuse euery thinge that hathe byn commended to vs by tradicyon of our elders . . . And this they do with an extreme zeale, but nat accordynge to knowledge, but rather because they haue nat that same pure and lyghtsome eye that is spoken of Mat. 6. the lacke wherof causeth them to stande in theyr owne lyght, . . . This do I here touche the more apertly, by occasyon of this englyshe prymar of Sarum vse whiche when

---

Crede, and .x. *Commaundementes*" (*S.T.C.* 16819), wherein the reader is asked to pray "for the moste noble and royal estate of our prynce: Prynce Edwarde." For the use of the term, 'the Lord's Prayer,' in *S.T.C.* 16820, see the writer's article on this subject in *The Library Chronicle* of the University of Pennsylvania (vol. XVIII, p. 24).

it was fyrste imprynted lyke as it lackyd nat the vituperation and disprayse of some, so had it agayne the fauour and commendacion of the more lernyd sorte. Howebeit when it came so to passe that it was nat vtterly myslyked of the better partie, but that also it semed to men of authorite nat inconuenyent to passe amonge the comen people, it hathe anymated the setters forthe therof nat a lytle, to communicate the same eftsones agayne to the redynge of other, beyng more diligently correctyd, more purely imprynted, and metely wel purged of many thinges that semed no small faultes therin.

It would help a great deal if we could be certain whose words these were. Couched in the classic learned style, they are (considering the period) unusually well written. Could Redman himself write like that, or had he some prominent churchman to serve as his editor? Or could this, perchance, have been an early example of Richard Taverner's workmanship? The reference to the "englyshe prymar" is, of course, to the edition of 1535 now preserved at Paris; but who were "the more lernyd sorte" and "men of authorite" that gave it sanction? Or, for that matter, who were the rejecters of tradition, having zeal but no wisdom? Was it the more ardent reformers like Marshall and Joye, who were being inveighed against? or was it some heretic fringe like those who practiced self-baptism, against whom a royal proclamation was issued in 1535?

After the preface, Redman's 1537 Primer follows pretty closely the contents of the Rouen Primer of 1536 down to the beginning of Matins (fol. D1). Here, and at the beginning of each succeeding section of the Primer—Hours, Evensong, Compline, etc.—the Redman editor briefly elucidates the name traditionally belonging to each portion. The Rouen Primer had attempted such a thing at the beginning of Hours, but in crude verse. The explanations in the Redman Primer are in prose, rather carefully done, after the humor of a scholar. Concerning Matins, for example, we are told:

> For the more euident explanacion & vnderstandyng of this Primer, it is to be noted, that this worde (Matyns) is asmoche to say, as the mornyng houres. or morning seruice, & so is called because the same is and hath ben alwayes accustomed to be sayde and songen in the mornynge.

Notice again the use of parenthetical curves for quotations marks, as in the word "Matyns."

Concerning the Psalter of St. Jerome, so called, we are told (fol. FF3):

> By cause it is vnknowen who fyrst gathered all these verses together, that we call saynt Hieroms Psalter, therfor of the begynnyng and purpose of the seruice, I can declare nothynge for certayne: for though it go forthe vnder the name of saynt Hierome, yet it is vncertayne whether euer he were author therof or not, seinge it dothe not so apere ... but onely in a rubryke that is set before it in latyn, whiche maketh mention that the aungell of god shulde teache it hym, with suche other pretye persuasions. . . .

Similarly, a cautionary notice is prefixed to the "Fifteen O's" and a long preliminary 'argument' is supplied for both the Commendations and the Psalms of the Passion.

For the main body of the Primer, in both its liturgical and scriptural passages, the revision of the text of 1536 is more or less haphazard; yet where it does occur it is usually effective. None of these early Primers, in fact, shows evidence of what we would today call a critical and careful revision. Passages amended in one instance are left to appear unrevised elsewhere in the same volume. A few specific examples will show to what extent this new edition fulfilled the claim made in its preface that it was "more purely imprynted, and metely wel purged."

Perhaps some special care was given to the revision of the scriptural passages. The wording of the Lord's Prayer as given in the Rouen Primer (fol. C2ᵛ) , which was based on Tyndale's translation, began thus:

> Our father whiche arte in heuen, halowed be thy name. Let thy kyngdome cum vnto vs. Thy wyll be fulfylled as well in erthe, as it is in heuen. Gyue vs this daye our daylye breade. And forgyue vs our trespasses, as we forgyue them that trespas against vs.

In 1537 the Redman editor wrought several changes in this (fol. C2ᵛ) :

> Our father, whiche arte in heuen sanctified be thy name.
> Let thy kyngdome come.
> Thy wyll be done also in erthe, euyn as it is in heuen.
> Our dayly breade gyue to vs this daye.
> And forgyue vs our offences, euyn as we forgyue them that offende vs.

Yet in another place where this Prayer occurs (fol. D2), the Primer of 1537 disregarded most of these variations. But it mattered little, for the Redman wording was soon to be superseded, as we shall observe.

As for the Psalms, where the Rouen Primer had read rather clumsily in the 126th Psalm:

Then was our mouth ful of myrthe: and our tongue of wylfulnes. . . .
The lorde hath magnyfyed to do with vs . . .

the Redman Primer improved on this:

Than was our mouthe fulfylled with myrthe: and our tongue with ioyfulnes. . . . The lorde hath done greately for vs, [etc.]

In the first verse of Psalm 27, where the Rouen Primer had said, "The lorde is the defender of my lyfe: at whom shall I quake"; the edition of 1537 amended to read, "of whom shal I be a drad?"

In the 67th Psalm, referred to in the preceding chapter (see p. 136), the Redman editor not only restored its proper heading where it had been wanting in the Dirge, but he also made some emendations in the wording of the Psalm. Once again, however, the readings differ somewhat in the two places where it occurs. For example, where the Primer of 1536 had said (verse 6), "for the earth hath yolden forth her frute"; the 1537 edition read in one place (fol. E8), "for the earthe hath yelded her frute," and in the other (fol. AA2^v), "for the earthe hath brought forthe her frute."

The oft-reprinted 51st Psalm also came in for a full quota of amendments. For instance, among the Seven Psalms, the Rouen Primer, borrowing its reading from the treatise of Savonarola, had read in verse 4:

Agaynste the onely haue I synned/ & haue done euyll in thy syght that thou mayste be iustefyed in thy wordes/ and haue the victory when thou haste iudged.

Here the Redman Primer changed the final clause to read: "& vanquishe whan thou arte iudged." In verse 12, the Rouen Primer read:

Make me agayne to reioyse in thy sauynge helthe/ and strengthen me with a pryncipall spiryte.

Redman's Primer, taking a hint from the Joye Psalter of 1534, made this read:

Restore vnto me the gladnes of thy saluacion: and strengthen me with a principall herte.

But in another context (in Matins) the Rouen version of this verse was left unchanged by the Redman editor; and in the Psalter of St. Jerome, the whole Psalm was copied almost exactly as it was given in the corresponding section of the Rouen Primer.[5]

Mr. Edwyn Birchenough, in his article on "The Prymer in English,"[6] makes a special point of one alteration introduced by Redman in one of the 'responses' occurring near the end of the Dirge. Actually, this particular response occurs a number of times in the service and prayers for the dead; but at this particular place the earlier Redman Primer of 1535 had read: "I trust to se ye lorde. In ye lande of lyuers." The Primer of 1536 (fol. S1) copied this as it stood, but in the 1537 Primer (fol. BB2) it was amended thus: "I truste to se the goodes of the lorde. In the lande of the lyuynge." But, as we have seen, variety abounds in these Primers. In another place (fol. X4ᵛ) the 1537 edition renders the first clause as, "I truste to se the goodnes of the lorde:" and in still other places the wording is copied unrevised from the Primer of 1535: "I trust to se the goodes of the lorde. In the lande of lyfe." The Latin text, of course, is the same in all these passages.

At the end of the Rouen edition of 1536, it will be recalled, were printed three prayers taken from Redman's earlier volume entitled *Prayers of the Byble*. In his 1537 Primer Redman enlarged the allotment to nine,[7] all taken from his earlier collection practically without change. In the prayer of Solomon, however, which was quoted above (see p. 88), beginning, "Two thynges (Lorde) I demaunded," the wording is now softened to read: "Two thynges (Lorde) haue I requyred the that

---

[5] See below, Appendix III.

[6] See *The Library*, Series IV, vol. 18, p. 177.

[7] Beside the three already used (see above, p. 133) the six additional citations were: Acts 4:24-30; John 17:1-26; Wisdom 15:1-3; Job 1:20,21; Tobit 3:2-6; Jeremiah 17:14,17,18. Some of these were mistakenly cited, just as they were in *Prayers of the Byble;* e.g., Acts 4 is given as "Actes the xiiii. Chap."

thou woldest" etc. This change was perhaps made under the influence of the Coverdale Bible, which read, "Two thinges I requyre of the, that thou wilt not denye me before I dye."

Moreover, in his 1537 edition Redman decided to insert the prayer of Jonah before the Psalms of the Passion (fol. DD3): "The prayer of the prophete Ionas de-‖ delyuered [sic] out of the whales belly." But for reasons best known to himself the editor did not use the version of this prayer that was given in Redman's own *Prayers of the Byble* but chose instead the wording he found in the Marshall Primers as printed by Byddell.

Enough has been said to show that this 1537 Primer of Redman evinced a good deal of fresh editorial revision. Following the text of the Primer and bound with it comes a section devoted to the treatises of Savonarola on the 51st and 31st Psalms.[8] This section has its own continuous pagination. Its text, in both Latin and English, seems to have been derived from the printing of these expositions that accompanied the Rouen Primer, but shows some traces of revision.

Lastly, there is yet a third section, also with fresh pagination, comprising the 'Epistles and Gospels' mentioned above. These are in English only, printed in double column and occupying some 68 leaves (i.e., 136 pages). The first leaf displays at the head of the first column (fol. ³A1) this title:

Here begynneth the Pystles and Gospels, of euery Sonday and holy daye in the yere.

At the end (fol. ²R4ᵛ) there is a full colophon, the only one in the entire volume:

⟨ : Imprinted at London by me Robert Redman dwellynge at the sygne of the George next to saynt Dunstons Churche.

These Epistles and Gospels, prescribed for public reading or private devotion on specified days throughout the year, coincide for the most part with those still read today in the services of the Church of England, although a number of

---

[8] The text of *S.T.C.* 21790 (as distinct from its title-page) is found to be identical with the text of Savonarola on the 51st Psalm as printed in this Primer (*S.T.C.* 15997). The title-page was erroneously supplied from some other edition. See the article cited above (p. 74n.) concerning these Savonarola expositions.

former saints' days are now no longer observed. As given in the Redman Primer these selected passages comprise a considerable portion of the New Testament, numbering over two hundred excerpts varying in length from a few verses to entire chapters, besides which there are about twenty others drawn from the Old Testament and Apocrypha—an 'epistle' and a 'gospel' for each day in the church calendar.

It is just possible that these Epistles and Gospels had already been printed in English before this, but the section in the 1537 Primer of Redman and the corresponding section in the Byddell Primer of the same year are the earliest we have record of. Consequently it is a matter of some interest to discover that the text of these selections is plainly based on the version of Tyndale. What we have observed before is true here, that the editors of these Primers did not always follow Tyndale word for word, but in general the version is unmistakably his. It is based apparently on the earliest edition of his New Testament rather than on the later ones, though in some places the text of 1534 is used. There are other instances where the phrasing momentarily departs from Tyndale altogether. Furthermore, a few of these selections Tyndale had not included either in his New Testament or in his 'epistles' taken from the Old. For Tyndale either overlooked or else rejected a few of the prescribed 'holy days,' evidently regarding them either as nonessential or as remnants of the usage of the Church of Rome. In such instances where Tyndale had contributed nothing, the editor of these Epistles and Gospels, instead of making use of the version in the Coverdale Bible (which included both Testaments as well as the Apocrypha), preferred to strike out for himself and to improvise new renderings. In these few passages, therefore, taken chiefly from the Apocryphal Books, these Primers of 1537 furnish us with an independent version of these fragments.[9]

Concerning one of these selections, the epistle for St.

---

[9] Selections thus translated afresh include: The Epistle for the Decollation of John the Baptist (Proverbs 10:28-32; 11:3,6,8-11); for Eleven Thousand Virgins' Day (Wisdom 4:1-7); for the Translation of Edward the Confessor (Ecclesiasticus 39:5-9); for Relic Sunday (Ecclus. 44:10-14); and for St. Margaret's Day (Ecclus. 51:9-12).

Katherine's Day, a curious fact has come to light. According to the use of Sarum, the Scripture appropriated for this day was Ecclesiasticus 51:1-8; but Tyndale had unwittingly adopted the 'use of Hereford' for this occasion; so when the epistle was printed at the very end of his New Testament in 1534, he made use of verses 9-12 from the same chapter. Now these particular verses were, by Sarum use, appropriated to St. Margaret's Day, a holiday which Tyndale did not choose to celebrate. When George Joye in January of 1535 issued his revised New Testament, he gave the correct citation for St. Katherine's Day according to a version of his own; and when Tyndale put forth his final revision early in 1535 he too included his own rendering of the proper verses, 1-8. But what did the editor of our Epistles and Gospels do, when he was preparing this text for the Redman Primer? Why, for St. Katherine's Day he copied the unauthorized selection from the Tyndale Testament of 1534, namely verses 9-12, using Tyndale's own version of it; but for St. Margaret's Day, having no precedent in Tyndale, he undertook a fresh translation of the very same verses! No attention was paid to the revised New Testaments of 1535, and this very neglect might seem to be an argument for concluding that the first edition of these Epistles and Gospels must have been earlier than 1537; if so, the earlier printing has not been preserved. In any case, the editing was far from meticulous in those days.

As to the translation of those selections that were not borrowed from Tyndale, it is not very skillful. It resembles somewhat the kind of translating that we noticed in Redman's *Prayers of the Byble*—perhaps done by the same person; certainly no better than that. One feels that a competent schoolboy could do as well. Here, for example, is a portion of the famous 44th chapter of Ecclesiasticus which begins, "Let us now praise famous men." This selection (verses 10-14) comprised "The Pystel on Relyke So*n*daye" as printed in Redman's Primer of 1537 (fol. ²O4):

These are y*e* men of mercy, whose ryghteousnes are nat torgotten [*sic*]. Goodnesse abyde with the seede of them: theyr kynsfolke, are an holy enheritaunce, and theyr seed hath stande in wytnesses/ and the sones of them abyde vnto ye worldes ende for the*m*/ the generacyon of them/ and the glorye of them shall nat be left, theyr bodyes are buried in peace, and theyr names shall lyue in the worldes, al people shall tel the wysdome of them, and all the congregacyon of sayntes shall shewe the laude of them.

At times the translation is so puerile as barely to escape being gibberish. Perhaps some old Lollard manuscript of the Apocryphal Books in an earlier English version was consulted for such passages; yet they do not resemble the Wycliffite Bible. Perhaps—for it is conceivable—the editor of these Epistles and Gospels was a Dutchman or a Fleming with an inadequate grasp of the English tongue.[10] Consider, for instance, the epistle for the obsolete holiday of St. Ursula and her eleven thousand virgins: the prescribed Scripture was the first portion of the fourth chapter of the Wisdom of Solomon, celebrating chastity. Part of this (verses 3-5) reads as follows in the Redman Primer (fol. ²Q3ᵛ):

. . . a great multytude of wicked men shal nat be profytable and euil plantes shal nat bring forth hyest trees, neyther shall set a suer grounde, and if they spryng in tyme in bowes/ they shal be unsuer put, they shal be moued with the wynde, & shall be plucked vp with the vehemency of the wynde/ the vnparfyte bowes shal be broken/ and the fruyte of them shall be vnprofytable and bytter to eate/ & profitable to nothynge, . . .

Myles Coverdale, translating from the same Latin text, but with the assistance of Luther's version, had been able to bring some coherence into this same passage:

But the multitude of vngodly childre*n* is vnprofitable, and the thinges y*t* are planted with whordome, shal take no depe rote, ner laye eny fast foundacion, Though they be grene in the braunches for a tyme, yet shal they be shake*n* with the wynde: for they stonde not fast, & thorow the vehemence of the wynde they shalbe roted out. For the vnparfecte braunches shalbe broken, their frute shalbe vnprofitable & sower to eate, yee mete for nothinge.

[10] In 1538 a certain John Hollybush was in the employ of James Nicolson in an editorial capacity. He is identified by E. G. Duff in *A Century of the English Book Trade* (p. 141) as Hans van Ruremond, a relative of the Antwerp printer, Christopher van Ruremond, alias Christopher of Endhoven. See below, p. 177.

Strange though it may seem that the editor of these Epistles did not make use of Coverdale (unless we assume them to have been edited before 1536), it is likewise inexplicable why he chose at times to introduce into the material taken from the New Testament a few sporadic departures from the text of Tyndale. Some of these readings go back to the period of Wycliffe; and though we cannot guess their source, they are not without interest. In the parable of the unjust steward, when he is called to account, his lord says to him, according to Tyndale's wording (Luke 16:2), "Geve a comptes of thy steward shippe: For thou mayste be no longer stewarde." But in the Redman Primer (fol. ³K1) he says, "Gyue accomptes of thy baylyshyppe, for thou mayste be no longer bayly." This old form of "bailiff" was a Wycliffite word, but why the change? Again, in the account of the beheading of John the Baptist, Tyndale had said that the daughter of Herodias asked to have John's head brought to her "in a charger," which term is still used in the Authorized Version (Mark 6:25); but the Redman editor changed this to "in a dishe," which was also Wycliffe's word.

Then there are occasional interpolations. At the beginning of the second chapter of Acts, Tyndale had said simply, "When the fyftith daye was come"; but now the epistle for Pentecost begins thus: "When the fyftyth daye was come which is witson sondaye/" etc. For the third Sunday after Easter the epistle was from the second chapter of I Peter. After the eighteenth verse the Latin text of the Vulgate reads, *Haec est enim gratia,* which Wycliffe had rendered literally, "For this is grace." In 1526 Tyndale translated this from the Greek as "For it commeth off grace"; but in his 1534 edition he revised this to read, "For it is thankeworthye," etc. In the Redman Primer (fol. ²G2) the epistle concludes with the words: "for it commeth of grace in Chryst Iesus our lorde."

Concerning this 1537 edition of the Redman Primer as a whole it should be said, not only did it contain the first printing in English (so far as we know) of these liturgical Epistles and Gospels, but it also marked a considerable advance editorially over the two former Latin-English editions of the Primer according to the use of Sarum. It was copied rather extensively during the short time that it remained preëminent, which was about two years.

During the period 1535-40, Robert Redman and John Byddell were engaged so frequently in publishing the same, or nearly the same, materials that it is difficult to tell whether they were vying with each other in strenuous competition or whether they were collaborating. One or the other of them evidently had some means of entrée to the favor of Cromwell. Byddell was inclined to be more venturesome, Redman more conservative. There are grounds for believing that Byddell was in sympathy with the more advanced members of the reforming party and had perhaps some understanding or working agreement with Marshall or with Joye. The Primer which he put forth in 1537 gave further evidence of this.

This Primer of Byddell's (*S.T.C.* 15999)[11] is furnished with an interesting title:

❡ The prymer with the pystles and gospels in Englysshe of euery sonday & holyday in the yere, reuised & diligently corrected/ and ye forme of the new bedis/ with diuers other thynges very necessary for yonge curates, and for all other men women and chyldren.

The make-up of the book is curious: the first two signatures, containing the preliminary material, have their leaves numbered at the top from 1 to 16; the body of the Primer itself is printed on unnumbered leaves, with a colophon (fol. M8ᵛ); and the remainder of the volume, comprising Epistles and Gospels and a table how to find them, is on numbered leaves beginning with "fol. xvii" where the preliminary signatures had left off. There is another colophon at the end (fol. R10ᵛ). Neither one gives any date, simply stating, "Imprynted at

---

11 The volume consists of 250 leaves, in eights, as follows: ✠8, ✻ 8, A-I8, K-M8; 2A-I8, 2K-M8, N-Q8, R10. The most perfect copy, at Balliol College, lacks two leaves, fol. ✠3 and 6. As noted before, *S.T.C.* 15990, at Emmanuel College, is identical with 15999, comprising signatures A to M of this Primer. The earlier *S.T.C.* entry (15990) is therefore mistaken and superfluous.

London in Flete strete, at the sygne of the Sonne, by me Iohan Byddell."

Almost certainly, this arrangement of the numbered leaves shows that the body of the Primer was printed separately, probably earlier, and then bound between the preliminary signatures and the Epistles and Gospels. Concerning the Primer itself not a great deal need be said. It was Byddell's first attempt to publish a Latin and English edition of the *Goodly Primer*—with hybrid results. He gave what might be called the bare text of the Primer according to the Marshall version, leaving out the expository treatises and meditations, and omitting even the 'argument' at the head of each Psalm in the Dirge. Wherever the Marshall Primer coincided with the use of Sarum, Byddell gave the Latin text along the margin; where it diverged, the English stands alone. In the Litany, for example, the two tongues appear side by side until the words, "That it mought please the lord to gouerne and leade thy holy catholyke churche," where the Latin is discontinued.

The two preliminary signatures are of considerable interest. "The Prologe" begins on the reverse of the title-page; it is a new introduction, not derived from the former "Admonition to the reder" in the *Goodly Primer*. Vigorously Protestant in tone, it outruns the position of the English Church in this respect. After assailing the "bisshop of Rome" as Antichrist and acknowledging the King as "supreme heed in erth immediatly vnder god, of the churche of Englande," it proceeds:

. . . Wherfore the kynges grace calling to his remembraunce the power charge & commissyon gyuen to hym of almyghty god/ and vpon a vehement loue & affection towardes his louyng & faythful subiectes, and that they shold not perysshe or faynt for lacke of spyrytuall foode, hath straytly charged & commaunded all his sayd bysshops and other of his clergye to declare, teache & preache vnto the people euery sondaye, & other hygh feestes through the yere, the true, mere, and syncere worde of god: without any maner colour, or dissimulacion: . . . Whiche worde of god is now of late well set forth, & preched in dyuers places of this realme. And the very Chrystyans of the same are greatly desyrous to haue the sayd worde of god in theyr mother tonge, & specially the pystles & gospels, whiche are red euery sondaye & other holy dayes in the churche, that they may therby the better vnderstande the precher in his sermon. And bycause the worde of god may the better go forwarde/ and for as moche as the pryce of the hole newe testament is somwhat hye, and specially for them that haue lytle money. And also that children and other hauyng lytle cunnynge or experience can not bryuely [i.e., *briefly*] fynde the said pystles and gospels in the sayd newe testament. Therfore I haue set forth and compiled in this boke al the pystles and gospels togyther, that are red in the churche euery sonday & other holy dayes in the yere, . . .

The reference to the cost of the New Testament reminds us that during 1536 there were at least seven printings of Tyndale's New Testament beside the editions put out by Tyndale and Joye in 1534 and 1535. Another item, often overlooked, which corroborates the widespread use of the New Testament at that period is a Concordance to the New Testament, which drew its citations from the Tyndale Testament of November 1534, and was published by Thomas Gybson in 1535 (*S.T.C.* 3046) with this title:

(The Concordance of the new Testament/ most necessary to be had in ye handes of all soche as [delyte] in the communycacion of any place contayned in ye new Testament.

Byddell's remark that the Word of God "is now of late well set forth" may refer not alone to the preaching in church, but also to this comparative opulence of publication, and it may perhaps have been inspired by the appearance of the so-called Matthew Bible, a handsome volume, the cost of which had been underwritten by Richard Grafton and Edward Whitchurch. But as Byddell points out, being a good salesman, in none of those books were the Epistles and Gospels conveniently arranged according to the usage of the Church calendar.

After the prologue comes "(The forme of the newe bedes," of which only half a page remains. The leaf which follows is lacking in the only surviving copy of this portion of the Primer; it may have contained some notice about the abrogation of certain holidays, as in the handbooks of the Paternoster which were mentioned earlier in this chapter. After the missing leaf comes the almanac, and then the calendar. The first date for Easter shown in the almanac is for 1537, and this tallies with other indications that point to this same year as the date of publication.

The 'form' of the new beads, for instance, begins thus:

Ye shall praye for the hole congregacion of Chrystes churche, & specyally for this churche of Englande, wherin first I commende to your deuout prayers ye kynges moost excellent maiestie,

—with no mention of his Queen. In the Litany also, where the *Goodly Primer* named, beside the King, "his most gracious quene Anne, all theyr posterite, ayders, helpers, and true subiectes," this new edition of the Primer reads (fol. G2):

That thou vouchesafe to preserue our moost gracious souereigne lord & kynge, Henry the eyght/ & all his true subiectes: we praye the to heare vs.

The omission suggests that the Primer portion of this volume was printed after May 1536 and before October 1537, when the Prince was born.

Following the Primer, we are told ("Fo. xvij."): "⟨ Here begynneth the pistles and gospels on the Sondayes." And later on ("Fo. C.xi." verso): "⟨ Here foloweth the pystles and gospels on sayntes dayes." These Epistles and Gospels contain many points of curious interest.

To begin with, it is demonstrable that this version of Byddell's and the one in the Redman Primer are based on Tyndale's work and that they represent a common text; for certain errors, interpolations, and peculiarities are common to both. Byddell, for instance, prints "baylyshyp" and "dishe" as does Redman. Those epistles from the Apocryphal Books that were not included by Tyndale are rendered alike in both Primers. Both make similar false ascriptions in citing chapters from the Bible, as in calling Jeremiah 23 chapter 33, and printing John 4 where they should have said John 3.

But besides these little peculiarities shared by both publications, the Byddell text gives frequent evidence of having been purposely edited and "corrected" to accord with some particular editor's theological predilections. The problem of determining which of the two printings was the earlier is therefore quite a problem! Altogether, it appears that the variations between them can be more readily explained if we assume either that Byddell took his text from Redman, or else that both drew from some previous edition no longer extant.

Byddell's prologue and the wording of his title-page both imply that he was offering something new to the public; yet there is one strand of evidence indicating that his edition of the Epistles and Gospels, rather than Redman's, was really the secondary one, as the following facts bear witness:

The epistle for St. Nicholas' Day was drawn from the 44th chapter of Ecclesiasticus. Instead of presenting the prescribed epistle (verses 19-23), Tyndale had printed in his Testament of 1534 an assortment of verses selected from chapters 44 and 45, commencing:

Beholde an excellent Preste which in his dayes pleased God/ & was founde righteous/ & in tyme of wrath made an atonement: Lyke to him there is not founde/ that kept the lawe of the moost hyest. And he was in covenaunt with him/ & in his flesshe he wrote the covenaunt/ & in tyme of temptacyon he was founde faythfull.

Redman, looking to Tyndale, followed these words exactly, except for a mistake in the first sentence, which he printed as "Beholde an excellent preest which is in his dayes pleased god/" etc.

Later on, near the end of the volume, the epistle prescribed for St. Martin's Day calls for a repetition of the same Scripture. But Tyndale had not recognized St. Martin's Day; so Redman, rather than print the selection over again, refers the reader back to it, thus:

Beholde an excellent preest. &c. Ye shal fynde this pis-|| pystel [sic] on saynt Nycholas day . . .

Now Byddell's editor was not content to use for St. Nicholas' Day the composite selection that Tyndale had given; he chose instead to present the regular epistle for that day, namely, verses 19-23. These he found ready to his hand in the

New Testament that George Joye had issued in January 1535. In publishing this edition of his Testament Joye called attention to his "pistles" and alleged their superiority to those in Tyndale's edition:

Whiche thys my laboure in translatyng these pistles in correcking & redressing them to make them correspondent wyth the chapters alleged in the byble/ and with the pistles red in the chirche/ whether yt be more diligent than hathe ben shewd hitherto/ let the indifferent reders be iuges [i.e., *judges*].

In the Joye New Testament the first of "The Pistles of the olde testament for the Sayntis" was "for S. Nicholas and S. Martyne." It began thus:

Abraham was a grete father of many nacions/ and there was none founde lyke hym in glorie. He kept the lawe of the hygh god/ and was in couenant wyth him/ In hys flesshe he dyd set faste the couenant/ & in his temptacion was he proued & founde faithfull.

The Byddell editor, accordingly, reprinted the epistle for St. Nicholas' Day from Joye, making two alterations: he did not finish out verse 23, but stopped with "and confirmed his couenant ouer Iacobs head"; and in verse 21 he departed from Joye's wording to adopt the Tyndale phraseology in the first part of this verse.

This was all most careful; but it so happened that when Byddell's editor came to the epistle for St. Martin's Day he was not so watchful. For at this point (fol. R4), in referring the reader back to St. Nicholas' Day, he not only misquoted the chapter as "Eccl. xiiii" but also neglected to check his cross-reference, which he printed in the same words that Redman used: "Beholde an excellente preest. &c. ye shall fynde this pystle on saynt Nicolas daye." In Redman's Primer the reference was of course correct, but in Byddell's it was not; which seems to indicate that Redman was the first to set up this passage in print.

In other minor instances also the variations peculiar to Byddell's Epistles and Gospels show the influence of Joye's publications. In Romans 12:13, Tyndale had written a hurried revision into his New Testament of 1534 as follows: "Distribute vnto the necessite of saynctes & diligently to harboure." This latter clause, which in the 1526 edition had been omitted entirely, Tyndale revised again in 1535 to read, "& be readie to harboure." In Joye's ill-starred revision of August 1534, he had given it as "kepe hospitaliter" (or at least so it was printed); and this rendering is the basis of the one in Byddell's Epistles and Gospels (fol. ²B7ᵛ): "& kepe hospitalite." Again, in the epistle for Annunciation Day taken from Isaiah 7, where Redman had followed Tyndale's wording in verses 13 and 14, this Primer of Byddell's (fol. N8) has a reading not so very different from the text of the Authorized Version:

> Is it not ynoughe to vexe men, but you must wery my god to? The lord therfore his owne selfe shal gyue you a token.

This turns out to be the translation given in Joye's *Prophete Isaye,* which he published back in 1531.

That Byddell's editor was either Marshall or Joye or a person of like stamp is evident from certain doctrinal emendations that were introduced into the 'epistles' drawn from the New Testament. Perhaps these were what Byddell was calling attention to in his title-page where he used the words "reuised & diligently corrected." In such 'corrections' we catch a glimpse of the theological quarrels that plagued the early Protestants. In the famous thirteenth chapter of I Corinthians, where Tyndale had written, "Though that prophesyinge fayle/ . . . and oure prophesyinge is vnperfet:" Byddell's editor took exception to the word "prophesying"; he also emended the "soundinge brasse" of Tyndale's version. Accordingly, where this chapter occurs in the Byddell Primer (fol. ²C7) as the epistle for the Sunday before Lent, it reads in part as follows:

> Brethren, though I speke wt the tonges of men & aungels, & yet had no loue, I were but as soundyng tyn, or as a tinkling cymball. . . . Though yt the interpretyng of scriptures fayle/ eyther tonges shall cease/ or knowlege vanysshe awaye/ yet loue falleth neuer away: for our knowlege is vnperfyte/ & our interpretacion is vnperfyte: but whan our perfection is ones come, than shal our imperfection be done away.

It will be recalled that a similar antipathy to another word, *resurrection,* precipitated the famous quarrel between Tyndale and Joye over the New Testaments.

Yet these independent renderings in the Byddell Primer sometimes obtain a merit of their own, as in the suggestive use of "perfection" and "imperfection" above. Again, in the epistle from the sixth chapter of Ephesians (fol. ²M2) , we find a certain fresh and forthright quality in a passage like this:

> My brethren, be stronge in the lorde/ . . . yt ye may stand stedfast against ye crafty awayte layinges of the deuyl/ for we wrastle not agaynste flessh & blode, but agaynst rulers/ against power/ & agaynst ye worldly lordes & rulers of the darknes of this worlde/ euen agaynst the spiritual craftynes aboue ye erth. For this cause take vnto you ye complete armure of god/ yt ye may resist in ye troublous tyme, & to stande vp after all the batayle be done.

For a last instance, in the 'gospel' for the second Sunday after Easter (fol. ²G4ᵛ) , this Primer introduces for the first time the word "hireling" into the tenth chapter of John (verse 13): "The hyerling flyeth, bicause he is an hyerling, and careth not for the shepe." The first New Testament to use this term was the Latin-English edition put forth in Coverdale's name before July 1538 (*S.T.C.* 2816); Tyndale had written "heyred servaunt." Would it not be interesting to know whether the pseudonymous "Iohan Hollybushe" who edited this Latin-English Testament had picked up this word out of the Byddell Primer? It eventually found its way into the Authorized Version.

At the close of his Epistles and Gospels Byddell provided a table showing which page each one is on. At the end of this he had room enough beneath the colophon for one of his rectangular printer's devices, enclosing his initials set off by fronds and scrolls against a black ground and, in the sill below, his name, "Iohan Byddell."

Chapter XIV

The Effect of the Injunctions
and the Royal Proclamation
(1538)

IT APPEARS that the Epistles and Gospels in English were printed at the same time as the Redman and Byddell Primers with which they were bound—that is, toward the latter half of 1537; but the first official pronouncement concerning their use in church is in the injunctions formulated by Bishop Shaxton of Salisbury. These were printed by Byddell in 1538 (*S.T.C.* 10326). As quoted by Frere and Kennedy in *Visitation Articles and Injunctions of the Reformation* (vol. II, p. 53), the second item of the bishop's injunctions said:

Item, That all such, having cures, do every Sunday and holyday continually recite, and sincerely declare in the pulpit, at the High Mass time, in the English tongue, both the Epistle and Gospel of the same day (if there be time thereto), or else the one of them at the least; . . .

That this represented some concerted agreement by Convocation or other authority is evident from similar provisions in the injunctions issued in 1538 by Archbishop Lee of York and Bishop Voysey of Exeter. Since John Byddell was already in the field with printed copies of his "pystles and gospels in Englysshe," so that the owners of them might (as he says) "therby the better vnderstande the precher in his sermon," it is obvious that Byddell—and Redman too—were kept abreast of the latest developments.

During 1538 each of these printers brought out another new edition of the Primer, Byddell's probably in the early part of the year and Redman's near the end. The new Byddell edition (*S.T.C.* 15998) was a reprint of the *Goodly Primer* of 1535 with but few alterations. It was not in both Latin and English, nor did it include the Epistles and Gospels; in other words, it was not modeled on the Byddell Primer discussed in our last chapter but on the edition of 1535. The title was worded as in 1535 but the title-page bore no royal coat-of-arms. It included all the materials featured in the *Goodly Primer,* and in addition it contained at the end (fol. ²V1) a new printing of Savonarola's Meditation on the 31st Psalm, here called "the .xxx. psalme."[1]

Were it not for certain special changes in the text, we should naturally assign the volume to an earlier year than 1538, for the almanac commences with 1535. But in the calendar of saints' days there is a new entry for July 12th: "Erasm*us* of Roterdame desessed. 1536." And in the Litany, where the *Goodly Primer* had mentioned Queen Anne, this new reprint reads:

. . . our moste gracious soueraigne lorde and kyng, Henry the eyghte, his most gracious sonne prince Edwarde, all theyr posterite, ayders, helpers, & true subiectes.

This substitution, of course, dates the edition as later than October 1537.

There is no colophon in this volume, neither is the 'patent' reprinted from the *Goodly Primer,* though the six years had not yet expired. In the place where these had been, Byddell now prints a pious tribute extolling the King as the dispenser of God's Word (fol. ²T4ᵛ), which begins:

The prophetes, as they were all taught, sterid vp, and thrusted forth of one sprite to preache, and write the worde of the lorde, folowyng all one lyne, attendyng vnto one ende, euen our sauiour Iesus Christ ye perfit some, and ful conclusion of all the law & prophettes. Euen by the same sprite hath god ye father of our sauiour Ihesu Christ, raysed vp our moste gracious prynce, Henry the .viii. to set forthe his moste holy wyll and worde, to attempte ye thynges that doth not a lytle auaunce goddes glorie, whiche hath longe ben obscured and darkened, yea and in maner clene abolyshed.

1 See the article cited above (p. 74*n.*) concerning these Savonarola items.

Once more, in this, we pick up the trail of George Joye; for, though the substance and application of this eulogy are new, as befitted the year 1538, the opening lines borrow their phrasing from Joye's *Ieremy the Prophete* (1534), the preface of which started out by connecting the mission of the prophets with the theme of the New Testament, in these words:

> The Prophetes/ as they were al taught/ stered vp/ and thrusted forth of one spirit to preche and wryte the worde of the Lorde: so folowed they al one threde and lyne tendyng vnto one ende/ euen our sauiour Iesus Christe the parfait some & ful conclusion of al the lawe & Prophetes.

Thus we note again that the Primers which Byddell printed, in the construction put upon their contents, went as far as they dared in the direction of contemporary Protestant interpretation. The name of Erasmus among the saints, the congratulation of the King with a view to spurring him to greater efforts in behalf of the Word of God in English—these are zealous touches that Henry himself would hardly have sanctioned or supported. They remind us of the lesson read to young Queen Elizabeth, in 1560, by the Genevan exiles in the preface to their English version of the Bible, imploring the young Queen to take advantage of her unusual opportunity to further the cause of true religion. Henry was perhaps even less impressed by such exhortations than was Queen Elizabeth. Yet there is reason to suppose that Byddell was "folowyng all one lyne" with the policy of Thomas Cromwell. For in the summer of 1538 Cromwell reached the peak of his Protestantism in politics when he tried to arrange for some coalition between his King and the Protestant Princes of Germany, whose envoys were sent to London at Cromwell's invitation. In the outcome, Henry was unresponsive to the scheme; so long as he could retain his title as supreme head of the Church of England, he was content to cling to the Catholic doctrine of his forbears. Cromwell, however, was undeterred, and went ahead with his plans for a new approved edition of the English Bible.

In the spring of 1538, Myles Coverdale went to Paris to supervise the editing of what has come to be known as the

Great Bible. Grafton and Whitchurch went also to superintend the business arrangements for publication, which they were able to conclude with the eminent Parisian printer, François Regnault. Coverdale had left instructions with his London printer, James Nicolson, to bring out a Latin-English edition of his New Testament; but when it appeared, he was so dissatisfied with it that he had Regnault print him a revised edition of it in November 1538. During the same year, Nicolson brought out still another edition, giving the editor's name as John Hollybush; while Redman published a Latin-English edition of Tyndale's New Testament, and Thomas Gybson put out an English New Testament based on the so-called Matthew Bible.[2]

Because of hostility on the part of the French Court, and the influence of the Inquisition, the printing of the Great Bible was not able to be consummated in Paris, nor was it finally completed until April of the following year, after the equipment and some of the printed sheets had been purchased and removed to London. Nevertheless, in September 1538, Cromwell drew up a set of royal injunctions (S.T.C. 10086) looking forward to the completion of the new Bible and providing that each church in the realm was to supply itself with one.

Meanwhile, the account of the English Primers also shifts to France; for in 1538 François Regnault and his associates were among the most active publishers of new editions. In fact, during the year at least five new editions of the Primer were printed at Rouen and Paris for the use of readers in England.

A few years before, at the beginning of 1534, the printers and booksellers of London tried to get Parliament to erect some sort of legislative barrier against the importation of printed books, already bound, from France and Flanders. While it did not prohibit wholesale trading in such books, Parliament did enact at that session

... that no person or persons, resiant or inhabitant within this realme, after the sayd feast of Christmas next coming, shal bie to sel ageine

2 See *S.T.C.* 2815-18 and 2841.

any printed bookes brought from any parties [i.e., *foreign parts*] out of the kynges obeysance, redyebounden in bordes, lether, or parchement, . . .

How severely this restriction worked against the business of foreign publishers like Regnault we do not know, but it was clearly intended to protect the interests of printers and binders in London. Apparently Regnault, who as a young man had resided in London at the turn of the century, felt that he too was entitled to some protection; for about 1536, he addressed a plea to Thomas Cromwell (in French) in which he states that he had for many years been active in supplying Missals, Breviaries, and Books of Hours after the use of Sarum, for the English trade; that he had never been forbidden to do so, but rather found his products welcomed. But now he understands that the English booksellers wish to prevent him from printing such books and to confiscate those already on hand; wherefore he asks for permission to continue to sell the said 'usages' in London and its environs. Whether this plea produced any effect is not definitely known; but when Coverdale and Grafton sought to do business with Regnault in 1538, they found him still apprehensive about his English trade.

Writing to Cromwell about the Great Bible negotiations on September 12, 1538,[3] Coverdale and Grafton refer to Regnault's plight at some length:

. . . we are instantly desyred of oure hoste (whose name is Fraunces Reynold a frenchman) to make supplicacion for him vnto your lordshippe. Where as of long tyme he hath bene an occupier in to England more than xl. yere, he hath allwayes provyded soche bookes for England, as they moost occupied, so that he hath a great nombre, at this present in his handes, As prymers in Englishe, Missales with other soche like: Whereof now (by the company of the booksellers in London) he is vtterly forbydden to make sale, to the vtter vndoyng of the man, Wherfore moost humbly we beseke your lordshippe to be gracious and fauourable vnto him, that he maye have lycence to sell those which he hath done allready, so that herafter he prynte nomoo [i.e., *no more*]

---

[3] The letter is printed in A. W. Pollard's *Records of the English Bible* (1911), p. 238. For a synopsis of Regnault's letter to Cromwell in 1536, see *Letters and Papers of the Reign of Henry VIII*, vol. XI, no. 1488.

in the english tong, onlesse he have an english man that is lerned, to be his corrector; and that is the man well contented withall.

From the foregoing it is plain, not only that the London printers—Byddell, Redman, Godfray, and the rest—were interested to halt this influx of books printed abroad, but that also the Church authorities seem to have been distressed at the great number of errors that inevitably found their way into these volumes at the hands of compositors who understood little or no English.

As it turned out, Regnault lost his plea. For on November 16, 1538, a royal proclamation was issued (*S.T.C.* 7790) banning the importation "of bokes imprinted in the englyshe tonge, brought and transported from outward parties." The proclamation, aimed at suppressing heresies, touched on different topics arising out of the King's being informed

that sondry contentions and sinyster opinyons, haue by wronge teachynge and naughtye printed bokes, encreaced and growen within this his realme.

It specifically provided that no person should

transport or bringe from outwarde parties, into this his realme of England, or any other his gracis dominions, any maner bokes printed in the englyshe tonge, nor sell, gyue, vtter, or publishe any suche bokes from hensforthe.

In particular it decreed that no person

from hensforth shall printe or bryng into this his realm any bokes of diuine scripture in the englishe tonge, with any annotations in the margyn, or any prologe or additions in the calender or table, . . . but onely the playne sentence and texte.

Such publications, especially "bokes of scripture in the englishe tonge," had first to be reviewed by some member of the Privy Council or by a bishop, whose name was to be mentioned; also the name of the translator was to be published; and every book printed in English was not to display the words *Cum privilegio regali* without also adding the words *ad imprimendum solum,* which meant that the royal privilege extended only to the printing of the book, and could not be construed as a license approving of its contents.

Another point of interest covered in the proclamation concerned the name of Thomas Becket, who had been canonized by the Church of Rome since the twelfth century on account of his martyrdom while upholding the authority of that Church against the English King Henry II. With this background of historical association his veneration as a saint was peculiarly distasteful to Henry VIII. Accordingly, in the autumn of 1538, a royal commission visited the shrine of St. Thomas at Canterbury Cathedral—long famous in the literary world through Chaucer's *Canterbury Tales*—and there despoiled his tomb and scattered his relics. Finally, in the proclamation it was ordered that Thomas Becket be no longer regarded as a saint and that the day set aside for his commemoration be stricken from the Church calendar.[4] Since the Primers had customarily listed his name in the calendar of saints' days and in the Litany, the omission of all mention of 'St. Thomas of Canterbury' helps to determine the date of issue. Such an omission, together with the use of the words "ad imprimendum solum" in title or colophon, implies that such Primers were not printed before 1539.

For the proclamation went into effect fairly promptly. Coverdale and Grafton were naturally disturbed by some of its provisions, in view of the New Testament in English and Latin which Regnault had just printed for them as well as the impending publication of the Great Bible. Each wrote to Cromwell for clarification as to how matters stood—Grafton on December 1, and Coverdale on December 13. Coverdale was instructed to withhold the annotations which he had intended using in the margin of the Bible, and thus the pathway was cleared for its publication. Eventually, in a later edition of November 1540, the title-page was reworded to provide for the approval of the text by two bishops, Tunstall and Heath, "at the comaundement of the kynges hyghnes." But so far as the English Primers were concerned, the importation and

4 See R. Steele, *Tudor and Stuart Proclamations* (Oxford, 1910), I, 19.

publication of such as were printed in France was virtually stopped by the proclamation of 1538.

Turning now to the five English Primers that Regnault and his associates printed during that year, we find little that need delay us very long. All of these books merely reproduced earlier material; all were dated 1538 and presumably issued in advance of the King's proclamation in November. In view of Grafton's assertion on September 12, that Regnault had "a great nombre, at this present in his handes," it is likely that most of these Primers appeared during the first half of the year. Four out of the five list the name of St. Thomas of Canterbury in the calendar under July 7 and December 29, as well as on January 5 (which was the 'octave' of the 'feast' celebrated on December 29). The fifth Primer of the series, however, is known in two different issues: the earlier one includes the three listings of St. Thomas just mentioned, while the latter omits his name on the two regular days for his commemoration but inadvertently retains it on January 5. This alteration was effected by substituting a new sheet (signature B) containing the latter half of the calendar together with a different preface, as will be described below.

From this it appears that this latest issue of Regnault's Primer was published about October 1538, in which month the shrine of Becket was desecrated at Henry's instigation.[5] For on September 5, when Cromwell drew up his injunctions in his own handwriting, he included no admonition about the commemoration of St. Thomas of Canterbury; but when these injunctions were printed by Berthelet, the King's printer, under date of 1538 (*S.T.C.* 10087), additional sections forbade the celebration of certain holidays in the churches, among which we find:

. . . Excepted also the commemoration of Thomas Bekket, sometyme archbishop of Canturburie, whiche shall be cleane omitted, and in the stede therof the feriall seruice vsed.

While it is not easy to determine the exact order in which

[5] See H. A. L. Fisher, *The History of England from the accession of Henry VII to the death of Henry VIII* (London, 1906), p. 426.

these five Primers were published, we may construct the following table giving their approximate sequence:

S.T.C. No.	Hoskins	Place	Printer	Source of Text
16003	133	Paris	Regnault	R36 (S.T.C. 15993)
16004	135	Rouen	LeRoux	R37 (" 15997)
16007	139	Rouen	LeRoux	R37 (" ")
16006	138	Rouen	[Marchant]	R37 (" ")
16005 (A) [6]	—	Paris	[Regnault]	R36 (" 15993)
16005 (B)	136	Paris	[Regnault]	R36 (" ")

Inasmuch as the ones that were printed at Paris were based on the Rouen Primer of 1536, it is convenient to refer to the entire series as Rouen Primers.

The first one (S.T.C. 16003) was unusual in both title and colophon. It was entitled:

Here after foloweth the Prymer in Engysshe [sic] and in latin sette out alonge: after the vse of Sarum. M.D.xxxviij.

This form of title, "Hereafter followeth," generally implied that the work was intended to accompany some other book bound in the preceding part of the same volume; but we know of no such forerunner in this instance. The colophon, equally careless, left out the words "in the year" and read:

Imprynted in Paris be me Fransses regnault of our Lorde Mil. d. xxxviij.

Small wonder that the London trade complained of foreign importations!

This Primer is found to be a reprint of the Rouen edition of 1536, excepting that where the 1536 edition reproduced nearly all of the preface as found in the Redman Primer of 1535, this new publication made use of "The preface and maner to lyue well." This substitution was in the Catholic, rather than the Protestant, tradition. In its English version this particular preface had originally appeared in the Primer printed by Christopher of Endhoven (S.T.C. 15966) of which we have spoken before, where it was headed:

[6] The two issues of 16005 here designated as (A) and (B) are not differentiated in S.T.C. The earlier one (A) is apparently represented by only one copy located in the British Museum (C.52.f.16); the later (B) is known through several copies.

The maner to lyue well/ deuoutly and salutaryly euery day for all persones of meane estate. Compyled by mayster Iohan quentin doctour in dyuinyte at Parys. Translated out of frenche in to englysshe by Robert Copland prynter at London.

The second Primer in the series (*S.T.C.* 16004) has the distinction of being the earliest Primer of Sarum use to give the main body of its text in English unaccompanied by the Latin. Its title so indicates, though it is cast in a similar form to that noticed above; it reads:

Hereafter Foloweth the Prymer in Englysshe sette out alonge/ after the vse of Sarum 1538

It is a small, well-printed volume, embellished with woodcuts and ornamental initials. A handsome copy is preserved in the Pierpont Morgan Library, New York City. In spite of the printer's pains, however, numerous verbal inaccuracies in the text belie the claim made in the colophon (fol. T4):

Thus endeth the Prymer in Englysshe after the vse of Salysbury/ dilygently correcte & newly imprynted at Rowen by Nycholas le Roux for Franchoys Regnault. M.D.xxxviij.

This edition was reprinted from the Redman Primer of 1537 and included the Epistles and Gospels; only it too declined to use the Redman preface and substituted "ye maner to lyue well" by John Quentin. It also supplemented this with another feature taken from older Primers in the Catholic tradition, namely, "A very be houefull techyng & remedy" compiled by another doctor of divinity, John Gerson, one time Chancellor of the University of Paris. In its Latin form this item was known as the "three verities"; an English version of it had appeared in a Primer printed by Regnault in 1531 (*S.T.C.* 15973). Nevertheless, in common with other Rouen Primers, this edition (*S.T.C.* 16004) continued to denominate each pope listed in the saints' calendar as "Bysshop of Rome."

The next two editions on our list (*S.T.C.* 16007 and 16006) not only were based on the Redman Primer of 1537 but followed it so faithfully as to contain all of the Redman preface in its expanded form. The title-page of No. 16007 is also similar to Redman's, the title appearing over a summary of the contents:

⫷ Thys prymer in Englyshe and in Laten is newly translated after the Laten texte. M. D. xxxviij.

Even the almanac begins with the year 1537. This Primer is accompanied by the treatises of Savonarola as well as by a section of Epistles and Gospels. The latter has a separate title-page which carries the initials "I. G." in the sill at the bottom of the border. These probably refer to some French bookseller or perhaps to a London stationer, John Growte, who is known to have traded with the Rouen publishers.[7] The colophon at the end of Savonarola on the 31st Psalm informs us that the book was "Imprynted by me Nicolas le Roux."

Likewise LeRoux may well have been the printer of the other edition (*S.T.C.* 16006) although the title-page of this Primer displays the elaborate device of "Iehan le Marchant" —a bookseller in Rouen for whom the work was undertaken. This particular volume, though also based on the Redman Primer, shows traces of some independent editing. The almanac begins with 1538; the preliminary material includes the "forme of the bedes" as well as an earlier form of the act abrogating certain church holidays which makes no reference to Thomas Becket. The volume contains no Epistles and Gospels. The printing is none too careful and betrays the lack of an English proof-reader. For example, two stray items from Hamilton's *Common Places,* were apparently appropriated from the Gough Primer of 1536, where they occurred near the end of "The Paradise of the Soul," (see above, p. 128); they are printed after this fashion in the LeMarchant Primer (fol. B2ᵛ):

⫷ The rule of Charyte is this. Do as thou woldest be done to/ for charyte holdest [*sic*] all a lyke/ the ryche and the poore/ the frende and the foo.

⫷ A compariso/ betwene Fayht/ Hope & charite

7 See E. G. Duff, *The Printers, Stationers and Bookbinders of Westminster and London from 1476 to 1535* (Cambridge, Eng., 1906), p. 204; also Hoskins, *op. cit.,* p. 46 (No. 123). In the New York Public Library is another edition of Epistles and Gospels with the initials "I. G." on the title-page, quite similar to those bound with *S.T.C.* 16007, yet not identical.

Fyrst [sic] commeth of the worde of god: hope commeth of Fayth: and Charyte spryngeth of them bothe.

As was pointed out above, the last Primer of this series (*S.T.C.* 16005) is known in two different issues. The earlier one is a fairly close reprint of the Rouen Primer of 1536.[8] Its almanac begins with 1536, but the colophon declares: "Imprynted in Parys the yere of our Lorde 1 5 3 8." Soon after it was printed, the publisher, Regnault, must have been given to understand that the name of St. Thomas of Canterbury would no longer be tolerated in Primers intended for the English market. Whereupon he canceled an entire sheet of this Primer (namely, the eight leaves of signature B) and prepared another sheet to take its place. The canceled signature contained the name of St. Thomas opposite July 7 and December 29 of the calendar, and it also contained the Redman preface to the reader as it was given in the Rouen Primer of 1536. In the new sheet the two dates were left blank and the Redman preface was replaced by the Quentin preface entitled "The preface and maner to lyue well, deuoutly and salutarily." This seems to indicate that Regnault felt that the older preface was perhaps too outspoken, or at least was not essential nor timely.

The rest of the volume was left intact, the publisher overlooking the fact that in signature A, at the beginning of the calendar, the name of St. Thomas still appeared on the fifth of January. Bound with certain copies of this Primer (comprehending either issue) are the two treatises of Savonarola both in English and Latin as well as a separate section of Epistles and Gospels.[9] In the latter the name of St. Thomas occurs again, once for a Sunday lection and later for the feast commemorating his 'translation.'

So much for the Rouen Primers. Meanwhile, over in London, the publication of the King's proclamation brought some

[8] The two issues are both represented in the British Museum; the earlier is listed as C.52.f.16, the later as C.35.c.13. See the article by E. C. Birchenough in *The Library* (Series IV, vol. 18, p. 187).

[9] These items are also known in the form of separate books. For example, *S.T.C.* 2965 and 21791, listed as separate items, are identical with those that are bound with the Primer (*S.T.C.* 16005).

uneasiness to Robert Redman; for it outmoded his Primer of 1537, which had freely mentioned St. Thomas of Canterbury thrice in the church calendar, once in the Litany, and twice among the Epistles and Gospels. Therefore, near the end of 1538 he brought out yet another edition (*S.T.C.* 16008) with this title standing at the head of the summary of its contents:

: This prymer in Englyshe and in Latyn is newly correctyd thys presente yere of our Lorde M. CCCCC. XXXVIII.

This seems to have been tantamount to notifying the public that already in the year 1538 (which was sometimes reckoned to extend to the next Lady Day, March 25) here was a Primer for the devout reader which conformed to the very latest proclamations and injunctions.

Of course all reference to Thomas Becket was removed, and there are further evidences of fresh revision; yet as a whole the text is very close to the edition of 1537, and little effort was made to harmonize the variant readings found within that volume. Comparing the list of contents in each, we notice that the new edition omits the days of the week 'moralized' and also the preface. Perhaps Redman had observed the reluctance of the French publishers to insert his preface; perhaps he felt that the temper of the times was shifting somewhat. Another omission was of the address to the Virgin beginning "Stella coeli" and of the collect against pestilence.

Of new material there is very little. The summary of contents lists, along with the Paternoster and Creed, the "x. Commaundementes of the laste settyng forthe by the kynges hyghnes & his moste honorable counsel." This probably takes into account the so-called 'Bishops' Book' issued in 1537. Furthermore, where Redman prints the Lord's Prayer in the preliminary portion of his Primer (fol. B5), instead of the usual wording, "And lead us not into temptation," he introduces the alteration, "And let vs nat be led in to temptacyon." This change reflects a doctrine then in vogue to the effect that while man is not entitled to claim exemption from all temptation, he might pray that God would not suffer him to be led into it. Perhaps some such pronouncement had been promulgated at a recent session of Convocation; at any rate, the new reading, which first appears in this Primer, became standard and approved usage for some dozen years. Nevertheless Redman's revision was not very thorough; for where the Prayer occurs again in the Matins of this Primer (fol. C2ᵛ), the wording formerly used in the edition of 1537 is allowed to stand.

Another additional feature of the new Primer was the insertion of the prayer of Hannah, taken from the second chapter of I Samuel. For his rendering of this, Redman went to his *Prayers of the Byble,* yet not without revising it somewhat. In verses 2 and 3, the *Prayers* had read:

There is none holy as is the lorde, for there is none other besyde the, and there is none stronge as is our god. Do nat multiplie to speke hyghe thynges gloriyng. Let the olde passe and departe from your mouthe, for god of sciences is the lorde and thoughtes and prouisions ar prepared vnto hym.

In the Primer (fol. G8) this reading, reminiscent of Wycliffe's day, was improved at least slightly:

There is none so holy as is the lorde, for there is none other besyde the, and there is none so stronge as is our god. Do nat endeuour to speke hyghe thyng*es* in boste Let the olde passe and departe frome your mouthe, for the lorde is god of sciences and thought*es* and prouisions are prepared vnto hym.

Perhaps the Coverdale Bible may have smoothed the way for this emendation by its reading, "Let go yo*ure* greate boostinge of hye thynges." The remaining biblical prayers as given in the new Primer are copied from the 1537 edition; even the prayer of Jonah is repeated again in the version that Marshall had taken over from the Joye Hortulus.

Similarly, the section of Epistles and Gospels was taken over from the 1537 edition with apparently no changes in the version itself, except that once more St. Thomas of Canterbury is now passed over in silence. Otherwise we have the same errors and peculiarities here as were noticed in our last chapter. The colophon also, which occurs after a table of contents at the end of the 'Epistles,' resembles the earlier one:

Imprynted at London in Fletestrete/ by me Roberte Redman/ dwellynge at the sygne of the George nexte to saynt Dunstons Churche.

All in all, 1538 was a fruitful year. Beside the Primers already described, there were other publications bordering on the fringe of our subject. Some of these were commentaries, such as that by Heinrich Bullinger on II Thessalonians, or by Lancelot Ridley on Jude, or by Tyndale and Ridley on the three Epistles of John (*S.T.C.* 4045, 21042, and 24444). Another volume, very little known, which appeared in either 1537 or 1538, was based on the Coverdale Bible and has sometimes been ascribed to Coverdale himself. But John Bale, in his *Illustrium scriptorum* (1548), assigned it to Lancelot Ridley.[10] It was evidently published by Thomas Gybson, though his name is not given, and was entitled:

⟨[Annotations in the boke of Iosue shewynge breflye in euery chapter by comon places how this boke seruyth for oure learnynge, what is ye profyt and the vse therof whyche is the fyrst boke of the seconde part of the Bible.

In a foreword, "The printer to the reader," we catch yet another echo of Joye's Jeremiah in the opening words:

Goode Reader, lyke as God stered vp all the prophetes through one spryte in the old tyme, euen so hathe he Reysed vp in this perelous times his elect prophetes and enteyre louers of his worde . . .

The publisher goes on to explain that—

. . . because that euery man can not carye about wyth hym the Byble I haue here prynted at the latter ende of these comen places the hole story or boke of Iosue, and as I perceyue by ye auctor that yf the Reader be thankfull, as he hath begon and done this so entendithe he to do mo of this second parte of the Byble, whyche the Lord graunte to whom I commit the. Amen.

---

[10] This rare volume, which is not listed in the 1926 edition of *S.T.C.*, was mentioned in Cotton's *Editions of The Bible and Parts Thereof in English* (edition of 1852, pp. 16, 308) as having been part of the Lea Wilson collection, and is now preserved in the New York Public Library. The ascription to Gybson's press rests on the border design of the title-page, which corresponds to No. 33 in McKerrow and Ferguson, *Title-page Borders Used in England and Scotland, 1485-1640.* The slot in the sill of the border is blank. Rev. J. F. Mozley drew my attention to the fact that Bale assigns the work to Ridley.

The version of Joshua which is thus appended is taken directly from the 1535 edition of the Coverdale Bible. Since there is no "Cum priuilegio" nor any use of the words "ad imprimendum solum," it is likely that this publication antedated the proclamation of 1538.

Somewhat nearer to our theme are two other publications dated this same year. One was "An exposicion vpon the songe of the blessed virgine Mary, called Magnificat" (S.T.C. 17536). This not only included text and commentary on the Magnificat, Benedictus, and Nunc Dimittis, but also gave Solomon's prayer for wisdom. It also attempted to refute the use of the prayer *Salve Regina* and gave a version of the alternative Protestant prayer, *Salve Rex*. The work was published by Nicolson, who attributed the compilation of it to the persistent "Ihon Hollybush."[11] The scriptural texts were taken from the Coverdale version of the Bible.

The other volume was entitled "Certeine prayers and godly meditacyons very nedefull for euery Christen." It states that it was printed "at Malborow" (that is, Marburg in Germany) by "Ioannem Philoponon" (S.T.C. 20193); but this has been shown to be a pseudonym used by Johannes Hoochstraten.[12] Its contents reproduce quite a good bit of material from Redman's *Prayers of the Byble,* including the rare item of a "Consolation for Troubled Consciences"; but its section of prayers is restricted to those few that appeared in the Redman Primer of 1537—doubtless here reprinted by Hoochstraten without consent.

Lastly, in or about 1538—the booklet being undated—we have the first, or rather the earliest printed one to be preserved, of those little books put out especially for the use of children, comprising the ABC, the Paternoster, the Creed, and the Commandments, together with such other religious morsels as the publisher thought good to include. It is more than likely that

11 There is, I believe, some possibility of identification of this person with the *Hans* who was related to Christopher of Endhoven, known also as Hans van Ruremond. See Duff, *Century of the English Book Trade*, p. 141.

12 See the article by M. E. Kronenberg, "Notes on English Printing in the Low Countries" in *The Library* (Series IV, vol. 9, p. 158).

many such books once in circulation have disappeared on account of the small value set upon them both by their publishers and by their owners.[13] The carelessness with which printers tossed off these little books is evident in the errors that were allowed to stand in both title and colophon of this ABC assigned to 1538 *(S.T.C.* 19). In fact, even the entry in the *Short-title Catalogue* is incorrect! The actual title of the booklet, which comprises but eight small leaves without signature, reads: "⟨ The .BAC bothe in latyn and in Englysshe." It is preserved in the library of Emmanuel College, Cambridge. The colophon is a bit more elaborate, but scarcely more careful:

> Thus endeth the .A B C translated out of Laten to to[*sic*] Englysshe with other deuoute Prayers.
> ⟨ Imprynted at London in Paules Chyrcheyarde at the sygne of the maydens heed by Thomas Petyt.

The title is printed at the head of the first page, and below it comes an alphabet with the words "est Amen" at the end of it. Whether this signified "So be it" or whether the "est" was given as a specimen of the simplest of Latin words, I do not know; but it was not unusual to precede the alphabet with the sign of a cross and follow it with "est Amen."[14] In this booklet, below the alphabet comes a list of vowels in their several consonantal combinations, beginning with *ab eb ib,* etc., down to *ug* and *gu.* This is followed by the Paternoster in Latin and then in English. The English version includes the rendering, "And let vs not be ouercom by temptacyon," which suggests the influence of the same doctrine as mentioned above, though not cast in the approved form of wording. It also reinforces the year 1538 as a likely date for this little ABC. The Lord's Prayer is followed by the Ave and the Credo in

---

[13] "The primer in English for children, after the vse of Sar*um*" (listed in *S.T.C.* as No. 16000) is not as early as the assigned date of 1537? would indicate. For evidence that this particular Primer was published about 1557, see the writer's article, "Early Primers for the Use of Children," in *Papers* of the Bibliographical Society of America (vol. 43, p. 374).

[14] Mr. Edwyn C. Birchenough, conversing with the writer, advanced the plausible suggestion that these words represent a remnant from the service of the Mass, which concludes with the Latin words, "Ite missa est. Amen."

both languages; and then (fol. 2ᵛ) we come upon a collection
of Latin phrases from the service-books, commencing with
Confitemini. These are printed under the caption: "To helpe
a prest to syng." This curious feature seems to imply that the
booklet was designed to assist children to bear their part in
the regular services of the church.

Next come various graces to be said before or after meals,
the first of which begins much like the grace that Joye taught
to young Dick Purser:

The eyes of euery thynge do loke vp/ and they hope in the good
lorde/ & thou gyuest them theyr fode in tyme conuenient.

It ends: "The kynge of eternall glory make vs to be pertenars
[i.e., *partners*] of the celestyall mele. Amen." There is also the
following rhymed benediction (fol. 5):

God preserue his chyrch vnyuersal
And this chyrch of england speciall
And the supreme heed therof oure kynge.
And graunt vs the blysse without endynge. Amen.

And the same grace that we met with in the Gough Primer
reappears here (fol. 6ᵛ):

Blyssed be our Lorde which of his grace.
Hath sende vs our fode/ good tyme/ and space.

Among special graces are some for Easter and "for fysshe
dayes." The grace "at Ester afore dyner" (fol. 7) concludes
with a few lines from I Corinthians (5:7) which are based
on the Tyndale version but somewhat modified to read:

Cast ye out clene the olde leuen that ye maye be newe dowgh as ye
are the swete brede/ for Chryst our Ester Lambe is offered for vs/
therfore let vs fede in our lorde. Amen.

The Ten Commandments are not printed in the usual way,
but near the end of the booklet they too are given in a rhymed
synopsis which begins:

Lord graunt me grace to honor the
One god & neuer to swere in vayne
The holy day to be kepte by me.
My parentes to obey & maynteyne . . .

After a few further rhymes presenting the seven works of mercy and the "Capitall synnes," the colophon as given above occurs at the bottom of the last of the eight leaves in the booklet.

Since this was the sort of children's book that bequeathed the name of *primer* to its successors and their more modern counterparts, we have given it special attention, even though it was not strictly a Primer according to the meaning of the term as used in that period, because it contained neither Psalms nor Hours.

It is plain, then, that while this year of 1538 saw, on the one hand, the stoppage of imported Primers intended for the English reader, it also saw on the other hand a much freer, less restricted publication in England itself of books and pamphlets ministering to the religious needs of the people. The publishers evidently knew that Cromwell was behind them, being aware of his zeal in promoting the forthcoming edition of the Great Bible. The lean years of English Scripture were at an end for a brief season.

Chapter XV

Bishop Hilsey's *Manual of Prayers*
(1539)

WITH the issuing of Cromwell's injunctions requiring an English Bible to be made available in every church, and of the King's proclamation forbidding the importation of printed books, the publishers of London saw a large new territory unrolling before them. The first English New Testament to have been published in London, a small folio edition in 1536 (*S.T.C.* 2831), is assigned by most authorities to the press of Thomas Godfray, though formerly it was thought to have been done by Thomas Berthelet, the King's printer.[1] We have noted that in 1538 other Testaments were published by Nicolson, Redman, and Gybson; but until 1539 the only complete Bibles in English to have been printed in England were those put forth by James Nicolson in 1537 containing a reprint of the Coverdale version.

By the end of 1538 it was clear that the new Great Bibles would not be ready as soon as had been expected. It seems to have been during this period of uncertainty that Thomas Berthelet undertook, as an alternative enterprise, the publication of a revised edition of the so-called Matthew Bible. The work of preparing the new edition was entrusted to Richard Taverner, who complains more than once that he could have done a more thorough job if he had not been so pressed for time. Perhaps the Matthew Bibles had all been disposed of, and Berthelet may have tried to appease in this way the popular demand for Scripture during the interim before the

---

[1] This particular New Testament in its marginal references makes use of the reversed 4 which was cited above (see p. 78, note) as typical of Godfray's press; and this peculiarity practically settles the question.

181

Great Bible could be got ready. At any rate, it seems logical that he would have launched such a venture before, rather than after, the Great Bible made its appearance, which was in April 1539. The task of printing the Taverner Bible was turned over to the shop of John Byddell; its title-page announces that it was "Prynted at London in Fletestrete at the sygne of the sonne by Iohn Byddell, for Thomas Barthlet." The date "M. D. XXXIX" is shown, but there is no indication of the time of year. Assuming, then, that it came out before April, it was our forward-looking friend, John Byddell, who was the first Londoner to share with Nicolson the honor of printing an English Bible.

Richard Grafton and Edward Whitchurch were not long behind. When the publication of the Great Bible had been interrupted at Paris in December 1538, they salvaged as much of the project as they could and transferred their base of operations to London. John Foxe intimates that they had to flee from Paris to avoid arrest. In his *Ecclesiastical History* (edition of 1570, p. 1362) he tells us:

... but hauyng some warnyng what would folowe, the sayd Englishemen posted away as fast as they could to saue them selues, leauyng behynde them all their Bibles ...

and he continues:

But notwithstandyng the sayd losse, after they had recouered some part of the aforesayd bookes, and were well comforted and encouraged by the Lord *Cromwell,* the sayd Englishemen went agayne to *Paris,* and there gotte the presses, letters, and seruauntes of the aforesayd Printer [i.e., Regnault], and brought them to London, and there they became Printers them selues (which before they neuer entended) and Printed out the said Bible in London, and after that Printed sundry impressions of them: ...

Since the first edition of the Great Bible was inadequate to supply the requirements under Cromwell's injunctions, fresh editions were prepared that included some revision of the text. On November 14, 1539, Cranmer writes to Cromwell

... to signifie unto your Lordeship that Bartelett and Edward Whitecherche hath ben with me, and have, by thair accomptes, declared thexpensis and charges of the pryntyng of the great bibles.

When two new editions came out, April 1540, one of them (*S.T.C.* 2069) announced that it was "Prynted at London by Thomas Petyt, and Roberte Redman for Thomas Berthelet." Thus the field was enlarged, and other names that we have met in the history of the Primers now take their place among the printers of the English Bible.

A new Parliament had assembled in April 1539, the first in nearly three years. Its temper was reactionary, opposed to further reforms, especially in religion. At the King's insistence and in spite of Cromwell's reluctance, this Parliament enacted the Six Articles, which reaffirmed salient points of Catholic doctrine in behalf of the Church of England. There ensued a struggle for prestige between the Duke of Norfolk, Thomas Howard, and the King's Vicegerent, Thomas Cromwell, which Cromwell eventually lost. But while the contest lasted, Cromwell went forward determinedly with his favorite policies, trying to tie Henry's reign into the sphere of Protestant influence, dissolving the larger monasteries, and encouraging the widespread use of the English Scriptures.

One of those who looked to Cromwell for patronage and support was John Hilsey, Bishop of Rochester. Hilsey had succeeded to this bishopric when the illustrious John Fisher fell a victim, along with Thomas More, to the King's unscrupulous ambition. Hilsey was a conscientious conformist who might have become a more important figure in this history but for his death in 1539. He labored to bring forth a new sort of Primer which he called the *Manual of Prayers* and which he doubtless hoped would be accepted as authentic and final, superseding the several versions of the Primer up to that time. Though it was received with some favor, its vogue proved to be brief, both on account of Hilsey's proximate decease and Cromwell's subsequent fall from power.

Through Cromwell's encouragement, Hilsey's *Manual* was published on July 15, 1539. It was encumbered with much

arduous explanation and no little apology. The unusual collation of the volume (*S.T.C.* 16009) suggests that it was put
together under difficulties and interruptions. It was entitled:

⟨ The Manual of prayers/ or the prymer in Englysh & Laten set out
at length, whose contentes the reader by ye prologe next after the Kalender, shal sone perceaue, and there in shall se brefly the order of the
whole boke . . .
⟨ Set forth by Ihon by Goddes grace, & the Kynges callyng,[2]
Bysshoppe of Rochester at the commaundemente of the ryghte honorable lorde Thomas Crumwell, lorde Priuie seale, Vicegerent to the
Kynges hyghnes.

The colophon (fol. Vv4^v) introduces a new name among publishers of the English Primers, that of John Wayland:

⟨ Imprinted at London in fletestrete by me Iohan Wayland in saynt
Dunstones parysh at the signe of the blewe Garland next to the
Temple bare. In the yere of our Lorde God a M.D.xxxix. the xv. daye
of Iuly. Cum priuilegio ad Imprimendum solum.

The volume was a small quarto, rather well printed but not
well edited. By July, either Bishop Hilsey was already in uncertain health, or the publisher, John Wayland, was involved
in his recurrent financial difficulties; the editing suffered as a
consequence.

Beside its numerous prologues, another distinctive feature
of Hilsey's *Manual* was his attempt to collect the contents
of the ordinary Primers into three sections, dealing with faith,
prayer, and works. The first section was brief and centered
around the Creed and the Passion. The second comprised
what we generally think of as the Primer from Matins to Dirge,
with preliminary prayers and graces. The final section was
also brief and was concerned with three classes of good works,
featuring the Ten Commandments and the Office of All
Estates.

Certain of the prologues have their own points of interest.

2 Some copies read, "by Goddes grace, at the Kynges callyng,"—an earlier imprint,
perhaps mistaking *et* for *at*. This earlier issue also neglected to mention Psalm 51
at the top of fol. D1; the omission was corrected in the reissue. Both issues use the
same colophon and have the same collation, namely: A4 2A4 BB-DD4 EE2 3A4 B-Z4
Aa-Ii4✠2 Kk-Vv4 (296 leaves).

The first, following the title, was by way of dedication to Lord Cromwell. Next was a brief prologue commenting on the new arrangement of the church calendar. Then came "The prologe to the whole worke" (fol. ²A4ᵛ) mentioned on the title-page. This one began as follows:

> I haue here set forth (moost deare reader) a rude worke, whome it hath pleased me to cal (the manual of prayers, [*sic*] because it is so commenly had in hande wyth the people, which before was called the prymer, bycause (I suppose) y*t* it is the fyrst boke that y*e* tender youth was instructed in.

After explaining the three divisions of the work, the prologue directs attention to the English version of the Psalms:

> . . . But where there shal seme to the reader in the psalmes ony differ-ence between the Laten and Englysh, let the same reme*m*ber that the englysh is accordaunt to the Hebraicall psalter translated by saynt Ierome, and the laten is the vsuall psalter, whych in some places are not correspondent in all thynges, and thus haue I ioyned the*m*, that such as delyteth in the englysh, myght haue the playner sente*n*ce, & that y*e* other y*t* redeth the late*n* shuld not thynke that we shulde brynge in ony strau*n*ge psalmony.

Later (fol. EE2) there is "A preface to the Matyns & the other houres." There are also prefatory paragraphs to Lauds, Evensong, and Seven Psalms, borrowed from the Redman Primer. Following the Litany, there is a special introduction with which Hilsey took great pains, entitled "An instruccio*n* of the maner in hearing of the Masse." This is printed in a smaller type (fol. Ff3ᵛ) and goes on for several pages, being followed by prayers pertaining to the celebration of Mass. In it Hilsey, apparently mindful of the recent enactment of the Six Articles, which (by the way) he had opposed, expostu-lates on the folly of those who question the doctrine of the 'real presence.' There is also a new short prologue to the Dirge, and a longer discourse (in the third section of the *Manual*) on those works that be of man's tradition.

This third section, in English only, is likewise printed in smaller type than the main body of the book. It concludes with various scriptural admonitions suitable for the various 'estates' of society. As in earlier Primers, this feature is called "The offyce of all estates"; but it is now considerably expanded beyond the text that Marshall and Redman had used. Hilsey seems to have been specially anxious to uphold the position of the King; therefore he begins with paragraphs from the Bible dealing with the duty of kings and of "the leage [i.e., *liege*] people of all estates vnto theyr Prynce"—the latter item having been adapted from Luther, it appears. The excerpt which Tyndale had labeled "The comens" is now enlarged by further verses from Leviticus and appears under a new caption: "Euery Christian to hys euen christen."[3] Finally, to show his zeal in the King's cause, Hilsey closes his Primer with an excerpt from II Peter which he levels against "The Bysshope of Rome wyth hys adherentes destroyers of all estates."

The immediate sources of this *Manual of Prayers* seem to be the Primer that Redman published in 1538 and the Coverdale version of the Bible that Nicolson published in 1537. Bishop Hilsey showed a good deal of originality, however, in departing from the use of Sarum, especially in his selection of devotional passages from the Scriptures. At the beginning of Matins he favored the response used by Joye and Marshall, starting "Come vnto me," instead of the more usual "Hail, Mary." Neither did he adhere to the traditional choice of Psalms as prescribed for the regular offices from Matins to Compline, although he did include the Seven Psalms and the Fifteen Psalms and the usual Psalms of the Dirge.[4] He omitted the Commendations and the Psalms of the Passion altogether, as well as the so-called Psalter of St. Jerome; nor did he add any group of selected prayers at the end of his Primer. In the Dirge he seems to have been particularly displeased with the 'lessons' from Job which the Sarum Primers regularly con-

---

[3] See above, p. 109. Hilsey's term, "his euen Christen," recalls the complaint of the grave-digger in *Hamlet* that great folks are given leave to do away with themselves "more than their even Christian." This expression for one's fellow-Christian has been traced back to the age of Chaucer.

[4] For detailed list see below, Appendix II.

tained, evidently feeling that they offered small consolation to the bereaved. In general, he incorporated in his *Manual* more excerpts from other portions of Scripture outside the Psalms than had been included in the Redman Primers. Some of his innovations were not forgotten when, in 1545, an 'authorized' edition of the Primer was at last achieved.

The way in which Hilsey made use of his sources is of some interest although it is not clear by what rules he was governed. From the Redman Primer of 1538 he took the 'approved' wording of the Lord's Prayer, the text of the Passion according to the Gospel of John, the Ten Commandments as "expounded by Christe," the wording of the Seven Psalms and of the first half-dozen of the Fifteen Psalms; also much of his liturgical material, such as the hymns and collects, the wording of which he often revised. The Sarum Primers had contained in all fifty-eight different Psalms; of these Hilsey appropriated the Redman wording in less than twenty. The remainder, including fourteen new ones which he himself substituted, as well as his incidental excerpts from other parts of the Bible, all were taken from the Coverdale version. Lest it seem unusual that Hilsey did not make use of the Matthew Bible, it should be borne in mind that by 1539 the Matthew Bible was out of favor with the King, after it was discovered to have reproduced so much of Tyndale's work, including his controversial prologues to certain books of the Bible. As for the Great Bible, which had been issued with official approval in April, we must suppose that Hilsey began to compile his *Manual of Prayers* before this Bible was published.

In the lessons of the Dirge it will be recalled that the Redman Primer of 1538 used a number of rhymed adaptations from the Book of Job. These Bishop Hilsey dispensed with; instead he used other excerpts from the Scriptures and even from the writings of St. Augustine; and in the three passages from Job which he retained, he chose the prose rendering of the Coverdale Bible.

In some respects the *Manual of Prayers* showed a more consistent policy in its composition than some of its predecessors. As a rule, when the same Psalm was printed more than once, it was given the same rendering each time. For some reason, the 130th Psalm proved troublesome: in the Seven Psalms it appears in the Rouen or Redman wording; but in the Fifteen Psalms and the Dirge it appears in a rendering combined partly from Coverdale and partly from Redman. Similarly with the Office of All Estates: what Hilsey appropriated from the Redman Primer is given as it stood, in Marshall's wording; but the expanded or added portions are copied from the Coverdale Bible. Another deviation occurs in a passage from the sixth chapter of Deuteronomy (verses 6-9), which the Redman Primer adduced in support of the Ten Commandments: here likewise (fol. Tt2) Hilsey took over the passage as it stood, derived from Tyndale's Pentateuch of 1530; but when a portion of the same chapter appears as one of the 'lessons' in Matins (fol. C2), the same verses are given according to the text of the Coverdale Bible.

Sometimes, in the Psalms cited from this Bible, Hilsey has slightly modified the Coverdale wording to accord with the Latin text, so as to reduce the divergencies that he spoke of in his prologue. That he made use of the Nicolson reprint, rather than of the original edition of 1535, is plain from the reading of the seventh Psalm, second verse. Coverdale, who was a north-country man, had written this verse:

Lest he hantch vp my soule lyke a lyon, & teare it in peces, whyle there is none to helpe.

This obscure old word, meaning to snap up, was evidently puzzling to James Nicolson, of Southwark, who reprinted it in 1537 as "catch vp my soule"; and in the Hilsey *Manual* it thus appears (fol. Mml) with an extra clause tacked on to conform to the Vulgate text in the margin:

Lest he catchvp my soule lyke a lyon & teare it in peces/ while ther is none to helpe/ that can saue me.

As soon as the *Manual of Prayers* had come from the press, Cromwell submitted a copy to Archbishop Cranmer for his approval, and on July 21, 1539, Cranmer replied as follows:[5]

My very singuler good Lorde After my moste hartie commendations, theis shalbe to signifie vnto your Lordeship, that I haue ouersene the prymer whiche you sent vnto me, and therin I haue noted and amended suche fawtes as ar moste wurthie of reformation/ Diuers thinges ther ar bisides therin, whiche if committed vnto me to ouersee, I would haue amendid/ Howbeyt thei be not of that Importaunce, but that for this tyme thei may be well enowgh permitted and suffered to be redde of the people, And the boke it self no doubte ys very good and commendable/ Thus my lorde moste hartly faire you well/ At Croydon the xxj[th] Daye of Julye/

Some of Cranmer's notations may have been embodied in the corrected reissue of the English-Latin edition to which reference was made above.

On the 29th of July, Hilsey wrote to Cromwell on another matter from his episcopal residence at Lambeth Marsh. In the course of his letter he mentions 'being sore sick in bed,' and says that he has sent a message to the Bishop of London only to receive a report that Stokesley also 'was sick and asleep, and his servants refused to wake him.'[6] At about the same time Hilsey sent another letter to Cromwell by his publisher, John Wayland, asking apparently for some sort of patent to protect the publication of the *Manual:*

These shalbe to desyre your Honorable Lordeshipp, Even as ye have declarede me your mynde concerninge the forther Impressions of the prymer that we haue sett owt, That it may please your Lordeshippe in lyke maner to declare vnto this berer the prynter therof the pryuylage yt he shall obteyn by your Lordeshipp favorable kyndenes bytwen this and Chrystmas for the Impressions of the sayde boke/ Certyfienge hym further wyther yt may please your Lordeshipp that the commandement to the rest of the prynters shalbe declarede vnto them by your messinger other els prynted in the prymer and thus Iesus preserue your Lordeshipp.

[5] For the text of the letter see an article by H. J. Byrom entitled "John Wayland— Printer, Scrivener, and Litigant" in *The Library*, Series IV, vol. XI, pp. 319-341 (London, 1931). The letter is summarized in *Letters and Papers of Henry VIII*, vol. XIV, no. 1293.

[6] The two letters from Bishop Hilsey are abridged in the *Letters and Papers*, vol. XIV, nos. 1328, 1329. The full text of the second is given in the article by Byrom cited above.

If this "pryuylage" was some special right of publication pertaining to the *Manual of Prayers,* over and above the privilege *ad imprimendum solum* that was required by the royal proclamation, no record exists that Wayland ever obtained it from Cromwell even though it had been promised. Indeed, the promise of such a privilege was made part of an agreement that Wayland entered into with another printer, John Mayler, on the first of September, 1539. Under this indenture Wayland also turned over to Mayler the bulk of his printing equipment. Mayler on his part agreed to pay a certain sum and to print for Wayland any further editions of the *Manual.* Each of the two men being quarrelsome and litigious, they were shortly involved in lawsuits that lasted for several years.

Pursuant to the agreement, Mayler brought out at least two editions of the *Manual of Prayers,* one in English without the Latin, and one arranged for children. In the meanwhile Hilsey had died; and on September 8 Stokesley, the Bishop of London, also died. Edmund Bonner was appointed to fill Stokesley's place, and the following year Nicholas Heath succeeded Hilsey as Bishop of Rochester. Because Mayler's shop was not in one of the busier parts of London, the sale of the new Primers was assigned to two booksellers. The titles and colophons of these two editions reflected the foregoing developments. It seems likely that the Primer for children (*S.T.C.* 16011) was published first; its title-page read:

❡ The Primer in English moste necessary for the educacyon of chyldren extracted oute of the Manuall of prayers or Primer in Englishe and laten, set forth by Iho. laet byshop of Rochester, at the commaundement of the ryght honorable, Lord Thomas Crumwell, lorde priuie seale, Vicegerent to the Kynges hyghnes.

❡ Imprynted in Fletestrete by Ihon waylande at the signe of the blew garlande, & be to sell in Powles churcheyarde, by Andrew Hester at the whyt horse, and also by Mychell Lobley, at the sygne of saynte Mychell. Cum Priuilegio ad imprimendum solum.

The colophon was short: "❡ Imprynted by Ihon Maylart/ for Ihon Waylande."

This was an octavo volume of 92 leaves. Its text was derived from the *Manual*, but was not divided in three parts nor did it contain Hilsey's laborious prologues. After an almanac and a calendar of holy days with their prescribed lessons from the Scriptures, this Primer gave the ABC. The alphabet was printed first in small letters and then in capitals, with the word "est" at the end of the former but no "Amen." Then came the vowels in combination, as in the ABC of 1538 (*S.T.C.* 19). The prayers and graces followed the wording in Hilsey's *Manual;* the body of the Primer began with Matins and concluded with the Litany, as was customary with Primers issued for children. As a further concession, it was printed throughout in a larger size of type.

The other edition (*S.T.C.* 16010) was based on the corrected issue of the *Manual of Prayers* referred to above. It gave only the English text,[7] which was faithfully reproduced from the Latin-English edition. Its title began as follows:

¶ The Manuall of prayers, or the prymer in Englyshe, set out at lengthe, whose contentes [etc., as in *S.T.C.* 16009].

¶Set forth by Ihon late bysshoppe of Rochester at the commaundement of the ryght honorable Lorde Thomas Crumwel, [etc.]

In the colophon at the end of the Primer are given both Mayler's address and those of the booksellers mentioned above:

¶ Imprynted in bottoll [i.e., *Botolph*] lane, at the sygne of the whyt beare by me Ihon Mayler for Ihon Waylande, and be to sell in powles churchyarde, by Andrewe Hester at the whyt horse, and also by Mychel Lobley, at the sygne of saynt Mychell. Cum priuilegio ad imprimendum solum. 1539.

Presumably this edition was printed about October 1539. As in the English-Latin edition of the *Manual*, the calendar is given in its new arrangement. This represented a distinct innovation in that it omitted the manifold entries of traditional saints' names and showed only the regular holy days of the Church; also it specified the Epistles and Gospels appro-

---

7 This English text, in abridged form and modern spelling, is available in Burton's *Three Primers Put Forth in the Reign of Henry VIII*, published at Oxford in 1834 (second edition, 1848).

priated to each Sunday and saint's day, and carried in the margin additional recommendations for other readings from the Scriptures.

Not only so, but there was prepared a new edition of the Epistles and Gospels to accompany this Primer which should conform to the new calendar, starting with New Year's Day instead of with the first Sunday in Advent as earlier editions had done. One of the main points of interest about this new printing of the Epistles and Gospels is that its phrasing is occasionally influenced by the text of the recently published Great Bible, or at least by the New Testament thereof which had separately appeared (*S.T.C.* 2843). Thus these Epistles and Gospels add their mite to the scanty evidence available indicating that the Great Bible, or at least the New Testament, was actually circulated during 1539.

They are entitled:

Here begynneth the Pystels and Gospels of the Sondayes and festyuall holy dayes, newly corrected and amended.

The style of the colophon at the conclusion of them is so similar to the one in the Primer with which they are bound (*S.T.C.* 16010) as to argue that both were printed at the same time, namely, October 1539. This colophon reads:

᚛ Imprynted in Botulph lane, at the sygne of the whyt beare, by me Ihon Mayler, for Iohn Waylande: and be to sell in powles church yarde, by Andrew Hester, also at the whyt horse, & Michel Lobley, at the sygne of saynt Mychell.

The text of these Epistles and Gospels follows the line of Byddell's edition, echoing its overtones from the renderings of George Joye; indeed, most of the text seems to have been copied directly from Byddell's Primer of 1537 (see above, p. 157). The following comparison will make this clear:

In the 'epistle' for St. George's Day, drawn from the first chapter of James, the Byddell edition had read (verses 4 and 5):

. . . and let pacience haue her perfyte worke, that ye may be perfyte & hole, that nothyng be lackyng vnto you. Yf any yt is among you lak wysdome, let hym aske it of god (whiche gyueth to al men abundantly *with*out fraude, and casteth no ma*n* in the teeth) and it shal be geuen hym/ . . .

Now Tyndale's wording of this, which was adopted by the Redman Primer, had read, "parfecte and sounde/" and "which geveth to all men indifferentlie." But in Hilsey's—or more properly, Mayler's—edition the wording not only copies Byddell's but actually misreads the contracted form of "p*er*fyte" as though it were "p*ro*fyte," and the passage is printed: "let pacience haue her profyte worke, that ye maye be profyte and hole."

Yet at times Mayler departs from Byddell, making use of words that do not appear elsewhere except in the Great Bible version. For instance, in the 'gospel' for the first Sunday in Lent, the temptation of our Lord is in part narrated in these words (Matthew 4:6):

> Then the deuyll taketh hym vp into the holy citye and setteth him on a pinnacle of the temple, & sayeth vnto hym. If thou be the sonne of god, cast thy selfe downe headlyng: . . .

—wherein the curious word "headlyng" [i.e., headlong] is peculiar to the New Testament of the Great Bible. And again, in "The Pistle on mydlent Sondaye," we read these words from Galatians (4:24): ". . . which thynges are spoke*n* by an allegory for these are two testame*n*tes," etc., wherein the word "allegory" is found to be borrowed from the Great Bible. Tyndale's phrase had been "Which thinges betoken mystery"; while the Coverdale Bible had simply said, "These wordes betoken somwhat."

On other occasions, however, this editor of Mayler's can strike out for himself. In Philippians 4:5, where the Authorized Version says, "Let your moderation be known unto all men," the Tyndale reading was "Let youre softenes be knowen"; whereas these Epistles and Gospels have "youre frendship." And in the 60th chapter of Isaiah—"The Epystle on twelfte day"—we find that the translation commences like the Great Bible and then diverges, resulting in this unique rendition:

And therfore get the vp by tymes, (o Ierusalem) for thy lyght cometh, and the glory of the lorde is rysen vp vpon the. Then take heade, for whyle the darkenes and myste couereth the earthe & the people, the lorde shal shewe the lyght, & his glory shall shyne by the. The Heythen shall come to thy lyght, & the Kynges to the lyghtnes yt is rysen ouer ye, . . . When thou seyst thys, thou shalte maruell exceadingly, & the lawe wyll go to thy harte, So thus she may be conuerted vnto the, that is, the strenght of the hethen shall come vnto the . . .

This is like no other version I know of—especially the clause, "the lawe wyll go to thy harte"—and seems to have been improvised for the occasion, "newly corrected and amended."

During September 1539, Cromwell, still trying to bolster the Protestant alliance, negotiated arrangements for the marriage of the King, now two years a widower. Henry had been favorably impressed by the portrait of a German princess, Anne of Cleves. Obediently the bride-to-be set out from her native land for England, where she landed on December 27. Henry's disappointment on seeing her in person, and his unwilling marriage to her in the following week, were at least contributory factors in the downfall of Thomas Cromwell.

Accordingly, it must have been near the end of the year that Richard Taverner brought out his *Epitome of the Psalmes;* for in the dedicatory address to the King he voices the high hopes which Cromwell's partisans entertained of the coming marriage. He hopes that God will vouchsafe

. . . to sende you the thynge that the most wyse kynge Salomon estemed for the swetest and beste porcion of mans lyfe, and for a treasure inestimable, that is to wyte, a prudent and wyse lady to your maiesties wyfe and to youre moost addicte subiectes Quene, . . . What shall we saye? God hath alredy herde our moost ardent vowes and peticions. Thys lady moost excellente is prepared of thalmyghtye for your maiestye, she is in iorney readye to be transported into your graces realme.

This volume (*S.T.C.* 2748, 23710) has place in our story because it was fitted out with an additional section of scriptural prayers. Its full title ran:

An Epitome of the Psalmes, or briefe meditations vpon the same, with diuerse other moste christian prayers, translated by Richard Taverner. Cum priuilegio ad imprimendum solum. 1539.

The name of the printer is not given, but the colophon (fol. ^{2}F7^v) is sufficient to identify him as Richard Bankes, for it says, "Imprinted at London in Fletestrete at the signe of the whyte hart." Bankes did several other books for Taverner at this same address.

What appears to have been an earlier edition of this very work, but not containing the section of prayers taken from the Scriptures, is preserved in the Lambeth Palace library.[8] It was entitled:

The Svmme or pith of the .150. Psalmes of Dauid, reduced in to a forme of prayers and meditations, with certayne other godlye orysons, very necessary for all sortes of people to say dayly, translated by Richard Taverner. Cum priuilegio ad imprimendu*m* solum.

Fortunately the colophon is also preserved, disclosing that the book was published by Byddell, who had likewise brought out the Taverner Bible at about the same time:

⁋ Imprynted at London in Fletstrete, at the signe of the Sonne by Ihon Byddell, the .v. daye of Apryll. M.D.xxxix.

In the *Epitome* the original author of these brief meditations on each of the Psalms is not named; but in *The Summe or pith* there was a prologue, "Richard Tauerner to the Christen readers" (fol. a2), in which the work is referred to as

. . . this very fruitefull boke of prayers, lately set forth by the right excelle*n*t clerke Capito, a boke doubtles neuer to be layde out of your ha*n*des, but contynually to be redde, reuolued, and deuoured gredily euery daye, yea, euery houre, as well in chambers and closettes priuilye, as in churches and assemblyes openly, and not onelye to be deuoured outwardly with the lyppes, but inwardly to be chawed, eaten downe and digested in the harte, for let noman thynke that it is y*e* nombre

---

8 See S. R. Maitland, *A List of some of the Early Printed Books in the Archiepiscopal Library at Lambeth* (London, 1843), p. 206, no. 454. This edition, not recorded in the 1926 edition of *S.T.C.*, includes (fol. Q2) "A meditation to be sayde afore the Lordes prayer & other prayers also." Its collation is: a-b8, A-Q8, R4. Signature B is missing in the Lambeth copy.

and multitude of wordes or moch pytter pattryng of lyppes, that maketh vs to be harde of God the father.

The mention of the author's name, Wolfgang Capito, represents another link with Protestant Germany, for Capito was one of Luther's followers who settled at Strassburg where he was contemporary with Martin Bucer. The prologue continues:

If ye shall lyke it, (as I trust surelye ye shall) thank not me for it, but gyue the hole thankes and glory to god, whiche by his myghty hande hath raysed vp oure mooste drad soueraygne Lorde Kynge Henry the eight with such godly counsaillours and furtherers as my Lorde priuie seal is, (at whose request I haue translate it,) to set vp agayne his fallen and decayed glory, maugre the hed of our capitall enemye the byshop of Rome, with all his vngodly lymmes, conspiratours, and adherentes.

The reference to "my Lord priuie seal" as the instigator of this translation recalls the fact that Taverner, in 1532, had appealed in distress to Cromwell for his patronage, and was known the following year as Cromwell's 'client.' Born about 1505 of good family, Taverner had been educated at Cambridge, whence he was transferred to Oxford by Wolsey, only to return to take his master's degree at Gonville Hall in Cambridge in 1530. Cromwell thought well of him, appointed him clerk of the privy seal, and evidently made good use of his literary talents. Before he was employed in the revision of the Matthew Bible, Taverner had become known through his translation of the Augsburg Confession, with Melanchthon's Apology in defense of the same; and also of the *Common Places of Scripture* by Sarcerius.[9]

The style of the two excerpts cited above from the prologue of *The Summe or pith* suggests that Taverner could adopt one tone of speech toward his "Christen readers" and another more learned style toward his sovereign King. For in the *Epitome* his

---

[9] *The confession of the fayth of the Germaynes . . . at Augusta . . . To which is added the Apologie of Melancthon* (S.T.C. 908) was printed by Redman in the first half of 1536; *Common places of scripture . . . by the ryght excellent clerke Erasmus Sarcerius* (S.T.C. 21753) was published by Byddell in 1538. The latter is mistakenly listed in *S.T.C.* (No. 10465) as one of the works of Desiderius Erasmus, some of whose writings Taverner also translated. See the article on Taverner in the *Dictionary of National Biography*.

preface addressed to the King is full of lavish compliment and written in his best latinical manner, sometimes skillful enough in its command of rolling English rhythms to resemble the later achievements of Milton and Sir Thomas Browne. He begins by reminding the King that some three years ago Cromwell had procured him the opportunity of using his literary talents in the King's service, and that among other works on which he might exercise his abilities Cromwell had suggested this one which he now presents. In a passage that comes off well, considering its early date, Taverner goes on to say:

> Truth it is, that my poore degre & basenesse of condicion is farre vnmete to offer any thynge vnto your moost excellent hyghnes. Howbeit, yf Hethen kinges haue very thankfully receyued of their subiectes handes, Pome granates, hand fuls of water, and such other tryflyng thynges, estemyng rather the prompt and ready wyl of the gyuers, than the pryce of the thynges gyuen, yf also Christ hymselfe our myghty sheperde (whose vicare for the church & realme of Englande youre maiestie is recognised) not onely accepted but also preferred the two minutes of ye poore wydowe afore the precious oblacions of the rych personages, I doubt not, but your maiestie beyng a christian Kynge and such a kynge, woll not ingratelye receyue at youre humble seruauntes hande, these hys symple lucubracions whych tende to the hygh benefyte, edificacion, and commoditie of youre graces people. But leste wyth my loquacitie I myght be an impediment vnto youre moost serious occupacions, I make an ende.

Typically enough—not to say ironically—he does not actually "make an ende," but spins out his dedication for another couple of pages.

The collection of "moste christian prayers" that Taverner included in his *Epitome of the Psalmes* was drawn mostly from the Scriptures. The section had a subtitle of its own (fol. ²Al):[10] "The Principall Prayers of the Byble moste necessary for christen men, gathered out by Richard Tauerner." In general he used the version of the Matthew Bible, which had been the basis of Taverner's own revision earlier in the year. It is worth remarking that in these prayers he did not follow his

---

[10] The collation of the *Epitome* volume is: Four unsigned leaves; then A-P8, 2A-F8; with fol. 2F8 blank.

own revision where this was different from the Matthew Bible, but rather ventured occasionally on some fresh variations of his own.

The selections themselves recall Redman's *Prayers of the Byble,* often comprising the same excerpts and occurring in the same sequence. The prayers are divided into four groups which correspond to the first four of Redman's headings. Yet Taverner was not a mere copyist; he verified certain citations that had been habitually cited amiss. His literary mannerisms are in evidence, and were not always consistent. Like Joye, he would never have been irked to find that he had rendered the same text differently at different times. In his translations from the Bible he affected a popular rather than a learned turn of phrase, and his work is earmarked by certain peculiarities of speech, such as the use of "to thintent that" etc.

In the prayer of Solomon taken from the thirtieth chapter of Proverbs, Taverner's *Epitome* reads (fol. ²D8):

Two thinges I require of the, that thou wylte not denye me before I dye. Remoue from me vanitie and lyes, gyue me neyther pouertie nor ryches, only graunt me a necessary lyuyng, least yf I be to ful I mought happely denye the, & say what felow is the lorde? or constrayned through pouerty, I mought fal vnto stealyng, & forsweare the name of my god.

Here he departs from Coverdale's rendering (in the Matthew Bible) by introducing the words "mought happely" and by shortening Coverdale's words, "And lest I beinge constrained" to the simpler form of "or constrayned."

In his version of the Magnificat (fol. ²D5ᵛ) Taverner departs from Tyndale's translation (Luke 1: 51, 52) and says:

He vttered strength with his arme, he disperpled the proude in the imaginacion of their hertes. He deposed the myghty from their seates, and aduaunced them of lowe degre.

The Matthew Bible, following Tyndale, had said: "He sheweth strength . . . he scattereth them that are proud . . . He putteth doune the myghty . . . and exalteth them of lowe degre."

Taverner shows some predilection for words of medieval flavor. In the prayer of the early Church, for instance, as recorded in the fourth chapter of Acts, he cites the chapter correctly (it had long been given in the Primers as Acts 14) but in verse 27 he rings in a new and colorful term (fol. ²E4) :

For suerly agaynst thy holy son Iesus, whom thou hast anoynted, both Herode and also Poncius Pylate with the Panyms and the people of Israel gathered them selues togyther . . .

This word "Panyms" instead of "heathen" occurs elsewhere in these prayers from Taverner's *Epitome;* it is derived from the French word for "pagan."

A few years before, a work similar to Capito's was brought out in an English translation by Myles Coverdale. This was a paraphrase of the Psalms made by Joannes Campensis.[11] In 1539, impressed perhaps by the success of Taverner's efforts, another publisher, Thomas Gybson, issued a reprint of Coverdale's translation (*S.T.C.* 14620) with the title:

A Paraphrasis vpon all the Psalmes of Dauid, made by Iohannes Campensis, reader of the Hebrue lecture in the vniuersite of Louane, and translated out of Latine into Englysshe.

This time the name of the translator was withheld. The Campensis volume, however, contained no additional section of prayers from the Bible.

11 I am informed by Rev. J. F. Mozley that an edition of Coverdale's Campensis belonging to 1535 is preserved in the library of Lincoln Cathedral.

Chapter XVI

Editorial Enigmas
(1540)

AFTER it had been arranged that Anne of Cleves was to be the next Queen of England, she made the King a gift of a Sarum Primer in Latin, published at Paris about 1533.[1] In it she wrote the following inscription:

> I beseche your grace humble when ye loke on this remember me
> your graces assured anne the dowther of cleves

But Henry's second Anne was not to his liking; he married her under protest. She was Queen only from January 6 to July 9, 1540, whereupon she was given what amounted to an honorable discharge with pension.

Quite a while before this divorce was ratified, the King had already determined to get rid of his chief minister, who had engineered the marriage. For in the meantime the whole course of European politics had taken a turn contrary to Cromwell's plans and expectations, and the King no longer felt it necessary to conciliate the Protestant Princes of Germany. So, without warning, on the tenth of June Cromwell was arrested as a traitor; and while in the Tower awaiting sentence and execution he willingly subscribed to the King's contention that the German marriage was not valid because the King had withheld his free consent thereto.

At his execution Cromwell professed that he had always been a loyal Catholic, notwithstanding that one of the charges laid against him had to do with his heretical and 'Lutheran' opinions. What Cromwell's real opinions were will probably

[1] Preserved at the Folger Library in Washington, this volume (*S.T.C.* 15982) was entitled *Enchiridion preclare ecclesie Sarisburiensis deuotissimis precationibus* [etc.]; its supplementary prayers are more numerous than in the ordinary Primer.

never be known. Though he had numerous agents, emissaries, clients, and dependents, he had few, if any, friends. He was first of all a politician, and it is not incredible that he should have fomented various Lutheran reforms without actually adopting the Lutheran theology as his own. Anne of Cleves, though herself a Catholic, had Protestant connections through her family; so it is not to be wondered at, that in Cromwell's eyes she seemed an ideal choice for the Queen.

With Cromwell's overthrow the Duke of Norfolk took a prominent place among the King's advisers, while Stephen Gardiner, Bishop of Winchester, obtained an influential voice in the shaping of religious policy. When the King was in need of a new Queen, it was to the Catholic family of the Howards that he turned, abetted by Bishop Gardiner, and on August 8 he married young Katherine Howard, a niece of the Duke of Norfolk.

The trend toward reform in religion, furthered under Cromwell and Cranmer, was now checked; the Six Articles were put in force, and old charges of heresy renewed. So strong was the tide of reaction that it carried the Lutheran preacher, Robert Barnes, and two of his associates to a martyr's death. On the same day three Catholic priests were also executed for treason because they would not acknowledge the King as Supreme Head of the Church. This was on the 30th of July, two days after Cromwell's execution. Forewarned by these commotions, both Coverdale and Joye took flight again across the Channel in search of refuge on the Continent.

The Archbishop, however, seems to have weathered the storm by virtue of the King's personal intervention; for Henry persisted in holding Cranmer in high regard in spite of his Lutheran leanings, and he in turn seems to have been sincerely attached to his King. Thus it fell to Cranmer's lot to champion the cause of the English Scriptures, as the only one who could and would. With the Archbishop's support, Great Bibles continued to be printed for use in the churches; in fact he composed for them a long and eloquent prologue encouraging their use; but editions published in July 1540 and thereafter had Thomas Cromwell's coat-of-arms carefully expunged from its place in the decorative scheme of the title-page. During 1539 and 1540 Grafton and Whitchurch also brought out at least three editions of the New Testament according to the version printed in the Great Bible.

Was it perhaps one of these Testaments that William Maldon learned to read as a boy of fifteen, in spite of the angry opposition of his father? Maldon's account, written some twenty-five years after the event,[2] is very vague as to dates, but vivid in its recollection of the monstrous punishment meted out to him at home. He was brought up, he says, in the town of Chelmsford, in Essex, where he studied an English Primer in order to learn to read the New Testament. He begins by mentioning that in King Henry's time the Scriptures were set forth "to be rede in all chvrches in ingelonde," and goes on to say:

... & Imedyately after dyueres poore men in the towne of chelmysford ... bought the newe testament of Jesus chryst & on svndayes dyd syt redyng in lower ende of chvrche, & many wolde floke abovte them to here theyr redyng then I cam amonge the sayd reders to here them, ... then thovghte I I will learne to read engelyshe, & then will I haue the newe testament & read ther on myselfe, and then had I larned of an engelyshe prymmer as fare as patris sapyentia[3] & then on svndayes I plyed my engelysshe prymmer, the mayetyd [i.e., *May-tide*] folovyng I & my fathers prentys, thomas Jeffary layed our money to gether, & bought the newe testament in engelyshe, & hydde it in our bedstrawe & so exersysed it at convenyent tymes, ...

When this was discovered, he was severely thrashed and threatened with an impromptu hanging by his irate father, who accused him, as he recalls, of speaking against "the kynges injvntyones."

But when was all this? In May of what year? There is, alas, no certainty about the date, save that it probably took place

---

[2] Reprinted from the British Museum MS., Harley 590, in A. W. Pollard, *Records of the English Bible* (Oxford, 1911), p. 268.

[3] An anthem near the end of Lauds, which in the English version current at the time commenced:

He that is the greate profounde sapyence,
And dyuyne truthe of the father on hye: [etc.]

between 1539 and 1542. Neither can we tell which English Primer it was that Maldon learned to read from.

But it is true that certain Primers put forth in 1540 likewise bear mute testimony to the religious and political dislocations of the period. There is, for example, a curious fragment of a Hilsey Primer consisting of two uncut and unbound sheets (*S.T.C.* 16017) on which were printed the first sixteen leaves (i.e., 32 pages) of a projected issue. This was probably printed by John Mayler under the terms of his agreement with John Wayland. Cromwell's name appears on the title-page and Queen Anne's name is found in the 'bidding of the beads'; the almanac is dated 1540. The title is of special interest:

> The Manuall of prayers or Primer in englysh ¶ Set forth by Ihon by goddes gra[ce] late bysshop of Rochester at the commaundement of the ryghte honorable Lorde Thomas Crumwell, Lorde Priuie seale Vicegerent to the Kynges hyghnes, for an vniuersall vsage to his graces louyng subiectes.

This fragment must have been printed after the sixth of January, while Anne was seated insecurely on the throne, and before the middle of June, when Cromwell was arrested for treason. A significant part of the title is that which proclaims the book "an vniuersall vsage" to the King's subjects. For this involves the unanswered query whether this edition was suppressed before it was well under way on account of its assuming to be authorized when it was not, or on account of Cromwell's sudden disappearance from his post as the King's vicegerent, or simply because Wayland and Mayler may have been at loggerheads and unable to come to terms. It seems logical to conjecture that Cromwell perhaps intended to issue a uniform and authorized Primer but was deprived of his power before the edition could be printed.

Another Primer printed at this same time "by Ihon Mayler at the signe of the whyte Beare in Botulph lane" (*S.T.C.* 16018) also shows the influence of Hilsey. Though dated 1539 in the almanac, the bidding of beads stipulates that prayers are to be offered for the King "and quene Anne his wife, and for the prosperite of the noble Prynce Edwarde his sonne." The book is not labeled a *Manual of Prayers* nor does it conform altogether to Hilsey's edition; it was a composite volume, lying perhaps outside the scope of the agreement between Wayland and Mayler. Besides the Primer itself it included not only a section of Epistles and Gospels but also the two expositions by Savonarola. It was entitled:

> The Primer in Englisshe and Laten set out at length with the exposicion of Miserere and In te domine speraui and with the Epistles and Gospels thorowe out all the whole yere.

Only two copies are known, both at the Bodleian Library, one in the Selden, the other in the Douce collection. Although but a slipshod publication, it achieves a kind of importance through a strange and unexplained discrepancy between the two extant copies. These agree everywhere except in signatures D to I. Here the Selden copy is the earlier and more regular, while in the Douce copy four new gatherings (D-G) have been substituted for the six (D-I) in the other copy.[4]

Taking the volume as a whole, it was apparently Mayler's intention to put out a Primer that would combine features drawn from both the Hilsey *Manual* and the Sarum Primers. The calendar, for instance, follows the use of Sarum, while the preliminary chapters from the four Gospels represent a combination of those used by Hilsey and Redman. Indeed, so little attention was paid to the editing that on one leaf (fol. C6) the selection from Mark 16 is printed in the Tyndale version, as Redman had given it, while on the next leaf (C7) it appears again in the Coverdale version which Hilsey had used, the two translations being very much alike.

Starting with signature K (near the end of Compline) and going on through Litany and Dirge, the text in both copies is simply a reprint of the Hilsey *Manual*, except that Hilsey's long "Instruction" and prayers for the saying of Mass are omitted, as are also the "Fifteen O's" which Hilsey had included. Mayler also reproduces the 'third part' of Hilsey's

---

4 The collation of the entire volume would be: A-I, K-S8; Aa-Cc8 2D8 2E10; 2A-C8 3D,E8 2F-I,K,L8. The Selden copy lacks fols. A1, 2E5,6; the Douce copy has no signature H or I and lacks the blank leaves 2E10 and 2L8.

Manual dealing with Good Works. For the two expositions of Savonarola, which are here given in English only, Mayler turned to the text that had accompanied the 'Rouen' Primer which was printed at Paris in 1538 (*S.T.C.* 16005; see above, p. 173). But for the version of his Epistles and Gospels he went directly to the English edition of the Hilsey *Manual* (*S.T.C.* 16010), reprinting even the same errors, such as "her profyte worke" for "her perfect work" (see above, p. 193). This time, however, in the colophon at the end of the volume Wayland's name no longer appears, but only Mayler's:

⟨ Imprynted in Botoulph lane, at the sygne of the whyt beare, by me Ihon Mayler.

Returning now to the body of the Primer—the portion most in use, from Matins to Compline—we find in the Selden copy that Matins begins on fol. C8. Then in signatures D to H the editing follows a fairly consistent pattern, utilizing the framework of the Hilsey *Manual* while at the same time disregarding Hilsey's innovations in the choice of unfamiliar Psalms. Only in Prime (the first of the Hours) are the Hilsey Psalms preferred; elsewhere in these particular signatures the Psalms accord with the regular use of Sarum, while other items, the hymns, prayers, and responses, are copied from Hilsey. But in signature I, for whatever reason, this plan is not followed through. For after the Sarum version of Psalm 131 (fol. I4) the text deserts the Hilsey framework entirely for some half-dozen pages, reverting to it again at the exact point where the Sarum version was about to launch into the prayer *Salve Regina,* which was anathema to the reformers. Then, a few pages later on (fol. K2ʳ), Mayler gives the Protestant counterpart of this prayer, *Salve Rex,* as it occurs in the Hilsey *Manual.*

It must have been shortly after the Selden copy of this Primer had been printed that Mayler decided for some reason to reissue the volume with a new set of signatures (D-G) containing an all-Sarum text. This second issue is preserved in the Douce copy. But here Mayler did a very unusual thing, for which no explanation is at hand: he started off his new substitute signatures (fol. D1) with a fresh beginning of Matins, wholly ignoring the fact that in the earlier issue Matins had already commenced on the last leaf of the preceding signature (fol. C8) ; nor did he take the trouble to cancel this former leaf. The result is that in the Douce copy we have two successive leaves showing the beginning of Matins. Moreover, there is a difference in the version used, so that the two leaves are not identical, though at first they may so appear. For on fol. C8 (as in the Selden copy also) it is Hilsey's version of the opening Psalm that is used, with its responses, "Come unto me," etc., drawn from the Marshall Primers; whereas on fol. D1 (in the Douce copy) it is the Sarum text of the Psalm that is used, with its traditional responses of "Hail, Mary" and "The Lord is with thee."

In making this substitution of signatures it is plain also that Mayler was greatly concerned about space: he crowds his pages with type and employs frequent contractions in the spelling. In the outcome he finds that by merely citing the Psalms of Evensong instead of printing them out at length (for they were already printed among the Hours), and by making some drastic short cuts towards the end of Compline, avoiding once again the use of *Salve Regina*, he is able to wind up his text at exactly the same point as in the Selden copy, but with a saving of two whole signatures![5]

But why the substitution? why go to all this trouble? This is still an enigma. In view of the evidence there would seem to be only two motives for such a change: one would be to save a certain quantity of paper, and the other would be to present a straight Sarum text in the main body of his Primer, without admixture from the Hilsey *Manual*. In the first case, we could assume that some negligent printer had run off too many sheets of the first three and the last nine signatures, and too few of those in between (D-I); and that Mayler's problem was how to make use of the extra sheets with the least expense of fresh paper; and that he hit upon the solution of using a somewhat

[5] For further details of these alterations, see below, Appendix I (B).

shorter version and tailoring the last leaf to make the wording fit into what was already printed.

In the other case, if Mayler was trying to supplant one version with another, there might be two sorts of explanation: Either he was apprehensive of the orthodox reaction that set in after Cromwell's fall and, recalling that Cromwell had been Hilsey's patron, sought to give his Primer a less Protestant complexion; or else he found he had run afoul of his agreement with John Wayland, which stipulated that editions of Hilsey's *Manual* were to be printed for Wayland; and after Mayler got his Primer under way and had issued the Selden copy, he may have been apprised that Wayland would raise objection to it on the ground that it was virtually an edition of Hilsey's *Manual* and therefore subject to the terms of their agreement.

Of these several hypotheses, I incline toward the explanation that it was the fall of Cromwell which unsettled the status of all those who were engaged in printing portions of the English Scriptures.

Another who suffered the loss of a patron in the fall of Cromwell was young Richard Grafton, member of the Grocers' company. With Edward Whitchurch he was engaged in publishing Great Bibles. Cromwell had provided a place for these two to conduct their Bible publication, namely, the premises of a recently dissolved monastery in London. It has been suggested that, having invested heavily in printing equipment which had been imported from Paris, Grafton was now obliged to take up the trade of publisher for his livelihood.[6] If this be so, then one of the first books (other than Bibles) to issue from his press was a small English-Latin Primer (*S.T.C.* 16015) entitled:

> The prymer both in Englishe and Latin Anno. M. D. XL. Prynted in the house late the graye freers [i.e., *Grayfriars*] by Rychard grafton and Edward whytchurche. . . . ❡ Cum priuilegio ad imprimendum solum.

[6] See J. A. Kingdon, *Richard Grafton Citizen and Grocer of London* (London, 1901), p. 12.

This Primer, too, presents enigmas of its own—certain extraordinary features for which there is no ready explanation unless it were the stress and uncertainty of the times. Like Mayler's, it was based essentially on the Hilsey *Manual* and, like his, it combined materials from other sources. Also, a section of Epistles and Gospels is appended to the volume.[7]

The three main sources out of which Grafton compiled this Primer are the Hilsey *Manual*, the Gough Primer of 1536, and the Marshall *Goodly Primer*. Not only do these three volumes supply materials for different portions of this Primer, but at one point there is some evidence of another cancellation or substitution such as was noticed above in the Mayler Primer.

The title of Grafton's Primer, announcing that it was printed in 1540, occupies but the upper half of the first page, the lower half remaining blank. On the reverse side, an almanac begins with the year 1539, which is not surprising since the two preliminary signatures were copied entirely from the Hilsey *Manual* of that year (*S.T.C.* 16009). What is peculiar is that below the almanac appear seven lines of type constituting an isolated and irrelevant fragment of text which seems to have been lifted bodily from a leaf near the end of the Primer (fol. L3). There, in their proper context, the identical lines occur near the bottom of the page. The explanation is that a printer's error was responsible for this excrescence on the reverse of the title-page; for it is assumed that the compositor picked up a stray block of type that was in process of being distributed after the printing of signature L, and stuck it in the space below the almanac, intending to use it as blank 'furniture'; but that some negligent or ignorant workman, instead of masking it to keep it from being imprinted, mistook it for something relevant and proceeded to ink it in.

In the calendar that follows, Hoskins[8] notes that St. Katherine's Day is entered against the 20th of November instead of

---

[7] Two copies are known, one in the British Museum, the other in the Folger Library at Washington. Collation: ✠8 *8 A-L8; 2A-K8. The Museum copy lacks fols. G1, 2; the Folger copy lacks fol. *1.

[8] *Op. cit.*, p. 219.

the 25th. This was due to a typographical disparity between Grafton's Primer and the *Manual of Prayers* in which Hilsey first introduced his revised calendar. In the calendar of the *Manual*, the column numbering the days of the month was set in much larger type than were the saints' names and the lessons that made up the body of the calendar; consequently, the corresponding entries at the end of November could be condensed into the space allotted to the last five days of the month. Whereas in Grafton's Primer the type used for such entries was of the same size as that used in the column of days, so that here the very same entries took up the equivalent of ten days, thus lifting the position of St. Katherine's name to the level of the 20th of the month.[9]

Apart from such peculiarities, the make-up of the Grafton Primer is also remarkable in that its signatures fall apparently into certain groups with respect to their source-material. Those signed ✠ and * (as was said) are copied from the Hilsey *Manual;* signatures A to D are based on the text of the Gough Primer; most of signature E is taken from Marshall's *Goodly Primer;* while the remainder (from F to L) reverts to Hilsey again. Moreover, between signatures D and E there is a strange lapse in continuity which suggests some shift of purpose rather than simple negligence.

In general, the text of Matins, Hours, and Evensong (signatures A to D) represents a combination of Sarum and Marshall ingredients—the same combination as Gough had used in his Primer of 1536 *(S.T.C.* 15992). That is, the Psalms are after the versions of George Joye as Redman had printed them in his first edition of the Sarum Primer (see above, p. 96); while the prayers, lessons, anthems, etc., are drawn from Marshall's materials based on the Joye Hortulus. That Grafton depended specifically on the Gough Primer is shown not only by certain transpositions in the sequence of prayers during the Hours, but also by the peculiar wording of the 'third lesson'

---

[9] It is curious that in the unbound fragmentary *Manual* mentioned first in this chapter *(S.T.C.* 16017) the calendar of saints, which was modeled after Redman instead of Hilsey, makes the same mistake of assigning St. Katherine's Day to November 20.

in Matins. Here Joye had said of those who walked not after the will of God, "Fearfullye and shortlye shall he appere vnto you"; but in the Gough Primer, and likewise in Grafton's, this is copied as "Fearfully and sharply."

Grafton did not, however, utilize all of Gough's materials. For example, in the Lauds he omitted the collects pertaining to various saints; and in the Compline he not only avoided the *Salve Regina,* as Mayler had done, but also adopted the shorter form which Marshall had given for the entire office of Compline. The reason for these preferences is plain: Grafton was a firm adherent of the Reformation and, while he attempted to use most of the Sarum version where the Latin text called for it, he ruled out what he considered to be undue veneration of the Virgin and of saints.

It is therefore significant that at the beginning of Compline we find a break in the continuity of the text and that this is observable in both the known copies of this Primer. As printed on the final page of signature D, the thirteenth Psalm is in the version of the Joye Psalter of 1534 just as Gough had given it in his Primer; but on the next page—the first in signature E— the Psalm is concluded in the version of 1530 as given in the *Goodly Primer* of Marshall. Moreover, the reading is not consecutive and the catchword is inapplicable. In other words, from one signature to the next, the wording skips inadvertently from Gough to Marshall, creating this effect:

[Fol. D8ᵛ] My herte hoppeth for ioye at the comyng of thy sauyng
    helth that
        [Catchword]   I myght
[Fol. E1] I shall gyue thankes to my lorde/ for he hath rewarded me.

In the Gough Primer the Psalm would have concluded: ". . . that I myght prayse the whan thou haste geuen it me."

Now if this *non sequitur* indicates another substitution of material while the Primer was still in the course of publication, it shows the same tendency we noted in the Mayler Primer, namely, to supplant a 'reformed' Marshall text with something more nearly resembling an orthodox version in the early signatures of the volume. And this too may have been out

THE GRAFTON-WHITCHURCH PRIMER OF 1540

Showing Psalm 13 in Compline (here cited as "xxii")
and the beginning of signature E

(From the copy in the Folger Shakespeare Library by permission)

of deference to the alteration that had come over the political and religious atmosphere of the times.

After the Compline come the Seven Psalms, and here in the midst of the 51st Psalm, and in this same signature (fol. E7), Grafton quietly abandons the Marshall text; for after verse 12 ("let thy chief governing free spirit strengthen and lead me"— see below, p. 300) he definitely takes over the reading in the Hilsey *Manual*. Thereafter he pursues the Hilsey text not only through the rest of the Seven Psalms but also through the Fifteen Psalms that follow. Why he decided to make a shift in his source material at that particular point, only Grafton himself would know.

Litany and Dirge are both like Hilsey's also, save that Grafton, as Mayler had done, omitted the long exposition on the saying of Mass, as well as the "Fifteen O's." Grafton also gives us the 'third part' of Hilsey's *Manual* intact, at the close of which he inserts the graces and prayers which Hilsey had placed at the beginning of the 'second part' of his *Manual*.

Lastly, to fill up the last two leaves of signature L, with which the Primer portion comes to a close, Grafton introduces two new collects, each of which was to reappear in later publications. The first of these is "❡A prayer and thankes gyuynge to the heuynly father for all his benefyces shewed to vs"; the second, "❡A prayer for trewe faythe." The latter commences thus, with the opening verse of Psalm 18:

> I wyll loue the o Lorde my strenghth
> The Lorde is my stablyshement and refuge.

O Lord make vs to haue a perpetuall feare and loue to thy holy name for thou neuer leuest those destytute of thy gouernayle/ whom thou hast fyxed in the steadfastnes of thi love.

This crude rendering seems to have been hastily contrived to fill up the last leaf of the Primer section. The lower part of the page has a dated colophon (1540) which begins:

❡ Imprynted in London in the house late the graye fryers by Rychard Grafton and Edward Whytchurche/ and be to sell in Paules churche yearde at the sygne of the Byble.

The volume is rounded out with a section of Epistles and Gospels which displays the same style of title as was used in Hilsey's *Manual* (*S.T.C.* 16010), claiming that the text is "newly corrected and amended." But whereas Hilsey did interject some new readings, Grafton reprints mostly the older version given in Redman's edition (*S.T.C.* 16008).[10] Again, Hilsey had rearranged his Epistles so that they began with January first; but Grafton adopts this arrangement only for the Sundays and holidays. When he came to the saints' days, he reverted to the old sequence, commencing with St. Andrew's Day instead of with Candlemas. Finally, at the close of his volume is another dated colophon.

Before the year was out, still another London printer made free with the text of Hilsey's *Manual,* adopting it as the basis for at least one new edition of the English Primer (*S.T.C.* 16016). This was Nicholas Bourman, whose Primer was dated 1540 on its title-page, according to the record of the antiquarian, William Herbert. Its almanac also starts with this year.

Bourman's Primer was of curious shape, about seven inches tall and only three inches wide. It was literally a 12mo, each of its signatures comprising twelve leaves, of which the first seven leaves were signed. It was printed down the page in short lines of rather small type, and its colophon said simply, "Imprynted at London in Aldersgate strete, by Nycholas Bourman." The title-page of the copy preserved at the Library of Lambeth Palace is mutilated, but its long detailed title begins as follows:

A Primer or boke of Prayers/ set forth at longe, wherin are conteined the houres of our Lady, of the Passion, and of the holy gho[st] . . .

From Matins to Dirge the text of this Primer is simply a reprint of the Hilsey *Manual,* except that Bourman did not

---

[10] In printing his Epistles and Gospels, both here and in *S.T.C.* 2971 (see below), Grafton showed his ingenuity in the 'gospel' for the Fifteenth Sunday after Trinity. In Matthew 6:24 Tyndale had written, ". . . or els he shall lene to the one and despise the other:" but in the Redman and Rouen editions this was misprinted, "he shall leue to the one" etc. This Grafton amended to read, "he shall cleaue to ye one and despise ye other."

include Hilsey's lengthy "Instruction" concerning the Mass, though he gives the accompanying prayers. Neither did he include the third portion of Hilsey's Primer concerning Works, but stopped his text with the ending of the Dirge.

A unique feature of Bourman's Primer was the Catechism that came after the calendar. Though resembling the older "Dialoge" which Marshall and Godfray had used, it was furnished with a new heading and its wording was freely amended. It was now entitled:

A Cathechismus, or chyldesshe instruction, which all parentes are bounde to se theyr chyldren to knowe by rote, set forthe question and answer wyse.

It begins in such a manner as to suggest that it is presented in place of the more elaborate materials that Hilsey had assembled for the first portion of his *Manual;* for it says:

This Catechismus consystethe in the thre chyefe poyntes of the whole scripture, namely: fayth, workes, and prayer, wheroute all parentes maye teache theyr chyldren . . .

The printing shop in Aldersgate Street where Bourman worked seems to have belonged to John Herford, a printer who had removed to St. Albans until he was returned to London in 1539 under suspicion of having printed heretical books. Accordingly, it may possibly have been either Herford or Bourman who put forth another edition of the Primer in English and Latin, of which a unique copy is now preserved in the Folger Shakespeare Library (Hoskins, No. 153). Though the copy is imperfect and shows neither date nor printer, its text resembles Bourman's, in that it is based even more closely on Hilsey's work but closes with the Dirge.

Moreover, both these Primers—Bourman's and the one at Folger—are fitted out with an additional section of Epistles and Gospels. And in their text of these, both editions, though plainly taken from the Hilsey *Manual* (*S.T.C.* 16010), have many peculiar variations in common. An analysis of such variant readings points to the likelihood that the Folger volume is the later imprint. For instance, in the epistle for Candlemas

Day from the third chapter of Malachi, the sentence, "Beholde, he commethe, sayeth the Lorde of powers," which Byddell had taken over from the 'epistles' in Joye's second edition of the New Testament, was retained by both Mayler and Bourman, but the Folger volume omits the sentence entirely.

Not only so, but there is another separate printing of these Epistles and Gospels, a small undated quarto, "Imprinted at London in Aldersgate strete by Ihoan Herforde" (*S.T.C.* 2973); and the same unusual variations of text are evident here that were also found to be peculiar to the two Primers just described. In other words, the volume at the Folger Library belongs to the same family of texts as the Bourman Primer and the Herford Epistles and Gospels.

How it happened that Grafton and Bourman, and perhaps Herford, felt free to make unrestricted use of the Hilsey *Manual* within one year of the time when the publication of Hilsey's volume was made the basis of an agreement between Mayler and Wayland, we do not know. It is not certain that Cromwell ever acceded to Hilsey's request that Wayland be granted a virtual monopoly of the printing of his *Manual;* and it is likely, in any case, that once Cromwell was out of the way, there was no real validity left in any such agreement as Mayler and Wayland had made with each other. The publication of Primers was by now an open field, and the names of new publishers begin to appear in them.

The same is also true of the Epistles and Gospels. In addition to those already mentioned there were at least three other editions brought out in 1540 or thereabouts. One was by Richard Grafton (*S.T.C.* 2971), remarkable especially for the fact that its title reversed the usual order and read:

℘ The Gospelles and Pystles of all *ye* So*n*dayes & sayntes dayes that are red in the churche, all the whole yere. Richardus Grafton excudebat. 1540.

Another (*S.T.C.* 2972) probably belonging to this same period was "Imprynted at London in Pater noster rowe, by me Ioha*n* Redman"—who is supposed to have been a relative of Robert.

The text of this edition, as one might guess, followed in the tradition of the Rouen and Redman Primers.

Then there was also a very elaborate edition of the Epistles and Gospels prepared by Richard Taverner, who supplied a comment or "Postil" upon each lesson (*S.T.C.* 2967), and this was published for him by Richard Bankes. It is worth noting that Taverner now dedicates his work to the King, with no mention of his defunct patron, Thomas Cromwell. Through all the ups and downs of this uncertain period Taverner was one of the few who managed to retain the good opinion of the King in spite of his adherence to the "New Learning" of the reformers.

From the foregoing it is plain that the Primers and their accompanying Epistles and Gospels were now being issued in a multiplicity of forms and editions. As if to add to this variety, it was probably during this same period—that is, about 1540— that there appeared still another composite edition of the English Primer, embracing a strange assortment of miscellaneous ingredients. Assigned doubtfully to the year 1539 by Hoskins, this edition might have appeared as late as 1542; but the only surviving copy, which is now in the library at St. Paul's Cathedral in London, is so imperfect as to lack both title and colophon; hence printer and date are both problematic.[11] It is a little book, cheaply printed in spite of its rubrication, yet its text is not without interest. It was edited rather carelessly and with an eye to saving space; e.g., "vnto" was usually shortened to "to." The opening leaves, which doubtless contained a calendar, were printed in small type, but only one of these remains, showing part of the 'Weekdays Moralized' (as in the Redman Primer of 1537). The bulk of the Primer is printed in a much larger letter, running only seventeen lines to a full page. A somewhat similar format, it may be recalled, had been tried in the Godfray Primer of 1535. But in this Primer at St.

---

11 Listed by Hoskins as No. 150, it is unrecorded in *S.T.C.* At least nine leaves are missing from the beginning and a few others from the end, while more than two signatures are wanting in the body of the book. The collation of the 135 surviving leaves is: B2-8, C2-7, D-E8, F2-7, G-M8, P2-8, Q-V8, X2-6.

Paul's, commencing with signature T, the type suddenly shifts back to the smaller size for the rest of the volume, and this without any ado, the shift occurring in the middle of a word!

From careful examination of the contents, and specially by the analogy of another Primer published about 1543, it is possible to hazard the guess that this little Primer (which we may refer to as Hoskins 150) was from the press of Robert Copland or his successor. Possibly, also, it was printed for Richard Kele, who likewise published the edition of 1543 (*S.T.C.* 16030). For in the main body of the text—from Matins through to the Psalms of the Passion—these two editions have many peculiar points in common. The 1543 edition was set in similar type, seventeen lines to the page, and its title would have applied equally well to the book we are considering (Hoskins 150), for it read: "⟨This is the Primer in Englysh set out a longe with dyuers additions."

In the Primer portion both editions use the same basic text, showing that at least they were derived from an identical source. This was a text based on the Marshall Primer except for the Psalms, most of which are in the Rouen version. Neither edition contains the Dirge or the Commendations. In Evensong, where Joye and Marshall had used Psalms 1-3 instead of those prescribed by the use of Sarum, these little Primers follow the Marshall version; but in the regular Psalms —such as the Seven Penitential and the Fifteen Gradual Psalms—it is the Rouen version that is followed, and also in the Psalms of the Passion, with which the Primer portion ends.

Certain features of the text, such as the hymns and the Litany, betray a heavy-handed, somewhat jumbled editing, evincing no definite policy or predilection. Much of the text, except the Psalms, varies uncertainly between those readings that were peculiar to the *Goodly Primer* of 1535 and those derived from the Joye Hortulus. Remembering that Byddell had obtained a patent for six years on his *Goodly Primer*, it is remarkable that this adaptation of his materials should have appeared when it did, unless we assume that Hoskins 150 was not printed until 1541 or 1542. But perhaps, with Cromwell removed from the stage, Byddell's patent rights were considered negligible.

At the beginning of Matins, Psalm 95 is given in the wording of the Redman Primer of 1537 but with the responses of Marshall. Now, Hilsey had used this same combination in his *Manual,* but these undated Primers do not keep to the Hilsey pattern; for the first hymn, which follows immediately, is in the older Sarum tradition, commencing, "The gouernour of the triple engin," etc. Nearly all the remaining hymns, however, are modeled on the Marshall Primer, most of them indeed on the earlier Marshall text or on the Godfray Primer.

In the Litany are several noteworthy peculiarities. The edition of 1543 (the corresponding leaves are missing in Hoskins 150) invokes but few of the saints, and those the more prominent, grouping the rest together (Mary Magdalene, St. Anne, and "the holy matrons"; St. Katherine, St. Margaret, and "the holy virgins"); while, by way of response to these invocations, it uses the unique expression, "Pray with vs," instead of "for vs." This no doubt reflects the much-debated issue of improper veneration of the saints. For the remainder of the Litany, the text is drawn not from Marshall, but from the Gough Primer of 1536, given in much condensed form. For example, at one point in the Litany the Gough Primer with its wretched spelling had read (fol. N2^r):

> That thou vouchsaufe to gyue vnyuersall pees to zesar [i.e., *to Caesar*] & amonge al kyngys vniuersall We pray the to here vs.
>
> That yu vochesaufe to preserue our kyng Henry & all his ayders & helpers. We pray the to heare vs

In Hoskins 150 (fol. P2), and similarly in *S.T.C.* 16030, this portion reads:

> That yu vouchesafe to gyue peace to oure kynge (Henry) [*sic*] and amonge all kynges vniuersall. We praye the to here.

But perhaps the chief interest of this undated Primer (Hoskins 150) lies in its extrinsic or additional material. Here it differs quite considerably from its analogue (*S.T.C.* 16030). In its preliminary pages, the material is drawn mostly from the

Redman edition of 1537, including the Gospel selections and the Commandments as "expounded by Chryste."[12] But when the Lord's Prayer and Commandments are presented farther on (fol. E4), they are given in the 'approved' wording which did not come into vogue until 1538.

Again, at the close of the Primer, after the Psalms of the Passion, we are treated to a bewildering array of "additions," comprising many old favorites both orthodox and reformed, and here concocted with a fine impartiality. We find, for instance, the prayer of Isaiah as given in the Joye Hortulus, along with the *Salve Rex;* and on the other hand we have the "Fifteen O's" and "The maner to lyue well." There is also the "Rule of Charity" from the Gough Primer, and there is the very same assortment of *Prayers of the Byble* that Redman had used in his Primer of 1537. Also we have the Act abrogating certain holidays and the approved form for the bidding of beads (see above, p. 143). In this last-named item, prayers for the King, Henry VIII, are specified but no Queen is mentioned; and the Prince is referred to in the following style (fol. V2ᵛ): "And for the most noble & royal estate of our prynce: Prynce Edwarde." Now this particular style of wording was rather unusual, but is also to be observed in Redman's little booklet on the Lord's Prayer published in 1539 (*S.T.C.* 16819).

Two of these additional items deserve special attention since the name of Robert Copland appears in connection with their background. For example, "The maner to lyue well" was originally translated by Copland from an exhortation by John Quentin (see above, p. 171), and had been included in certain of the Rouen Primers; but in Hoskins 150 the text does not follow these Primers exactly, but has been somewhat abridged, and not too carefully. Again, there is a very unusual version of the "Fifteen O's," followed by several other devout prayers (fol. V5 to X3). The text of these goes clear back to

---

12 See above, p. 142. Hoskins 150 repeats the Redman error in Mark 4 (*S.T.C.* 15997 and 16819) which says that the care of this world and the deceitfulness of riches "choke the worlde" instead of "the worde." But *S.T.C.* 16030 surprises with the reading, "the deceytfulnesse of rychesse cloketh al the worlde" (fol. R6ᵛ).

the edition printed by William Caxton toward the end of his career, about 1491 (*S.T.C.* 20195). Wynkyn de Worde had used this same material in his Primer of 1494 (see above, p. 6), and Redman had printed a slightly modernized version of it in his first Sarum Primer of 1535. In 1536, however, the Rouen Primer introduced a good many alterations in the text of the "Fifteen O's"; while Gough, in his "Paradise of the Soul," had included what appears to be an entirely independent rendering. Nevertheless our little Primer at St. Paul's (Hoskins 150) not only harks back to the very wording of Caxton but also appends the five devout prayers which follow, just as Caxton had done. Now Robert Copland had been in the employ of both Caxton and de Worde. Not only so, but there is a unique edition of this same material which Copland himself printed in 1529 (*S.T.C.* 20196).[13] The colophon of this edition reads:

Here endeth the .XV. OOS. *in* Englysshe *with* diuers other prayers. Emprinted at London in the Flete Strete at the sygne of the Rose Garlande by Robert Copla*n*de. Anno Dni. M.CCCCC .XXIX.

Probably it was from this very booklet that the editor of Hoskins 150 derived his text for these prayers.

It remains to record that, besides the Great Bibles that were beginning to pour forth for use in the churches, a few other books of scriptural content were issued in 1540, thus touching upon the theme of our story. Next to the New Testament, the most popular parts of the Bible for separate reprinting were, first, the Psalter, and second, the writings of Solomon.

Back in 1537, James Nicolson had published in a separate volume "The bokes of Salomon" including the Wisdom of Solomon and Ecclesiasticus as well as Proverbs and Ecclesiastes.[14] For this issue Nicolson used the same text that he had just published in his reprint of the Coverdale Bible. Then in 1540, Robert Redman, following his example, brought forth

13 This little tract of 20 leaves is preserved in the library of St. Mary's College at Blairs, outside of Aberdeen, Scotland. It is bound with eight other religious tracts, all printed by Copland between 1522 and 1531.
14 Not recorded in *S.T.C.*; a unique copy is preserved in the library of St. Paul's Cathedral, London.

a new edition of the Proverbs of Solomon, "Wherunto is added dyuers other Bookes of the Byble" (*S.T.C.* 2753). In addition to those listed above, Redman's volume contained also the Song of Solomon or (as it used to be called) "Salomons Balettes." For the text of his volume Redman drew upon the edition of the Great Bible which he and Petyt had printed for Thomas Berthelet in the preceding April. This little collection must have been among the last products to come from Redman's press, for he passed away about the first of November, 1540, after an honorable career.

During this year Grafton also ventured to bring out a new version of the Psalter (*S.T.C.* 2368).[15] This translation was probably prepared by Myles Coverdale before he left his native land. It was entitled:

The Psalter or boke of Psalmes both in Latyn and Englyshe. wyth a Kalender, & a Table the more eassyer and lyghtlyer to fynde the psalmes contayned therin.

A second title-page adds the information: "Translated in Englyshe out of the comon texte in Latyne, which customably is redde in the churche." The Latin text of the Vulgate is printed in parallel columns with the new translation. But Coverdale's name is not mentioned anywhere in the volume—a sign that Grafton was treading cautiously.

[15] Still another Psalter (*S.T.C.* 2373) has been doubtfully assigned to the year 1540 and to the press of Edward Whitchurch. Recent investigation indicates, however, that this edition, based on the version in the Coverdale Bible, was printed about 1548, either by Nicholas Hill or by John White.

Chapter XVII

Stress and Counter Stress
(1541-1542)

U PON the loss of their patron, Thomas Cromwell, it appears that Grafton and Whitchurch felt the need of some safeguard lest their forthcoming editions of the Great Bible should be repudiated by the King's new advisers. For the title-page of the edition published in November 1540 was careful to announce that the Bible was "Ouersene and perused at the comaundement of the kynges hyghnes by the ryghte reuerende fathers in God, Cuthbert, bysshop of Duresme, and Nicolas bisshop of Rochester." These two prelates were, of course, Cuthbert Tunstall and Nicholas Heath, but there is nothing to show that their supervision was more than nominal; and indeed in later years they disclaimed any connection with this Bible.

Tunstall was a member of the King's Privy Council, as were also Cranmer and Gardiner and the Duke of Norfolk, and the Chancellor, Thomas Audley, as well as a dozen more. This formidable body, endued with fresh vigor and authority, busied itself with the welfare of the realm and also heard complaints involving disloyalty or disobedience to the laws. Stephen Gardiner's party was paramount just then, not only in the Council but likewise in the sessions of Convocation. As for Gardiner himself, the King had recently sent him on a special mission to Regensburg, in Germany, where a so-called 'interim Diet' was to be held the next spring to discuss the troublesome issues that were in dispute between Catholic and Protestant. He was absent for nearly a year on this important business, and during his absence dissension seethed at home.

Before long, Grafton, in spite of his apparent caution, found

221

himself in trouble with the Privy Council. The new Queen, Katherine Howard, had for a tutor one Thomas Smith, who in the latter half of 1540 turned his hand to doggerel verse and put forth a 'ballad' containing derogatory remarks about the late vicegerent, Thomas Cromwell. The latter's partisans willingly took up the gauntlet, finding a spokesman in a pamphleteer named William Gray, who replied to Smith in kind. There ensued an exchange of some half-dozen broadside 'ballads' pro and con, printed by various hands.[1] Among the publishers' names were some already known to us: Richard Bankes, John Gough, John Redman, etc. Finally the Privy Council took cognizance of the affair, and Bankes was called to account inasmuch as his name appeared as the printer of "An answere to mayster Smyth" signed by "W. G." Bankes pleaded that he was not the prime mover in the controversy and laid the blame at the door of Robert Redman (now deceased) and Richard Grafton. Grafton was summoned to appear before the Council and was further charged with having circulated a seditious epistle written by Melanchthon against the Six Articles.[2] On January 6, 1541, he was sentenced to a term in prison, but after he had served some weeks in jail he was released by order of the King. Cranmer no doubt would have been glad to spare him this sentence; but had not Gardiner been abroad at the time, Grafton might not have got off so lightly.

Two things are clear from this episode: first, that there was a kind of tug-of-war going on over the Six Articles between the supporters of orthodoxy and of reform, headed respectively by Gardiner and Cranmer; second, that there existed some sort of fraternal understanding among the publishers of the day. Perhaps the bond that united them was merely of defense against the risk of inquisition; but those printers and booksellers who were aligned with the reformers seem to have

[1] The series is reproduced in facsimile in J. A. Kingdon's *Incidents in the Lives of Thomas Poyntz and Richard Grafton* (London, 1895), p. 84.

[2] After Henry's death, when Edward had come to the throne, this Epistle of Melanchthon was printed in England (*S.T.C.* 17789) apparently for the first time.

known one another's business pretty well and to have employed or assisted one another in various ways. Books occur, for example, printed by Mayler for Gough,[3] or by Bankes for Whitchurch; and it is no accident that works by Erasmus or Taverner were published sometimes by Byddell, sometimes by Robert Redman, sometimes by Grafton or by Richard Bankes; and so on.

We catch hints of what the printers were faced with in those troublous times from the pages of Foxe's *Ecclesiasticall History* (1570) wherein he gathers a list, several pages long, of those who were reported to the Bishop of London (Edmund Bonner) "in the time of the Six Articles" for failure to comply. In the course of this list, arranged according to the parishes of London, we come across these familiar names:

(p. 1377)
    S. Owins Parishe.   *Grafton* and *Whitchurch* suspected not to haue bene confessed.
    S. Butolphes . . . *Iohn Mayler.*   To be a Sacramentarie & a rayler agaynst the Masse.
(p. 1378)
    S. Butolphes . . . *Iohn Mayler, Grocer.*   For callyng the Sacrament of the aultar, the baken God: and for saying, that the Masse was called beyonde the Sea, Misse, for that all is amysse in it.

Possibly these last two were not the same Mayler; but recollecting that Grafton was also a Grocer, it is likely that both entries refer to the printer. On page 1379 we are told of Thomas Lancaster, a priest of the parish of St. Katherine's, who was imprisoned in "the compter in the Poultry" for importing prohibited books; whereupon we read: "Item, *Gough* the Stationer troubled for resorting vnto him."

How much persecution or actual interference resulted from all these complaints we cannot say, but in Gough's case it is clear that he did not escape; for a minute in the proceedings of the Privy Council for January 8, 1541, reads:

---

[3] During 1542 and 1543 Thomas Becon put forth ten different treatises, mostly on scriptural themes, under the pseudonym of Theodore Basille. All of these, together with reprinted editions of the same, were printed by Mayler for Gough (see *S.T.C.*, Nos. 1713-1776, *passim*).

John Gough of London prynt*er* was sent to the Flytt [i.e., *Fleet prison*] for prynting and selling of sedycyous book*es*.

Neither is it likely that anyone as outspoken as the complaints against Mayler would indicate that he was, could escape notice.

When the Six Articles were not involved, the Council might be more considerate. After Grafton was released from prison, he and Whitchurch were in need of additional funds if they were to bring out further editions of the Great Bible, since all the churches in the realm were by no means yet supplied with them as the King's injunctions had required. So the two printers turned to a prosperous citizen of London, Anthony Marler, a member of the Guild of Haberdashers, to underwrite their Bibles. In April, Marler obtained a ruling from the Council on the price at which the new Bibles were to be sold, and on the first of May he appealed to the Council to see to it that a fresh proclamation should be issued reiterating that each church must be provided with a Bible; otherwise he complained that he would lose all he had put into the venture, saying that in such a case

. . . my grete sute, that I have made herin is not only frustrate and voyde, but also being charged as I am with an importune somme of the said bookes now lying on my hande, [I] am undone for ever.

The Council was favorably impressed and on May 6 the new proclamation was issued in the King's name, calling on each church to be provided with a Bible by November first. Accordingly, a new edition of the Great Bible was printed in May. The proclamation itself, incidentally, bore the imprint of Grafton and Whitchurch (*S.T.C.* 7793).

Such activity would seem to betoken Cranmer's influence in the Council, but it should be recalled that Gardiner was still abroad, not returning till September. Also the times were still mightily unsettled. During the summer of 1541 persecutions broke out afresh—against the Catholics for political reasons and against the Protestants for heresy under the Six Articles. The populace knew not what to expect next. The aged Countess of Salisbury, when members of her family were implicated in a plot against the King, was haled out of prison and beheaded. A prominent young nobleman, Thomas Fiennes, Lord Dacre, was executed for riotous conduct. On the other hand, an obscure boy of fifteen, Richard Mekins, who had come under the spell of Barnes's oratory, was reported to the Council for heresy and put to death.

This last was too much for George Joye, who was writing pamphlets from abroad against Gardiner and his party. Joye inveighed especially against the enforcement of celibacy among the clergy and bewailed his own exile as a married priest. In 1541 he put forth three such books under assumed names and with fictitious colophons, which all appear to have been printed at the same press.[4]

Notwithstanding this background of stress, a few new editions of the Primer continued to make their appearance in London. Perhaps the official support given to the circulation of the Great Bible made it look safe to undertake the publication of works of this kind, which were still much in demand.

Thomas Petye, "in Paules church yerde/ at the sygne of the Maydens heade," was evidently intent upon filling the post of Robert Redman in this department; for in 1541 he brought out two Primers, one in Latin and the other in both Latin and English. The latter (*S.T.C.* 16020) is a conservative text "after the vse of Sarum," complete with Epistles and Gospels and the two expositions of Savonarola.[5] But at the outset of this Primer (fol. B1) we are presented with a new statement of

---

[4] These were (1) *S.T.C.* 24217, dated April 27: "A frutefull treatis of Baptyme [*sic*] and the Lordis Souper"; (2) *S.T.C.* 17798, dated August: "A very godly defense/ full of lerning/ defending the mariage of Preistes" (under the assumed name of "Iewes beuchame," translated from Melanchthon); (3) *S.T.C.* 21804, dated August: "The defence of the Mariage of Preistes: Agenst Steuen Gardiner bisshop of Wynchester/ Wylliam Repse bisshop of Norwiche/ and agenst all the bisshops and preistes of that false popisshe secte" (under the assumed name of James Sawtry). It is in the last that Joye lashes out against what he calls the murder of young Richard Mekins.

[5] The title-page of this edition reads: "The prymer in Englysshe and Laten. after the vse of Sarum, set out at length with many goodly prayers, & with the exposicion of Miserere, & In te domine speraui with the Epystles and Gospels throughout the hoole yeare. M.D.XLI. Cum priuilegio ad imprimendum solum." Notice the modern form "at length" in place of the usual "set out a longe." Hilsey was the first to make this change, in his *Manual* of 1539 (*S.T.C.* 16009; see above, p. 184).

the King's pleasure in the matter of the Lord's Prayer and the Commandments, etc. So far I have been able to find no direct antecedent for this pronouncement, yet it has an official sound and may have stemmed from some act of Convocation. It is here worded as follows:

> The kynges hyghnesse greatly tenderynge the welthe of his realme hath suffered heretofore the .Pater noster, Aue, Crede, and the .x commaundementes of god, to be had in ye Englysh tongue. But his grace perceyuynge nowe the great diuersyte of the Translacyons hath wylled them all to be taken vp, and in stede of them hath caused an vniforme translacyon of the sayd Pater noster, Aue, Crede, & .x. commaundementes, to be set forth, as hereafter foloweth, Wyllynge all his louyng subiectes to learn, and vse the same, . . .

The "vniforme translacyon" given in this Primer of Petyt's is no different from the one approved during 1538, which first appeared in the Redman Primer of that year. But this is the earliest *authorization* of it that has come to my notice. The very same statement, in a corrected print, is also incorporated in another Primer of this same period, a Latin edition published by Mayler (*S.T.C.* 16022).[6] The upshot of it, of course, was to debar the use of such booklets on the Paternoster and Commandments as had been published previously by John Byddell.

There has been preserved one copy of a tiny folder of four leaves belonging probably to 1541 or 1542, containing this approved material, along with the alphabet. This little waif, typical of much that has been lost, now reposes in the library of the University of Illinois. Its title no doubt refers to the statement cited above, for it reads:

> The a b c with the Pater noster Aue Credo and .x. commaundementes in Englysshe newly translated and set forth at the kynges moste gracyouse commaundement.
> ⟨ Printed at London in the Old bayly by Richard Lant

6 Another curious feature of this Latin Primer (*S.T.C.* 16022) is its concluding item, an English rendering of "The offyce of all estate" (fol. S7v), wherein the wording is copied, not from Marshall or Hilsey, but from the original Tyndale reading in the "G-H" New Testament, except that now the admonition to "Rulers" is put ahead of the one addressed to "Bysshoppes."

The reverse of the title-page is taken up with five alphabets printed in different styles, two of which have the tag words "Est. Amen" at the end. Then comes the material specified in the title, all standard items of religious education, given in their approved form. The last page is devoted to two rhymed graces, for before and after meals, the latter of which is perhaps appealing enough to deserve quotation:

> Thankes to that lorde that all hath sent
> For this our fode conuenient
> And for his worde/ which is our helth
> And lyfe of soule as scripture telth.

Richard Lant, the printer of this ABC, was an obscure publisher whose name appears in connection with some fifteen or twenty titles. We shall hear of him again briefly in the next chapter.[7]

Presumably it was also in 1541 that Edward Whitchurch brought out an interesting edition of the Psalms in English (*S.T.C.* 2374), bearing the following title:

☞ The Psalter of Dauid in english truly translated out of Latyn Euery Psalme hauynge his argument before, declaryng brefely thentent & substaunce of the whole Psalme. Whervnto is annexed in thende certayne godly prayers thorowe-oute the whole yere, commenly called collettes.

This, of all things, is a faithful reprint of Joye's earlier version of 1530. Godfray had likewise reprinted it in 1534 or 1535, but now the title omits all mention of the text of "Feline" on which it was based. Moreover, the volume is now enlarged by the addition of certain collects and canticles. Certainly it is astonishing to find Joye's workmanship being published in London at this particular juncture. It argues that Whitchurch must have been feeling pretty sure of his ground now that the Great Bible had been given a new lease of life, or else that he

---

[7] On the subject of contemporary ABC's, see Butterworth, "Early Primers for the Use of Children" in the *Papers* of the Bibliographical Society of America for 1949 (vol. 43, p. 374).

calculated no one would recall that the version had been
Joye's.[8]

The collects at the end of the Psalter are of special interest,
partly because they were reprinted in at least two Primers belonging to this same period, and partly because many of them
found their way, in revised form, into the Book of Common
Prayer later on. They cover the whole year of the church calendar and consist of a short prayer, some four or five lines
long, appropriate to the day observed, preceded by a brief
'versicle' or 'introit' composed of two lines from the Bible,
mostly from the Book of Psalms. The Bible excerpts do not
conform to the wording of any published version but show
originality of treatment, as do the prayers likewise. These collects are translated from a Latin source,[9] but no translator's
name is appended. The style of the writing, however, suggests
that they may have been done by Taverner. The opening verse
of Psalm 93 is rendered in this form (fol. P4):

> The Lorde reygneth, and hath put on beautyfulnesse.
> The Lorde hath put on strength & hath gyrded hym selfe.

The following specimen is typical, intended for the first Sunday after Easter (fol. P7):

> Verse. Our Easter Christ is offered
>   Let vs feast in vnleuended [sic] breade of purenes
>   and truth
> O God whyche alwayes makest thy churche mery & glad wyth some
> newe byrth, which hast made this paschall sacrament for a couenaunt
> of mans reconciliation gyue to our soules, that we maye folowe in
> effecte that we celebrate in profession, thorough the Lorde Iesus Christ.

---

[8] In this or the following year (1542) Whitchurch also brought out a sort of
companion volume entitled "The bokes of Salomon, namely: Prouerbia. Ecclesiastes.
Sapientia, and Ecclesiasticus, or Iesus the sonne of Syrach." This item is misdated in
S.T.C. (No. 2754); it was printed "in London in the olde Iury," whither Whitchurch
had removed after separating from Grafton, perhaps on account of the latter's im-
prisonment. For the text of this edition Whitchurch reprinted the Coverdale version
which Nicolson had issued in 1537. It is remarkable that neither in his Psalter nor
in his Solomon did Whitchurch utilize the version of the Great Bible which he helped
to produce.

[9] For the corresponding Latin see J. H. Blunt, *The Annotated Book of Common
Prayer,* under *Collects* (edition of 1899, pp. 243 ff.).

A more familiar example is the collect "For peace" (fol. Q7):[10]

> Verse. Let peace be in thy strength
> And aboundaunce in thy towres
>
> O God of whome holy desyres good purposes, & good workes haue theyr begynnynge gyue to thy seruauntes that peace whych ye worlde can not gyue, that both our hertes may be gyuen to thy commaundementes, and also be quyete by thy protection wythout the feare of enemyes.

Two other points may be singled out for special attention. First, the reader may remember that Grafton had printed at the end of his Primer of 1540 a "prayer for trewe fayth" (see above, p. 211). The material for this is found to correspond to the collects given by Whitchurch for the second and third Sundays after Trinity; only, in the Whitchurch Psalter the rendering is now refurbished, so that the first of them appears now in this form (fol. P8ᵛ):

> Verse. I wyll loue the O God my strength
> The Lorde is my sure hold, and refuge
>
> O Lorde let vs haue perpetuall loue and also feare of thy holy name, for thou neuer takest thy gouernaunce from them, whome yu enstructest in the suertie of thy loue, thorowe our Lorde.

Second, the collect for St. Bartholomew's Day ends in this unusual fashion (fol. Q4):

> . . . graunt to thy church we beseche the, to loue yt, that he beleued, & to preach that, that he taught: tho.

Now this final "tho" was evidently intended for an abbreviation of the familiar closing words, "thorowe our Lorde" (as above); but at any rate, when these collects were reprinted in current editions of the Primer, this same "tho" duly reappears at the end of this particular passage without enlargement or explanation. The printers were copyists and spared no time to ask questions.

Two editions of the Primer, distinctive for their reproduc-

---

10 For earlier renditions of this same collect, see above, p. 93.

tion of these collects, survive in what are apparently unique copies. One (*S.T.C.* 16021) is at the Folger Library in Washington; the other (Hoskins 156), lacking several leaves at the beginning and the end, is at Cambridge University. A brief notice of them will suffice.

The Folger edition (*S.T.C.* 16021) is undated save for the almanac, which gives the Easter date for 1541 at the top of the list. Its title, standing above a table of contents, reads as follows:

A Prymar of Salisbery vse/ set out a longe in Englyshe and Latyn, and a prayer for euery sondaye and holy day in the yere/ besydes these folowynge. [Referring, of course, to the contents.]

It is significant that the collects are featured in the title, which publishers often used to advertise their wares. At the end of the Primer section (fol. Y8ᵛ) there is a colophon, bringing forward the name of a new publisher: "¶Prynted in Pauls churche yarde by Roberte Toye." Toye was apparently a bookseller, like Gough, rather than a printer, and it is thought that this volume, his first Primer, may have been printed for him at the press of John Herford, who succeeded to Nicholas Bourman.

Though drawn largely from the text of Robert Redman's edition of 1538, Toye's first Primer departs from strict Sarum usage in that it employs the same 'lessons' in Matins which Hilsey had used, in which passages from the Scripture were substituted for the more usual addresses to the Virgin. This Primer also contains both the prayer *Salve Regina* (in Compline) and its counterpart, the *Salve Rex*, which Redman did not give. The volume concludes with the expositions of Savonarola and a section of Epistles and Gospels.

The other Primer, preserved at Cambridge, is hard to identify since it lacks both title and colophon.[11] It is not identical with Toye's and seems to adhere more closely to the Sarum tradition. It contains a few of the *Prayers of the Byble* as some

---

[11] Listed by Hoskins as No. 156, it is unrecorded in *S.T.C.*

of the Rouen Primers did, and its printing of the Whitchurch collects discloses quite a few errata, which would lead to the conclusion that it was probably the later printing.

There is yet another feature which these two editions of the Primer also have in common. It is a new item occurring toward the end of the Primer and comprising five prayers under the heading:

Dyuers goodly and necessarie prayers to be sayde moste specyally at the houre of deathe.

These hail from various sources, and some of them we have met before or will meet again. The first of them is based on a Latin prayer by Erasmus and begins, "O Lorde Iesu, whiche arte the onely healthe of all men lyuynge." It is the only one of the series that contemplates the approach of death. The next is the very same prayer of thanksgiving to the heavenly Father that Grafton had printed near the end of his Primer of 1540 (see above, p. 211). Then there is a biblical prayer for meekness and chastity, drawn from the 23rd chapter of Ecclesiasticus. This was an old favorite, though not heretofore included in the Primers. Brunfels had used it in his Latin *Precationes;* Redman had printed an English version in his *Prayers of the Byble;* and Taverner had included it in his volume, *Epitome of the Psalmes.* Significantly, it is Taverner's version which is now reproduced in the Primers.

It was also to Taverner that these two Primers were indebted for the most interesting of these final items, namely, a prayer which in both editions is entitled, "⟨For a swete and yll harte. Psalmus .xli." Now this too was copied (or rather miscopied) from the *Epitome;* for in 1539 Taverner, in treating of the 41st Psalm, had prefixed the title, "For a swete and styll herte." The same misprint in both of the Primers shows them to be interrelated in their text. One excerpt from the prayer itself will exhibit Taverner's individuality of style:

. . . delyuer me from enemyes, which busye them selues to noye me that they reioise not ouer me. Herby I may vnderstande thy good wyll towardes me, in that thou vouchsauest to cut myne enemyes combes: soo that they triumphe not ouer me, whych had thought to haue gyuen me a foule fall.

To give a person "a fall" is still intelligible, but to "cut their combs" is now obsolete; it meant to disable or to overthrow, and was doubtless borrowed from the cock-fighting that was then a part of fashionable entertainment.

When Bishop Gardiner returned to England in the autumn of 1541 after fruitless disputation with other theologians at Regensburg, he was informed that Cranmer had been showing great leniency toward certain prebendaries of Canterbury who were expounding Lutheran views. This aggravated the long climactic struggle between Cranmer and Gardiner for control of the King's religious establishment. Henry, however, was shrewd enough to play one off against the other and to act as umpire without committing himself irrevocably to either side. He preferred to be able to utilize the abilities of both men; and so long as both were loyal to the King, he was minded to get rid of neither. That Gardiner's party eventually came to grief several years later, whereas Cranmer officiated at the coronation of Henry's only son, was due rather to political than to religious pressures.

But toward the end of 1541 the orthodox party suffered a setback or a decline of prestige when it became known that the Queen, Katherine Howard, had been guilty of immoral behavior. Henry was greatly affected by the news of this when the Archbishop communicated it to him early in November. When fuller investigation had brought out the questionable conduct of the Queen, at least prior to her marriage with Henry, there was no other way but to get rid of her, and she was beheaded on February 15, 1542.

Meanwhile there were developments concerning the Bible. The royal proclamation of May 1541 had stipulated that Bibles were to be in all the churches by All Saints' Day; but the order met with only dilatory compliance, so that fresh editions of the Great Bible were issued in November and December. The proclamation had also warned the people to be reverent in their public reading of the Bible and not to interfere with the regular services in the church. But feelings were still running high, and there was enough disorder and excitement to persuade some of the clergy that the status of Bible-reading ought to be restricted. Those who opposed a vernacular Bible altogether were now insistent that the Great Bible should be revised, and this question was laid before Convocation early in 1542. On February 3, it was voted to undertake a new translation of the Bible, one that would be more orthodox in tone. But Cranmer still wielded enough influence with the King to be able to announce to Convocation on March 10 that it was the King's pleasure that the proposed revision should be examined by the two universities of Oxford and Cambridge. The upshot was that, once sidetracked, nothing was done about the project at all.

On the other hand, no further editions of the Great Bible were published during Henry's reign. We gain some insight into the political tug-of-war going on behind the scenes from the fact that, despite the absence of any new editions, Anthony Marler was granted a royal patent for exclusive printing of the Bible for the next four years.[12] This was on March 12, just two days after the King had referred the matter to the Universities. No doubt Marler and his friends felt that they had scored a notable victory, for the patent read in part:

We late you wytt that we, for certayne Causes convenyent, of our Grace especiall, have Gyven and Graunted to our Welbelovyd Subject Antony Marlar Citezyn and Haberdasher of our Citie of London only to Prynte the Bible in our Englishe Tonge, Auctorysed or hereaftre to be auctorysed by Us, hymselfe or his Assignes,

And We Command that no maner Person withyn thies our Domynyons shall Prynte the saide Byble, or any parte therof, within the space of Foure Yeres next ensuynge the Pryntyng of the said Booke by our saide Subject or his Assignes, . . .

This certainly sounded as if the Bible was about to be published again, but it was a hollow triumph.

12 See Rymer's *Foedera* (vol. XIV, p. 745). The patent is reprinted in modernized form in Anderson's *Annals of the English Bible* (edition of 1845), vol. II, p. 152.

Somewhat earlier, Edmund Bonner, who succeeded Stokesley as Bishop of London, had issued an admonition to those
desiring to make use of the Bibles set up in the churches. He
sought to reinforce the demand in the King's proclamation
that quietness should be maintained during divine service.
Bonner asked in particular

> ... that no number of people be specially congregate therefor to make
> a multitude, and that no exposition be made thereupon otherwise than
> is declared in the book itself; and that especial regard be had, that no
> reading thereof be used aloud, and with noise in the time of any divine
> service or sermon, or that in the same be used any disputation, conten-
> tion, or any other misdemeanour; ...

Bonner likewise issued a set of episcopal injunctions and
followed these with an up-to-date list of prohibited books in
1542.[13] Among the latter we come upon this item: "The Preface made in the English Prymmers, by Marshall." Evidently,
by this time, the preface in the Marshall Primers had been
traced to its source and branded as one of Luther's stepchildren. The entire text of the *Goodly Primer* is not specifically
forbidden, only the preface. Of Marshall himself we hear no
more.

The demand for English Primers was unflagging; but the
publishers now seem to strike a note of caution by reverting to
the older texts in the Sarum tradition and by printing the
Latin in parallel columns with the English. Thus Thomas
Petyt publishes a dated Primer (*S.T.C.* 16028) with this title:

> ⁋ The Prymer in Englysshe and Laten, after the vse of Sarum set
> out at length with many goodly prayers With the Epystles and Gospels
> throughout the hoole yeare. M.D.XLij.

But the volume is in no way distinguished, being largely a reprint of the Redman Primer of 1537.

At least two other editions appeared this same year, or
rather, two issues of the same edition; for although the titles

---

[13] The several documents issued by Bonner are recorded in G. Burnet, *History of
the Reformation of the Church of England* (see edition of 1865, vol. IV, pp. 509-
519). Bonner's list is long and also mentions "The Preface before the Psalter in
English." Neither Whitchurch's edition of this Psalter nor the earlier printing by
Godfray had included Joye's original preface.

and colophons designate two different publishers, the contents of the volumes are identical, word for word. The printer's name, as given, is either Robert Toye or William Bonham. Copies evidently were prepared for one or the other of these two stationers.[14] The actual printer's name does not appear. Though the books are tolerably well printed, the editing is careless. They are entitled:

⁋ The Prymer in Englyshe, and Latyn wyth the Epystles and Gospelles: of euery Sonday, & holye daye in the yere, and also the exposycion vpon Miserere mei deus. wyth many other prayers.

Again the text of this edition is conservative, based almost entirely on the Rouen Primer of 1536. It is perhaps of interest to note that in the exposition of Savonarola on the 31st Psalm (fol. S8ᵛ), where earlier prints had read, "The Pater noster belongeth to all," this edition reads, "The lordes prayer belongeth to all"—a sign of the growing influence of English speech in the services of the church.[15]

Among the "other prayers" mentioned in the title we find the prayer of Erasmus to be said at the hour of death (fol. N8) but not the rest of the series (see above, p. 231). Then near the end of the Primer (fol. T2ᵛ) there is a new departure; we are presented with "⁋A prayer for the reader, expressynge after what sorte scrypture shuld be red." This had originally been incorporated in one of Grafton's editions of the New Testament (S.T.C. 2843) containing the version of the Great Bible, but (so far as I know) had not appeared before in any of the Primers. Couched in a style suggestive of Taverner's, it is strongly anti-Roman in its tone, as may be judged from these brief excerpts, appearing thus in the Primer:

... Graunte vs mooste fauorable Father, thys one of the greateste gyftes that euer thou gauest to mankynde, the knoweledge of thy holy wyl, and glad tydynges of our saluacyon, this great whyle opressed wyth ye

14 Listed in S.T.C. as 16026 and 16027. It is more than likely that another copy in the John Rylands Library (S.T.C. 16025) is of this same edition, but its title is wanting and it lacks the section of Epistles and Gospels.

15 Earlier uses of the term "the lordes prayer" occur in Byddell's little booklet of 1537 (S.T.C. 16820) and in Taverner's "Svmme or Pith of the .150. Psalmes." See the writer's article on this subject in The Library Chronicle of the University of Pennsylvania, vol. XVIII, p. 24 (1952).

tyrannye of thy aduersary of Rome, and hys fautors [i.e., *favorers*], and kepte close vnder his Latin letters, & nowe at lengthe prououlgate [*sic;* for *promulgate*] publyshed, and set at liberty by thy grace, powered [i.e., *poured*] into ye herte of thy supreme power our prince . . . Graunte Lorde vnto our most gracyous gouernoure & kynge that as he hathe gracyously begonne, and hetherto hathe thorowe thy mercye, hadde prosperous successe, in settinge forthe of thy holy worde (a seruyce, no lesse acceptable to the, than profytable to vs) that he maye vertuouslye acheue thys hys hye and goodlye enterprise, . . .

Suitable enough perhaps in 1539, this eloquent plea in behalf of the Great Bible wears a wry look in 1542, and comes unpropitiously into the Primers at a time when the publication of the Bible was about to be suspended for the rest of Henry's reign.

Chapter XVIII

Steps Towards Uniformity
(1543-1545)

THOUGHTFUL interpretation of the available evidence indicates that, in spite of the royal patent issued to Anthony Marler in 1542, the publication of the Great Bible, or portions thereof, was interrupted until November 1546, when Whitchurch brought out a dated edition of the New Testament. If Cranmer and his followers were able to prevent an orthodox reaction toward a less readable version, Gardiner and the conservative bishops were able to stifle the circulation of the Bible itself. But there seems to have been no similar interruption of the Primers.

In certain of the writings of Thomas Becon, published in 1542 and 1543, we find a selected Psalm or a chapter from the Bible included incidentally; but even this sort of thing was apparently frowned upon, for we hear of no publication of any of Becon's works between 1543 and 1549. He too was one of the Cambridge reformers, though younger than the rest.

Aside from the Primers, the nearest thing we have to a volume of scriptural content was a book of prayers chosen out of the Bible, which Grafton printed without any date (*S.T.C.* 20200) but which is probably to be assigned to 1543 or 1544. What appears to be the only surviving copy is now in the Huntington Library in California and is entitled:

Praiers of holi fathers, Patryarches, Prophetes, Iudges, Kynges, and renowmed men and wemen of eyther testamente.

As the title would imply, this unusual volume harks directly back to Robert Redman's *Prayers of the Byble* (see above, Chapter VIII). Like that, it is divided into six groups

237

of prayers, of which the first five cover almost precisely the same ground as in Redman's edition; that is, the same prayers recur in the same sequence with very few exceptions. But in general Grafton's edition does not reproduce the unique version that Redman employed. Instead, Grafton plainly preferred the text used by Taverner in his *Epitome of the Psalmes* (see above, p. 197).[1] Where the two books coincided in their material, this one was Grafton's preference, while for other passages not to be found in Taverner he apparently used the Coverdale Bible as a basis, reëditing the text in the light of Redman's volume.

For instance, in what Grafton calls "The prayer of Ionas when he was as yet in the fisshes bely," the Coverdale version, modeled upon Tyndale's *Prophete Ionas,* read as follows (Jonah 2:5):

The waters compased me, euen to the very soule: the depe laye aboute me, and the wedes were wrapte aboute myne heade.

In Redman's volume (fol. E4ᵛ) this passage read:

. . . waters haue compassed me rounde about euen to my very soule, and the depnes haue walled me in, the mayne see hath hylled my heed.

This was poor stuff, and Grafton's editor, sensing that "hylled" was then an obsolescent word, and perhaps knowing that the Vulgate Latin said nothing here about weeds, rendered the verse thus (fol. D4ᵛ):

The waters compassed me, euen to ye very soule, the depe laie aboute me and the snrges [*sic;* for *surges*] couered my hedde: . . .

There are other indications of reëditing. Certain errors are corrected, as where Redman had printed a prayer from Judith under the heading "Iudicum [i.e., *Judges*], the .xiii. chap." And in the sixth group, entitled "Certaine Praiers shorte and of dyuers sortes," Grafton's edition contains more excerpts from the Old Testament and fewer from the New than Redman had used.

---

[1] Specific evidence of dependence on Taverner's text is found in the prayer from the second and third chapter of Baruch, which is cited in both volumes as "Baruch 23"; whereas Redman had it correctly as "Baruch 2, 3."

Yet his indebtedness to Redman is unmistakable in at least two respects: First, the group composed of selected Psalms, after coming by progressive stages to the 150th, has Psalms 35 and 37 appended to it, just as in Redman's volume, although the same translation is not used in both books. Second, Grafton concludes his book with the "Testament of Moyses" (Deuteronomy 32) which Redman had used as a prefatory chapter; but this time Grafton reprints the Redman version without change.

The most striking bit of new material is the insertion of three Psalms (12, 20, and 83) near the end of Grafton's book under the heading, "Psalmes of David against tirauntes and persecutours of Goddes worde" (fol. N6^v). Here again we encounter suspicious traces of the hand of Richard Taverner; for the 83rd Psalm opens as follows:

Holde not thy tongue oh God, kepe not styll sylence: refrayne not thyselfe Oh God. For lo, thyne enemies a hurly burly: and they that hate thee: lyfte vp theyr heade.

This is not unlike Coverdale save for the telltale intrusion of "hurly-burly" where Coverdale in his smoother manner had written "make a murmurynge."

The colophon points to a new outlet for Grafton's publications:

¶ Imprinted in London by Richard Grafton. Cum priuilegio adimprimendum solum. These bookes are to bee solde at the Weste doore of P[aul]es in London. By Wyllyam Tylotson.

Several books of this period were assigned by both Grafton and Whitchurch to be sold by William Tillotson.[2] Why, we do not know; unless it had to do with the changing fortunes of this pair of printers as the prevailing winds of domestic politics shifted their direction during Henry's régime. Indeed, one might almost say that Grafton's career was like a sensitive barometer to pressures of his time.

[2] Tillotson's name may be of some help in dating the publication, for all of the dated volumes that were assigned to him belong either to 1543 or 1544. His name appears in connection with the following items: *S.T.C.* 393, 3327, 11968, 15835, 20116, 20200, 22129, 23712. The collation of *S.T.C.* 20200 is: A-O^8, P^4. The Huntington copy lacks fols. H1, H8, I1 and I8.

Robert Redman's old shop "at the sygne of the George" had been taken over by another printer, William Middleton; and it was perhaps about 1543 that the latter put forth a tiny unbound, undated booklet entitled: "⟨A boke of prayers called y*e* ordynary fassyon of good lyuynge." The Folger Library possesses what is probably a unique copy.[3] The only item of its contents relevant to our subject is an old friend, "The prayer of Salomon," which appears therein not so much in a new version as in a paraphrase, as if the publisher were chary of trespassing in the realm of translated Scripture. It now reads (fol. B5):

O lorde great ryches: or extreme pouerte gyue me nat: but prouyde for me in the meane: accordinge to thy wyl & pleasure for by hauyng the one I shal forget the, & by hauynge the other I shalbe dryuen to forsake the.

As to the Primers, we have already had occasion to describe the volume published by Richard Kele, listing the year 1543 at the beginning of its almanac (see above, p. 216). The colophon of this volume, undated, read:

⟨ Imprynted at London by Rycharde Kele dwellynge at the longe shoppe in the poultre vnder s. Myldredes churche.

This Primer will be recalled as a small book, seventeen lines to the page, comprising a variety of materials, a large part of which was drawn from the editions of Marshall and Joye.

In 1543 Thomas Petyt also put out still another Primer "at the sygne of the maydens heade" (*S.T.C.* 16029). This represented the conservative Sarum tradition, being essentially a reprint, and nothing about the volume need detain us here. Yet these two editions—Petyt's and Kele's—exemplify anew the marked divergence in materials that characterized the output of English Primers even as late as 1543.

Our story now turns to the growing desire on the part of King and clergy to provide a standard and uniform Primer that should be regular in its theology as well as in its form.

---

[3] Not listed in *S.T.C.*, the booklet comprises 18 leaves with a colophon "by Wyllyam Myddylton."

The first need, of course, was to agree on some platform of theology. This was intended to have been accomplished in the issuance of the Ten Articles of 1536 and in the Bishops' Book of 1537. But events had disavowed the stated purpose of the Ten Articles "to stablyshe christen quietnes and vnitie"; the Six Articles had displaced the Ten, and it was now incumbent on the clergy to revise their statement of doctrine. As early as 1540 this need was recognized, and Cranmer had circulated a questionnaire among the bishops to determine their views of disputed points. The ensuing consultations were long drawn out, but at last in the spring of 1543 a committee was at work drawing up a new formulation of the old doctrines. Most of this work was entrusted to four men in particular, Bishops Thirlby of Westminster, Heath of Rochester, Gardiner of Winchester, and Archbishop Cranmer. The King was duly impressed with the gravity of the work; glad to be consulted on matters of doctrine, he sometimes took a hand in the dissertations.

All these developments were not unknown to Parliament, which reconvened on the 22nd of January and sat until May 12. They too were animated by the zeal for orthodoxy and uniformity. The foremost statute enacted at this session enjoined further restrictions on the reading of religious books. Bible-reading in public was disapproved, and even in private it was limited to those having some background of gentility or education. In particular, the writings of William Tyndale were stringently prohibited from being bought or sold or read. This led to some extraordinary provisions in the statute which wholly ignore the fact that the Great Bible itself was based in large part on the work of Tyndale. Primers also were specifically exempted from the provisions of the act.

Since repeated reference to the Primers brings this whole statute into the focus of our history, it will be well to cite actual excerpts defining more exactly what the act of 1543 provided.[4] Among other provisions, the new act specified

4 First printed by Berthelet, June 1, 1543 (*S.T.C.* 9407).

... that all maner of bookes of the olde and newe testament in english, being of the crafty, false, and vntrue translation of Tindal, and all other bookes and writynges in the englishe tongue, teachyng or comprisyng any matters of christen religion, articles of the fayth, or holy scripture, or any part of them, contrary to that doctrine, which . . . shalbe set forthe by his hyghnes, . . . shalbe . . . clerely and vtterly abolished, extinguished, and forbydden, . . .

Prouided alwayes, that the bibles and new testamentes in englysshe, not being of Tindalles translations, shall stand in force, and not be comprised in this abolition or acte.

The following list of books, printed before 1540, was likewise specifically exempted from the act: "proclamations, iniunctions, translations of the Pater noster, the Aue Maria, and the Crede, the psalters, prymers, prayers, statutes and lawes of the realme, cronicles, Canturbury tales, Chaucers bookes, Gowers bookes, and stories of mennes lyues."

Permission to read the Bible in their own homes was granted to "euery nobleman and gentylman being a householder" and "euery marchant man being a householder, and occupieng the feat of marchaundise" and "euery noble woman and gentilwoman." For the rest, "no women, nor artificers, prentises, iorneymen, seruinge men of the degrees of yomen or vnder, husband men, nor labourers" were allowed to read the Bible either privately or openly. But here again an exception was made concerning "the psalters, primers, Pater noster, Aue and Crede in englysh, and all suche bookes and writynges whiche be aboue specyally named"; these might be read or taught by every person in his own home,— "So they do the same quietlye, and wythoute disturbance of good ordre."

From all this it is apparent that the lawmakers were finding it difficult to know where to draw the line between what was and what was not approved reading! Small wonder, then, that the publishers, as well as the general populace, were perplexed. Between Gardiner's determination that heresy should be extirpated and Cranmer's insistence upon sufficient reservations to guarantee that all that had been gained would not be lost, the law was so encumbered with doubtful meanings that only the Council, interpreting the statute according to what appeared to be the King's pleasure and purpose, could really decide what was illegal.

The minutes of the Privy Council for April and May disclose these pertinent entries concerning printers and booksellers whose names are already familiar to us:[5]

(April 8, 1543)

Whitchurche, Beddle [i.e., Byddell], Grafton, Middleton, Maylour, Petye [i.e., Petyt], Lant, and Kele, printers, for printing off suche bokes as wer thowght to be unlawfull, contrary to the proclamation made on that behalff, wer committed unto prison.

(April 22)

Beddell, Myddleton, Kele, Lant, and Maylar, printers, having been committed unto the Fleete, wer this day delivered and bounde by recognisance as hereafter ensueth.

Their "recognisance" is thereupon recorded as obligating them to make in writing a true declaration of

. . . what nomber off bookes and ballettes they have bowght wythin thiese iij yeres last past, and what they have sowlde in grosse, and what marchauntes they know to have browght in to the Realme any Englisshe bookes of ill matter.

By recourse to such means the Council could spread its dragnet to include fresh suspects.

(April 26)

Beddle, Myddleton, Lant, Kele and Maylor browght in this daye theyre certificat in writing according to theyre recognisance taken off them the xxij day off April.

(May 2)

The Kinges plesor was declared towching the dismissing out off the Towre off Thomas Wiatt, . . . and off Grafton and Whitchurche out off the Fleete.

Concerning Thomas Petyt nothing definite is said, but he must have been released all in due time, as he printed other Primers the following year. As for Grafton and Whitchurch, they appear to have been citizens of sufficient consequence so that

[5] See *Acts of the Privy Council of England*, New Series, edited by J. R. Dasent, vol. I (London, 1890).

the King was led to believe that they could be of some professional service to him.

At length, May 29, 1543, Thomas Berthelet, the King's
printer, published the book that had been so long preparing;
it was entitled:

A Necessary Doctrine and ervdition for any Christen man, sette
furthe by the kynges maiestie of Englande &c.

A suitable preface was prepared in the King's name—quite
likely by his own hand—and the volume became known as the
'King's Book' in contradistinction to the previous 'Bishops'
Book.' It went through a number of editions in a short time
(*S.T.C.* 5168-5177) as befitted so important a pronouncement.
It is not requisite to our present history for us to delve into
its theological propositions; suffice it to say that it set up a
standard of religious belief and worship representative of its
own particular period.[6] It might have been of more permanent
significance had its sponsor lived a great while longer; but
when Henry departed from the stage in 1547 the 'King's
Book' declined with him, and in Edward's brief reign it was
but little regarded.

Then too Henry had other matters on his mind beside religion and conformity. His realm had been involved in wars
with Ireland and Scotland. He thought to settle the troubles
in Ireland by assuming the title of King of Ireland, which he
did in January 1542, but a few years later they broke out
afresh. At the beginning of June 1543 he patched up a peace
with Scotland, but this too lasted for only a few years. Then
no sooner had he thus made a truce with Scotland than he
embarked upon a war with France.

Moreover, on July 12, 1543, he took unto him his sixth and
last wife, Catharine Parr, a devout woman of moderate views
who, when she married the King, was already twice a widow
at the age of thirty-two. She stood loyally by the King, sup-

---

6 The religious aspects of the 'King's Book' have been treated in a number of
works. For discussion of the modifications made in comparison with the 'Bishops'
Book,' see for example E. G. Rupp, *Studies in the Making of the English Protestant
Tradition* (Cambridge, Eng., 1949), p. 149; and H. M. Smith, *Henry VIII and the
Reformation* (London, 1948), p. 375.

porting him in his wars, tending him in his sickness, and looking out for the interests of his children.

On August 2, 1543, Berthelet printed a royal proclamation announcing the war with France. To make this palatable to the populace it had to be given the color of a religious crusade against the Turk.[7] Nothing was said of Henry's alliance with Emperor Charles V against the King of France; instead the opening of the proclamation was couched in these terms:

For as moche as by credyble meanes it hath bene declared to the kynges maiestie that the frenche kynge . . . hath not onely by a longe tyme and season ayded the great Turke, common ennemye to christendome, [etc.]

Though not a Protestant herself, the new Queen was sympathetic toward those who favored the "New Learning." Her influence, fortunately, was on the side of moderation; for earlier in the year persecutions for heresy had flared up again. One of the King's agents had uncovered notorious heresies among the citizens of Windsor, three of whom were burned at the stake. The evidence pointed to possible incrimination of certain members of the royal household. Through Catharine's mediation the King was brought to view these charges in a tolerant light and even to express concern over the sad lot of those humble citizens of Windsor who had suffered death. Yet the law under which they were condemned was allowed to stand.

The feud between Gardiner and Cranmer also broke out afresh. The latter's secretary tells the story of how Gardiner and his party sought to entrap the Archbishop in connection with an examination into charges of heresy alleged to be rampant in the archdiocese of Canterbury; and how the King, being apprised of Cranmer's alleged heresies, viewed the

[7] How popular this device was can be gauged perhaps from the wording of the title of the 1542 edition of one of Becon's religious treatises (S.T.C. 1735) which read: "The new pollecye of warre, wherin is declared not only how ye mooste cruell Tyraunt the great Turke may be ouercome, but also all other enemies of the Christen publique weale." Again, in Grafton's Praiers of holi fathers the heading over the prayer from II Chronicles 14 is "In warres againste Turkes and inuadours, the prayer of kyng Asa." This was taken over from Taverner's Epitome of the Psalmes. See H. C. White, Tudor Books of Private Devotion (1951), p. 135.

charge indulgently. Then when the examination had back-fired, one of its chief instigators, a relative of Gardiner's, was seized and put to death for treason, for denying the royal supremacy as head of the Church of England. This conspiracy was probably maturing during 1543 and 1544; and from that time on, Cranmer's position was never seriously in danger as long as Henry lived.

The Archbishop himself during this period was meditating a plan whereby the forms of worship in the English Church could be simplified and made more uniform and at the same time be celebrated in the English tongue. The ultimate outcome of this labor was the Book of Common Prayer, but the intermediate steps included an approved form for rehearsing the Litany in English as well as an authorized edition of the Primer. It may be that while considering these projects Cranmer remembered the usefulness of Grafton and of Whitchurch, for on January 28, 1544, a royal patent was issued vesting in them the sole rights to print editions of various service books used in the King's realm. The patent (as reprinted in Rymer's *Foedera*) reads:

We doo you to understand, that where in tymes past it hathe been usually accustomed that thies Bookes of Divine Service, that is to say, the *Masse Booke,* the *Graill,* the *Antyphoner,* the *Himptuall* [i.e., the Hymnal], the *Portans,* and the Prymer, bothe in Latyne and in Englyshe of *Sarum use,* for the Province of Canterbury have been Prynted by Strangers in other and strange Countreys . . . We of our Grace especiall have Graunted and Geven Privilege to our welbiloved Subjects *Richard Grafton* and *Edward Whitchurch* Citezeins of London, that they and their Assignes and noon other Person nor Persons saving the said *Richard* and *Edward* and their Assignes onely, have Libertie to Prynte the Bookes abovesaid . . . whiche either at this present Daye arre in use or hereafter shal be auctorysed for *Sarum use* within any parte of oure Realmes or Domynions, . . . within the space of Seven Years next ensuing the Printing of every suche Booke or Bookes, so Printed by our seid Subjects . . . Witness our self at *Westminster,* the twenty eighth Day of Januarye.

Apparently it was under the terms of this patent that Grafton and Whitchurch brought out their 1544 edition of the

Latin Breviary after the use of Sarum (known also as a Porti-forium—*S.T.C.* 15835—or a "Portans") . Yet it is to be re-marked that when the new Litany in English was ready for the press, the first issue seems to have been published by Thomas Berthelet, the King's printer, although other edi-tions followed from the press of Petyt and of Grafton.[8]

When Cranmer's English Litany first appeared, under date of May 27, 1544, it was in connection with an Exhortation to Prayer, and was entitled:

An exhortation vnto prayer, thoughte mete by the kinges maiestie, and his clergy, to be read to the people in euery church afore pro-cessyons. Also a Letanie with suffrages to be said or song in the tyme of the said processyons.

The custom of observing special holydays with an outdoor re-ligious procession headed by the clergy, with the parishioners chanting appropriate responses, was soon to give way to the use of the Litany within doors as part of the church service; so we need spend no time here on the prescribed Exhortation to Prayer for use on such special occasions. The setting up of a standard form for the English Litany was, however, of great importance; for the Litany thus compiled by Cranmer became the regular usage and was adopted not alone in the Primer of 1545 but also in the Book of Common Prayer, where it per-sists to this day with certain modifications.

We have already noted how an English version of the Litany was incorporated in the Sarum Primer first printed by Red-man in 1535 (see above, p. 93) and how it was adapted and amplified in the *Goodly Primer* of the same year (see p. 111). Compared with those earlier forms, Cranmer's composition achieves a literary excellence that is still generally acknowl-

---

8 One of the few emendations discoverable in Berthelet's editions of the Litany may serve as a clue to the sequence of their publication: In *S.T.C.* 10620, dated May 27, one petition concerning the King reads, "That it may please the to rule his hart in thy faithe, feare, and hole"; in *S.T.C.* 10621, of the same date, this was corrected to "fayth, feare, and hope"; whereas in *S.T.C.* 10622, printed by Grafton for Berthelet on June 16, the reading is "in thy fayth, feare, and loue"—which was the wording as finally approved. This approved reading also appears in Berthelet's undated issue, *S.T.C.* 10619. The edition by Petyt (*S.T.C.* 10623) is dated October 12. Incidentally, Grafton's edition contains some musical notation.

edged. He was able to do this partly by taking the separate items used in the older forms and combining them into a series of well-organized petitions, with great gain in the sustained rhythms of the prose. He also abandoned the long catalogue of individual saints formerly invoked, substituting for this a single comprehensive appeal addressed to patriarchs, prophets, apostles, martyrs, confessors, virgins, "and all the blessed company of heauen." The latter was a radical innovation, since the traditional list embraced fifty-eight saints' names, shortened by Bishop Hilsey to thirty-eight in his *Manual of Prayers.*

Those familiar with the oft-repeated phrases of the Litany as given in the Book of Common Prayer may enjoy seeing the exact form in which Cranmer wrought them in this little book of 1544; so even at the risk of repetition it is well to cite here some of the more famous passages as they were first printed (*S.T.C.* 10620):

From all euyll and mischief, from sinne, from the craftis and assautes of the deuyll, from thy wrathe, and from euerlastynge damnation, Good lord delyuer vs. . . .

From fornication, & al deadly synne, and from all the deceites of the worlde, the flesshe, and the deuil, Good lord delyuer vs.

From lightnyng and tempest, frome plage, pestilence, and famine, frome battayle and murder, and frome sodayne deathe, Good lorde delyuer vs.

From all sedition and priuey conspiracy, from the tyranny of the byshop of Rome, and all his detestable enormities, from all false doctrine and heresy, from hardnes of hart and contempte of thy word and commandement, Good lorde delyuer vs. . . .

That it may please the to gyue to all nations vnitie peace and concorde We beseche ye to here vs good lord.

That it maye please the to bring into the way of truthe, all suche as haue erred & ar deceiued, We beseche the to here vs good lord.

That it maye please the to strengthen suche as do stande, and to comforte and helpe the weake harted, and toraise vp theim that fall, and fynally to beate downe Satan vnder our fete. We beseche the to heare vs good lorde. . . .

That it maye please ye to giue to our vse the kindly fruites of the erthe, so as in due tyme we maye enioy them: & to preserue them. We beseche the to here vs good lord.

The petition for deliverance "from battayle and murder, and frome sodayne deathe" acquired an added timely point from the continuance of the French war. In another of Berthelet's publications (*S.T.C.* 3002), printed May 25—two days before the Exhortation and Litany—we catch an echo of those martial days. This book was entitled "Psalmes or prayers taken out of holye scripture";[9] and its final items were a prayer for the King and "A prayer for men to saie entryng into bat-taile." The latter (fol. L7) exhorts us to remember how God gave unto David

. . . both courage and strengthe, beyng but a little one, vnarmed, and vnexpert in feates of warre, with his slinge to set vpon, and ouerthrowe the great huge Goliath.

In its earliest form this popular work comprised fifteen "Psalmes" which were really nothing but long compilations of selected verses from the Bible, chiefly from the Psalms, often rhetorically enlarged in the translation. For instance, a familiar verse from the 23rd Psalm appears in this style (fol. K5):

And therfore if it shuld fortune me to passe thoroughe the darke vale of death: I wyll go without feare: for thou wilte be with me, thy rod and thy staffe shall comfort me.

The volume concludes with a rendition of two biblical Psalms in their entirety, the 22nd and the 100th. The rendering is not without a certain air of its own; indeed the unknown author's style, though sometimes pompous, is often as affecting as it was affected—witness these lines from Psalm 22 (fol. L3):

Deliuer my soule from daungier of the swerde, and kepe my life, destitute of all mans helpe, from the violence of the dogge. Saue me from the mouthe of the lion, and take me from the hornes of the vnicornes. . . . For the lorde hath a power royall, and an imperiall dominion ouer the heathen.

It is no wonder that such swelling words should have been

9 This first issue may have been farmed out by Berthelet since the printing shows some unusual quirks; e.g., several of the so-called psalms are headed "spalme." For further discussion of this book, which went through many editions, see Helen C. White, *The Tudor Books of Private Devotion* (1951), p. 48.

well received and republished in the great age of Queen Elizabeth.

Later editions of this work came to be known as the 'King's Psalms'; and almost exactly a year later—June 2, 1545—Berthelet put out a companion volume, ascribed to the pen of Catharine Parr, that came to be known as the 'Queen's Prayers.' It too concluded with the prayers for the King and for men entering into battle. The first edition (*S.T.C.* 4818) bore a lengthy title in which the Queen was accorded her full style:

Prayers or Meditations, wherin the mynde is styrred paciently to suffre all afflictions here, . . . collected out of certain holy woorkes by the most vertuous and gracious princes Catharine, Quene of Englande, France, and Irelande.

No doubt Catharine knew what it was to suffer afflictions patiently; she may also have had some feeling of what it might be like to be the Queen of France; for in July 1544 Henry himself had set forth at the head of an invading army and crossed the English Channel. He laid a long siege to the town of Boulogne, which finally capitulated on September 14. But at this point Henry's ally, the Emperor Charles V, deserted him and made a separate peace with the King of France; so Henry was left to carry on the war alone. Henry himself returned to England in October, and the war dragged on ineffectually till, after two more years, both sides were weary of it and agreed to conclude a peace.

But few Primers were published in 1544, and these were of the traditional sort. Perhaps the publishers knew that some standardization was in the making and so felt uncertain of their market; or perhaps Grafton and Whitchurch, under the new patent granted them, were restricting the publication of Primers to their own assignees. In any case, only Petyt put forth a couple of issues bearing the date of 1544, one in English and Latin, the other in Latin. The former was simply a new edition (*S.T.C.* 16033) of the same sort of Sarum Primer that Redman had formerly published in 1537.

The Latin edition (*S.T.C.* 16032) was dated "the xii. day of Septembre," while the King was still besieging Boulogne. Though the body of the Primer was in Latin only, there were several items in English both at the beginning and at the end.[10] In the 'bidding of the beads' (fol. Y4ᵛ) Queen Catharine's name appears for the first time among the members of the royal family: we are admonished, "Also ye shal pray for quene katherinthat [*sic*] nowe is, and for our most noble Prynce Edwarde." It should be mentioned, however, that Catharine's name likewise appeared in the English Litany which Berthelet had brought out in May.

Indeed, before he left for France Henry had appointed Catharine as Regent in his absence. And during this time she won the respect of her three stepchildren, Mary, Elizabeth, and Edward. Princess Mary was but five years younger than the Queen, while Edward was only a boy of seven.

It is apparent that the King had provided that the Prince's education was not to be neglected in spite of his fragile health. In the British Museum there is an ABC that was specially printed by Berthelet for little Edward's use in 1543 under the title, "Alphabetum Latino anglicum." It was specially bound in a volume containing two other standard textbooks of the period, William Lily's "Introduction of the Eyght Partes of speche" and the *Institutum* of Erasmus (see above, p. 7).[11] These two items Berthelet had published as a single volume in the preceding year (1542) "by the commaundement of our most gracious souerayne lorde the King."

From this edition of Lily's Introduction to Latin Grammar we learn that the King, amid his manifold distractions, had been revolving in his thought how the education of children could be brought to a more uniform standard. For he himself

---

[10] The preliminary material includes the King's pleasure concerning the Lord's Prayer and so on (see above, p. 226); also a 'devout prayer' which begins, "My souerayne lorde Iesu the very son of almyghty god," representing an inheritance from the 'devout prayers' that Wynkyn de Worde had used (see above, p. 6).

[11] Cf. *S.T.C.* 15605. The shelf-mark of the volume in the British Museum is C.21.b.4. The text of the whole, including the ABC, is reprinted in the *Shakespeare Jahrbuch*, vol. 45, p. 84. See also T. W. Baldwin, *William Shakspere's Petty School* (Urbana, Illinois, 1943), pp. 35, 42.

wrote a brief foreword to this grammar-book addressed to all schoolmasters and teachers of grammar within his realm, specifying that this particular "Introduction" and "the lateyne grammer annexed to the same, and none other," should be used to teach the Latin language to children. For, as he says—

... we forgette not the tendre babes, and the youth of our realme, whose good education and godly bryngyng vp, is a great furniture to the same and cause of moche goodnesse.

Right after the King's foreword comes a preface to the reader, in which the unknown editor encourages the schoolboy with the promising example of little Prince Edward (then aged five!):

You tender babes of Englande, shake of slouthfulnes, set wantonnes a parte, apply your wyttes holy to lernyng and vertue, wherby you maye doo youre duetye to god and your kyng, make gladde your parentes, profytte your selues, and moche auaunce [i.e., *advance*] the common weale of your countery. Let noble prynce Edwarde encourage your tender hartes, a prynce of great towardnes, ... nowe almost in a redynesse, to rounne [i.e., *run*] in the same rase of lernyng with you.

Such was the volume to which was prefixed a special ABC designed for the Prince's use. The latter consists of but four leaves. Inside a colored border are printed seven styles of alphabet. Next—first in Latin, then in English—come the Lord's Prayer, Ave Maria, Creed, and Commandments; the last expanded to include the two commandments of Christ Jesus from the Gospel of Matthew. Then come two special prayers in Latin and English: "A prayer to God for deuoute feare, out of the seconde Psalme" and "An other prayer for aptitude to learne godlynesse." The fourth leaf of this ABC is rounded off with a rendering of James 1: 17, wherein the final phrase is varied from the version of the Great Bible under the prevailing influence of a latinical style, thus:

Euery good gifte, and euery perfect gift is from aboue, commyng downe from the father of lyghtes: with whom is no variablenes, nor shadowing of mutabilitie.

Beneath this is a Latin colophon dated 1543.

We may conclude, then, that while Cranmer was engaged in reformulating the service books of the English Church, the King was devoting some of his attention to the preparation of standard manuals for education. These included first a grammar, second an ABC book, and lastly a new Primer. The prescribed form of the ABC was not like the one specially put forth for the Prince. We know that an ABC was prescribed because there is reference to it in the preface of the Primer of 1545. But of the text of the ABC itself there is but one surviving copy (S.T.C. 20), the title of which imports that it is of the approved edition, though the contents are a little less than convincing.[12]

This particular copy is undated but belongs presumably to 1545 or 1546. It is a little booklet of eight leaves printed by William Powell, having the following title:

> The A. B. C set forthe by the Kynges maiestie and his Clergye, and commaunded to be taught through out all his Realme. All other vtterly set apart as the teachers thereof tender his graces fauour.

Although this copy may have been issued later than the authorized Primer of which we shall speak in the next chapter, we will treat of it here inasmuch as it is the only specimen we have of what the official ABC may have been like; so great was the mortality among these cheap and fugitive little booklets.

The first page shows three alphabets, and then come the Lord's Prayer, Ave, Creed, and Ten Commandments, all in the approved version as in the Primer. Then come the graces before and after dinner and supper, just as in the Primer. Next comes Psalm 130 in English, of the same translation as that given among the Seven Psalms in the authorized Primer. After this there are a few snatches of Latin based on *Confitemini*, similar to those that occurred in the ABC of 1538 (see above, p. 179). The last three leaves are set in smaller type, and commencing with fol. 6 we have a form of catechism entitled: "⁋ These questions the master ought to demaunde and to

12 For other discussion see Butterworth, "Early Primers for the Use of Children" in the *Papers* of the Bibliographical Society of America, vol. 43, p. 378.

lerne his scolers." This is indeed a curious feature to appear in an authorized ABC, for it is taken bodily from the Gough Primer of 1536.[13] The final leaf is taken up with the prayer to the Trinity ("Holy trinity, be helping vnto me") and with two more graces, the last of which begins:

Nowe you haue well refresshed your bodies, remember the lamentable afflictions and miseries of many thousands of your neighbours and brethren in Christ. . . .

The booklet concludes with a benediction and a colophon, thus:

God saue the Kynge the Queene and the Realme, and send vs peace in Christ Amen.
₵ Imprinted at London by Wyllyam Powell.

It remains to say that shortly after the King returned from his victorious siege of Boulogne, he appointed Richard Grafton as printer to the young Prince.[14] This amounted to putting Grafton on the royal payroll at a modest stipend. Accordingly, it must have been late in 1544 or early in 1545 that Grafton published a small Primer, of which only a few leaves now remain (*S.T.C.* 16031). It was printed in good-sized type, only seventeen lines to the page, as in the Primer of Richard Kele. Fortunately, the colophon has been preserved:

₵ Imprynted in London by Rycharde Grafton dwellynge within the circuite of the late Gray fryers, prynter to the Prynces grace. (✠) Cum priuilegio ad imprimendum solum

The surviving leaves indicate, however, that this little Primer was of a different text from Kele's, more like the one that Grafton issued in 1540; for the portion that has been preserved is the conclusion of the Dirge, with which the edition ended, and this is identical with the version used by Hilsey

[13] Specific dependence on the Gough Primer is demonstrated by a portion of the answer to the question, What is God? Where the original text had said, "unto whom also I fly . . . as unto a present and alone sufficient help for me," the Gough Primer read: "as vnto a presente all alone is sufficient helpe for me"; and this is the reading also in the Powell ABC.

[14] See J. A. Kingdon, *Richard Grafton Citizen and Grocer of London* (London, 1901), p. 21.

in his *Manual of Prayers*. Later than May of 1545 such a version would hardly have been encouraged, since it was then superseded, as we shall see, by the authorized Primer which Grafton and Whitchurch were specially commissioned to publish.

Chapter XIX

The Authorized Primer of Henry VIII
(1545)

THE first edition of the Primer of Henry VIII (*S.T.C.* 16034) was published by Grafton on May 29, 1545. It was a well-printed quarto, well spaced and generous in its use of blank paper, and bore the following title:

> The Primer, set foorth by the Kinges maiestie and his Clergie, to be taught lerned, & read: and none other to be vsed throughout all his dominions. M. D. XLV.

In the colophon, which was printed beneath a device showing Prince Edward's crest and initials, Grafton gave a definite date and proudly displayed his new title:

> Imprinted at London vvithin the precinct of the late dissolued house of the gray Friers, by Richard Grafton Printer to the Princes grace, the xxix. daye of May, the yere of our Lord, M.D.XLV. Cum priuilegio ad imprimendum solum.

During this and the following year the book went through a number of editions: ten in English, two in English and Latin, and one in Latin.[1]

The King plainly took the new project most seriously. On May 6 he drew up an injunction setting forth the royal purpose and pleasure in the Primer, assigning its function in the educational system of the day, and setting up the use of English on an equality with Latin. Part of this reads:

---

[1] The collation of *S.T.C.* 16034 is: *4, [*]*4, ****4, A-V4, AA-KK4, LL2 (134 leaves). The authorized Latin edition (*S.T.C.* 16042) was issued early in 1546 with the title, *Orarium seu libellus precationum per Regiam maiestatem & clerum latine oeditus.* In spite of the official declaration that no other Primer was to be used, it appears that Petyt was permitted to bring out an unauthorized Sarum edition in Latin on November 25, 1545 (*S.T.C.* 16041).

Emong the manyfolde busines, and moste weightie affaires apper-
tainyng to our regall authoritee and office, we, muche tenderyng the
youthe of our realmes, . . . for diuers good consideracions, & specially
for that the youth by diuers persones are taught the Pater noster, the
Aue maria, Crede, and .x. commaundementes all in Latin and not in
Englishe, by meanes wherof the same are not brought vp in the knowledge of their faith, dutye and obedience, . . . And fynally, for the
auoydyng of the dyuersitie of primer bookes that are nowe abroade,
wherof are almoost innumerable sortes whiche minister occasion of
contentions & vaine disputations, rather then to edifye, and to haue one
vniforme ordre of al suche bokes throughout all our dominions, bothe
to be taught vnto chyldren, and also to be vsed for ordinary praiers of
al our people not learned in the Latin tong: haue set furth this Primer
or booke of praiers in Englishe to be frequented and vsed in and
throughe out al places of our said realmes and dominions aswell of
the eldre people, as also of the youth, for their common and ordinarye
praiers, willyng, commaundyng, and streightly chargyng, that for the
better bringyng vp of youth in the knowledge of their dutye towardes
God, their prince, & all other in their degre, euery schoolemaster &
bringer vp of yong beginners in lernyng, next after their A.B.C. nowe
by vs also set furth, do teache this Primer or boke of ordinary praiers
vnto them in Englishe, and that the youthe customably & ordinarily
vse the same vntyl they be of competent vnderstandyng and knowledge
to perceyue it in Latin. At what tyme they may at their libertie either
vse this Prymer in Englishe, or that whiche is by oure authorytie like-
wyse made in the Latyn tong, in all poinctes correspondent vnto this
in Englishe.

This was printed at the beginning of the Primer, and is of
value as showing that Primers were designed either for the
use of the youth or for "eldre people." The ABC, including
Paternoster, Ave, etc., was evidently considered a more elementary textbook than the Primer.

At the end of the volume was printed a special license for
the publication of this Primer, drawn up by the King on
May 28, assigning exclusive rights for printing and selling the
same unto Grafton and Whitchurch.

When a diglot edition of the new Primer was issued, September 6 (S.T.C. 16040), it was furnished with still another
foreword, printed in both English and Latin and set in ahead
of the injunction at the beginning of the volume. This was a

preface made by the King's most excellent Majesty, addressed to all his subjects, both laity and clergy. Where the injunction had spoken of the Primer as a "boke of ordinary praiers" and treated of it as an educational instrument, the new preface takes up its religious and devotional aspects. It seems to bear the imprint of Cranmer's composition, particularly as it refers to other efforts being made toward greater uniformity of worship. Parts of it are worth quoting. It commences with a discussion of acceptable and effectual prayer, pointing out that we must pray with both the spirit and the understanding

> . . . lest when the spirite dooeth praie, the mynde take no fruite at al, & the partie yt vnderstandeth not the pith or effectualnes of the talke yt he frankely maketh with God, maie bee as an harpe or pype geuyng a sounde but not vnderstanding the noise yt it self hath made.

Whereupon it proceeds:

> AND forasmuche as wee haue bestowed right greate labour & diligence aboute settyng a perfecte staigh [i.e., *stay*] in ye other partes of our religion: wee haue thought good to bestowe our earnest labour in this parte also, beyng a thyng as fruictefull as the best, that men maie knowe, bothe what thei praie, & also with what woordes: lest thyngs special good & principall, beyng enwrapped in ignoraunce of the woordes, should not perfeictely come to the mynde & to the intelligence of men: . . . IN consideration wherof we haue sette out & geuen to our subiectes a determinate fourme of praiyng in their owne mother toung, to thentente that suche as are ignoraunt of any straunge or foren speche, maie haue what to praie in their owne acquainted & familiar language with fruicte & vnderstanding: . . .

Then, bearing in mind the predilection of certain bishops for the continued use of Latin in the church services, the King (or Cranmer or whoever wrote this preface) is careful to balance the claims of both English and Latin and to stress the need for harmony:

> NEVERTHELESSE to thentente that suche as haue vnderstanding of the latine toung, & thinke that thei can with a more feruent spirite make their praiers in that toung, maie haue wherin to dooe their deuocion to God beyng none acceptour neither of any persone ne toung: we haue prouided theself same fourme of praiyng to be sette foorth in latin also, whiche we had afore published in englishe, to thentente,

that we would bee all thynges to all persones, & that all parties maie
at large bee satisfied, and as well the willes & desire of theim that
perceiue bothe tounges as also the necessitee and lacke of theim that
dooe not vnderstande the latin. AND wee haue iudged it to bee of no
small force for ye auoidyng of strife and contencion, to haue one
vniforme maner or course of praiyng throughout all our dominions:
and a veraie greate efficacie it hath to stirre vp the feruentenesse of the
mynde, if the confuse maner of praiyng bee somewhat holpen with the
feloship or annexion of vnderstandyng: . . .

The concluding paragraph is very well managed as an effective encouragement to the sluggish:

WHEREFORE as greate as our will and forewardenesse hath been to set
foorth and publishe these thynges, so greate ought your diligence and
industrie to bee towardes well & fruictefully vsing the same, that when
al thynges hath been prepared and sette foorth to the glorie of God &
for your welthe: your selfes onely maie not bee slacke or negligente
towarde your owne behouf and towarde your owne benefites.

We have devoted generous space to these documents—the
preface and the injunction—in the belief that they exhibit
quite distinctly the attitude and religious tone that prevailed
in the closing years of Henry's reign. For the launching of the
new Primer was regarded by those in charge of it as part of a
general campaign, and much care was given to its revision.
All in all, it was a simpler compilation than its forerunners,
plain in arrangement, moderate in temper, and considerably
revised, not to say renovated.

Turning now to the first edition (*S.T.C.* 16034) we see
from the table of contents that it is divisible into three main
portions, though not actually subdivided as was the Hilsey
Manual. First there are the usual preliminary features—calendar, Lord's Prayer, Ave Maria, etc., with graces for dinner
and supper (12 leaves in all); then the regular offices corresponding to the familiar core of the Primer—from Matins to
Compline and from the Seven Psalms on through Litany,
Dirge, and Commendations, to the Psalms of the Passion (80
leaves); and lastly the Passion according to St. John, followed
by a large and unusual collection of prayers (42 leaves).

The calendar of Henry's Primer is positively bare in comparison with the older Sarum calendars; it averages about seven or eight entries per month for saints' days and holydays, where the older form called for twenty-five or more. Understandably, some preference is shown for Anglican saints, though quite a few obscure names are inexplicably perpetuated, such as Sts. Alphege and Protus and Hyacinthus. The new calendar also specializes in chronological information, registering the sun's progress through the zodiac and recording days of the month after the Roman system of kalends, nones, and ides.

The section devoted to the Lord's Prayer, Commandments, etc., is presented of course in the wording that was approved in 1538. The graces that follow show marked kinship with those that were used in the ABC's; at least one of which— the first, beginning "The eyes of all thinges trust in the, O Lorde" (see above, p. 179)—is paralleled by a grace in Luther's *Betbüchlein*.

In the main body of the Primer, although the general outline of Sarum usage is adhered to, there are many innovations, the more conspicuous of which deserve our attention. For instance, there are new departures in the sequence and selection of the Psalms. Indeed, the Seven Penitential Psalms and those traditionally associated with Matins are the only groups allowed to come through intact. Furthermore, the total number of Psalms has been cut down to thirty-six in all (including the Seven Psalms) as compared with fifty-eight in the Sarum Primers.[2] And of these thirty-six only twenty-eight had belonged to the older use of Sarum. The Fifteen Gradual Psalms are now omitted altogether, and the Psalms of the Passion are represented by a brand-new selection. Of the five new Psalms in this Primer that make their appearance for the first time in any English Primer, three are included in the Psalms of the Passion. It is true, as we shall remark in the section devoted to Prayers, that several of these latter prayers are based on other Psalms, but these, properly speaking, are paraphrases or meditations rather than actual translations.

[2] See below, Appendix II.

As to what version of the Psalms was utilized in the Primer of Henry VIII, it has been demonstrated that for the most part the Psalms were drawn from what we have referred to as the Rouen version, set forth in the Primer of 1536 and emended in the Redman Primer of 1537. Wherever the translation varies from that version, it is apt to show the influence of the Cranmer Bible of 1540, which the editor evidently felt free to consult. Also he bore in mind the claims of the Latin Vulgate text, which was to appear in the margin of the diglot edition. For example,[3] here are the opening verses of the 27th Psalm as they occur in the Dirge of the authorized Primer (fol. O1):

> The Lorde is my light, and my helth, whom shal I feare?
> The Lord is the defender of my life, of whom shal I be a frayd?
> Whilest the malitious approch vnto me for to deuoure my fleshe?
> Myne enemies which trouble me, they were made weke, and fell downe.
> If they pitche pauilions against me, my hart shal not feare.
> If a battayle rise against me, I shal trust in it.

Only twice does this depart from the Rouen version of 1536. That had said, "The lorde is the defender of my lyfe: at whom shall I quake?" and here the Cranmer Bible read, "of whom then shall I be afrayed?" Again, the Rouen Primer had said, "Whylste euyll doers approche vnto me," etc. For the term "the malitious" (Vulgate, *nocentes*) the Primer of Henry VIII had no earlier precedent, the nearest being George Joye's "the maligne myscheuouse" in 1534.

When it came to Psalms that were not represented in the regular Sarum Primers, it seems to have been the practice of the new authorized Primer to base its version on the Cranmer Bible, introducing such modifications as might accord with the Latin Vulgate. There was also available, of course, the diglot Psalter attributed to Coverdale which Grafton had published in 1540 (*S.T.C.* 2368), but as a rule this seems not to have been consulted. A case in point is the second Psalm,

---

[3] For other examples see below, Appendix III; also, H. C. White, *Tudor Books of Private Devotion*, p. 113, and Butterworth, *Literary Lineage*, etc., p. 148.

which now appears as one of the Psalms of the Passion (fol. V2ᵛ), beginning, "Why hath the Hethen raged? and why hath the people imagined vaine thinges?" These opening words, it happens, are closer to the Coverdale diglot Psalter than to the Cranmer Bible; yet a little later in the same Psalm the Cranmer Bible is followed almost word for word:

> He that dwelleth in heauen, shall laugh them to scorne, and the lorde shal haue them in derision.
> Then he wil speake vnto them in his wrathe, and vexe them in his sore displeasure.

Finally, at the end of the Psalm the authorized Primer departs from all the preceding versions and reads:

> Get discipline, that the lord be not angry, & ye perishe from the right way
> Whan his anger shalbe kindled for a shorte whyle, blessed are all thei that trust in him.

There is perhaps something typical of Henry's reign in the translation of the Latin text so literally into "Get discipline." The usual Bible reading here was "Kisse the sonne, lest he be angrye"; only in the Taverner Bible do we find a similar rendition, "Embrace instruction, least the Lorde be angrye." And this similarity, too, may not be accidental; for Taverner's name will appear again in our discussion of this authorized Primer.

Coming now to Matins, not only are the Psalms like those in the Sarum Primers (as was said), but the traditional response of "Hail, Mary" is retained in the invitatory Psalm. On the other hand, a different set of 'lessons' is introduced. Instead of the three traditional 'lessons' in praise of the Virgin, the Primer of Henry VIII uses selections from the Bible, as Joye and Hilsey had done; but the choice of Scripture is new, the first lesson coming from chapter eleven of Isaiah, about the Rod of Jesse, and the remaining two from Luke, comprising between them the entire account of the Annunciation (Luke 1: 26-38). Here again, the editor is not content to make use of current versions of the Bible; he makes his own rendering, though keeping fairly close to the wording of the Great Bible. Mary is described as "a virgin which was ensured to a man, whose name was Ioseph." The account of the angel's appearing to her continues in this style (fol. B2):

And when the virgin heryng these wordes was troubled with them, and mused with her selfe what maner of salutacion it shulde be: the Angel said to her. Feare not, Mari, be not abashed, for thou hast founde fauour in the sight of God.

The opening Psalm of Lauds—Psalm 67—likewise gives evidence of careful emendation. While the version is that of the Redman Primer of 1537, it is freely modified, especially toward the close; and this time the alteration seems to suggest the diglot Psalter of Coverdale. A comparison of the final verses (5-7) runs as follows:

Redman   —People knowledge the   to be god, let all   nacyons
Coverdale —Let the people   prayse ye   O god, let all   people
Henry VIII—Let the people magnify the, o god, let all ye people

confesse the: for the earthe hath brought forthe her frute.   Blesse vs
prayse   the: the erth   hath geuen   hyr frute.   God, euen
magnify the,   the yearth hath brought furth   her fruite.   God

our god: and all that inhabyte the earthe,   that all the partes
oure awne God geue vs his blessynge, God blesse vs, and let all the coastes
our   God   blesse vs, God blesse vs, &   all the costes

therof   may feare the.
of the erthe   feare hym.
of the yearth feare hym.

The new Primer is also fitted out with fresh renditions of the hymns. These strike a simple and pleasing note, at least compared with the sombre tones of the older hymns in the Sarum or Marshall Primers. Take for example the opening stanzas of the first hymn in Matins (fol. A2):

Now the cherefull day doth spryng.
Vnto God, praye we & syng.
That in all workes of the day
He preserue and kepe vs ay

> That our tong he may refrayne
> From all stryfe and wordes vayne
> Kepe our eyes in couerture
> From all yll and vayne pleasure

> That our hertes be voyded quyte
> From phansy and fond delighte
> Thinne, dyet of drinke and meat
> Of the fleshe, to coole the heat . . .

Though still bordering more closely on the ascetic than on the aesthetic, these hymns are said to have attracted the attention of Cranmer. The year before, Cranmer had tried his hand at English verses while at work on a revision of the *Processionale* (which apparently was never issued) and he had found the setting of English words to the ancient musical notes a difficult matter; for in a letter to the King,[4] dated October 7, he had said:

> . . . I have travailed to make the verses in English, and have put the Latin note unto the same. . . . I made them only for a proof, to see how English would do in song. But by cause mine English verses lack the grace and facility that I would wish they had, your majesty may cause some other to make them again, that can do the same in more pleasant English and phrase.

Many times the authorized Primer toned down the emphasis which the Sarum Primers had laid on the worship of the Virgin Mary. It also veered away from undue veneration of the saints. At the close of Lauds, for instance, the new Primer has but eight collects, and these are no longer addressed to individual saints. Yet of the material that is here employed, nearly all is derived from the usage of Sarum, probably by way of the Hilsey *Manual of Prayers;* witness, for example, the ancient collect for Peace (see above, p. 93).

How far-reaching these changes could be is exemplified in Prime and Hours. Each of the Hours is supplied with but a single Psalm, which is followed by an 'anthem' (or antiphon) together with a short prayer (or collect). But instead of the

---

4 Printed in the Parker Society edition of *Miscellaneous Writings and Letters of Thomas Cranmer,* edited by J. E. Cox (Cambridge, Eng., 1846), p. 412.

The fixt houre.

Ad releuaui oculos meos. Pfal.xxii.

¶ A prayer to be deliuered from the defpi-
tes of the wicked.

Haue lift vp myne eyes to the,
which dwelleth in heauen.

Beholde, euen like as the
eyes of the feruauntes wayt at
their maifters handes:

As the eyes of the handmaide be
vpon her maiftreffe: euen fo be our eyes
vpō our lord God, vntyl he haue mercy on vs.

Haue mercy on vs O lorde, haue
mercy on vs, for we be had in muche
contempt.

For oure foule is very full, beyng
fkorned of the riche, and defpifed of the
proude.

Glory to the father. &c.

¶ It is faid in the beginnyng. &c. Amē.

¶ The anetheme.

Bleffed are the mercyful, for they
fhall get mercy. Bleffed are the
cleane

The fixt houre.

cleane in harte, for they fhall fee God.

¶ The verficle.   Deliuere my paper.
¶ Anfwere. And let my cry come to the.

¶ Let vs pray.

Orde Jefu Chrift, whofe proper
ty is to be mercyfull, whiche art
alway pure and clene without fpot of
fynne, graunt vs the grace to folowe
the innercifulnes towarde our neighboures, and alwayes to beare a pure
harte, and a clene confience towarde
the, that we may after this lyfe fee
the in thy euerlafting glory: whiche liueft and reigneft God
worlde without ende.

Amen.

F.i.

THE AUTHORIZED PRIMER OF HENRY VIII

(May 29, 1545)

Showing the anthem and collect for Sixth Hour

(From the copy in the Divinity School library of the Protestant Episcopal Church, Philadelphia, Pa.)

celebration of the Virgin we find a whole new idea: each anthem is fashioned out of two of the Beatitudes, and the accompanying prayer extols the Saviour for his embodiment of the particular qualities named in the beatitude. The unified effect is illustrated, for example, in the Sixth Hour, where the anthem is: "Blessed are the merciful, for they shall get merci. Blessed are the cleane in harte, for they shall see God." Thereupon the prayer begins as follows (fol. F1):

Lorde Iesu Christ, whose property is to be mercyfull, whiche art alway pure and clene without spot of synne, graunt vs the grace to folowe the in mercifulnes towarde our neighboures, and alwayes to beare a pure harte, and a clene conscience towarde the, . . .

The office of Evensong is devoted more specifically to the commemoration of the Virgin, and in it of course occurs the Magnificat (Luke 1: 46-55). It is worth a mention that here again the authorized Primer introduces new variations into the version of the Magnificat that had come down from Tyndale through the Rouen and Redman Primers. Perhaps the most striking of these is the noteworthy alteration in the rhythm whereby the Tyndale reading, "He hath filled the hongry with goode thinges: And hath sent awaye the ryche empty," now becomes: "He hath filled the hungry with good thinges, and the riche he hath sent empty away." This particular turn of phrase thence established itself in the Prayerbook and later in the King James Bible.[5]

The Compline was brief and retained only two of the Psalms traditionally belonging to it. The Seven Psalms, as has been said, were the same as had always been used, barring an occasional change in the phraseology; but the collect at the end of them was fashioned anew and began with the words, "Remembre not (O Lorde God) our olde iniquities, but let thy merci spedely preuent vs."

The Litany of the new Primer was copied word for word from the edition that Cranmer had prepared the year before, including the brief foreword to instruct the layman how it ought to be used. Part of this now reads (fol. L^v):

5 See Butterworth, *Literary Lineage,* etc., pp. 156, 334.

. . . it shalbe euery christen mans part reuerently to vse the same, to the honor & glory of almighty God, and the profyte of theire owne soules. And suche amonge the people as haue bokes, and can reade may reade them quietly and softly to them selfe: and suche as cannot read, let them quietly & attentiuely geue audience in time of the saide prayers, hauyng their myndes erect to almighty God, and deuoutly praiyng in their hartes, the same petitions which do entrein at their eares, so that with one sounde of the hart, and one accorde, God may be glorified in his church.

The half-dozen 'suffrages' or prayers at the end of the Litany are brief, and although their wording has been retouched, evidently by Cranmer, several of them are very similar in tone to those in the older Primers. They conclude with a prayer of St. Chrysostom, commencing, "Almighty God, which haste geuen vs grace"; but the designation of the prayer as his was omitted in the first edition of Henry's Primer.

The office of the Dirge has been drastically shortened, partly by omitting a number of the Psalms and partly by reducing the 'lessons' from nine to three. In this revision the Hilsey *Manual of Prayers* was found useful. There is no ostensible division of the office into *Placebo* and the Matins of the Dirge, as there was in Hilsey and the older Primers, but the essence of each was maintained, and each portion is concluded with the ancient formula, "God haue mercy on all christen soules. Amen." Where Hilsey had used five prayers at the end of *Placebo,* the authorized Primer chose only three of these, all representative of material venerable with tradition. The second one, transferred from the usage of Sarum, now reads (fol. N3ᵛ):

O God the lorde of pardon, graunt vnto the soule of .N. thy seruaunt (the yeres mynde of whose death, we haue in remembraunce) a place of rest, the blesful quiet & clerenes of thy lyght, Thorough Christ our Lorde.

It is perhaps typical of the renovations which took place that the special 'anthem' which gave its name to the office of the Dirge ("Dirige, Domine"—or as Hilsey had it, "Dyrecte good lorde/ my way in thy syght") was altogether left out in the Primer of Henry VIII. Moreover, the use of Sarum had called for nine 'lessons' in the Dirge, all taken from the Book of Job and all dwelling fondly on the sorrows of mortality and its mortification. Hilsey had sought to relieve the gloom of this by selecting three lessons from Job, three from St. Augustine, and three from the New Testament. Henry's Primer had only three altogether, one from Job and the other two from the New Testament, each fitted with an antiphon or 'anthem.'

In case the reader would like to compare it with earlier translations, the passage from Job (10: 8-12) which we have noticed before (see above, pp. 102, 115) is rendered as follows in the authorized Primer (fol. O3ᵛ):

Thyne *handes* hath made me & fashioned me al together round aboute, & wilt thou destroy me so sodenly? O remembre: that thou madest me as moulde of the yearth, & shalt bryng me into dust againe, hast thou not put me together, as it were milke, and hardened me to cruddes like chese? Thou hast couered me with skinne and fleshe, and ioyned me with bones & sinowes. Thou hast graunted me life and mercy, and the diligent heede that thou tokest on me, hath preserued my spirit.

The 'anthem' for this begins, 'I knowe that my redemer liueth." The version resembles that in the Great Bible.

The other two 'lessons' are drawn from material that Hilsey had used, passages from the fifth chapter of John and from the fifteenth of I Corinthians. Yet in spite of the more hopeful tone prevailing in the Dirge of Henry's Primer, the old theology reasserts itself in the 'anthem' accompanying the third of these lessons. Apparently it was felt that Paul's expectancy of the resurrection should be counterbalanced by a reminder of doomsday and the fiery pit; for we read (fol. P1):

Deliuer me good lorde from eternal death, in that dreadful day, when that heauen and yearth shalbe moued, & thou shalt iudge the worlde by fyre. Thys day is the day of ire, of wretchednes and misery, the great day and very bitter.

This prepares the way for the prayer of Hezekiah from Isaiah 38, the rendering of which keeps fairly close to the version in the Rouen-Redman Primers, but with some modifications as before. The four prayers at the end of the Dirge are taken from the Hilsey *Manual,* which in turn had adapted all but the first of them from the use of Sarum.

'Commendations' in the authorized Primer consists only of the 119th Psalm. The text of this is plainly modeled upon the Rouen version as that had been reworked for the 1537 edition of Redman's Primer. It is now fitted out by the new editor with a brief 'argument' at the beginning, as are all of the Psalms in the authorized Primer. But the argument for this particular Psalm is cast in a curious style and commences thus (fol. Q2ᵛ):

⟨ This psalme is the .A.B.C. of godly loue, the paradise of learning, the shop of the holy Gost, the scole of truth. In which appereth how the saintes of God esteme his holy lawes, how feruently they be giuen vnto them, [etc.]

This brings to mind again the whimseys of Richard Taverner,[6] especially the phrase, "the shop of the holy Gost." At any rate it seems to foreshadow the use of unrestrained 'conceits' by the later Elizabethan poets.

The next portion of the Primer has to do with the Passion: first the Psalms of the Passion, then the account according to John's Gospel, followed by half a dozen prayers. We have already pointed out that these Psalms of the Passion included several newcomers and that to a large extent they depended for their wording on the version in the Cranmer Bible. The Gospel account, on the other hand, follows the translation used in the Hilsey *Manual,* which was descended from the Tyndale Testament of 1534. This was the longest consecutive passage from the Bible to be contained in the Primer of Henry VIII; for this Primer did not include the traditional four selections from the Gospels pertaining to the beginning and end of the Saviour's career, nor was any special provision made for a section of 'Epistles and Gospels.' The fact that the Passion ac-

---

[6] To my ear it is not far afield from the famous announcement attributed to Taverner in his later days (perhaps apocryphally) when he is said to have told a group of Oxford students in a sermon that he was bringing them "some fine biskets baked in the oven of charity, carefully conserv'd for the chickens of the Church, the sparrows of the spirit, and the sweet swallows of salvation." See the *Athenae Oxonienses* of Anthony à Wood (edition of 1721), vol. I, p. 183.

cording to John is placed, not at the beginning, but near the end of the volume along with other Passion material, is another indication of the care and intelligence with which this Primer was edited. Indeed, the Passion from John initiates a new series of signatures in the first edition of the Primer (fol. AA1).

The six prayers on the Passion introduce a remarkable section of Prayers of all sorts with which the authorized Primer comes to an end. The prayers dealing with the Passion are in a solemn and stately vein and were probably a contribution by Cranmer himself. In this Primer they fill the place, more or less, that was formerly occupied by the "Fifteen O's" in the Sarum Primers.

The miscellaneous prayers that follow amount to thirty-five in all, drawn from several different sources and dealing with all sorts of themes. In the diglot edition of the Primer they are given in both English and Latin. The morning and evening prayers include "A prayer at your uprising" (fol. CC2^v) taken from the *Precationes aliquot novae* of Erasmus published in 1537. This became a well-known prayer which in its English rendition began as follows:

O Lorde Iesu Christ, which art the verye bright sonne of the worlde, euer risyng, neuer falling, which with thy holsome loke engendrest, preseruest, norishest, & makest ioyfull all thinges that are in heauen and in yearth.

Then we come upon "A praier for trust in God" (fol. CC4) commencing:

The beginnyng of the fall of man was trust in him self. The beginnyng of the restoring of man was distrust in him self & trust in God.

This forthright petition was translated from the *Preces et meditationes generales* of the Spaniard, Juan Luis Vives, published in 1539.[7] Later on in this Primer there are at least four other prayers taken from this same source. Today Vives is remembered more for his pedagogical theories, especially for

[7] For further mention of the prayers of Erasmus and Vives, see H. C. White, *Tudor Books of Private Devotion* (1951).

his advanced ideas on the education of women, than for his religious writings. His reputation for scholarship stood high in the England of Henry's time, for Catherine of Aragon, the King's first Queen, had brought him from Spain to be her tutor. It is perhaps a point of political interest that his work, though not his name, should now be permitted to appear in a volume "set foorth by the Kinges maiestie and his Clergie" nine years after his deposed pupil had passed to her reward.

Next come a group of six prayers based on certain of the Psalms. One significant point about them is that they are copied directly from Taverner's *Epitome of the Psalmes,* and therefore in their Latin form they represent the work of Wolfgang Capito (see above, p. 195).[8] They are followed by a series of eleven prayers from the Bible, many of which we have already met, such as the prayer of Solomon for a competent living, the prayer for chastity from the Apocryphal Book of Ecclesiasticus, and the prayer of the early Church from the fourth chapter of Acts. These too are all in the particular wording used by Taverner at the end of his *Epitome,* though they might also have been supplied from the *Praiers of holi fathers* which Grafton himself had published a couple of years before. But the evidence seems to indicate that they were taken from the *Epitome* rather than the *Praiers.* In the prayer from Acts, for instance, Taverner's flavorful term, the Paynims, reappears here in the King's Primer (see above, p. 199).

Two other items also from the last pages of Taverner's volume are included at this point in the authorized Primer. These are a long prayer "for the peace of the Churche" and a shorter one "for the kepyng of a good name." The former was a translation of one of the *Precationes aliquot* of Erasmus, mentioned above, and constituted an eloquent plea for the remedy of abuses. While the substance of it would appeal to the reformers, its statements were moderate enough in tone and

---

[8] The prayers selected—they were meditations, not translations of the Psalms—were those belonging to Ps. 60, 68, 140-143. No reason is apparent for this particular choice. That the editor took them directly from the Taverner edition of 1539 is proved by a reversed numeral. In the *Epitome* the prayer on Psalm 143 was headed "Psalm 134" and it appears in Henry's Primer as "Ps. cxxxiv."

regular enough in form to make it acceptable also to the upholders of tradition.

Then, after a few prayers of defense against particular sins or the perils of adversity and of prosperity, we come upon two other favorites which we have noticed before: one, the ever-popular "O bone Iesu" by St. Bernardine of Siena, which Marshall found room for in his *Goodly Primer;* and the other, the prayer of Erasmus to be said at the hour of death, which had found its way into the Toye Primers of 1541 and 1542 (see above, p. 235).

The King's Primer brings its collection of prayers to a close with a "generall confessyon of sinnes"—also reprinted from Taverner's book—followed by two more prayers taken from the Latin of Vives, one against the devil, and the last one of all, "For the desire of the lyfe to come" (fol. LL1). While it was not unnatural for the volume to close on the note of expectancy of bliss, it was still quite typical of the period that this final prayer should start off with the cheerless theme of body versus soul:

> This my body is the very darke and filthy prison of the solle, this worlde is an exile, and a banysment [*sic*]: this lyfe is care & mysery, but where thou arte (O Lorde) there is the very countrey of libertie, & euerlastyng blessednes.

It is the age-old plaint of mortal man engaged in contemplating immortality, and may be said to have its roots in those words of the Apostle to the Gentiles: "Who shall deliver me from the body of this death?" and "Where the Spirit of the Lord is, there is liberty" (Romans 7:24; II Corinthians 3:17).

Reviewing the authorized Primer as a whole, it was plainly more than a mere continuation or refurbishment of the traditional Book of Hours of the Blessed Virgin Mary, as its ancient origins might lead one to suppose; it also emerges as a new and contemporary "boke of ordinary praiers" for the use of young or old, just as the injunction of the King described it. Moreover, it was obviously part of a national effort to reduce religion to a greater uniformity; and it is clear also that this program was agreed upon between the King and the clergy.

In keeping with the attempt to set up uniformity, many diverse strands were woven together to produce this Primer of 1545. Cranmer seems to have interested himself personally in the project, but we do not know who was the actual compiler or editor. Taking the book just as Grafton first published it, there is at least some support for the hypothesis that it was the work of Richard Taverner. We have seen from time to time recurrent inklings of his individual style. Certainly, if this Primer was not his work, it contained a surprisingly large proportion of material that had already been issued over his name.

It evinced a careful and thorough revision. On the other hand, it is likewise true that many of those figures whom we have met in the course of this history would have been able to pick out familiar ingredients among the contents of this Primer. It might be serviceable here to summarize its ancestry in this way, remembering that such a conspectus is designed to be merely suggestive, not exhaustive.

Wynkyn de Worde or François Regnault, as publishers of Sarum Primers for many years, would doubtless have been amazed at the number of changes to be encountered in this Primer of Henry VIII, but they would also have observed that not everything was strange. The general pattern of the work, the old familiar Psalms in Matins and the Seven Psalms, together with a venerable prayer or collect here and there, would have duly reminded them of the long line of Latin *Horae* according to the use of Salisbury.

Neither ought those eminent Continental scholars who composed their works in contemporary Latin be wholly forgotten: Luther, Brunfels, and Capito, Erasmus and Vives—names all known to one another—each might claim some shadow of representation in the King's Primer.

Likewise the three pioneers in translating the printed Bible into English—Tyndale, Joye, and Coverdale—would have been able to recognize certain contributions of their own.

Tyndale would have found the wording of the Magnificat or of the Passion according to St. John very largely as he left it. Joye, on the other hand, despite his earlier work on the Primers, would have found little still having a familiar ring. The overthrow of Thomas Cromwell spelled an end to much of what Joye had sought to accomplish. About all he would have recognized of his *Ortulus anime* in the Primer of Henry VIII would be a phrase here and there, such as the opening lines of the first grace, or a turn of speech in the prayer of Hezekiah ("Myne eyen daseled with loking on high") transferred from his own 'Commendations'; or a line from the invitatory Psalm in Matins, "The sea is his, for he hath made it, & his handes haue fashyoned the earth also." But Coverdale would have found much of his own handiwork intact, by virtue of his having edited the Great Bible and having revised the translation for the Cranmer Bibles.

The unknown translator of Redman's *Prayers of the Byble* might have observed some of the same selections, though not often the words, in those prayers taken over from Taverner's *Epitome of the Psalmes*. And the unknown translator of the Rouen Primer of 1536 would have felt even more at home, for he would be greeted with accustomed turns of speech in nearly every Psalm. So also would Bishop Hilsey have felt at home, particularly in the Dirge of the new Primer.

Among the publishers, John Byddell might have recognized the version of the 51st Psalm as derived from the text of the Exposition by Savonarola which he printed for William Marshall. Or Robert Redman might have spotted the prayer "O bone Iesu" which he had incorporated in his Sarum Primer of 1535. Again, Redman could have recognized many an emendation that appeared for the first time in his Primer of 1537. And Thomas Berthelet, the King's printer, who had just published the Litany, would have seen it reproduced in the very same form in the new Primer. Even Thomas Petyt might have caught an echo from the grace before dinner ("The kyng of eternall glory, make vs parteners of the heauenly table") not so different from the one in his ABC; while Robert Toye could have spotted a familiar prayer or two. As for Grafton and Whitchurch, they of course were involved in the publishing of the book itself.

And what was to lie ahead for the authorized Primer of Henry VIII? Inside of two years the King was dead, and the reigns of Edward his son and of Mary his elder daughter were both characterized by violent reactions. Nevertheless, all three of his children were to sponsor fresh editions of the Primer. In Edward's reign, the Primer of 1547 (*S.T.C.* 16048) reëmbodied virtually the whole of Henry's Primer. In Mary's reign, though much was brushed aside with the return of Roman Catholic influence, yet the "vniforme and Catholyke Prymer" of 1555 (*S.T.C.* 16060) retained a great many of the same Psalms and prayers that were in her father's edition. Even as late as the beginning of Elizabeth's reign, an authorized Primer was set forth (*S.T.C.* 16087) to carry on the long tradition. But soon thereafter its usefulness declined.

Why was this? In the first place, the Protestant ascendancy during the reign of Edward VI resulted in the free use of the mother tongue in all the services of the Church. This first began to prevail during Easter season of 1548, and by the next year the Book of Common Prayer was formulated. It was then no longer necessary to carry a Primer to church with you in order to take an intelligent part in the service because you knew no Latin. The new Prayer Book was also made available for use at home, that is, for *private* as well as for *common* prayer. Subsequently, in response to a popular demand for private prayers, suitable for repeating in one's personal devotions, there grew up a veritable multitude of books catering to this need.[9] Meanwhile, for purposes of instruction in the field of education, newer fashions were coming into vogue with the rise of more grammar schools. The content of the older Primers was thereby transmuted into a whole series of books—hornbooks, ABC's, Catechisms, Primers, etc.—until

[9] For material of this kind see Hoskins or White, *op. cit.*; and for educational textbooks see T. W. Baldwin, *William Shakspere's Petty School* (1943).

the name *Primer* became simply a synonym for any elementary reading book, of whatever sort.

While Latin was officially reinstated in the Church during Mary's reign, and while its use was permitted even in the earlier years of Elizabeth, it was inevitable that English should supersede it both for religious service and for prayer. Here the English Bible was destined to play a dominant part. After 1575 the Bible began to be published in larger and larger quantities until the Geneva version had won its way into the homes of ordinary families. Often bound with it in the same volume was the Book of Common Prayer or the Sternhold and Hopkins metrical version of the Psalter, or perhaps a Concordance. Thus the English nation was given fresh impetus toward becoming a Bible-reading people, the roots of Puritanism were nourished, and the way was prepared for the widespread reception of the King James version of the Bible. Toward this culmination the English Primers were but a preliminary chapter.

Appendices

I. (A)   Martin Luther and the Marshall Primers

   (B)   The Two Issues of Mayler's Primer of 1540

II.   Synopsis of Scriptural Passages in the Primers

III.   Specimens of Variant Readings:

        1. Psalm 51: 1-12

        2. The Lord's Prayer (Matt. 6:9-13)

Appendix I

(A)

Martin Luther and the Marshall Primers

THE Marshall Primers owed more than a little to the work of Martin Luther. Though the debt was not acknowledged in the Primers themselves, the clerical authorities of Henry's reign must almost certainly have been aware of the connection. In the 1534 edition of the Primer the indebtedness is more obvious, for in the revision of June 1535 Marshall often expanded the wording with interpolations of his own. Not much is known of the actual process by which the Lutheran ideas were incorporated into the Primers, but the following information can be set down.

Two of Luther's sermons, which were published in German in 1519 and subsequently rendered in Latin, reappear in the Marshall Primer. One was "Ein Sermon von der Betrachtung des heiligen Leidens Christi," comprising fifteen brief topics (see Weimar edition of Luther's *Werke,* vol. II, p. 131). In 1521 a Latin version appeared at Wittenberg under the title, "Sermo . . . de Meditatione Dominice Passionis e vernaculo in latinum versus." Later it was included in the collected editions of Luther's *Opera* as part of his "Aliquot Conciones" under the heading, "Quomodo Christi Passio Sit Meditanda" (see Luther's *Opera,* Wittenberg edition, vol. I, p. 83ᵛ; Jena edition, vol. I, p. 323ᵛ). It seems to have been the Latin version which was turned into English for the Primer, wherein (fol. 13ᵛ) it appears as "A deuoute frutfull & godly remembrance of the passion of our sauyour Iesu Christe." The dependence of Marshall upon the Lutheran sermon was remarked by Rev. Constantin Hopf in an article, "A Sermon of Martin Luther in the English Primer," printed in the Oxford *Journal of Theological Studies* (vol. 43, p. 194).

The other sermon used by Marshall was "Ein Sermon von dem Gebet und Procession in der Kreuzwoche" (see Weimar edition of the *Werke,* vol. II, p. 172). Originally it comprised seven topics, of

279

which the first five had to do with Prayer. Later, when Luther published his *Betbüchlein* (or Little Prayer Book) in 1522, these five sections were treated as a separate sermon, and in 1529 they were so rendered in Latin under the title of "Concio quo modo sit orandum ad Deum." This Latin text was included in the composite edition of Brunfels' *Precationes Biblicae* which de Keyser published at Antwerp in 1531; it was also included in the Wittenberg edition of Luther's *Opera* (vol. I, p. 70ᵛ) and in the Jena edition (vol. I, p. 332ᵛ). The Latin text appears to have been the basis for the English rendering in the Primer (fol. E5), where it is entitled, "An oration or sermon/ howe and in what maner/ we oughte to pray to almyghty God."

In 1520 Luther put forth a small treatise called "Eine Kurze Form der Zehn Geboten, des Glaubens, und des Vater Unsers" (see Weimar edition, vol. VII, p. 204). This material he used again in the forepart of his *Betbüchlein,* which in its content was roughly the equivalent of a Lutheran Primer. The *Betbüchlein* was evidently very popular with adherents of the Reformation, both in England and elsewhere. In Wittenberg, in August 1529, Johannes Lufft published a Latin edition of it under the title, *Enchiridion piarum precationum cum Calendario et passionali.* This was reprinted in 1543 under a slightly different title, and the first part of it was again reprinted at Wittenberg in the 1558 edition of Luther's *Opera* (vol. VII, p. 118ᵛ). In this 1558 collection no date is assigned to the material from the *Enchiridion,* but from the context it has been mistakenly assumed that it harked back to a Latin edition of 1520 or 1521; notwithstanding that the Weimar editor of the *Werke* mentions no Latin edition of the *Enchiridion* earlier than the one of 1529 (see vol. XXX, part 1, pp. 585, 671). A considerable portion of this 1529 text was also included in the 1531 edition of Brunfels' *Precationes Biblicae* spoken of above.

While one hesitates to run counter to the findings of a German editor in the field of Luther's early editions, it is by no means certain that the *Enchiridion piarum precationum* appeared for the first time in 1529. It seems to have been known in England as early as 1526 or 1527. It may be well to digress for a moment to present such evidence as we have, though the form of the title varies and the dates are not too clearly fixed.

In the Folger Shakespeare Library at Washington is a copy of a later edition of Marshall's Primer (*S.T.C.* 15998) on the flyleaf of which there is a handwritten notation dating from about 1650 which says that the preface of the Primer, the introduction and discussion of the Commandments, Creed, and Paternoster "you shall finde set forth formerlie in Latine in a Manuall of Praiers intituled *Precationum aliquot et piarum Meditationum Enchiridion* printed in xvjº Anno 1526 mense Nouember: the author nor printers names & the place where it was printed are not expressed."

In Foxe's *Acts and Monuments* there are references to a similar volume. In his edition of 1563 (p. 450) there is a short list of books accompanying a prohibition issued by Bishop Tunstall of London in October 1526; this includes a "Piae precationes." Following this is a long list of Latin titles prohibited "within a short time after"; this includes both "Lutheri Cathecismus Latina" and "Enchiridion piarum precationum M. Lutheri."

Further along in the same volume (fol. Vv6ᵛ—the paging is confused) we come across "Articles obiected againste Ieffrey Lom somtime porter of S. Antonies schole" as taken from Bishop Tunstall's register about the year 1528:

Inprimis for hauinge and dispersynge abrode sondry bookes of Martin Luthers, & others as also for translating into the English tounge certain chapters . . . of a certen boke called *pie predicationes* wherin diuers workes of Luther be comprehended.

This might well have referred to the same work, with the title misquoted.

Next, in the correspondence having to do with Thomas Garrard (or Garret), printed among the addenda to Foxe's book (see Pratt's edition, vol. V), Rev. J. F. Mozley has directed my attention to several references to a similar work. The correspondence is assigned to the year 1528. In a list of books (p. [874]) recommended by Garret to one John Mayhew occurs the title "Pie precationes de canonica"—evidently a small book of which many copies were found. In a letter from John London to the Bishop of Lincoln (p. [875]) the "Enchiridion precationum" is said to have been one of the books loaned to Anthony Dalaber by Master Clark, formerly of Cambridge. Again, in Tunstall's letter to Cardinal Wolsey (p. [879]) a Dutchman of Antwerp named Theodoric is said to have imported certain forbidden books the year before, including a "Precationes Piae."

All of these may not have been the same book, of course; but the foregoing references all seem to antedate the year 1529. We have already mentioned the item of "Godly prayers" which Foxe lists among the English books covered in the royal Proclamation of June 1530, and which may have been some English adaptation of Luther's *Enchiridion;* and there was also an item on Bishop Stokesley's list of 1531 called "Pre precaciones" which looks like a false entry for some similar title. Lastly, there is in the John Rylands Library at Manchester an early undated compilation called "Deuout prayers in Englysshe of thactes of our redemption," printed by Redman and assigned without much certainty to the year 1531. These prayers are not biblical and the item is not listed in the *Short-title Catalogue.* It would be interesting to know whether this rare volume is also of Lutheran extraction.

Returning now to the *Betbüchlein,* we find that in 1531 the Danish reformer, Christiern Pedersen, published at Antwerp a treatise called "Den rette vey till Hiemmerigis Rige" which was based on material gathered partly from Luther's *Betbüchlein* and partly from the writings of Urbanus Regius. Two years later, at Malmö in Sweden, a Scotchman, John Gau, put forth a translation of Pedersen's treatise into his own native tongue,[1] having the following title:

The richt vay to the Kingdome of heuine is techit heir in the x commandis of God/ And in the Creid/ and Pater noster/ . . .

Therefore, in addition to the Joye Hortulus, all the Lutheran materials cited above would have been available to Marshall in 1534. It is not easy to determine which of these he used; whether the German or Latin form of the *Betbüchlein,* or the de Keyser printing of Brunfels' *Precationes;* or whether he was also acquainted with the treatise of John Gau. Some of the evidence inclines one way, some another.

Take, for example, Marshall's "Preface to the reader" (fol. B1), which in the Primer of 1534 begins:

Among other innumerable pestilent infections of bokes & learnynges/ with the which christen people haue been pytyously seduced and deceyued/ . . .

---

[1] See *S.T.C.* 11686 and 19525. The original Gau edition is now in the Folger Shakespeare Library. It was reprinted for the Scottish Text Society in 1888 (vol. 12), edited by A. F. Mitchell.

This does not occur in the earlier "Kurze Form" of Luther or in the Brunfels *Precationes*, but it is found in the *Betbüchlein* of 1522 in these words (Weimar edition, vol. X, part 2, p. 375):

Unter andern viel schedlichen leren unnd buchlin, da mit die Christen verfuret unnd betrogen unnd untzehlich missglawben auffkommen sind, . . .

In the *Enchiridion* of 1529 (Wittenberg *Opera,* vol. VII, p. 118ᵛ) the Latin version read:

Inter multos alios perniciosos libros ac dogmata, quibus Christiana religio obscurata est . . .

while the Scots version of John Gau (1533) began as follows:

Amangis many oder skaithful bukis and fals doctrine with the quhilk the pepil hes ben falslie dissauit . . .

Not only did the *Betbüchlein* contain this preface, but in at least some of its editions (including the *Enchiridion*) it gave also the two sermons referred to above. But only one of these was contained in the *Precationes* of 1531. Again, either the *Betbüchlein* or the *Precationes* might have supplied Marshall with any of the following items which he appropriated to the use of his Primer, but whether he took them from German, Latin, or Scots, we cannot always tell:

(fol. B2) The introduction which starts, "It was neuer ordeyned withoute ye synguler prouidence of god," etc.
(B3) The entire treatise on the Ten Commandments, divided into two tables and discussed as to the transgression and fulfilment of each command.
(C4) The treatise on the three parts of the Creed.
(D1ᵛ) The brief interpretation and the longer commentary on the "seven petitions" of the Lord's Prayer.
(E3ᵛ) The comment on the Ave Maria.[2]

In his exposition on the Ten Commandments, Luther divides them so that the last two together comprise what we usually now think of as the tenth commandment. At this point, the Latin version in the *Enchiridion* breaks out into a long interpolation concerning the Jews: "Postrema duo praecepta maxime ad Iudaeos

---

2 Fol. E4, containing most of this comment, is missing in the Bodleian copy of the Marshall Primer of 1534, but the text can be supplied from the copy in the Boston Public Library.

pertinent," etc. The German text of the *Betbüchlein* did not contain this; neither did the *Precationes* of 1531, in which the passage is given simply as: "Postrema duo praecepta docent & conuincunt nos de naturae malicia," etc. This latter reading is closely followed in the Marshall Primer and seems to indicate that here Marshall used the text of the *Precationes* rather than of the *Enchiridion* itself.

In 1529 Luther issued his *Kleiner Katechismus* (or Shorter Catechism) and many of its features were incorporated the same year in Latin form in his *Enchiridion*. One of these was what he called "Haustafel"—that is, a series of brief excerpts from the Bible setting forth in tabular form the Christian duties of various sorts of persons. These ranged from the duties required of rulers and of their subjects down to those of parents and children (see Weimar edition of Luther's *Werke,* vol. XXX, part 1, pp. 326-338).

When Tyndale was preparing his last revision of the New Testament—the "G-H" edition—early in 1535, he picked up the idea of Luther's "Haustafel" and imitated it under the heading, "The office of all estates," setting this among the preliminary materials in the front pages of the volume. From here it was taken over by Marshall, who included it with very slight revisions in his *Goodly Primer* of 1535 (fol. ²D3). The office comprised eleven short sections, of which the following were copied directly from Luther's Catechism: Bishops, wives, fathers and mothers, children, servants, and widows. Other sections of Luther's table were included by Bishop Hilsey in his *Manual of Prayers,* and the office was reprinted in a number of English Primers prior to the appearance of the authorized Primer of 1545, when it was omitted.

Also in the *Kleiner Katechismus* Luther included certain graces and prayers, which were likewise turned into Latin and reprinted in the *Enchiridion* as well as in de Keyser's edition of the *Precationes* (see *Werke,* vol. XXX, part 1, pp. 320-324). Several of these appeared also in the Joye Hortulus of 1530, from which they were copied into the Godfray Primer of 1535 (*S.T.C.* 15988a). But Marshall added still others which seem to be derived from Luther. Also, in the Gough Primer (*S.T.C.* 15992) and in the ABC of about 1538 (*S.T.C.* 19) we find other additional graces; but these show considerable diversity and can hardly be said to point to any specific Lutheran source.

Again, it was no doubt Luther's recognition of the two expositions by Savonarola on the 51st and 31st Psalms which paved the way for the favorable reception of these among the English reformers. These expositions had been published in Latin at Wittenberg in 1523 with a foreword by Luther himself (see Weimar edition of his *Werke,* vol. XII, p. 248). They were also included in the 1531 edition of Brunfels' *Precationes;* and it is likely that Marshall and Redman took them over from this source.

The lasting influence of Luther can be illustrated by a single example taken from the "sixth petition" of the Lord's Prayer.[3] In his "Kurze Form" of 1520 we come upon these words (Weimar edition, vol. VII, p. 227):

Drei vorsuchung oder anfechtung haben wir, das fleisch, die welt, den teufel. Darum bitten wir: Lieber Vater, gieb uns gnade, das wir des fleisches lust zwingen, *etc.*

In the *Enchiridion* and also in the *Precationes* we read:

Triplici genere tentationum vexamur, Carne, Mundo & Sathana, Oramus igitur, Bone Pater, adsis nobis tua gratia, ut domare carnalem libidinem possimus, *etc.*

In the Marshall Primer (fol. E1ʳ) the same passage goes:

We ar assaulted with thre maners of temptation/ the flesshe/ the worlde & the deuyll. Therfore we desyre the more dere father to endowe vs so with thy grace/ that we may withstonde the desyres of the flesshe.

Likewise in the Godfray Primer *(S.T.C.* 15988a), though the wording does not agree with Marshall's exactly, it follows the sense so literally as to make it certain that this Primer also was indebted to Luther (fol. C8):

Thre temptacyons haue we as namely/ the flesshe/ the worlde/ and the deuyll. Therfore praie we. O dere father/ gyue vs grace to ouercome the luste of the flesshe.

Eventually Cranmer embodied this idea in the Litany of the Church of England, which first appeared in print in 1544 *(S.T.C.* 10620), wherein the phrase was immortalized in the following form:

From fornication, & al deadly synne, and from all the deceites of the worlde, the fleshe, and the deuil, Good lord delyuer vs.

---

[3] The germ of Luther's idea is, of course, much older. For instance, in Plimpton's *Education of Chaucer* there is reproduced a children's Primer in manuscript dating from about 1400, wherein we read: "Strengeth stondith in myghti withstonding the temptacions of our iij enymes that is the fend the world & thyn own flessh."

Appendix I
(B)

The Two Issues of Mayler's Primer of 1540

THE alterations which Mayler introduced in the two issues of his Primer of 1540 (see above, p. 205) may help to elucidate methods of procedure as practiced by the printers of that period. As stated, the earlier or Selden copy follows a fairly consistent pattern until signature I. Here in the Compline (fol. I4) Mayler uses the Sarum text for the Psalms, but at the close of Psalm 131, instead of resuming with the Hilsey readings, he continues to follow the Sarum text for several pages, abandoning it for the Hilsey version at the place where *Salve Regina* is about to commence. From here (fol. I7ᵛ) throughout the rest of the Primer, the Hilsey *Manual* is followed.

This shifting from Hilsey to Sarum and back again in signature I involves a certain amount of duplication of material. For instance, on fol. I6 where the hymn occurs, "O blessyd Christe these houres canonycall," the concluding words of the hymn are:

> Make me accordynge to my busynes
> Paterne of thy crowne & glory endles.

Here the word *pattern* was a misprint for *partner;* and this particular misprint is found both in the Rouen Primer of 1536 and in the reprinted edition thereof which was published at Paris in 1538 *(S.T.C.* 16005). Other peculiarities of this Rouen text of 1536 are also to be found in Mayler's Selden copy; and since he likewise made use of the same text of the Savonarola expositions as was bound with *S.T.C.* 16005, it is logical to assume that he was copying the text of his Primer from this particular edition.

Later in the same signature (fol. I8ᵛ) the hymn recurs as part of the Hilsey text, and this time it is printed according to the wording given in the *Manual:*

286

> Make me, accordynge to thy busynes
> Partener of thy crowne and glory endles.

Incidentally, in the Redman Primer of 1538 *(S.T.C.* 16008) a different version was given of the next to last line: "Make me, Lorde, through thy goodnes Partener" etc. Perhaps Hilsey had been influenced by this reading to use "thy busynes" in his *Manual* instead of the older form, "my busynes."

In the Douce copy of Mayler's Primer a new set of substitute signatures was introduced drawn entirely from the Sarum version. Here, for reasons of his own, Mayler did not use again the Rouen Primer *(S.T.C.* 16005) but turned instead to the wording of the Redman Primer of 1537, which he follows quite literally.

But now he must also watch his spacing so as to make his material come out even at the end of a signature, so that it will join without a break with the beginning of signature K, as in the Selden copy. Therefore he compresses his text wherever he can and omits quite a little of the latter portion of the Compline. By this means he manages to print in a single signature (G of the Douce copy) the equivalent of his combined materials, partly Sarum and partly Hilsey, which in the Selden copy had occupied two signatures and a half (fol. G5^v-I8^v). Where the hymn cited above appears for the first time, Mayler now attaches to it the versicle and response that accompanied it in the *Hilsey* text, and he wholly omits its second appearance with all the material intervening; thus he tailors his text to make the G signature of the Douce copy end at the same point as the I signature of the Selden copy.

Appendix II

Synopsis of Scriptural Passages in the Primers

(A) Psalms[1]

	Matins	Lauds	Hours (I)
Sarum	95, 8, 19, 24, 51;	93, 100, 63, 67, 148-150;	54, 117, 118;
Joye	95, 8, 19, 24; —	93, 100, 63, 67, 148-150;	54, 117, 118;
Marshall	95, 8, 19, 24; —	93, 100, 63, 67, 148-150;	54, 117, 118;
Hilsey	95, 5, 25, 86; —	— 103, 104, — 148-150;	54, 118, 146;
Henry	95, 8, 19, 24; —	— — — 67, 148; —	— 118; —

Hours (cont'd)

	(III)	(VI)	(IX)
Sarum	120-122;	123-125;	126-128;
Joye	120-122;	123-125;	126-128;
Marshall	120-122;	123-125;	126-128;
Hilsey	33, 119 (1-16), 147;	34, 119 (17-24), 117;	67, 119 (25-32), 145;
Henry	— — 120; — —	— — 123; — —	— — 15; — —

	Evensong	Compline	Seven Psalms
Sarum	122-126;	13, 43, 129, 131, 130;	6, 32, 38, 51, 102, 130, 143;
Joye	1-3, 115;	13, 43, 129, 131; —	6, 32, 38, 51, 102, 130, 143;
Marshall	1-3, 115;	13, 43, 129, 131; —	6, 32, 38, 51, 102, 130, 143;
Hilsey	112-115, 135, 136;	4, 31(1-6), 134, 138;	6, 32, 38, 51, 102, 130, 143;
Henry	— 113, 135, 138;	13, 43; — — —	6, 32, 38, 51, 102, 130, 143;

	15 Psalms	Placebo[2]	Dirge
Sarum	120-134;	116, 120, 121, 130, 138, 146;	5-7; 23, 25, 27;
Joye	— —	— — — — — —	— — — —
Marshall	— —	116, 120, 121, 130, 138, 146;	5-7; 23, 25, 27;
Hilsey	120-134;	116, 120, 121, 130, 138, 146;	5-7; 23, 25, 27;
Henry	— —	116, 41, — — — 146;	5; — — 27;

[1] Citations are according to the King James version, which is based on the Hebrew Psalter. The numbering in the Latin Psalter is different, the comparison being as follows:

Hebrew 1-8, 9, 10, 11....113, 114, 115, 116, 117....146, 147, 148-150.
Latin 1-8, 9, 10....112, 113, 114, 115, 116....145, 146, 147, 148-150.

[2] Joye's Hortulus and Marshall's first Primer contained neither Placebo nor Dirge, but the Marshall *Goodly Primer* included them.

	Dirge (cont'd)	*Commen-dations*	*Ps. of the Passion*[3]
Sarum	40-42; 51, 65, 63, 67; 148-150, 30, 142;	119, 139;	22-31(5).
Joye	— — — — — — — — — —	119; —	— ——
Marshall	40-42; 51, 65, 63; — 148-150, 30; —	119; —	22-31(5).
Hilsey	40-42; 51, 65, 63, 67; 148-150, 30; —	— —	— ——
Henry	— 42; — — — — — — 30, 71;	119; —	22, 69, 88, 2, 59.

(B) *Other than Psalms*

In the Joye Hortulus:

Ex. 20:3-17 (Ten Comm.); I Sam. 2:1-10; Isa. 57:20, 21; 59:1; 63:15—64:12; Dan. 9:4-19; Jonah 2:1-10; Wisd. 5:2-7; 6:4-6; Dan. 3:34-67 (Song of the Three Children[4]); Matt. 6:9-13 (Lord's Prayer); 10:16-20; 11:28; Luke 1:46-55 (Magnificat); 1:68-79 (Benedictus); 2:29-32 (Nunc Dimittis); John 16:1-3; Rom. 15:1-3; Ephes. 2:8, 9; Hebr. 12:1-7; I Peter 2:6, 7.

In Marshall's *Goodly Primer,* in addition to the above:

In the Office of All Estates: Levit. 19:15, 36; Wisd. 1:1; Ephes. 5:22-29; 6:1-4; Col. 3:22-24; 4:1; I Tim. 3:2-4; 5:5.

And in the Dirge: Job 7:16-21; 10:1-12, 18-22; 13:23-28; 14:1-6, 13-16; 17:11-15; 19:20-27; Isa. 38:10-20.

In Redman's first Primer (1535) were the passages just cited from the Dirge and these in addition:

Prov. 30:7-9; Dan. 3 (Song of Three Children); Matt. 2:1-12; 6:9-13; Mark 16:14-20; Luke 1:26-38, 46-55, 68-79; 2:29-32; John 1:1-14; 18:1—19:42.

In Redman's later Primer (1538), in addition to the 'Epistles and Gospels' were these citations:

Ex. 20:2-17; Levit. 19:15, 36; Deut. 6:6-9; I Sam. 2:1-10; I Kings 3:6-9; Job 1:20, 21; Prov. 30:7-9; Isa. 38:10-20; Jer. 17:14, 18; Jonah 2:1-10; Tobit 3:2-6; Wisd. 1:1; 9:1-11; 15:1-3; Dan. 3 (Song of Three Children); Matt. 2:1-12; 5:21, 22, 33-37, 40, 42-45; 6:9-13; Mark 12: 29, 30; 16:14-20; Luke 1:26-38, 46-55, 68-79; 2:29-32; John 1:1-14; 17:1-26; 18:1—19:42; Acts 4:24-30; I Cor. 6:7, 8; Ephes. 4:25, 28, 29, 31; 5:4, 22-29; 6:1-4; Col. 3:22-24; 4:1; I Tim. 3:2-4; 5:5; 6:6-10.

---

[3] After Psalms of the Passion, Sarum Primers gave the Psalter of St. Jerome, made up of excerpts from the Psalms, including Ps. 51 entire. In the Gough Primer we also find the "Matins and Hours of the Name of Jesus" comprising the following: 95; 66:1-4; 143:8-12; 86:9-12; 51:10-12; 111:9,10; 13:3-6.

[4] This canticle from the Apocryphal addition to Daniel is variously cited as to verses.

In Hilsey's *Manual*:

Gen. 50:24-26; Ex. 20:2-17; Levit. 19:11-15, 36; Deut. 6:1-9; Job 7:1, 2, 5-7; 14:1-5, 7-16; Isa. 38:10-20; 40:6, 7; Wisd. 1:1; 6:1-3, 9-11; Dan. 3 (Song of Three Children); Matt. 1:18-25; 5:21, 22, 33-37, 40, 42-45; 6:5-13; 11:28; Mark 12:29, 30; 16:14-20; Luke 1:46-55, 68-79; 2:29-32; 24:1-12; John 5:24-29; 18:1— 19:42; Rom. 3:19-26; 13:1-6; I Cor. 6:7, 8; 15:20-23, 50-54; Ephes. 2:8, 9; 4:25, 28, 29, 31; 5:4, 22-29; 6:1-4; Col. 3:22-24; 4:1; I Thess. 4:13-18; I Tim. 5:5; 6:6-10; Titus 1:7-9; I Pet. 2:13, 14; 3:8, 9; 5:1-4; II Pet. 2:1-3, 13-15.

In the Authorized Primer (1545):

Ex. 20:3-17; II Chron. 14:11; Job 1:20, 21; 10:8-12; 19:25-27; Prov. 30:7-9; Isa. 11:1-5; 38:10-20; Jer. 17:14, 17, 18; 31:18, 19; Wisd. 9:1-11; 15:1-3; Ecclus. 23:4-6; 51:1-30; Dan. 3 (Song of Three Children); Prayer of Manasses; Matt. 5:3-10; 6:9-13; Luke 1:26-38, 46-55, 68-79; 2:29-32; John 5:24-29; 18:1— 19:42; Acts 4:24-30; I Cor. 15:50-57; I Thess. 4:13, 14.

Appendix III

Specimens of Variant Readings

THIS appendix is designed to illustrate the remarkable variety of versions in the translation of Scripture during the period of this history. For this purpose two selections are used which were perhaps the most frequently published. Just as the Psalms were printed more often than other portions of the Old Testament, so the 51st was doubtless the most often reprinted of the Psalms; for in certain Primers it occurs three or four times in the same volume. Likewise, the Lord's Prayer was printed over and over again, and is likely to have had the distinction of being the passage from the New Testament most frequently reprinted. The Magnificat was probably its nearest competitor in this.

Accordingly these two specimens—the first portion of the 51st Psalm and the Lord's Prayer—are here presented in such a way as to show all variant readings for each clause as printed during the years 1523-45. Wherever any given edition is not represented, this means that it simply repeated the wording already given in some earlier edition. Significant misprints are relegated to footnotes. It will be recalled that during 1538 an attempt was made to set up a standard version of the Lord's Prayer for public worship; so there is less change to be recorded in this Prayer after that year than before.

For purposes of comparison it was thought helpful to supply the text of these two selections in the Wycliffite and the King James versions also. The former, which appears first, is cited as representative of the state of the text during the period preceding the introduction of printing; while the Authorized Version is shown at the bottom of the list as printed in the King James Bible of 1611.

It is a surprising fact that simply to canvass the verbal variations occurring in these two selections during the period of our study requires the citation of at least thirty-five different editions. These include Primers, Psalters, Testaments, Bibles, and a few books of biblical selections or exposition. The sources are cited in chronological order and are indicated by the use of symbols. For the explanation of these, the following table may be consulted:

Date	Symbol	Edition
1390	WPv	Purvey's revision of the Wycliffite Bible (ed. Forshall and Madden)
1523	W23	De Worde's edition of the *Horae*, *S.T.C.* 15934 (fol. xi)
	K23	Kaetz's edition of the *Horae*, *S.T.C.* 15935 (fol. ✠8)
1525	T25	Fragment of Tyndale's first New Testament (ed. Arber)
1530	P30	First English Psalter by Joye
	H30	Joye's English Hortulus
	M30	*Mirror of Our Lady*, *S.T.C.* 17542 (fol. H1^v)
1532	T32	Tyndale's *Exposition* of Matthew v, vi, vii, *S.T.C.* 24439 (fol. i5^v)
1534	GJP	Joye's Psalter of 1534
	M34	Marshall's first English Primer (fol. D1^v)
	Sav	Savonarola on the 51st Psalm (bound with foregoing)
	T34	Tyndale's revised New Testament, November 1534
1535	PBR	Redman's *Prayers of the Byble* (fol. E2)
	PnR	Redman's booklet of the Paternoster, etc., *S.T.C.* 16815
	Fnt	The *Fountain of Lyfe*, *S.T.C.* 11211 (fol. C2, C7)
	G35	Godfray's English Primer
	R35	Redman's Sarum Primer in English and Latin (fol. I8, A5^v)
	Cov	First edition of the Coverdale Bible
1536	G36	Gough Primer of 1536 (fol. L7^v, T5)
	R36	Rouen edition of English-Latin Primer (citations are from 'St. Jerome's Psalter'—fol. X2^v—unless otherwise specified)
	StP	*Stories and Prophecies of Holy Scripture*, *S.T.C.* 3014 (fol. L1)
1537	InB	*Institution of a Christian Man* ('Bishops' Book') *S.T.C.* 5163 (fol. V3^v)
	Mat	The Matthew Bible, first edition
	PnB	Byddell's booklet of the Paternoster, etc., *S.T.C.* 16820 (fol. A4^v)
	R37	Redman's English-Latin Primer of 1537, *S.T.C.* 15997 (fol. P4^v, C2^v)
1538	CLN	Nicolson's edition of the Coverdale diglot Testament, *S.T.C.* 2816
	ABC	Petyt's ABC in Latin and English, *S.T.C.* 19
	R38	Redman's Sarum Primer 'newly corrected', *S.T.C.* 16008 (fol. B5)
1539	Tav	The Taverner Bible, folio
	Grt	First edition of the Great Bible
	M39	Mayler's Primer for Children, *S.T.C.* 16011
1540	Gt2	Berthelet's edition of the Great Bible, *S.T.C.* 2069
	G40	Grafton's Primer in English and Latin, *S.T.C.* 16015
	PLG	Coverdale's diglot edition of the Psalter, *S.T.C.* 2368
1543	K43	Kele's Primer in English, *S.T.C.* 16030 (fol. K6^v)
1545	H45	Authorized Primer of Henry VIII (fol. K3)
1611	KJ	First edition of the King James Bible

(A)

PSALM 51:1-12

WPv (1390)	God haue thou merci on me;				bi thi greet
P30 (1530)	Have mercy vpon me	(god)		for	thy ientle-
H30 (1530)	Haue mercy vpon me	(God)		for	thy fauour-
GJP (1534)	Haue mercy vpon me oh god/	accordinge vnto	thy good-
Sav (1534)	Haue mercy vpon me (oh god)	accordynge to	thy greate
Fnt (1535)	Haue mercy on me o lorde/	accordynge to	thy great
Cov (1535)	Haue mercy vpon me (o God)		after	thy good-
R36 (1536)	Haue mercy on me	god,	accordynge to	thy greate
Grt (1539)	Haue mercy vpon me (O God)		after	thy (greate)
PLG (1540)	Haue mercy on me o god,	accordyng to	thy great
KJ (1611)	Haue mercie vpon mee, O God, according to	thy louing

WPv	merci. And bi the mychilnesse of thi merciful doyngis;
P30	nes sake:		for	thy grete mercyes sake
H30	able goodnes: . . .		. . .
GJP	nes:		for	thy grete infinite mercyes
Sav	mercye	And accordinge to	the multitude of thy compassions
Fnt	mercy/	and accordynge to	the gretness of thy pyte.
R35 (1535) . . .		. . .	For	thy gret infinite mercyes
Cov	nes,	& acordinge vnto	thy greate mercies,
R36	mercye.	And accordynge to	the multytude of thy mercyes,
StP (1536) . . .		and for	thy manyfolde mercyes
Grt	goodnes:	according vnto ye	multitude of thy mercyes,
PLG	mercy	And accordynge to	the multitude of thy louynge
KJ	kindnesse:	according vnto the	multitude of thy tender

WPv		do thou awei my wickidnesse.	More
P30		wype awaye my sinnes.	And yet ageine
GJP		do awaye my transgressions.	Nowe & yet agene
Sav		wype awaye myne iniquite.	Yet
Fnt		take away myne iniquite.	. . .
R35		do[1] awaye myne iniquite.	. . .
Cov		do awaye myne offences.	
R36		put awaye my wyckednes.	And
StP		wype awaye my synnes.	. . .
Grt		do awaye mine offences.	
PLG	kyndnesses do	awaye myne iniquyte.	
H45 (1545)		. . .	. . . More & more
KJ	mercies	blot out my transgressions.	

[1] G36 (fol. L7v) omits the word "do."

WPv	waische thou me	fro	my	wickidnesse; and clense thou

P30	washe	me	more/	fro	my	wikednes	and make	me
GJP	washe	me		from	my	wikednes/	and pourge me
Sav	washe	me	more	from	myne iniquite ·	and clense	me
Cov	Wash	me	well	fro	my wickednesse, . . .
R36	wasshe	me	clene	from	myne vniustyce/	and clense	me
R37	(1537) Washe me more	from	myn iniquitie:[2]	and clense	me
Grt	Wash	me	thorowly	fro	my wickednesse, . . .
PLG	Wash	me	yet more	fro	myne iniquyte, . . .
H45	washe	me		from	myne iniquitie, . . .

KJ	2 Wash mee throughly from mine iniquitie,	and clense me

WPv	me	fro my synne.	For Y	knouleche my wickidnesse;
P30	cleane fro my vngodlines.	For my grevous sinnes do I knowledge:
GJP		fro my sinne.	For my transgressions do I knowlege/[3]
Sav		from my synne.	For I	knowlege myne iniquyte,
Cov		. . .	For I	knowledge my fautes,
R36		from my faultes.	For I	do knowe myne iniquite
R37	more	from my synne.	. . .
PLG		. . .	For myne iniquite do I knowe,

KJ	from my sinne.	For I	acknowledge my transgressions:

WPv	and my synne	is euere agens me.
P30	and my vngodlynes	is ever before myn eyes. Ageinste the/
GJP	and my sinne neuer	gothe out of my mynde. Agenst the
Sav	and my synne	is euer before myne iyes. Agaynst the
Cov	and my synne	is euer before me. Agaynst the
R36	& my synne	is euer agaynste me.
PLG	& my synne	is alwaye in my syght. . . .
H45	. . .	. . . To the

KJ	and my sinne	is euer before mee. 4 Against thee,

---

[2] R36 (fol. L4ᵛ) likewise reads: "Wasshe me more frome myne iniquite:" etc.
[3] PBR (1535) has "my transgressyon do I knowlege" (fol. F4).

WPv   I haue synned to the aloone,

P30   ageinste y*e*/ only   have I sinned/
GJP   onely to haue so sinned it beruweth me and it rep*en*teth
Sav   only   haue I synned:
Cov   only, agaynst the haue I synned,
R36   I haue synned to the alonely/
H45   alone   haue I sinned, . . .

KJ   thee onely   haue I sinned,

WPv   and Y haue do yuel bifor thee;   that thou

P30   and that at sore offendeth the have I done: wherfore
GJP   me to haue had done this greuouse sinne in thy sight: wherfore
Sav   &   haue done that which is euyll in thy sight: y*t* thou
Cov   and   done euell   in thy sight: that thou
R36   & I haue   done euyll before the,   that y*u*
StP   and yll haue I done in the presence/ . . .
R37   and haue   done euyll in thy syghte:[4]. . .
Grt   and   done this euell in thy syght: . . .
PLG   &   done euell before y*e*:   so that thou

KJ   and   done this euill in thy sight: that thou

WPv   be iustified   in thy wordis,   and ouercome

P30   very iuste shalt thou be knowne in thy wordis and pure/
GJP   iustifie me   accordinge to thy promise   and make me clene
Sav   maist be iustified   in thy word*es*:   and mayst haue y*e*
Cov   mightest be iustified   in thy saynges,[5]   and shuldest ouercome
R36   myghtest be iustefyed   in all thy wordes/   & that thou mayste
StP   . . .   . . .   when it shal be iuged
R37   . . .   . . .   & vanquishe
Grt   . . .   . . .   & cleare
PLG   mayest be fou*n*de true   in thy sayenges,   and ouer come
K43 (1543) . . .   . . .   and vanquysh
H45   . . .   . . .   and maist ouercome

KJ   mightest bee iustified   when thou speakest, *and* be cleare

[4] R36 (fol. L4ᵛ) also reads, "& haue done euyll in thy syght"; but on fol. C5ᵛ it
reads as in Sav above.
[5] Grt (1539) has "in thy sayinge," etc.

WPv		whanne thou art demed.	For lo!	Y was
P30		when it shalbe iudged of the.	Lo	I was
GJP		accordinge to thy equite.[6]	Behold with sorowe	
Sav	victorie	when thou art iuged.[7]	. . .	
R35		. . .	. . . Lo	I was
Cov		when thou art iudged.	Beholde,	I was
R36	ouercome	whan thou shalt be iudged.	Lo surely	I am
StP	of the	when thou ouercomes.	. . .	
R37		whan thou arte iudged.[8]	. . .	
Grt		when yu art iudged.	Beholde,	I was
PLG		whan thou art iudged.	For beholde,	I am
K43		when I shalbe iudged of the	. . .	
H45		when thou art iudged.	Beholde	I was
KJ		when thou iudgest.	2 Behold,	I was

WPv	conseyued in wickednessis;	and my modir conceyuede me in synnes.
P30	fashoned in wikednes:	and my mother conceyued me polluted
GJP	and payne was I borne;	and with sinne my mother conceiued
R35	begotten in wyckednes . . .	
Cov	borne in wickednesse,	and in synne hath my mother conceaued
R36	conceyued in iniquyte/	and my mother hathe conceyued me in
R37	. . .	and my mother conceyued me in synne. . . .
Grt	shapen in wickednesse, . . .	
PLG	conceaued in iniquyties,	& in synnes dyd my mother conceaue
H45	begotten in wickednes, . . .	
KJ	shapen in iniquitie:	and in sinne did my mother conceiue

WPv		For lo! thou louedist treuthe;
P30	with sinne. But lo/	thou woldst trowith to occupye and rule in my
GJP	me.[9]	
Sav		Lo thou hast, loued truth/
Cov	me.	But lo, thou hast a pleasure in the treuth,
R36	synnes.	Lo truely thou hast loued treuth
Grt		But lo, thou requirest treuth in the
PLG	me.	For lo, yu hast loued treueth:
KJ	me.	6 Behold, thou desirest treueth in the

[6] PBR (1535) has "thyne equite" (fol. F4).
[7] R35 (fol. B1) has "whan thou haste iudged." R36 (fol. L4ᵛ) reads: "and haue the victory when thou haste iudged."
[8] R37 (fol. E2) reads: "& mayst vanquyshe whan thou haste iudged."
[9] GJP (1534) omits the next two clauses entirely.

WPv	thou hast schewid to me the vncerteyn thingis, and
P30	inwarde partes: thou shewedste me wysdome which thou woldst to
Sav	ye vnknowne & secrete tgynges[10] of thy wysdome,
Cov	and hast shewed me secret wyszdome.
R36	the vncertayne & the secrete thynges of thy wysdome
Grt	inward partes, and shalt make me to vnderstonde wisdome secretly.
PLG	ye secretes & pryuities of thy wysdome hast thou de-
H45	the vnknowen and secret thinges of thy wisdome thou
KJ	inward parts: and in the hidden *part* thou shalt make me to know

WPv	pryuy thingis of thi wisdom.	Lord, sprenge thou me with
P30	sitte in the secrets of my harte.	Sprinkle me with
GJP	. . .	Bespreigne me with
Sav	haste thou vttered vnto me.[11]	Sprynkle me Lorde
Cov	. . .	O reconcile me with
R36	thou haste magnifyed vnto me.[12]	Thou shalt sprynkle me good lorde
Mat (1537)	. . .	O purge me with
Grt	. . .	Thou shalt pourge me with
PLG	clared vnto me.	Thou shalt sprynkle me with
H45	hast reueled vnto me.	Sprynckle me lorde
KJ	wisedome.	7 Purge me with

WPv	ysope,	and Y schal be	clensid; waische thou
P30	hyssope	and so shall I be	clene: thou shalt
GJP	ysope	and I shalbe	clene:
Sav	with ysope	and so shall I be	clene/[13]
Cov	Isope,	and I shalbe	clene: wash thou
R36	with hysope/	and I shall be made	clene, thou shalt
Mat	Isope/[14]. . .		
Grt	Isope,	and I shal be	cleane: thou shalt
PLG	ysope O Lorde,	& I shalbe	clensed:
H45	with Hysop,	and I shalbe	clensed.
KJ	hyssope,	and I shalbe	cleane:

10 *Sic.*
11 R36 (fol. L4v) reads: "haste thou vtterly vnto me."
12 R37 (fol. E2) reads: "hast thou reueled vnto me." But on fol. GG1v it has "magnifyed to me."
13 G36 (fol. L8) has "and than shal I be clene."
14 Tav (1539) reads: "Purge me with Isope," etc.

WPv		me,	and Y	schal be maad whijt more then snow.		
P30	wasshe	me/[15]	& then	shall I be	whighter	then snowe.
GJP	washe	me/	and so	shal I be	whyter	than snowe:
Cov		me,	and I	shalbe	whyter	then snowe.
R36	wasshe	me	and I	shall be made	whyter	than snowe.
Grt	wash	me,	and I	shalbe	whiter	then snowe:
KJ	wash	me,	and I	shall be	whiter	then snow.

WPv	Gyue thou ioie, and gladnesse to myn heryng;
P30	Powre vppon me ioye and gladnes/
GJP	Shewe me ioye and gladnes/
Sav	Vnto my hearynge shalte thou geue ioye and gladnes
Cov	Oh let me heare of ioye and gladnesse,
R36	To my hearyng thou shalt gyue ioye and gladnes,
Grt	Thou shalt make me heare of[16] ioye and gladnesse,
KJ	8 Make mee to heare ioy and gladnesse:

WPv	and		boonys maad meke schulen ful out make ioye.
P30	make my	bones	to reioyse which thou hast smyten.
GJP	and my	bones	shal reioyse/ which thou hast broken.
Sav	& my brosed	bones	shall be refreshed.
Cov	that the	bones	which thou hast broken, maye reioyse.
R36	& the humbled	bones	shall sprynge for ioye.
StP	and make me	bones	reioyse the which thou hast smyten.
R37	and my weykened	bones[17]	shalbe refreshed.
PLG	& the	bones	which are brought lowe, shall reioyse.
H45	and the brused	bones	shal reioyse.
KJ	*that* the	bones	*which* thou hast broken, may reioyce.

15 K43 (1543) omits the words "thou shalt wash me."
16 Gt2 (1540) has "make me heare ioye and gladnesse," etc.
17 M39 (1539) has "my weyked bones."

WPv	Turne awei	thi face fro	my synnes;	and do awei alle my
P30	Turne	thy face fro	my sinnes:[18]	& wype awaye all my
GJP	Auerte	thy face fro	my sinnes/	and do awaye al my
Fnt	Tourn away	thy face from	myn offences	& put away al my
Cov	. . .	. . .		and put out all my
R36	Torne thy face awaye frome my synnes/			and put awaye all myne
PLG	Turne awaye thy face from my synnes,			& put out al myne
KJ	9 Hide	thy face from my sinnes;		and blot out all mine

WPv	wickidnesses.	God, make thou a clene herte in me; and make thou
P30	wikednes.[19]	A pure harte create in me (Oh lorde): and a stedfaste
GJP	iniquites.[20]	Create a clene herte in me oh god and a stable
Sav		A pure herte create in me[21] oh god & an vpryghte
Fnt	wickednes.	Create in me a pure herte (o god) and renew a
Cov	myszdedes.	Make me a clene hert (o God) . . .
G36	(1536)	A pure hart lord creat in me and a stedfast
R36	iniquyte.	O god create in me a clene harte and renue a
StP		. . . and a ryght
PLG	iniquities.	Make a new hert within me o god, & renew a
H45		. . . and a perfite
KJ	iniquities.	10 Create in mee a cleane heart, O God; and renew a

WPv	newe a rightful spirit in my entrailis.	Caste thou me no awei fro
P30	right spyrit make a newe withyn me.	Caste me not awaye:
GJP	spirit renewe with in me.	Cast me not out of
Sav	spiryte make a newe within me.[22]	Caste me not away from
Fnt	right spirite within me.	Do nat cast me away from
Cov	. . .	Caste me not awaie from
G36	pure spryte renew with in me.	. . .
R36	ryghte spiryte in my bowels.	Put me nat away from
StP	stedfaste sprite make anewe with in me.	. . .
PLG	right sprete in my body.	. . .
H45	spirit renue within me.	. . .
KJ	right spirit within mee.	11 Cast mee not away from

18 Sav (1534) has "from of my synnes."
19 R35 (fol. 18) reads: "& wepe away al my wykednes."
20 PBR (1535) has "myne iniquities" (fol. F4).
21 R36 in the Dirge (fol. R2) has "creature in me."
22 In Matins, R36 (fol. C6) reads: "and an vpryght spiryte renewe within me."

WPv	thi face;	and take thou not awei fro me thin hooli spirit.	Giue
P30		and thy holy ghoste take not fro me.	Make
GJP	thy sight:	and thy holy spirit take not fro me.	Restore
Sav	thy face/	...	Make[23]
Fnt	thy face	and do nat take from me thyne holy spiryte.[24]	
Cov	thy presence,	and take not thy holy sprete fro me.	O geue[25]
G36	...	and thy holy ghost take not awaye frome me.	Make
R36	thy face	nor take nat awaye thy holy spiryte frome me.	Gyue
StP		...	...	Geue
R37		...	...	Restore
PLG		and take not thy holy ghoost awaye fro me.	Graunte
KJ	thy presence; and take not thy holy Spirit from me. 12	Restore

WPv	thou to me the gladnesse of thyn helthe;	
P30	me ageine to reioyse whyls[26] thou bryngest me thy savynge helthe:	
GJP	me the gladnes of thy sauinge helth:	
Sav	me agayne to reioyse in thy sauynge healthe/	
Cov	me the comforte of thy helpe agayne,	
G36	me agayne to reioyse whylys thou bryngest me my saluatyon/	
R36	vnto me the gladnes of thy helthe/	
StP	me agayne the reioysinge of thy helth	
R37	vnto me[27] the gladnes of thy saluacion.	
PLG	me the gladnesse of thy saluacyon agayne,	
KJ	vnto me the ioy of thy saluation:	

WPv	and conferme thou me with the principal spirit.	
P30	and let thy chefe governynge fre spyrit strengthen and lede me.[28]	
GJP	and sustayne me with thy fre benigne spirit.	
Sav	and strengthen me with a pryncypall spirite.	
R35	& strengthen me with a spirituall spirite.	
Cov	and stablish me with thy fre sprete.	
R36	and confyrme me with thy princypall spiryte.	
StP	& the principall gouernynge spirite strengthen in me.	
R37	and strengthen me with a principall herte.	
PLG	and stablishe me wyth thy princypall sprete.	
H45	and strengthen me with the principal spirit.	
KJ	and vphold mee *with thy* free Spirit.	

23 R38 (1538) has "Take me agayn" etc.
24 Fnt (1535) contains only verses 1 and 9-11.
25 Tav (1539) has "Gyue me the comfort" etc.
26 M34 (fol. O8ᵛ) has "whyle".
27 H45 reads: "Restore to me the gladnes of thy saluation," etc.
28 G40 (1540) follows the P30 text to this point, then changes to Cov for the remainder of the Psalm (fol. E7).

(B)

THE LORD'S PRAYER
(Matthew 6:9-13)

WPv (1390)	Oure fadir	that	art in heuenes,	halewid	be	
W23 (1523)	Our fader	that	arte in heuen	sanctyfyed be		
K23 (1523)	. . .		. . .	holy	bemade	
T25 (1525)	O oure father/	which	art in heven	halowed	be	
H30 (1530)	Owre father	whiche	arte in hevene	. . .		
M30 (1530)	. . .		. . .			Thy name
T32 (1532)	. . .		. . .	honoured be		
PBR (1535)	Our father	whiche	art in heuens,	. . .		
Fnt (1535)	O oure Father	that	arte in heuen/	. . .		
KJ (1611)	Our father	which	art in heauen,	hallowed	be	

WPv	thi name;	thi kyngdom	come to;
W23	thy name.	Thy kyngdome	come to vs.
K23	thy name	thy kyngdome muste come tho vs/ . . .	
T25	thy name.	Let thy kyngdom	come.
H30	. . .	Let thy kyngdome	come over vs.
M30	be halowed.	Thy kyngdome maye come.	
T32	thy name.	thy kyngedome	come.
PBR	. . .	Thy kyngdome	come vnto vs.
Fnt	. . .	let thy kyngdom	come to vs. . . .
R35 (1535)	. . .	let thy kingedome	com vnto vs. . . .
CLN (1538)	. . .	Let thy kyngdom	come nye.
KJ	thy name.	10 Thy kingdome	come.

WPv	be thi wille don		in erthe	as	in
W23	Thy wyll be done		in erth	as	in
T25	Thy wyll be fulfilled/	aswell in erth/		as hit ys in	
M30	So be thy wyl done		in erthe.	as yt ys in	
T32	Thy will befulfilled,	euen in erthe,		as it is in	
PBR	Thy wyll be fulfylled		in erth	as it is in	
Cov (1535)	Thy wyll be fulfilled	vpon earth		as it is in	
R37 (1537)	Thy wyll be done	also in erthe, euyn as it is in			
InB (1537)	Thy wyll be done and fulfylled in erthe,			as it is in	
PnB (1537)	Thy wyl be fulfylled	as wel in erth		as	in
R38 (1538)	Thy wyll be done		in earthe,	as it is in	
CLN	Thy wyl be done		in erth also as		in
Tav (1539)	Thy wyll be done,	as well in earthe,		as	in
Gt2 (1540)	Thy wyll be done	as well in earth,		as it is in	
KJ	Thy will be done,		in earth,	as it is in	

301

WPv	heuene;	gyue to vs this dai oure breed ouer othir substaunce;
W23	heuen.	Our dayly breed gyue vs to daye
T25	heven	Geve vs this daye oure dayly breade.
H30		Geve vs this daye oure sufficiente fode.
M30	heuen.	. . . . . .
T32	heauen.	. . . . . .
PBR	heuen.	Gyue vs to day our dayly bread.
Cov	heauen.	. . . . . .
PnR (1535)		Our dayly bred geue vs this daye.
R37	heuen.	Our dayly breade gyue to vs this daye.
InB	heuen.	. . . . . .
PnB	heuen.	. . . . . .
R38	heauen.	. . . . . .
ABC (1538)		Gyue vs this day our dayly fode.
CLN	heue*n*	Geue vs this daye our bread ouer other substau*n*ce
Tav	heauen.	. . . . . .
Gt2	heuen.	. . . . . .
KJ	heauen.	11 Giue vs this day our daily bread.

WPv	and forgyue	to vs oure	dettis,		as we	forgyuen
W23	& forgyue	vs our	dettys		as we	forgiue
K23	and forgyue	vs our	synnes/		as we	forgyue
T25	And forgeve	vs oure	treaspases/	even as we		forgeve
H30	And forgeve	vs ower	trespases		as we	forgeve
M30	And forgyue	vs oure	trespasses/		as we	forgyue
M34 (1534)	And forgyue	vs our	trespasses	euen as we		forgyue
T34 (1534)	And forgeve	vs oure	treaspases/	even as we		forgeve
PnR	Forgeue	vs our	trespasses	euen as we		forgeue
Fnt	And forgyue	vs our	offences/	lyke as we do		forgyue
Cov	And forgeue	vs oure	dettes,		as we also	forgeue
R37	And forgyue	vs our	offences,	euyn as we		forgyue
ABC	And forgyue	vs our	offences/		as we	forgyue
Tav	And forgeue	vs oure	dettes,	euen as we		forgeue
KJ	12 And forgiue	vs our	debts,		as we	forgiue

WPv	to oure dettouris;	and lede vs not in to
W23	our detters.	And lede vs not into
K23	other/	and suffer nat vs tho be
T25	them whych treaspas vs.	Lede[1] vs nott in to
H30	them that trespas ageinste vs.	. . . . . .
M30	oure trespassoures.	. . . . . .
PBR	. . . . . .	And bryng vs nat into
M34	theym whiche trespasse agaynste vs. . . .	. . .
T34	oure trespacers. . . .	
PnR	them that trespas vs. . . .	
Fnt	them that offende vs. . . .	
Cov	oure detters. . . .	
R37	them that offende vs. . . .	
ABC	them that offend vs.	And let vs not be ouercom
Tav	oure detters.	. . . . . .
R38	. . . . . .	And let vs nat be led in to
KJ	our debters.	13 And lead vs not into

WPv	temptacioun, but delyuere vs fro yuel. Amen.
W23	temptacyon. But delyuer vs from euyll. Amen.[2]
K23	tempted/ but delyuer vs from all euyll. Amen.
T25	temptacion. . . . . . .
H30	. . . But delyvre vs frome thevel spirit. Amen.
PBR	temptacyon but delyuer vs from the wycked. Amen.
InB	. . . But delyuer vs from the euyll. Amen.
ABC	by temptacyon. . . . . . .
R38	temptacyon. . . . . . .
KJ	temptation, but deliuer vs from euill:

T32	For thine is the kyngedome, the power and the glorie
T34	For thyne is ye kyngedome and ye power/ & ye glorye
Fnt	for it is thy kyngdome & power/ & glory
KJ	For thine is the kingdome, and the power, and the glory,

T32	for euer. Amen.
T34	for euer. Amen.
Fnt	for euermore.
KJ	for euer, Amen.

1 G35 (1535) has "Let vs nat into" etc. (fol. C3).
2 M34 (fol. D1v) has "So be it."

Bibliography

A.—PRIMERS, BOOKS OF HOURS, ETC.

(Listed chronologically)

[Page-numbers in brackets refer to this volume.]

[*Horae*] (Begins with calendar; Latin, with "Fifteen O's" and a few prayers in English [p. 6]). Colophon: "Thyse forsayd prayers as the .xv. oes in englysshe & ye other folowyng be enprynted by ye commaundementys of ye moost hye & vertuous pryncesse our lyege lady Elyzabeth by the grace of god quene of englond . . ." Wynkyn de Worde, c. 1494 (*S.T.C.* 15875).

[*Horae*] (Title-page wanting; Latin, with Ten Commandments in English rhyme [p. 6]). Colophon: "Thus endeth the matyns of our lady with many a prayer and deuoute lessone . . . Enlonged without inquysyon . . ." Wynkyn de Worde, 1513 (*S.T.C.* 15914).

Hore beate marie viginis [sic] *ad vsum Sarum pro pueris/ totaliter ad longum et sine require* . . . (Latin; contains an ABC [p. 6]). Francis Byrckman, Jan. 1, 1514 (*S.T.C.* 15916).

Hore beate marie virginis ad vsum insignis ac preclare ecclesie Sarum. (Latin, with rhymed prayer in English [p. 6]). Richard Pynson, May 12, 1514 (*S.T.C.* 15917).

Hore beatissime virginis Marie ad consuetudinem insignis ecclesie Sarum. (Latin, with Lord's Prayer in English [p. 8]). Wynkyn de Worde, Nov. 20, 1523 (*S.T.C.* 15934).

Hore beate Marie virginis secundum vsum Sarum: cum varijs orationibus/ cuilibet deuoto commodis. (Latin, with Lord's Prayer in English [p. 8]). Colophon wanting; almanac commences with 1523. Pieter Kaetz, c. 1523 (*S.T.C.* 15935).

This prymer of Salysbury vse is set out a long without ony serchyng . . . (Latin, with English title and rhymes [p. 9]). François Regnault, Dec. 13, 1527 (*S.T.C.* 15955).

Ortulus anime. The garden of the soule: or the englisshe primers . . . (Joye's Hortulus in English, revised edition [p. 21]). Marten de Keyser, 1530 (British Museum).

Hore beate marie virginis ad vsum ecclesie Sarum: cum multis ac variis orationibus multum deuotis. 1531 (Latin; contains "The Manner to Live Well" in English [p. 141]). Colophon dated October 1530. Christopher van Endhoven, 1531 (*S.T.C.* 15966).

Hortulus anime recenter diuersis/ ac odoriferis flosculis decoratus . . .

(Latin [p. 20, note]). Colophon wanting; printer unknown; June 30, 1531 (*S.T.C.* 15972).

[*Horae*] (Title-page wanting; begins on fol. a2; Latin; contains "Lesson for Children" in English [p. 122]). Colophon: "Robertus Wyer me excudebat, in parochio diui Martini . . ." Robert Wyer, c. 1533 (*S.T.C.* 15983).

Hore Beatissime virginis marie ad legitimum Sarisburiensis Ecclesie ritum . . . M.D.xxxiiij. (Latin [p. 71]). François Regnault, 1534 (*S.T.C.* 15984).

A Prymer in Englyshe, with certeyn prayers & godly meditations, . . . (Marshall's first edition [p. 52]). John Byddell for William Marshall, 1534 (*S.T.C.* 15986).

A Prymer in Englysshe/ with dyuers prayers & godly meditations (Godfray's edition [p. 73]). Thomas Godfray, c. 1535 (*S.T.C.* 15988a).

This prymer of Salysbery vse/ bothe in Englyshe & in Laten, . . . (Redman's first edition [p. 87]). Robert Redman, 1535 (Bibliothèque Nationale, Paris).

A goodly prymer in englyshe, newly corrected and printed, . . . (Marshall's revised edition [p. 104]). John Byddell for William Marshall, June 16, 1535 (*S.T.C.* 15988). *Note*: *S.T.C.* 15989 appears to be identical with this.

This prymer of Salysbery vse/ bothe in Englyshe and in Laten . . . (Gough's edition [p. 121]). John Gough, 1536 (*S.T.C.* 15992).

Thys prymer in Englyshe and in Laten is newly translatyd after the Laten texte. (First Rouen diglot edition [p. 131]). Colophon: "Imprynted in Rowen the yere of our Lorde 1 5 3 6." [Nicholas LeRoux for François Regnault ?], 1536 (*S.T.C.* 15993).

[*Primer in English and Latin*] (Title-page wanting; text said to resemble *S.T.C.* 15992) [p. 119, note]. Colophon wanting: [Nicholas LeRoux ?, c. 1536] (Hoskins No. 117*).

Thys prymer in Englyshe and in Laten is newly translated after the Laten texte. (Redman's revised edition, based on *S.T.C.* 15993 [p. 141]). Robert Redman, c. 1537 (*S.T.C.* 15997).

The prymer with the pystles and gospels in Englysshe . . . very necessary for yonge curates . . . (English and Latin; Byddell's diglot edition [p. 154]). John Byddell, c. 1537 (*S.T.C.* 15999). *Note*: *S.T.C.* 15990 is identical with this.

A goodly prymer in Englysshe, newely corrected and prynted, with certeyne godly meditations & prayers added to the same, . . . (Second edition of Marshall's Goodly Primer [p. 163]). Colophon lacking: [John Byddell ?, c. 1538] (*S.T.C.* 15998).

Here after foloweth the Prymer in Engysshe [sic] *and in latin sette out alonge: after the vse of Sarum. M.D.xxxviij.* (Similar to *S.T.C.*

15993 but with different preface [p. 170]). François Regnault, 1538 (*S.T.C.* 16003).

Here after Foloweth the Prymer in Englysshe sette out alonge/ after the vse of Sarum . . . 1538 (English only, save for a few Latin prayers; text based on *S.T.C.* 15997 [p. 171]). Nicholas LeRoux for François Regnault, 1538 (*S.T.C.* 16004).

Thys prymer in Englyshe/ and in Laten is newly translated after the Laten texte. M. D. xxxviij. (Virtually a reprint of *S.T.C.* 15997 [p. 172]). Nicholas LeRoux, 1538 (*S.T.C.* 16007).

Thys prymer in Englyshe and in Laten is newly translatyd after the Laten texte [Device of Jehan le Marchant]. Colophon reads: "Imprynted in Rowen the yere of our Lorde. M. CCCCC.XXX.-viij." [p. 172]. [Nicholas LeRoux for Jean le Marchant ?] 1538 (*S.T.C.* 16006).

Thys prymer in Englyshe and in Laten is newly translatyd after the Laten texte. (Known in two issues [p. 173]; based on *S.T.C.* 15993). Colophon reads: "Imprynted in Parys the yere of our Lorde 1 5 3 8." [François Regnault ?] 1538 (*S.T.C.* 16005).

This prymer in Englyshe and in Latyn is newly correctyd thys presente yere of our Lorde M.CCCCC.XXXVIII. (Further revision of *S.T.C.* 15997 [p. 174]). Robert Redman, 1538 (*S.T.C.* 16008).

The .BAC [sic] *bothe in latyn and in Englysshe.* (Earliest extant ABC book printed in English [p. 178]). Thomas Petyt, c. 1538 (*S.T.C.* 19).

The Manual of prayers/ or the prymer in Englysh & Laten set out at length, . . . Set forth by Ihon by Goddes grace, at the Kynges callyng, Bysshoppe of Rochester . . . (First edition of Hilsey's Manual; known in two issues [p. 184]). John Wayland, July 15, 1539 (*S.T.C.* 16009).

The Primer in English moste necessary for the educacyon of chyldren extracted oute of the Manuall of prayers or Primer in Englishe and laten, . . . (Drawn from English text of foregoing [p. 190]). John Mayler for John Wayland, 1539 (*S.T.C.* 16011).

The Manuall of prayers, or the prymer in Englyshe, set out at lengthe, . . . Set forth by Ihon late bysshoppe of Rochester . . . (Reprint of *S.T.C.* 16009 in English only [p. 191]). John Mayler for John Wayland, 1539 (*S.T.C.* 16010).

The Manuall of prayers or Primer in englysh . . . (Fragment of unfinished edition [p. 203]). (Contains reference to Anne of Cleves.) Printer unknown; colophon lacking. [John Mayler ?] 1540 (*S.T.C.* 16017).

[*Primer in English*] (Title-page and colophon both wanting; printer and date unknown [p. 215]). [Robert Copland ?, 1539-1541 ?] (Hoskins, No. 150). Copy in St. Paul's Cathedral.

The Primer in Englisshe and Laten set out at length with the exposicion of Miserere . . . and with the Epistles and Gospels . . . (Mayler's edition, known in two issues [p. 204]). John Mayler, 1540 (*S.T.C.* 16018).

The prymer both in Englyshe and Latin Anno. M. D.XL. Prynted in the house late the graye freers by Rychard grafton and Edward whytchurche. . . . [p. 207]. Richard Grafton and Edward Whitchurch, 1540 (*S.T.C.* 16015).

A Primer or boke of Prayers/ set forth at longe, . . . Here vnton [sic] *is added the Pistles & Gospels dayly red in the church. Anno 1540.* (In English only; based largely on *S.T.C.* 16010 [p. 212]). Nicholas Bourman, 1540 (*S.T.C.* 16016).

[Primer in English and Latin] (Title-page wanting; ends with the Dirge and without colophon; but has a section of Epistles and Gospels in addition, also without colophon [p. 213]). [John Herford ?, c. 1540.] Almanac commences with 1540; copy preserved in Folger Shakespeare Library (Hoskins No. 153).

The prymer in Englysshe and Laten. after the vse of Sarum, set out at length with many goodly prayers, . . . M.D.XLI. . . . [p. 225]. Thomas Petyt, 1541 (*S.T.C.* 16020).

*Hore beate marie virginis secundum vsu*m *insignis ecclesie Sariburisburium de nouo impresse:* . . . (Latin text; but contains "Office of all Estates" and the King's order concerning the Paternoster, etc., in English [p. 226]). John Mayler, c. 1541 (*S.T.C.* 16022).

A Prymar of Salisbery vse/ set out a longe in Englyshe and Latyn, and a prayer for euery sondaye and holy day in the yere/ besydes these folowynge. (Contains a set of collects in English [p. 230]). Robert Toye, c. 1541 (*S.T.C.* 16021).

[Primer in English and Latin] (Title-page and colophon both wanting; also contains collects in English [p. 230]). [Printer unknown; 1541-1542 ?] Preserved in Cambridge University Library (Hoskins No. 156).

*The abc with the Pater noster Aue/ Credo/ and .x. commaundementes in Englysshe newly translated and set forth at the kynge*s *most gracyouse commaundement.* . . . (A booklet of four leaves, now preserved in the library of the University of Illinois [p. 226]). Richard Lant, c. 1542.

*The Prymer in Englysshe and Laten, after the vse of Saru*m *set out at length with many goodly prayers . . . M.D.XLij. . . .* [p. 234]. Thomas Petyt, 1542 (*S.T.C.* 16028).

The Prymer in Englyshe, and Latyn wyth the Epystles and Gospelles:

of euery Sonday, & holye daye in the yere, . . . Prynted in London by Wyllyam Bonham . . . 1542. (Known also in another issue having the name of *Roberte Toye* on title-page instead of Bonham [p. 235]). William Bonham or Robert Toye, 1542 (*S.T.C.* 16025-27).

Alphabetum Latino anglicum (Special printing for Prince Edward, containing leaves bound at the beginning of *S.T.C.* 15605, preserved in the British Museum [p. 251]). Thomas Berthelet, 1543.

This is the Prymer in Englysh set out a longe with dyuers additions. (Text resembles that in Hoskins No. 150; almanac commences with 1543 [p. 216]). Richard Kele, c. 1543 (*S.T.C.* 16030).

The prymer in Englysh and latyn, after the vse of Sarum, set out at length with manye goodly prayers, . . . (Colophon dated "M. D. XLiij" [p. 240]). Thomas Petyt, 1543 (*S.T.C.* 16029).

[*Primer in English and Latin*] (Title-page wanting; colophon reads, "Printed at London in paules church yearde at the sygne of the maydens heed by Thomas petyt. M. D. xliiij" [p. 250]). Thomas Petyt, 1544 (*S.T.C.* 16033).

This prymer of Salysbury vse is set out a longe without anye searchynge with many prayers. Imprynted at London the xii. day of Septembre M.D.XLiiii (Latin text, with a few features in English [p. 251]). Thomas Petyt, Sept. 12, 1544 (*S.T.C.* 16032).

[*Primer in English*] (Fragment including leaves from the Dirge [p. 254]). Colophon cites "Rycharde Grafton" as "prynter to the Prynces grace." Richard Grafton, c. 1545 (*S.T.C.* 16031).

The A.B.C set forthe by the Kynges maiestie and his Clergye, . . . All other vtterly set apart . . . (Apparently, the ABC book authorized by King Henry VIII [p. 253]). William Powell, c. 1545 (*S.T.C.* 20).

The Primer, set foorth by the Kynges maiestie and his Clergie, to be taught lerned, & read: . . . M.D.XLV. (Quarto, in English; the first edition of the authorized Primer [p. 256]). The colophon is dated "the xxix. daye of May." Richard Grafton, May 29, 1545 (*S.T.C.* 16034).

The Primer in Englishe and Latyn, set foorth by the Kynges maiestie and his Clergie . . . (Diglot edition of the preceding [p. 257]). Colophon is dated "the .vi daye of Septembre." Richard Grafton, Sept. 6, 1545 (*S.T.C.* 16040).

The Primer set furth by the Kinges maiestie & his Clergie . . . (First edition of the authorized Primer in the reign of Edward VI [p. 274]). The colophon is dated "the laste daie of Nouember, in the firste yere of the reigne of our souereigne kyng Edward the vi." Richard Grafton, Nov. 30, 1547 (*S.T.C.* 16048).

An vniforme and Catholyke Prymer in Latin and Englishe . . . to be only vsed (al other sette a parte) of al the kyng and Quenes maies-

ties louinge subiectes . . . (First authorized Primer during the reign of Mary [p. 274]). John Wayland, June 4, 1555 (*S.T.C.* 16060).

The Primer set furth at large, with many godly and deuoute Prayers. Anno. 1559. . . . (The authorized Primer during the early years of Elizabeth's reign [p. 274]). William Seres for the assigns of John Wayland, 1559 (*S.T.C.* 16087).

B.—KINDRED BOOKS BELONGING TO THE PERIOD

1. *Bibles, Testaments, Psalters, Etc.*

Gospel of Matthew, i-xxii [title-page wanting]. Fragment of Tyndale's first quarto edition of the New Testament [Peter Quentel, Cologne, c. 1525 (*S.T.C.* 2823)]. Facsimile reprint (ed. Arber): *The First Printed English New Testament translated by William Tyndale, photo-lithographed from the unique fragment* . . . (London, 1871) [p. 32].

New Testament [title-page wanting]. Tyndale's first completed edition [p. 30] (*S.T.C.* 2824). [Peter Schoeffer, Worms, 1526]. Facsimile reprint (ed. Fry): *The First New Testament Printed in the English Language* . . . *Reproduced in facsimile* . . . (Bristol, 1862).

The Psalter of Dauid in Englishe . . . (Joye's first edition [p. 18]). Colophon dated: ". . . at Argentine in the yeare of oure lorde 1530. the .16. daye of Ianuary." Based on the Latin of Martin Bucer. [Marten de Keyser, 1530] (*S.T.C.* 2370).

The fyrst boke of Moses called Genesis (followed by the other four books of the Pentateuch; translated by Tyndale). Colophon is dated "the yere of oure Lorde. M.CCCCC.xxx. the .xvij. dayes of Ianuarij." [Johannes Hoochstraten, 1530] (*S.T.C.* 2350). Modern reprint: Mombert, J. I. (ed.) *William Tyndale's Five Books of Moses, called The Pentateuch* (New York, 1884) [p. 36].

The Prophete Isaye/ translated into englysshe/ by George Ioye [p. 25]. Colophon dated "in the year of our lorde 1531. the .x. daye of Maye." [Marten de Keyser, 1531] (*S.T.C.* 2777).

The prophete Ionas/ with an introduccion before . . . (Tyndale's Jonah [p. 37]). [Marten de Keyser, 1531] (*S.T.C.* 2788). Facsimile edition (ed. Fry): *The Prophete Jonas with an introduction* . . . *To which is added Coverdale's version* . . . (London, 1863).

Ieremy the Prophete/ translated into Englisshe: by George Ioye: . . . Anno. M.D. and xxxiiii. in the monethe of Maye [p. 164]. [Assigned to the press of the widow of Christopher van Endhoven, 1534] (*S.T.C.* 2778).

Dauids Psalter/ diligently and faithfully translated by George Ioye/
. . . (Joye's second version, this one based on Zwingli's Latin).
Marten de Keyser, August 1534 (*S.T.C.* 2372) [p. 81].

The new Testament as it was written/ and caused to be written/ . . .
(Joye's first reprint of Tyndale's New Testament [p. 160]). Widow
of Christopher van Endhoven, August 1534 (*S.T.C.* 2825).

*The Psalter of Dauid in Englysshe/ purely and faythfully translated
after the texte of Felyne* . . . (Reprint of the Psalter of 1530).
Thomas Godfray, c. 1534 (*S.T.C.* 2371) [p. 73, note].

*The newe Testament dylygently corrected and compared with the
Greke by Willyam Tindale:* . . . (Tyndale's first revision [p. 89]).
Marten de Keyser, November 1534 (*S.T.C.* 2826).

New Testament [title-page wanting]. Colophon begins: "The ende of
the hole new Testament with the Pistles taken out of the olde
Testament/" (Joye's second reprint [p. 42]). Widow of Christopher van Endhoven, January 9, 1535 (*S.T.C.* 2827).

The newe Testament yet once agayne corrected by William Tyndale:
. . . (Tyndale's last revision [p. 109]). Godfrid van der Haghen,
1535 (*S.T.C.* 2830).

Prayers of the Byble taken out of the olde testament and the newe, . . .
(Excerpts translated from Brunfels' *Precationes Biblicae* [p. 80]).
Robert Redman, c. 1535 (Pierpont Morgan Library).

*The Fountayne or well of lyfe/ out of whiche doth springe most swete
consolations/* . . . (Anthology of Bible texts, translated from *Fons
Vitae* [p. 78]). Thomas Godfray, c. 1535 (S.T.C. 11211).

*Biblia The Bible/ that is, the holy Scripture of the Olde and New Tes-
tament,* . . . *out of Douche and Latyn in to Englishe. M.D.XXXV.*
(First edition of the Coverdale Bible [p. 117]). [Ascribed to the
press of Cervicornus at Marburg], October 4, 1535 (*S.T.C.* 2063).

*The Newe testament yet ones agayne corrected by W. Tyndale: And
in many places amended/* . . . *Newly printed/ in the yere of our
lorde M. D. xxxvi.* (First edition to be printed in England [p. 181];
large quarto or small folio.) [Thomas Godfray], 1536 (*S.T.C.* 2831).

Storys and prophesis out of the holy scriptur/ . . . *Anno. M.CCCCC.-
XXXV.* (Bible excerpts "with deuoute praeirs/ and thanckgeuings
vnto God" [p. 292]). Simon Cock, c. 1536 (*S.T.C.* 3014). (The
colophon is dated "By my Symon Cowke. Anno. xxxvi.")

Biblia The Byble, that is the holy Scripture . . . *newly ouersene & corrected. M.D.XXXVII.* (Second edition of the Coverdale Bible
[p. 140]). James Nicolson, 1537 (*S.T.C.* 2064).

The Byble, which is all the holy Scripture: . . . *translated into Englysh
by Thomas Matthew* . . . *M.D.XXXVII.* (First edition of the so-

called Matthew Bible [p. 140]). [Assigned to the press of Marten de Keyser, Antwerp], 1537 (*S.T.C.* 2066).

Here begynneth the Pystles and Gospels, of euery Sonday and holy daye in the yere. (Earliest extant printed edition of the liturgical Epistles and Gospels, bound with Redman's Primer of 1537 [p. 149]). Robert Redman, c. 1537. *Note*: The Byddell Primer of the same year (*S.T.C.* 15999) contains a similar section.

The newe testament both Latine and Englyshe ech correspondent to the other . . . Faythfully translated by Myles Couerdale . . . (First edition of the Coverdale diglot Testament [p. 165]). James Nicolson, 1538 (*S.T.C.* 2816).

Here begynneth the Pystles and Gospels/ of euery Sonday and holy Daye in the yere. M.D.XXXviij (A reprint of the item above [p. 172, note]). The initials "I. G." are in the sill on the title-page; similar editions are bound with Primers of 1538 (*S.T.C.* 16004-07). [Probably printed by Nicholas LeRoux, perhaps for John Growte] 1538 (New York Public Library).

The Most Sacred Bible; Whiche is the holy scripture, . . . newly recognized . . . by Rychard Taverner . . . (First edition of the Taverner Bible [p. 182]). John Byddell for Thomas Berthelet, 1539 (*S.T.C.* 2067).

The Byble in Englyshe, that is to saye the content of all the holy scrypture . . . 1539. (First edition of the Great Bible [p. 182]). Richard Grafton and Edward Whitchurch, April 1539 (*S.T.C.* 2068).

The new testament in Englyshe translated after the texte of Master Erasmus Roterodame in anno 1539 . . . (The Great Bible version is used [p. 192]). Grafton and Whitchurch, 1539 (*S.T.C.* 2843).

Here begynneth the Pystels and Gospels of the Sondayes and festyuall holy dayes, newly corrected and amended. (A revised text, bound with *S.T.C.* 16010 [p. 192]). John Mayler for John Wayland, 1539.

The Byble in Englyshe . . . Prynted at London by Thomas Petyt, and Roberte Redman for Thomas Berthelet: . . . (Corrected edition of the Great Bible in smaller folio [p. 183]). Petyt and Redman for Berthelet, April 1540 (*S.T.C.* 2069).

The Byble in Englyshe, . . . with a prologue therinto, made by . . . Thomas archbyshop of Cantorbury . . . (First edition of the Cranmer Bible, with text revised from the Great Bible [p. 201]). Whitchurch or Grafton, April 1540 (*S.T.C.* 2070).

The Psalter or boke of Psalmes both in Latyn and Englyshe. . . . (A diglot Psalter, probably by Coverdale [p. 220]). Richard Grafton, 1540 (*S.T.C.* 2368).

The Gospelles and Pystles of all ye Sondayes & sayntes dayes that are red in the churche, all the whole yere. . . . (A separate item, but similar in text to the Epistles and Gospels bound with *S.T.C.* 16015 [p. 214]). Richard Grafton, 1540 (*S.T.C.* 2971). *Note:* Epistles and Gospels are also found bound with *S.T.C.* 16018 as well as with some later Primers.

Here begynneth the Pystles and Gospels, of euery Sonday and holy daye in the yere. (A separate item, but perhaps bound up with some missing edition of the Primer [p. 214]). John Redman, c. 1540 (*S.T.C.* 2972).

Here begynneth the Pistels and Gospels of the Sondayes and festiuall holy dayes, newly corrected and amended. (A separate quarto edition, based on the text bound up with *S.T.C.* 16010 [p. 214]). John Herford, c. 1540 (*S.T.C.* 2973).

The Psalter of Dauid in english truly translated out of Latyn. . . . Where vnto is annexed in thende certayne godly prayers . . . commenly called collettes. (A reprint of Joye's first Psalter, with collects added [p. 277]). Edward Whitchurch, c. 1541 (*S.T.C.* 2374).

Praiers of holi fathers, Patryarches, Prophetes, Iudges, Kynges, and renowmed men and wemen . . . (A revised edition of Redman's "Prayers of the Byble" [p. 237]). Richard Grafton, c. 1543 (*S.T.C.* 20200).

The Holy Bible, . . . (King James version, first edition). Robert Barker, 1611 (*S.T.C.* 2216). Modern reprint: Pollard, A. W. (ed.) *The Holy Bible An exact reprint in roman type, . . . of the Authorized Version* (Oxford, 1911).

2. *Prayers, Devotions, Commentaries, Etc.*

Caxton, ed. [Title wanting] (Begins: "O Ihesu endles swetnes of louyng soules" [p. 219]). William Caxton, 1491 (*S.T.C.* 20195). Facsimile edition: *The Fifteen O's and other Prayers . . . Reproduced in Photo-lithography by Stephen Ayling* (London, 1869).

[Chertsey, Andrew, trans.?] *Ihesus.* (⟨ *The floure of the commaundementes of god . . .* (Translated from the French; contains Ten Commandments in English rhyme [p. 89, note]). Wynkyn de Worde, Sept. 14, 1510 (*S.T.C.* 23876).

Luther, Martin. *Ein Sermon von der Betrachtung des heiligen Leidens Christi.* [p. 279] 1519 (See Weimar edition, vol. II, p. 131).

—— *Ein Sermon von dem Gebet und Procession in der Kreuzwoche . . .* [p. 279]. 1519 (See Weimar edition, vol. II, p. 172).

—— *Kurze Form der Zehen Gebote, des Glaubens und des Vater Unsers . . .* [p. 280]. 1520 (See Weimar edition, vol. VII, p. 204).

—— *Eyn bett buchlin . . . Gedruckt zu Wittemberg, 1522.* (First edition of the *Betbüchlein* [p. 61]). 1522 (See Weimar edition, vol. X, pt. 2, p. 355).

Brunfels, Otto. *Precationes Biblicae Sanctorum Patrum,* . . . (First edition [p. 79]). Johann Schott, Strassburg, 1528.

—— —— (Later edition [p. 79]). Marten de Keyser, Antwerp, 1531.

The XV. Oos in Englysshe with other prayers (See also under Caxton, above [p. 219]). Robert Copland, 1529 (*S.T.C.* 20196).

Bucer, Martin. *S. Psalmorvm Libri Qvinque Ad Ebraicum Veritatem Versi,* . . . *Per Aretium Felinum Theologum.* (Text and commentary on the Psalms [p. 19]). Ulrich Andlan, Strassburg, 1529.

Luther, Martin. *Der Kleine Catechismus für die gemeine Pfarrherr und Prediger* [p. 284]. Nicholas Schirlentz, Wittenberg, 1529.

—— *Enchiridion piarum precationum* . . . (Latin version of the foregoing [p. 280]). Joannes Lufft, Wittenberg, 1529. (See Weimar edition, vol. XXX, pt. 1, p. 264.)

[Gascoigne, Thomas ?] *Hereafter Foloweth the boke callyd the Myrroure of Oure Lady* . . . [p. 292]. Richard Fawkes, 1530 (*S.T.C.* 17542).

Pedersen, Christiern. *Den rette vey till Hiemmerigis Rige* . . . (The basis of Gau's treatise [p. 282]). Antwerp, 1531.

Tyndale, William. *An exposicion vppon the .v.vi.vii. chapters of Matthew* . . . [p. 292]. [John Grapheus ?], Antwerp, c. 1532 (*S.T.C.* 24439).

Gau, John. *The richt vay to the Kingdome of heuine is techit heir in the x commandis of God/ And in the Creid/ and Pater noster/* . . . [p. 282]. Johannes Hoochstraten, Malmö, October 16, 1533 (*S.T.C.* 11686, 19525).

Hamilton, Patrick. *Dyuers frutful gatherynges of scripture and declarynge of fayth and workes* (Translated by John Frith [p. 127]). Robert Redman, c. 1534 (*S.T.C.* 12733). *Note*: *S.T.C.* 12732 is now regarded as a later reprint, assigned to William Copland, c. 1549.

Savonarola, Girolamo. *An exposition after the maner of a contemplacyon vpon ye .li. psalme/ called Miserere mei Deus.* (Apparently the first printing in English, perhaps translated by William Marshall; bound with Marshall's first Primer [p. 66]). John Byddell for William Marshall, 1534 (*S.T.C.* 21795). *Note*: Subsequent editions, 1535-43, were issued in connection with the Primers; see under discussion of the individual Primer; also the writer's article in section C of this Bibliography.

—— *A meditation of the same Ierom/ vpon the Psalme of In te domine speraui whiche preuented by death he coulde nat fynyshe.* (Bound with Redman's "Prayers of the Byble" as the last section; apparently the first English printing; translator unknown [p. 84]). Robert Redman, 1535 (Pierpont Morgan Library). *Note*: Subsequent editions were issued in connection with the Primers; see preceding note.

(Lord's Prayer, Creed, Commandments, Ave Maria, etc.) *In the name of the Father/ of the Sonne/ and of the holy Ghoste. Amen. The pater noster in Englyshe.* (Bound with Redman's "Prayers of the Byble" as the second section [p. 82]). Robert Redman, 1535 (*S.T.C.* 16815).

—— —— *The Pater noster. ye Crede. & the commaundementes of god in englysh, with many other godly lessons/* . . . [p. 142]). John Byddell, 1537 (*S.T.C.* 16820). *Note*: Byddell and Redman put forth other editions in 1538 and 1539, respectively (*S.T.C.* 16821, 16819).

—— *The pater noster spoken of ye Sinner: God answerynge him at euery peticyon.* (Small booklet of eight leaves [p. 129]). Thomas Godfray, c. 1535 (*S.T.C.* 16818).

Capito, Wolfgang. *Praecationes Christianae ad imitationem Psalmorum compositae,* . . . *e Germanico versae in Latinum.* (Basis of Taverner's "Epitome"; see below). V. Richel, Strassburg, 1536.

Erasmus, Desiderius. *Precationes aliquot nouae,* . . . (Source of certain prayers in later Primers [p. 269]). Freiburg, 1537.

Ridley, Lancelot. *Annotations in the boke of Iosue* . . . [p. 176]. (Commentary with addition of the text of the entire Book of Joshua.) Copy preserved in New York Public Library [Thomas Gybson ?, c. 1538].

Certeine prayers and godly meditacyons very nedefull for euery Cristen. (Compiled from Redman's "Prayers of the Byble" [p. 177]). Johannes Hoochstraten (*alias* Philoponon), 1538 (*S.T.C.* 20193).

Hollybush, John (pseud.?). *An exposicion vpon the songe of the blessed virgine Mary, called Magnificat* . . . (Contains also the Benedictus, Nunc Dimittis, and Salve Rex [p. 177]). James Nicolson, 1538 (*S.T.C.* 17536).

Campensis, Johannes. *A Paraphrasis vpon all the Psalmes of Dauid,* . . . *translated out of Latine into Englysshe.* . . . (Translated by Myles Coverdale [p. 199]). Thomas Gybson, 1539 (*S.T.C.* 14620). *Note*: An earlier edition, dating from 1535, is preserved in the library of Lincoln Cathedral.

Taverner, Richard. *The Svmme or pith of the .150. Psalmes of Dauid, reduced in to a forme of prayers and meditations,* . . . (Based on the *Praecationes* of Capito; translated by Taverner [p. 195]). John Byddell, April 5, 1539 (Preserved in the Lambeth Palace library).

—— *An Epitome of the Psalmes, or briefe meditations vpon the same, with diuerse other moste christian prayers,* . . . (A revised and enlarged edition of the preceding [p. 195]). Richard Bankes, 1539 (*S.T.C.* 2748, 23710).

Vives, Juan Luis. *Ioannis Ludovici Vivis Valentini ad animae excitationem in Deum commentariunculae . . . Preces & meditationes quotidianae—Preces et meditationes generales.* (Source of certain prayers in the authorized Primer of 1545 [p. 269]). Ioannes Gymnicus, Cologne, 1539.

Taverner, Richard. *The Epistles and Gospelles with a brief Postyl vpon the same . . .* (Text and commentary; text drawn from Great Bible [p. 215]). Richard Bankes, 1540 (*S.T.C.* 2967).

A boke of prayers called ye *ordynary fasshyon of good lyuynge. . . .* (Booklet of eighteen leaves; author unknown [p. 240]). William Middleton, c. 1543 (Preserved in Folger Shakespeare Library).

Psalmes or prayers taken out of holye scripture. Anno domini M.D.XLIIII. (Not a Psalter but a cento of Bible verses; compiler unknown [p. 249]). Thomas Berthelet, May 25, 1544 (*S.T.C.* 3002).

Parr, Catharine. *Prayers or Meditations, . . . collected out of certain holy woorkes by . . . princes Catharine, Quene of Englande, . . .* [p. 250]. Thomas Berthelet, June 2, 1545 (*S.T.C.* 4818).

3. *Proclamations, Statutes, and Books Issued by Authority.*

A Proclamation for resystyng and withstandyng of moste dampnable heresyes . . . [p. 15]. [Richard Pynson ?], c. 1529 (*S.T.C.* 7772).

(Proclamation) *By the Kyng. For dampning of erronious bokes . . .* [p. 14]. Thomas Berthelet, June 22, 1530 (*S.T.C.* 7775).

(Statutes) *Anno .XXV. Henrici VIII. Actis made in the session of this present Parliament holden vppon prorogation at Westmynster, the .xv. daye of Ianuarye . . .* [p. 165] Thomas Berthelet, 1534 (*S.T.C.* 9379).

—— *Anno XXVI. Henrici VIII. Actes made in the session of this present parlyament holden vpon prorogation at Westm*[inster], *the .iii. day of Nouembre . . .* Thomas Berthelet, 1534 (*S.T.C.* 9385).

A Proclamation concerninge heresie. "For bycause that of late many straungers" etc. (Directed against the Anabaptists and others [p. 145]). Thomas Berthelet, c. 1535 (*S.T.C.* 7785).

(Proclamation) *Yet once agayne by the Kynge to the Shyryues* [i.e., sheriffs] . . . (Abolishing the authority of the Pope in England). Thomas Berthelet, June 9, 1535(?) (*S.T.C.* 7786).

(Statutes) *Anno XXVII Henrici VIII. Actes made in the session of this present parlyament holden vpon prorogation at Westm*[inster], *the .iiii. day of February, . . .* Thomas Berthelet, 1536 (*S.T.C.* 9390).

—— *Anno XXVIII. Henrici VIII. Actes made in the parlyament be-*

gonne and holden at Westm[inster], *the .viii. daye of Iune, . . .*
Thomas Berthelet, 1536 (*S.T.C.* 9394).

Articles deuised by the Kynges highnes maiestie, to stablyshe christen quietnes and vnitie amonge vs. (The so-called Ten Articles [p. 119]). [Printer not named], July 11, 1536 (*S.T.C.* 10033).

Iniunctions gyuen by auctoritie of the Kynges highnes to the clergie . . . [p. 119]. Thomas Berthelet, 1536 (*S.T.C.* 10085).

The Institution of a Christen man. (The so-called Bishops' Book [p. 140]). Thomas Berthelet, July 1537 (*S.T.C.* 5163).

Iniunctions for the clergy, 1538. Thomas Berthelet (*S.T.C.* 10086).

—— —— (Another edition) *Iniunctions exhibited. 1538.* [p. 169]. Thomas Berthelet, 1538 (*S.T.C.* 10087).

(Proclamation) "The Kynges Moste Royall maiestie being enfourmed, that sondry contentions and sinyster opinyons . . . (About printing and importing books [p. 167]). Thomas Berthelet, November 16, 1538 (*S.T.C.* 7790).

(Statutes) *Anno tricesimo primo Henrici Octaui. Henry the VIII. . . . helde his moste high courte of Parliament, begonne at Westm*[inster] *the .xxviii. day of April, . . .* Thomas Berthelet, 1539 (*S.T.C.* 9397).

A proclamacion . . . for the Byble of the largest and greatest volume . . . [p. 224]. Grafton and Whitchurch, May 6, 1541 (*S.T.C.* 7793).

A Necessary Doctrine and erudition for any Christen man, sette furthe by the kynges maiestie of Englande &c. . . . (The so-called King's Book [p. 244]). Thomas Berthelet, May 29, 1543 (*S.T.C.* 5168).

(Statutes) *Anno Tricesimo Quarto et Quinto Henrici Octaui. Actes made in the session of this present parlyament holden vpon prorogation at westm*[inster] *the .xxii. day of Ianuary/ . . .* [p. 241]. Thomas Berthelet, June 1, 1543 (*S.T.C.* 9407).

(Proclamation) "For as moche as by credyble meanes it hath bene declared to the kynges maiestie that the frenche kynge [etc.] (Declaring war with France [p. 245]). Thomas Berthelet, August 2, 1543 (*S.T.C.* 7801).

An exhortation vnto prayer, thoughte mete by the kinges maiestie, . . . Also a Letanie with suffrages to be said or song . . . (Probably composed by Thomas Cranmer [p. 247]). Thomas Berthelet, May 27, 1544 (*S.T.C.* 10620). *Note*: For editions of the authorized Primer of 1545, see section A of this Bibliography.

(Statutes) *In this volume are conteined the statutes* [etc.] (A collected edition; vol. II includes the reign of Henry VIII). Thomas Berthelet, 1546 (*S.T.C.* 9301).

The booke of common prayer and administracion of the Sacramentes . . . after the vse of the Churche of England . . . (First edition of the Prayer-book [p. 274]). Edward Whitchurch, March 7, 1549 (*S.T.C.* 16267).

(Ordinal) *The forme and maner of makyng and consecratyng of Archebishoppes Bishoppes, Priestes and Deacons. M.D.xlix* [p. 133]. Richard Grafton, March 1550 (*S.T.C.* 16462).

4. *Miscellaneous.*

Erasmus, Desiderius. *Christiani hominis Institutum in fide Iesus et in amore.* [p. 7]. Wynkyn de Worde, 1510 (*S.T.C.* 5162).

Colet, John. *Ioannis Coleti Theologi, Olim decani diui Pauli, aeditio, . . . Anno MDXXVII.* [p. 8]. [Printer not named] 1527 (*S.T.C.* 5542).

Tyndale, William. *The practyse of Prelates.* [p. 11]. [Johannes Hoochstraten ?], 1530 (*S.T.C.* 24465).

Joye, George. *The letters which Iohan Ashwel Priour . . . sente secretely to the Bishope of Lyncolne/ . . . with the answer of the sayed George vn to the same opinions* [p. 19, note]. [Marten de Keyser], c. 1531 (*S.T.C.* 845). *Note:* The colophon is dated Strassburg, June 10, but the place is fictitious.

More, Thomas. *The confutacyon of Tyndales answere . . .* [p. 23]. William Rastell, 1532 (*S.T.C.* 18079).

—— *The apologye of syr Thomas More knyght.* [p. 34]. William Rastell, 1533 (*S.T.C.* 18078).

[Marshall, William]. *A treatyse of the donation or gyfte . . . by Constantyne emperour of Rome . . .* [p. 57]. Thomas Godfray, March 1534 (*S.T.C.* 5641).

Watt, Joachim von (*alias* Vadianus). *A worke entytled of ye olde god & the newe/ . . . or orygynall begynnynge of Idolatrye. . . .* (Translated by William Turner [p. 59]). John Byddell, June 15, 1534 (*S.T.C.* 25127).

Joye, George. *The Subuersion of Moris false foundacion: . . .* [p. 35]. (The colophon, probably fictitious, reads "M.D.xxxiiij. at Emdon by Iacob Aurik.") 1534 (*S.T.C.* 14829).

—— *An Apologye made by George Ioye to satisfye (if it maye be) w. Tindale: . . .* [p. 50]. [Printer unknown], February 27, 1535 (*S.T.C.* 14820).

[Marshall, William]. *A treatise declaryng and shewing . . . that pyctures & other ymages . . . ar in no wise to be suffred in the temples or churches of Christen men. . . .* [p. 58]. Colophon reads: "Printed for W. Marshall. with the Kynges moost gratiouse priuylege." [Thomas Godfray ?], 1535 (*S.T.C.* 24238).

The Concordance of the new Testament/ . . . Anno. 1535 . . . [p. 156].

(The citations listed are apparently based on the Tyndale Testament of 1534.) Thomas Gybson, 1535 (*S.T.C.* 3046).

Becon, Thomas. *The new pollecye of warre, . . . lately deuised by Theodore Basille. . . .* (First edition; dedicated to "Syr Thomas Wyet" [p. 245]). John Mayler for John Gough, 1542 (*S.T.C.* 1735).

Lily, William. *An Introduction of the Eyght Partes of speche, and the Construction of the same, . . . Anno. MD.XLII.* [p. 251]. Thomas Berthelet, 1542 (*S.T.C.* 15605). *Note*: The British Museum copy is preceded by an ABC and followed by the *Institutum* of Erasmus; see above.

Bale, John. *Illustrium maioris Britanniae scriptorum summarium.* [p. 27]. (First edition) John Overton, 1548 (*S.T.C.* 1295).

C.—BOOKS TOUCHING ON THE HISTORY OF THE PRIMERS

(Listed alphabetically by authors)

Allnutt, W. H. *An Early Sixteenth Century ABC in Latin after the use of Sarum. With a few introductory Notes on the ABC and its History.* (London, 1891).

Anders, H. "The Elizabethan ABC with the Catechism" in *The Library,* Series IV, vol. 16, p. 32 (London, 1936).

Baldwin, T. W. *William Shakspere's Petty School* (Urbana, Ill., 1943).

Benton, J. H. *The Book of Common Prayer: Its Origin and Growth* (Boston, 1910).

Birchenough, E. C. "The Parallel Translation of the Sarum Prymer" in *Bodleian Quarterly Record,* vol. VII, p. 457 (Oxford, 1934).

—— "The Prymer in English" in *The Library,* Series IV, vol. 18, p. 177 (London, 1937).

Bishop, E. *Liturgica Historia: Papers on the Liturgy and Religious Life of the Western Church* (Oxford, 1918). *Note*: Chapter IX, "On the Origin of the Prymer," is reprinted from the second volume of *The Prymer or Lay Folks' Prayer Book,* edited by Littlehales (E.E.T.S., vol. 109; London, 1897) [see below, under Littlehales].

Blunt, J. H. *The Annotated Book of Common Prayer, forming a concise commentary on the devotional system of The Church of England* (London, 1866).

Bradshaw, H. *Collected Papers of Henry Bradshaw, late University Librarian* (Cambridge, Eng., 1889).

Brightman, F. E. *The English Rite, being a synopsis of the sources and revisions of the Book of Common Prayer*, . . . (2 vols., London, 1915).

Burnet, G. *History of the Reformation of the Church of England* (Revised and edited by N. Pocock, 7 vols., Oxford, 1865).

Burton, E. *Three Primers put forth in The Reign of Henry VIII viz. I. A Goodly Prymer, 1535. II. The Manual of Prayers or the Prymer in English, 1539. III. King Henry's Primer, 1545.* (First ed., Oxford, 1834).

Butterworth, C. C. "Bishop Tunstall and the English *Hortulus*" in *The Library Chronicle* (Univ. of Penna.) vol. XVI, p. 37 (Philadelphia, 1950).

—— "Early Primers for the Use of Children" in the *Papers* of the Bibliographical Society of America, vol. 43, p. 374 (New York, 1949).

—— "How Early Could English Scripture Be Printed in England?" in *The Library Chronicle* (Univ. of Penna.) vol. XIV, no. 2, p. 1 (Philadelphia, 1947).

—— *The Literary Lineage of the King James Bible, 1340-1611* (Philadelphia, 1941).

—— "Robert Redman's *Prayers of the Byble*" in *The Library*, Series V, vol. III, p. 279 (London, 1949).

—— "Savonarola's Expositions on the Fifty-first and Thirty-first Psalms" in *The Library*, Series V, vol. VI, p. 162 (London, 1951).

Byrom, H. J. "John Wayland—Printer, Scrivener, and Litigant" in *The Library*, Series IV, vol. XI, p. 319 (London, 1931).

Dasent, J. R. (ed.) *Acts of the Privy Council of England* (New Series; London, 1890).

Dixon, R. W. *History of the Church of England from the Abolition of the Roman Jurisdiction* (6 vols., London, 1887).

Dowden, J. *The Workmanship of The Prayer Book in its literary and liturgical aspects* (London, 1899).

—— *Further Studies in the Prayer Book* (London, [1908]).

Duff, E. G. *Horae Beate Virginis Marie Secundum Vsum Sarum. The unique copy printed at Westminster by William Caxton circa 1477.* . . . (London, 1908).

Foxe, J. *Actes and Monuments of these latter and perillous dayes, touching matters of the Church* . . . (First ed., John Daye, March 20, 1563; *S.T.C.* 11222).

—— *The First [Second] Volume of the Ecclesiasticall history contaynyng the Actes and Monumentes of thynges passed in euery kynges tyme in this Realme* . . . *Newly recognised and inlarged* . . . (2 vols., John Daye, London, 1570; *S.T.C.* 11223).

—— —— (John Daye, London, October 1583; *S.T.C.* 11225).

—— (ed. Pratt) *The Acts and Monuments of John Foxe. Fourth edition: Revised and Corrected, with Appendices, Glossary, and Indices*, . . . (8 vols., London [1877]).

Gairdner, J. *The English Church in the Sixteenth Century from the Accession of Henry VIII to the Death of Mary* (Vol. IV in History of the English Church; London, 1912).

—— *Lollardy and the Reformation in England: An Historical Survey* (4 vols., London, 1908).

Hennig, J. "Primer-Versions of Liturgical Prayers" in the *Modern Language Review*, vol. 39, p. 325 (Cambridge, Eng., 1944).

Hope, C. "The Story of the Passion and Resurrection in the English Primer" in *Journal of Theological Studies*, New Series, vol. II, pt. 1, p. 68 (Oxford, 1951).

Hopf, C. *Martin Bucer and the English Reformation* (Oxford, 1946).

—— "A Sermon of Martin Luther in the English Primer" in *Journal of Theological Studies*, vol. 43, p. 194 (Oxford, 1942).

Hoskins, E. *Horae Beatae Mariae Virginis or Sarum and York Primers with Kindred Books and Primers of the Reformed and Roman Use* . . . (London, 1901).

[Joye, G.] *Passion of our Saviour Christ according to the IV Evangelists, from the Goodley (?) primer of 1535* (Society of SS. Peter and Paul; reprint, [London?], 1916).

Kingdon, J. A. *Incidents in the Lives of Thomas Poyntz and Richard Grafton, Two Citizens and Grocers of London*, . . . (London, 1895).

—— *Richard Grafton Citizen and Grocer of London* . . . *A sequel to Poyntz and Grafton* (London, 1901).

Lacombe, P. *Livres d'Heures Imprimés au XVᵉ et au XVIᵉ Siècle conservés dans les bibliothèques publiques de Paris: Catalogue.* (Paris, 1907).

Lathbury, T. *A History of The Book of Common Prayer and Other Books of Authority;* . . . (2nd ed., Oxford & London, 1859).

Littlehales, H. *The Prymer or Prayer-Book of the Lay People in the Middle Ages, in English dating about 1400 A.D.* . . . (2 vols., London, 1891).

—— *The Prymer or Lay Folks Prayer Book. (With several facsimiles.) Edited . . . from the Ms. . . . 1420-30 A.D.* . . . (2 vols., Early English Text Society, Original Series, Nos. 105, 109; London, 1895, 1897. A different text from the preceding.)

Maskell, W. *Monumenta Ritualia Ecclesiae Anglicanae: The occasional Offices of the Church of England according to the old use of Salisbury, the Prymer in English, and other prayers,* . . . (3 vols., 2nd ed., Oxford, 1882).

Morison, S. *English Prayer Books: An Introduction to the Literature of Christian Public Worship* (revised ed., Cambridge, Eng., 1945).

Moultrie, G. *The Primer set forth at large for the use of the faithful in family and private prayer* (London, 1864).

Nicolas, H., ed. *Proceedings and Ordinances of the Privy Council of England* (7 vols., London, 1837).

Perry, G. G. *A History of the Church of England from the accession of Henry VIII to the silencing of Convocation in the eighteenth century . . .* (New York, 1879).

Plimpton, G. A. *The Education of Chaucer, Illustrated from the Schoolbooks in Use in his Time* (New York & London, 1935).

Ratcliff, E. C. *The booke of common prayer of the Churche of England: its making and revisions M.D.xlix-M.D.clxi. set forth in eighty illustrations . . .* (London, 1949).

Rupp, E. G. *Studies in the Making of The English Protestant Tradition (Mainly in the Reign of Henry VIII)*. (Second printing, Cambridge, Eng., 1949).

Shepherd, John. *A Critical and Practical Elucidation of the Book of Common Prayer, . . .* (2 vols., London, 1817; 1st ed., 1798?). *Note*: The opening pages of the "Introduction" constitute an early attempt to draw attention to the importance of the printed Primers.

Sheppard, L. A. "The Hortulus Animae in English, 1530" in *The Library*, Series V, vol. VI, p. 109 (London, 1951).

Shuckburgh, E. S. *The ABC Both in Latyn & Englyshe: being A facsimile reprint of the earliest extant English reading book. . . .* (London, 1889).

Smith, H. M. *Henry VIII and the Reformation* (London, 1948).

Strype, J. *Ecclesiastical Memorials, relating chiefly to Religion, and the Reformation of it, . . .* (3 vols. in 6 pts.; Oxford, 1822).

Tuer, A. W. *History of The Horn-Book* (2 vols., London, 1896).

Watson, F. *The English Grammar Schools to 1660: their Curriculum and Practice* (Cambridge, Eng., 1908).

White, H. C. *The Tudor Books of Private Devotion* (Madison, Wis., 1951).

Wordsworth, C. and Littlehales, H. *Old Service Books of the English Church* (London, 1904).

D.—BOOKS ON RELATED SUBJECTS

Anderson, C. *The Annals of The English Bible* (1st ed., 2 vols., London, 1845).

Bennett, H. S. *English Books & Readers 1475 to 1557 Being a study in the history of the book trade from Caxton to the incorporation of the Stationers' Company* (Cambridge, Eng., 1952).

Bishop, W. W. *A Checklist of American Copies of "Short-Title Catalogue" Books* (Ann Arbor, Mich., 1950).

British Museum. *Catalogue of Printed Books* (London; new edition uncompleted).

Butterworth, C. C. "The Term 'Lord's Prayer' Instead of 'Pater Noster'" in *The Library Chronicle* (Univ. of Penna.) vol. XVIII, p. 24 (Philadelphia, 1952).

Cambridge University Press. *A Photographic Reproduction of the original royal Injunctions issued under the authority of King Henry VIII* [1538] . . . (Pamphlet; London, 1938).

Cooper, C. H., and T. *Athenae Cantabrigienses* (3 vols., Cambridge, Eng., 1858).

Cranmer, T. (ed. Cox). *Miscellaneous Writings and Letters of Thomas Cranmer, Archbishop of Canterbury, Martyr, 1556* (Parker Society edition; Cambridge, Eng., 1846).

Deanesly, M. *The Lollard Bible and other Medieval Biblical Versions* (Cambridge, Eng., 1920).

Dibdin, T. F. *Typographical Antiquities; or The History of Printing in England . . . containing memoirs of our ancient printers . . .* (4 vols., London, 1809-19).

Dictionary of National Biography.

Duff, E. G. *A Century of the English Book Trade 1457-1557* (Reprinted edition, London, 1948).

—— *The Printers, Stationers and Bookbinders of Westminster and London from 1476 to 1535* (Cambridge, Eng., 1906).

Fisher, H. A. L. *The History of England from the accession of Henry VII to the death of Henry VIII* (Vol. V of the Political History of England; London, 1906).

Forshall, J. and Madden, F. *The Holy Bible, . . . in the earliest English Versions . . . by John Wycliffe and his followers* (4 vols., Oxford, 1850).

Frere, W. H. and Kennedy, W. M. *Visitation Articles and Injunctions of the Period of the Reformation* (2 vols., London, 1910).

Friedmann, P. *Anne Boleyn: A Chapter of English History 1527-1536* (2 vols., London, 1884).

Fry, F. *A Bibliographical Description of the Editions of The New Testament, Tyndale's Version in English, . . .* (London, 1878).

Furnivall, F. J. (ed.) *Political, Religious, and Love Poems* (Early English Text Society, Original Series, No. 15; reëdited, London, 1903).

Gairdner, J. (ed.) *Letters and Papers, Foreign and Domestic, of the reign of Henry VIII. . . .* (Series of vols., London, 1882 ff.).

Gardiner, R. B. *The Admission Registers of St. Paul's School* (London, 1884).

Hain, L. *Reportorium Bibliographicum* (Stuttgart, 1826).

Halle, E. *The Vnion of the two noble and illustre famelies Lancastre & Yorke, . . . to the reigne of . . . kyng Henry the eight, . . .* (Richard Grafton, London, 1548; *S.T.C.* 12722). [Known as "Hall's *Chronicle*."]

Haraszti, Z. "The First Book of Common Prayer" in *The Boston Public Library Quarterly,* Vol. I, p. 93 (Boston, October 1949).

Hughes, P. *The Reformation in England* (To be complete in several vols.; vol. I, New York, 1951).

Isaac, F. S. *English and Scottish Printing Types, 1501-41* [and *1535-58*] (2 vols., London, 1930-32).

—— *English Printers' Types of the Sixteenth Century* (Oxford, 1936).

Johnson, J. *Typographia, or the Printers' Instructor: including an account of the Origin of Printing, with Biographical Notices of the Printers of England, . . .* (2 vols., London, 1824).

Kronenberg, M. E. "Notes on English Printing in the Low Countries (Early Sixteenth Century)" in *The Library,* Series IV, vol. IX, p. 139 (London, 1928).

—— *Verboden Boeken en Opstandige Drukkers in de Hervormingstijd* (Amsterdam, 1948).

Lewis, J. *A Complete History of the several Translations of the Holy Bible, . . . into English, . . .* (2nd ed., London, 1739).

Luther, M. D. *Martin Luthers Werke: Kritische Gesamtausgabe* (The Weimar edition, begun in 1883; more than 60 vols. issued).

Maitland, S. R. *A List of some of the Early Printed Books in the Archiepiscopal Library at Lambeth* (London, 1843).

McKerrow, R. B. and Ferguson, F. S. *Title-page Borders Used in England and Scotland, 1485-1640* (London, 1932).

Merriman, R. B. *Life and Letters of Thomas Cromwell* (2 vols., Oxford, 1902).

Morrison, P. G. *Index of Printers, Publishers and Booksellers in . . . A Short-title Catalogue of Books . . . 1475-1640* (Charlottesville, Va., 1950).

Mozley, J. F. *William Tyndale* (London and New York, 1937).

Nijhoff, W. and Kronenberg, M. E. *Nederlandsche Bibliographie van 1500 tot 1540* (2 vols. and supplements, The Hague, 1926-40).

Pollard, A. W. *Records of the English Bible: The Documents relating to the Translation and Publication of the Bible in English, 1525-1611* (Oxford, 1911).

Pollard, A. W. and Redgrave, G. R. *A Short-title Catalogue of Books*

Printed in England . . . 1475-1640 (London, 1926). [Cited herein as *S.T.C.*]

Procter, F. and Frere, W. H. *A New History of the Book of Common Prayer with a Rationale of its offices* (Revised ed., London, 1910).

Reed, A. W. *Early Tudor Drama; Medwall, The Rastells, Heywood, and the More Circle* (London, 1926).

—— "The Regulation of the Book Trade Before the Proclamation of 1538" in *Transactions of the Bibliographical Society*, vol. XV, p. 157 (London, 1920). [Also reprinted as part of the preceding entry, p. 160.]

Reu, M. "Religious Instruction of the Young in the Sixteenth Century" in *Lutheran Church Review*, vol. 34, p. 566 (1915).

Rymer, T. *Foedera, Conventiones, Litterae, . . .* (20 vols., London, 1704, et seq.).

Sayle, C. E. *Early English Printed Books in the University Library Cambridge (1475-1640)* (4 vols., Cambridge, Eng., 1903).

Sergeant, P. W. *The Life of Anne Boleyn* (New York, 1924).

Sheppard, L. A. "The Printers of the Coverdale Bible, 1535" in *The Library*, Series IV, vol. XVI, p. 280 (Oxford, 1935).

Steele, R. "Notes on English Books Printed Abroad, 1525-48" in *Transactions of the Bibliographical Society*, vol. XI, p. 189 (London, 1912).

—— *Tudor and Stuart Proclamations, 1485-1714* (2 vols., Oxford, 1910).

Wilkins, D. *Concilia Magnae Britanniae et Hiberniae, . . .* (4 vols., London, 1737).

Wolf, A. *William Roye's Dialogue between a Christian Father and His Stubborn Son* (Reprint of original 1527 edition; Vienna, 1874).

à Wood, A. *Athenae Oxonienses* (Oxford, 1721).

Index
of
Scriptural Citations

Page

EXODUS
20:3 .... 35, 132
20:7 .... 36, 132

LEVITICUS
19:15 109

I SAMUEL
2:2, 3 175

JOB
7:17, 18, 21 101
10:8-12 .... 102, 115, 267
19:23-26 .... 101, 115

PSALMS
2:1, 4, 5 262
2:12 263
7:2 188
8:1-9 41
13:6 210
18:1 .... 211, 229
22:18 31
22:27, 28 249
23:1 97
23:4 249
27:1 .... 84, 147
27:1-3 .... 134, 261
27:13 148
48:3 229
51:1 .... 45, 124
51:1-12 293-300
51:4, 12 .... 147, 148
51:7-12 .... 68, 98
51:11 67
51:12 211
51:15 38
66:1-4 126
67:1-7 95
67:1, 4-7 136
67:5-7 263
67:6 147
83:1, 2 239
93:1 .... 94, 228
95:5 273
95:8-11 40

Page

PSALMS
111:10 .... 125, 126
119:64 .... 77, 97
126:1-6 .... 96, 97
126:2 147
130:1 135
145:15 .... 179, 260
145:15, 16 33
147:9-11 .... 33, 34

PROVERBS
21:1 65
30:7 148
30:7-9 .... 86, 88, 198, 240

ISAIAH
7:13, 14 160
38:12 114
38:14 273
38:14, 16 .... 99, 113
38:14-17 137
57:20, 21 110
59:1 46
60:1-5 194
64:1, 2 25
64:1-4 85

JONAH
2:3, 5, 6 37
2:5 238

MALACHI
3:2 214

WISDOM
4:3-5 152
5:2-7 42
6:5 210
9:4-6 86
15:1-3 85

ECCLESIASTES
44:10-14 .... 151, 152
44:16-20 158
44:19, 20, 23 159

Page

MATTHEW

4:6 193
5:7, 8........................ 265
5:34 142
6:9-12 146
6:9-13 ....9, 32, 33, 301-303
6:12 174
6:24 ....212n.
11:28 ....39, 94

MARK

4:19 ....142, 218n.
6:25 153
14:51 30

LUKE

1:29, 30 263
1:46, 47 99
1:51, 52 198
1:51-53 44
1:53 265
1:68-71 44
1:73, 74 114
2:29-32 43
16:2 153

JOHN

10:13 161
19:23 90

Page

ACTS

2:1 153
4:27 199

ROMANS

5:8, 9 32
7:24 271
12:13 160

I CORINTHIANS

5:7 ....179, 228
13:8-10 160

II CORINTHIANS

3:17 271

GALATIANS

4:24 193

EPHESIANS

6:10-13 161

PHILIPPIANS

4:5 193

JAMES

1:4, 5....................192, 193
1:17 252

I PETER

2:18 153

General Index

ABC Both in Latin and in English (1538), 177-180, 191, 253, 260, 273, 284, 292, 302, 303
"ABC of Thorpes" (see also *Examination*), 14
ABC set forth by the King's Majesty (1545), 253, 254, 257
ABC with the Pater Noster (Lant), 226, 227
Abrogation of Holidays, 143, 156, 172, 218
Acts and Monuments (1563), 11, 12, 14, 281
  (Pratt's ed.), 120n., 281
Acts of Parliament: (1534), 48, 50, 51, 165; (1536), 51; (1539), 183; (1543), 241, 242
Acts of the Privy Council, 243n.
Admission Registers of St. Paul's School, 7n.
Almanac for Easter, 3, 28, 53, 73, 87n., 88, 106, 107, 141, 157, 163, 172, 173, 191, 203, 208, 212, 230, 240
Alphabet (ABC), 3, 4, 6, 23, 32, 122, 178, 191, 227, 252, 253, 274
Alphabetum Latino Anglicum (1543), 251, 252
Anderson, Christopher, 16n., 233n.
Annals of the English Bible, 16n., 233n.
Anne Boleyn (Friedmann), 55n.
Anne of Cleves, Queen, 194, 200, 201, 203
Annotated Book of Common Prayer, 228n.
Annotations in the Book of Joshua, 176
Annunciation, 39, 92, 262
Answer unto Sir Thomas More (Tyndale), 11
Antwerp, 8, 11, 18, 19, 20n., 21, 25, 34, 49, 51, 72, 78, 79, 81, 116n., 117, 152n., 280-282
Apology (Joye), 27n., 50, 116
Apology (Melanchthon), 196n.
Apology (More), 34
Arber, Edward, 27n.
Argentine (Strassburg), 18, 21, 57
Articles Devised by the King's Majesty (see Ten Articles)
Arundel, Thomas, archbishop, 5

Aske, Robert, 140
Athanasian Creed, 124, 125, 144
Athenae Cantabrigienses, 54n.
Athenae Oxonienses, 268n.
Audley, Thomas, 48, 221
Augsburg, 20
Authorized Primer (see also Primer of Henry VIII), 183, 187, 203, 240, 246, 253, 255, 262, 264-267, 274, 284, 290
Ave Maria, 8, 32, 35, 44, 63, 83, 87n., 89, 94, 123, 143n., 178, 186, 206, 226, 242, 252, 253, 257, 259, 262, 283

Baldwin, T. W., 7n., 251n., 274n.
Bale, John, 27, 30n., 176
Balliol College, 154n.
Bankes, Richard, 120n., 195, 215, 222, 223
Barnes, Robert, 23, 201
Basille, Theodore (pseud.), 223n.
Basle, 62n.
Bayfield, Richard, 14, 16
Beads, Bidding of, 143, 154, 156, 157, 172, 203, 218, 251
Beatitudes, 83, 265
Beaton, David, cardinal, 128
Beckenth, Balthassar (pseud.), 25
Beckett, Thomas, archbishop, 168, 169, 172, 174
Becon, Thomas, 223n., 237, 245n.
Benedictus (Luke 1: 68-79), 43, 45n., 99, 114, 177, 289
Berthelet, Thomas, 120n., 169, 181-183, 220, 241n., 244, 245, 247, 249n., 250, 251, 273
Betbüchlein (Luther), 24n., 33n., 61, 63, 260, 280, 282-284
Beuchame, Lewis (pseud.), 225n.
Bible, English:
  Coverdale (1535), 2, 41, 46, 86, 117, 118, 138, 140, 143n., 149, 150, 152, 153, 175-177, 188, 193, 204, 238, 292-303
    (1537), 140, 181, 186, 188, 219, 228n.
  Geneva (1560), 164, 275
  Great (1539), 73, 164-166, 168, 180-182, 187, 192, 193, 207, 219, 221, 224, 225,

329

Bible, English *(Continued)*
  Great *(Continued)*
    227, 228n., 233, 235-237, 241, 252,
     263, 267, 273, 292-298
    (1540, Berthelet), 183, 220, 292,
     298n., 301, 302
    (1540-41, Cranmer), 201, 232, 261,
     262, 268, 273
    (1540-41, Tunstall and Heath),
     168, 221, 232
    King James (Authorized), 30n., 109,
     153, 161, 193, 265, 271, 275, 288n.,
     291-303
    Matthew (1537), 73, 140, 143n., 156,
     165, 181, 187, 196-198, 292, 297
    Taverner (1539), 181, 182, 195, 197,
     262, 292, 297n., 300n., 301-303
    Wycliffite (Forshall and Madden, ed.),
     5, 84, 101, 102, 138, 152, 153, 291-303
  Bible, German (Luther, 1534), 49
  Bible, Latin (Vulgate), 37, 68, 79, 86, 134,
   138, 153, 188, 220, 238, 261
  Bibliographical Description of Tyndale's
   New Testaments (Fry), 109n.
  Bibliothèque Nationale, Paris, 87
  Birchenough, Edwyn C., 87n., 148, 173n.,
   178n.
  "Bishops' Book" (see also *Institution*),
   140n., 174, 241, 244
  "Bishop Tunstall and the English *Hor-*
   tulus," 50n.
  Blairs (St. Mary's), 219n.
  Blunt, J. H., 228n.
  Bodleian Library, Oxford, 52, 54, 60n.,
   74, 121, 129-131, 204, 283
  Boleyn, Anne, Queen, 47-49, 51, 52, 54-
   56, 104, 118, 121, 123, 143, 157, 163
  Bonham, William, 120n., 235
  Bonner, Edmund, bishop, 62, 190, 223,
   234
  Book of Common Prayer (1549), 2, 32,
   39n., 93, 228, 246-248, 265, 274, 275
  Book of Hours, 2-4, 9, 93, 271
   Editions: (1477) Caxton, 3
    (1494) deWorde, 6, 219; (1503), 125;
     (1513), 6, 89n.
    (1514) Byrckman, 6; Pynson, 6
    (1523) deWorde, 8, 9, 89, 292, 301-
     303; Kaetz, 8, 9, 89, 292, 301-303
    (1527) Regnault, 9
    (1531) Endhoven, 141, 170; Regnault,
     171
    (1532) Kerver, 89
    (1533) Wyer, 122

Book of Hours *(Continued)*
  Editions *(Continued)*
   (c. 1533) *Enchiridion*, 200n.
   (1534) Regnault, 71, 72
   (c. 1541) Mayler, 226
   (1544) Petyt, 251; (1545), 256n.
Book of Prayers Called the Ordinary
  Fashion, 240
Book Prices Current (1919), 119n.
Books of Solomon (*see* Solomon)
Boston Public Library, 52, 60n., 283n.
Boulogne, 250, 251, 254
Bourman, Nicholas, 212-214, 230
Brief Dialogue between Father and Son
  (1527), 112n.
British Museum, 20, 50, 72, 100n., 170n.,
  173n., 202n., 208n., 251
Browne, Sir Thomas, 197
Brunfels, Otto, 37, 38, 79, 81, 86, 138,
  231, 272, 280
Bucer, Martin, 18, 19, 30, 39, 40, 77n.,
  196
Bullinger, Heinrich, 176
Burnet, Gilbert, 62n., 234n.
Burton, Edward, 106n., 111, 140n., 191n.
Butterworth, Charles C., 19n., 41n., 52n.,
  227n., 253n., 261n., 265n.
Byddell, John, 52, 53, 59, 61, 66, 73, 74,
  79, 83, 84, 95, 104, 105, 113, 116, 136,
  141-143, 149, 154-158, 160-164, 167,
  182, 192, 193, 195, 196n., 216, 217,
  223, 226, 235n., 243, 273
Byrom, H. J., 189n.

Calais, 117
Calendar, Saints', 3, 9, 11, 13, 22-24, 28,
  29, 50-52, 60, 61, 74, 88, 106, 107, 122,
  132, 141, 150, 156, 157, 163, 167-169,
  173, 174, 184, 191, 204, 208, 209, 213,
  220, 259, 260
Cambridge, Eng., 19, 93, 196, 230, 233,
  281
Cambridge University Library, 20n., 74n.,
  100n., 121, 131
Campensis, Johannes, 199
Candlemas Day, 212, 214
Canterbury, 232, 245, 246
Canterbury Tales, 3, 4, 168, 242
Capito, Wolfgang, 196, 199, 270, 272
Catechism, 7, 32, 35, 60, 65, 76, 213, 253,
  274
Catherine of Aragon, Queen, 47, 48, 51,
  118, 270

Catholic (Roman) influence, 10, 49, 139, 170, 171, 183, 274

Caxton, William, 1, 3, 6, 52n., 127, 219

Century of English Book Trade (Duff), 120n., 152n., 177n.

Certain Prayers and Godly Meditations (1538), 177

Chapin Library, 80n.

"Charity, Rule of," 128, 172, 218

Charles V, Emperor, 245, 250

Charterhouse, 56

Chaucer, Geoffrey, 3, 4, 186n., 242, 285n.

Chelmsford, 202

Christ-cross, 7, 122

Church of England, 2, 32, 48, 70, 71, 106, 110, 149, 155, 157, 164, 179, 183, 197, 246, 274, 275, 285

Clarendon, Constitutions of (1408), 5, 58

Coke, John, 25, 26n., 27

Colet, John, 7, 8, 89, 121

Collects:
  Against pestilence, 93, 94, 174
  For peace, 93, 229, 264
  For *Placebo*, 266
  For Seven Psalms, 265
  For true faith, 211, 229
  Sunday after Easter, 228
  Thanksgiving, 211, 231

Commendations, 22, 45, 60, 64, 77, 88n., 97, 100, 103, 113, 146, 186, 216, 259, 268, 273, 289

Common Places (Hamilton), 79n., 128, 172

Common Places of Scripture (Sarcerius), 196

Complete History of Translations of the Bible (Lewis), 96n.

Compline, 2, 5, 22, 40, 43, 45, 60, 64, 77, 88n., 145, 186, 204-206, 210, 211, 230, 259, 265, 286-288

Concilia Magnae Britanniae (Wilkins), 13n., 15, 70n., 143

Concordance of the New Testament (1535), 156

Confession, General, 3, 22, 36, 37, 60, 61, 76, 95, 121, 123, 271

Confession of the Faith of the Germans, 196n.

Confutation of Tyndale's Answer (More), 12, 23

Consolation for Troubled Consciences, 83, 177

Constantine, Emperor, 57

Convocation of Canterbury, 48, 49, 65, 70, 72, 119, 132, 143, 144, 162, 175, 221, 226, 233

Copland, Robert, 120n., 170, 216, 218, 219

Copland, William, 127n.

Cotton, Henry, 176n.

Coverdale, Myles, 34, 41, 66, 86, 117, 118, 126, 138, 140, 152, 153, 164-166, 168, 176, 187, 188, 198, 199, 201, 220, 228n., 239, 261, 272, 273

Cox, J. E. (ed.), 264n.

Cox, Leonard, 66

Cranmer, Thomas, archbishop, 39, 47-49, 72, 110, 133, 140, 141, 182, 188, 189, 201, 221, 222, 224, 232, 233, 237, 241, 242, 245-248, 253, 258, 264-266, 269, 272, 285

Creed, 3, 7, 32, 35, 56, 63, 74, 75, 82, 83, 87n., 89, 142, 143, 174, 177, 178, 184, 226, 242, 252, 253, 257, 281, 283

Crocus, Cornelius, 80

Cromwell, Thomas, 26n., 47-51, 56-58, 70, 118, 140, 141, 143, 154, 164-166, 168, 169, 180-185, 188-191, 194, 196, 197, 200-203, 207, 214-216, 221, 222, 273

Croydon, 189

Dacre, Lord (*see* Fiennes)

Dalaber, Anthony, 281

Dasent, J. R., 243n.

Dassett, John, 70

Deanesly, Margaret, 5n.

Defence of Peace, 56

Defence of the Marriage of Priests (see also *Very Godly*), 225n.

Devout Prayers in English (c. 1531), 282

Dialogue (More), 11, 12

Dialogue between Gentleman and Ploughman, 14

Dialogue for Children (*see also* Catechism), 22, 32, 35, 36, 65, 76, 111, 122, 213

Dibdin, Thomas, 55n., 120

Dictionary of National Biography, 56, 96n., 196n.

Dirge, 3, 5, 9, 17, 20, 23, 45, 60, 88n., 93, 96-101, 103, 104, 108-110, 112-115, 122, 134, 137, 138, 147, 148, 155, 184-188, 204, 211-213, 216, 254, 259, 261, 266, 267, 273, 288, 289

Divers Fruitful Gatherings (Frith), 79n., 127

Douce collection, 121n., 129, 131, 204-206, 287

Duff, E. Gordon, 120n., 152n., 172n., 177n.

Early English Printed Books in University Library Cambridge, 116n.
"Early Primers for the Use of Children," 178n., 227n., 253n.
Early Tudor Drama, 53n., 120n.
Ecclesiastical History (Foxe), 12, 14, 15, 182, 223
Ecclesiastical Memorials (Strype), 50n.
Editions of the Bible and Parts Thereof, 176n.
Education of Chaucer, 4n., 82n., 285n.
Edward VI, 75, 141, 143, 157, 163, 203, 218, 222n., 232, 244, 251, 252, 254, 256, 274
Elizabeth, Queen, 54, 55, 118, 143, 164, 250, 251, 274, 275
Elizabeth of York, Queen, 71
Emmanuel College, Cambridge, 154n., 178
Enchiridion Piarum Precationum, 24n., 33n., 80, 109n., 280-285
Endhoven, Christopher van, 21, 119, 141, 152n., 170, 177n.; Widow of, 121n., 129n.
English and Scottish Printing Types, 120n.
Epistles and Gospels, Editions:
    (1537), 141, 149-163, 171, 174
    (1538), 172, 173, 175, 192, 212n., 289
    (1539), 192, 193
    (1540), 204, 205, 208, 212-215
    (1541-45), 225, 230, 234, 235, 268
Epistles and Gospels with a Brief Postil (1540), 215
"Epistles" from Old Testament (see also Epistles and Gospels), 42, 72, 141, 150
Epitome of the Psalms (Taverner), 194-199, 231, 238, 245n., 270, 271, 273
Erasmus, Desiderius, 7, 56, 80, 105, 163, 164, 196n., 223, 231, 235, 269n., 271, 272
Evensong, 2, 22, 39, 40, 43, 64, 77, 88n., 96, 99, 115, 145, 185, 206, 209, 216, 265, 288
Examination of William Thorpe, 12n.
Exhortation unto Prayer (see also Litany and Suffrages), 247
"Exposition on the Seventh Chapter of I Corinthians" (1529), 13n.

Exposition upon Matthew v-vii (Tyndale), 292, 301-303
Exposition upon Psalm 51 (see also Savonarola), 53, 60n., 66-69, 73, 74, 80, 83, 95, 98, 111, 121, 129, 130, 135, 147, 149n., 235, 273, 292-300
Exposition upon the Magnificat (1538), 177

Felinus, Aretius (pseud.; see also Bucer), 18, 19, 67, 91, 92, 94, 96, 133-135, 227
Ferguson, F. S., 129n.
Ferrara, 66, 80, 130
Fiennes, Thomas, 225
Fifteen Gradual Psalms, 22n., 96, 134, 186-188, 211, 216, 260, 288
"Fifteen O's," 6, 88n., 106, 127, 146, 204, 211, 218, 269
Fish, Simon, 13n., 16
Fisher, H. A. L., 169n.
Fisher, John, bishop, 11, 12n., 48, 52, 118, 183
Florence, 66
Flower of the Commandments (1510), 89n.
Foedera (Rymer), 233n., 246
Folger Shakespeare Library, 200n., 208n., 213, 214, 230, 240, 280, 282n.
Fons Vitae, 78
Fountain of Life, 73n., 78, 292, 293, 299-303
Fox, Edward, bishop, 117, 140
Foxe, Francis (pseud.), 18, 21
Foxe, John, 11, 12, 14-19, 21, 24, 120n., 182, 282
France, War with, 244, 245, 249
Francis I, King, 250
Fratris Hieronymi Ferrariensis Expositiones, 66n.
Frere, W. H., and Kennedy, W. M., 162
Friedmann, Paul, 55
Frith, John, 13n., 16, 26, 79n., 127-129
"Fruitful Instruction for Children," 22, 32, 34, 35, 64, 76
"Fruitful Remembrance of Christ's Passion," 64, 128, 129, 279
Fruitful Treatise of Baptism (Joye), 225n.
Fry, Francis, 109n.
Furnivall, F. J., 16n.

Gairdner, James, 26n.
"Garden of the Soul" (see also Hortulus Animae), 16, 21, 61, 62

Gardiner, R. B., 7n.
Gardiner, Stephen, bishop, 201, 221, 222, 224, 225, 232, 237, 241, 242, 245, 246
Garrard, Thomas, 281
Gau, John, 282, 283
"Genesis" (Tyndale, 1530), 18; (1534), 49
Gerson, John, 171
Gifford, George, 70
"Gift of Constantine" (1534), 56, 57, 78n.
Godfray, Thomas, 73-79, 95, 105, 129, 130, 167, 181, 213, 227, 234n.
"Godly Prayers" (c. 1528), 24, 282
Golden Legend (Caxton, 1483), 52n.
Gonville Hall, Cambridge, 196
Goodly Primer (see Primer, English, 1535)
Gospels and Epistles (Grafton, 1540; see also Epistles), 214
Gough, John, 119-130, 210, 219, 222-224, 230
Gower, John, 242
Graces, 32-34, 64, 122, 179, 184, 191, 211, 227, 253, 254, 259, 260, 273, 284
Grafton, Richard, 156, 165, 166, 168, 169, 182, 202, 207-212, 214, 220-224, 228n., 229, 231, 235, 237-239, 243, 246, 247, 250, 254-257, 261, 270, 272, 274
Gray, William, 222
Growte, John, 172
Gybson, Thomas, 156, 165, 176, 181, 199

Haghen, Godfried van der, 73, 129n.
Hailes Abbey, 54
Hain, Ludwig, 20n., 62n.
Hamilton, Patrick, 127, 129
Hamlet, 94, 186n.
"Haustafel," 109n., 284
Heath, Nicholas, bishop, 168, 190, 221, 241
Henry II, 168
Henry VII, 71
Henry VIII (see also under Primer), 13, 47, 48, 52-54, 65, 72, 105, 118, 157, 163, 164, 168, 169, 184, 186, 187, 196, 197, 215, 217, 218, 221, 222, 224-226, 233, 240, 243-246, 247n., 249-253, 256-258, 270, 271, 274
—— and Cranmer, 47, 201, 232, 233, 245, 246, 253, 264
—— and Cromwell, 47, 164, 183, 190, 200, 203
—— and his Queens, 47, 48, 52, 55, 104, 121, 123, 141, 143, 157, 194, 200, 201, 203, 232, 244, 245, 251, 253, 270
—— and religion, 48, 49, 57, 70, 72, 119, 155, 163, 164, 167, 179, 183, 221, 226, 240, 241, 244, 258, 272
——, Reign of, 47, 103, 138, 183, 202, 233, 236, 239, 246, 259, 262, 270, 279
Henry VIII and the Reformation, 244n.
Herbert, William, 212
Hereford, Use of, 151
Heretical books, 10, 11, 13-16, 18, 23, 50, 62, 70, 72, 120, 167, 213, 223, 234, 242
Herford, John, 213, 214, 230
Hester, Andrew, 190-192
Hill, Nicholas, 220n.
Hill, William, 26
Hilsey, John, bishop (see also Manual), 183-191, 203-207, 209, 211-213, 217, 225n., 226n., 230, 248, 254, 262, 266, 267, 273, 284, 287
Historia Supplicii Domini Iesu, 30
History of England from Henry VII to Henry VIII, 169n.
History of the Reformation (Burnet), 62n., 234n.
Hitton, Sir Thomas, 11-14, 17, 23, 24, 28, 39, 47, 60
Hollybush, John, 152n., 161, 165, 177
Hoochstraten, Johannes, 11, 12n., 18, 21, 177
Hope, Constantin (see also Hopf), 30n., 77n.
Hopf, C., 19n., 279
Horae (see Book of Hours)
Horae Beatae Mariae Virginis (Hoskins), 6n., 8n., 20n., 30n., 119n., 126
Hortulus Animae, Dutch (see Ortulus)
English (see also Garden and Ortulus), 15n., 16, 17, 19-28, 32-45, 47, 51, 52, 59-61, 64, 65, 71, 74, 76, 77, 81, 85, 94, 95, 97-99, 105, 107, 109, 113, 116, 124, 135, 175, 209, 216, 218, 282, 284, 288, 289, 292, 293, 301-303
German (see Seelenwurzgarten)
Latin, 20, 62, 81
Hoskins, Edgar, 6, 20n., 87n., 105n., 126, 172n., 208, 215, 274n.
Hours, Saying of, 2, 132, 145
"How Early Could English Scripture Be Printed in England?" 52n.
Howard, Katherine, Queen, 201, 222, 232
Howard, Thomas (see also Norfolk), 183
Hugh of Lincoln, 3
Huntington Library, 237, 239n.

Hymns, 43, 77
"God be in my head," 6, 9
"Governor of triple engine," 217
"Now the cheerful day," 263
"O blessed Christ," 286, 287
"Patris sapientia," 202
"Praised be God," 107
"Veni Creator," 133

Illinois, University of, 226
Illustrium Scriptorum Summarium (Bale), 27, 30n., 176
Image of Love (Gough), 120
Incidents in Lives of Poyntz and Grafton, 222n.
Injunctions, Bishops': Bonner, 234; Lee, 162; Shaxton, 162; Voysey, 162
—— to Clergy: (1536), 119, 142, 143; (1538), 165, 169, 181, 182, 202, 224; (1545), 256-259
Inquisition, The, 117, 165
Institution of a Christian Man, 140, 292, 301-303
Institutum Christiani Hominis (1510), 7, 251
Introduction of the Eight Parts of Speech, 251, 252
Invitatory Psalm, 39, 94, 135, 206, 217, 262, 273
Isaac, F. S., 120n.
Isleworth, 54

Jeremy the Prophet (Joye), 49, 164, 176
"Jesus' Matins," 121, 125, 126, 289n.
Ioannes Coleti Theologi . . . Editio (1527), 8n.
"John Wayland—Printer," etc. (Byrom), 189n.
Journal of Theological Studies (Oxford), 30n., 77n., 279
Joye, George, 19, 21-27, 29, 32, 34-38, 42, 44, 49, 50, 52, 57, 60, 64, 72, 77, 85, 93, 96, 116, 117, 145, 154, 159-161, 164, 179, 201, 225, 272, 273
His work as translator (see also *Hortulus*), 16n., 19, 21, 24-27, 30-37, 39-46, 61, 63-66, 72, 73n., 76, 77, 81, 88, 94-99, 107, 113, 116, 126, 134-136, 141, 151, 156, 159, 160, 164, 176, 186, 192, 198, 209, 210, 216, 227, 228, 234n., 240, 261, 262, 273

Kaetz, Pieter, 8, 89
Kele, Richard, 216, 240, 243, 254

Keyser, Marten de, 18, 21, 25, 78-80, 82, 280, 282, 284
Kingdon, J. A., 207n., 222n., 254n.
"King's Book" (see also *Necessary Doctrine*), 244
"King's Psalms" (see also *Psalms or Prayers*), 250
Kiry, Walter, 15
Kleiner Katechismus (Luther), 33n., 109n., 281, 284
Kronenberg, M. E., 129n., 177n.
Kurze Form der Zehn Geboten (Luther), 280, 283, 285

Lacombe, P., 87n.
Lady Day, 12, 174
Lambeth Palace, 13n., 16n., 20n., 30n., 80n., 195, 212
Lancaster, Thomas, 223
Langham (Essex), 53
Lant, Richard, 226, 227, 243
Latimer, Hugh, bishop, 22, 25-27, 75
Latimer, William, 54, 55
Lauds, 2, 43, 94, 95, 99, 185, 202n., 210, 263, 264, 288
Lee, Edward, archbishop, 162
LeRoux, Nicholas, 131, 171, 172
Letters and Papers of Henry VIII, 16n., 25n., 26n., 50n., 53n., 55n., 58n., 59n., 70n., 117n., 166n., 189n.
Letters of John Ashwell (Joye), 19n.
Lewis, John, 96n.
Leyden, 20n.
Library Chronicle (Univ. of Penna.), 50n., 52n., 144n., 235n.
Library, The (Bibliographical Society), 18n., 20n., 74n., 80n., 83n., 87n., 117n., 148n., 173n., 177n., 189n.
Life of Anne Boleyn (Sergeant), 55n.
Lily, William, 7, 251
Lincoln Cathedral, 199n.
List of Early Printed Books in Lambeth Palace Library, 195n.
Litany, 3, 5, 16, 17, 23, 45, 60, 75, 88n., 92, 93, 104, 108-111, 121, 124, 155, 157, 163, 168, 174, 185, 191, 204, 211, 216, 217, 246-248, 251, 259, 265, 266
Litany and Suffrages (Cranmer), 110, 247-249, 265, 273, 285
Literary Lineage of King James Bible, 19n., 41n., 52n., 60n., 261n., 265n.
Littlehales, Henry, 4n., 5, 93n., 100, 101
Livres d'Heures (Lacombe), 87n.
Lobley, Michael, 190-192

Loci Communes (see also *Common Places*), 128
Lollard Bible (Deanesly), 5n.
Lollard sources, 83, 100, 123, 152
Lome, Geoffrey, 281
London, John, 281
Lord's Prayer (*see also* Paternoster), 8, 32, 62-64, 75, 76, 80, 83, 89, 122, 123, 146, 174, 175, 178, 187, 195n., 218, 226, 235, 251n., 252, 253, 259, 260, 283, 285, 289, 291, 301-303
Louvain, University of, 199
Lufft, Johannes, 18, 280
Luther, Martin, 20, 34, 38, 59-64, 67, 71, 79, 83, 108, 109, 128, 186, 196, 234, 272, 279-285
Lutheran influence, 10, 33, 36, 43, 49, 59, 61-63, 67, 69, 75, 76, 80, 83, 108, 129, 196, 201, 232, 279, 282, 284, 285
Luttrell, Narcissus, 21

Magnificat (Luke 1:46-55), 44, 45n., 99, 114, 115, 177, 198, 265, 273, 289
Maidstone (Kent), 11
Maitland, S. R., 195n.
Maldon, William, 202, 203
Malmö (Sweden), 282
"Manner to Live Well," 170, 171, 173, 218
Manual of Prayers (Hilsey):
    (1539) English, 190-192, 205, 212, 213, 217; English-Latin, 183-191, 204-209, 211, 212, 214, 225n., 248, 255, 259, 264, 266, 268, 284, 286-290; For children, 190, 191, 292, 298n.
    (1540) Fragment, 203, 209n. (*See also under* Primer.)
Marburg, 18, 177
Marchant, Jean le, 172
Marler, Anthony, 224, 233, 237
Marshall, William (*see also under* Primer), 28n., 52-62, 64-67, 73-77, 78n., 93-95, 97, 99, 104-117, 122, 128, 129, 134-136, 145, 154, 160, 175, 186, 188, 209, 210, 213, 216, 226n., 234, 240, 279, 282-285
Marsilius of Padua, 57
Martin Bucer and the English Reformation, 19n.
Mary (Tudor), Queen, 2, 139, 251, 274, 275
Maskell, William, 4n., 100n.
Mass, Celebration of, 88n., 103, 178n., 185, 204, 211, 213, 223, 246

Matins, 2, 5, 9, 32, 38-43, 60, 64, 76, 77, 87n., 88n., 92-95, 97, 98, 107, 109, 121, 123, 125, 135, 145, 146, 148, 175, 184-186, 188, 191, 205, 206, 209, 210, 212, 216, 217, 230, 259, 260, 262, 263, 272, 288
"Matins and Evensong," etc. (*see* Primer, 1529), 16, 21
Mayhew, John, 281
Mayler, John, 190-193, 203-207, 210, 211, 214, 223, 224, 226, 243, 286, 287
McKerrow, R. B., and Ferguson, F. S., 127n., 176n.
Meditation on Psalm 31 (see also Savonarola), 80, 84, 121, 129n., 130, 163, 172, 235
Mekins, Richard, 225
Melanchthon, Philip, 118, 222
Middleton, William, 240, 243
Milton, John, 197
Mirror of Our Lady (1530), 292, 301-303
Miscellaneous Writings of Thomas Cranmer, 264n.
Mitchell, A. F. (ed.), 282n.
Monumenta Ritualia (Maskell), 4n., 100n.
More, Sir Thomas, 7, 11-14, 17, 22-24, 27, 34, 35, 45, 48, 118, 183
Morgan Library, 80, 82, 83, 171
Mozley, J. F., 26n., 81n., 96n., 117n., 176n., 199n., 281

Necessary Doctrine for Any Christian, 244
Nederlandsche Bibliographie, 20n., 129n.
New Learning, 215, 245
New Policy of War (Becon), 245n.
New Testament, English, editions:
    (1525) Fragment, St. Matthew, 8, 32, 292, 301-303
    (1526) Tyndale, 10, 14, 15, 30, 32, 34, 42-44, 89, 90, 99, 114, 115, 142, 150, 153, 160, 179, 193, 204, 212n., 265
    (1534) Joye, 49, 160; Tyndale, 42, 49, 72, 89, 90, 115, 141, 150, 151, 153, 156, 158, 160, 268, 292, 302, 303
    (1535) Joye, 42, 72, 117, 141, 151, 159, 214; Tyndale, 73, 109, 151, 198, 226n., 284
    (1536) Tyndale, 119, 156, 181; (1538), 165, 181
    (1539) Great Bible, 192, 202, 235; (1540), 202; (1546), 237
    English-Latin: (1538) Coverdale, 161,

New Testament *(Continued)*
165, 168, 181, 292, 301, 302; Tyndale, 165, 181
New York Public Library, 172*n.*, 176*n.*
Newcastle (Eng.), 50, 51
Nicolson, James, 140, 152*n.*, 165, 177, 181, 182, 186, 188, 219, 228*n.*
Nijhoff, W., and Kronenberg, M. E., 20*n.*, 129*n.*
Norfolk, Duke of, 183, 201, 221
Northampton (Eng.), 70
"Notes on English Books Printed Abroad," 112*n.*
"Notes on English Printing in the Low Countries," 18*n.*, 177*n.*
Nunc Dimittis (Luke 2:29-32), 43, 177, 289

Obedience of a Christian Man, 13*n.*, 14
Of the Old God and the New, 59, 116*n.*
"Office of All Estates," 108, 123, 144, 184, 186, 188, 226*n.*, 284, 289
Opera (Luther), Jena ed., 279, 280; Wittenberg ed., 279, 280, 283
Orarium seu Libellus (Authorized ed.), 256*n.*
Orationale Paradisus Animae, 62*n.*
Order or Train of War (Gough), 120*n.*
Ordinal (Cranmer, 1549), 133
Ortulus Anime (Dutch), 20*n.*
(English: see also *Hortulus*), 16, 20, 21, 28, 35, 50, 52, 273
Oxford, 5, 196, 233

Papers (American Bibliographical Society), 178*n.*, 227*n.*
Parable of the Wicked Mammon, 13*n.*, 14
"Paradise of the Soul," 61, 62*n.*, 219; (1536 ed.), 121, 126-128, 172
Paraphrasis upon All the Psalms, 199
Paris, 6, 9, 20, 145, 164, 165, 170, 171, 173, 182; University of, 131, 171
Parliament, 48, 50, 51, 107, 165, 183, 241
Parr, Catharine, Queen, 244, 245, 250, 251, 254
Parvus Catechismus pro pueris (1529), 33*n.*
Passion according to St. John, 87*n.*, 90, 123, 184, 187, 259, 268, 269, 273
"Passion of Our Saviour" (Joye), 22, 29-31, 64, 76, 111
Patent, royal (*see also* Privilege), 105, 163, 189, 216, 233, 237, 246

Paternoster (*see also* Lord's Prayer), 3, 8, 9, 32, 35, 62, 63, 74, 75, 83, 87*n.*, 90, 142, 143, 156, 174, 177, 178, 226, 235, 242, 257, 281
"Pater Noster in English" (booklet):
(1535), 82, 292, 302, 303
(1537), 142, 143, 226, 235*n.*, 292, 301
(1538), 143*n.*
(1539), 143*n.*, 218
"Pater Noster Spoken of the Sinner," 129, 130
Paul's Cross (London), 16
Pedersen, Christiern, 282
Pennsylvania, University of, 50*n.*, 52*n.*, 144*n.*, 235*n.*
Pentateuch (Tyndale, 1530), 36, 109, 188
Persecution, paragraph on, 84, 108
Peterhouse, Cambridge, 19
Petyt, Thomas, 120*n.*, 178, 183, 220, 225, 234, 240, 243, 247, 250, 256*n.*, 273
Pfortzheim, printer, 62*n.*
Philoponon, Johannes (pseud.), 177
Piae Precationes (see also *Enchiridion*), 24, 281
Piers Plowman, 75
"Pilgrimage of Grace," 119, 140
Placebo, 266, 288
Plimpton, G. A., 4*n.*, 82*n.*, 285*n.*
Political, Religious, and Love Poems, 16*n.*
Pollard, A. W., 6*n.*, 166*n.*, 202*n.*
Popes (*see also* Rome):
Clement VII, 47-49, 57
Paul III, 48
Sixtus IV, 71
Sylvester, 57, 107
Portiforium (or Portans), 246, 247
Powell, William, 253, 254
Practice of Prelates (Tyndale), 11, 47
Pratensis, Felix, 96*n.*
Prayer and Complaint of the Plowman, 12*n.*, 23
Prayers: Acts IV, 199, 270
At hour of death, 231, 235, 271
At uprising, 269
Conditor coeli, 108, 133
Daniel, 37*n.*, 65, 71
Desire of life to come, 271
For a sweet and still heart, 231
For Bible readers, 235
For men entering battle, 249, 250
For trust in God, 269
Hannah, 37*n.*, 65, 77, 175
Hezekiah, 99, 112, 113, 137, 267, 273

Prayers *(Continued)*
  Isaiah, 24-27, 37, 65, 71, 77, 85, 116, 218
  Jonah, 37, 65, 116, 149, 175, 238
  Manasses, 290
  Mollifying of hard hearts, 65
  O bone Iesu, 88n., 103, 108, 271, 273
  Solomon, 86, 88, 103, 114, 125, 133, 148, 177, 198, 240, 270
Prayers of Holy Fathers (Grafton), 237-239, 245n., 270
Prayers of the Bible (Redman), 79-86, 88, 90, 91, 95, 96, 100, 108, 114, 125, 130, 133, 137, 138, 148, 149, 151, 175, 177, 198, 218, 230, 231, 237-239, 273, 292, 294n., 296n., 299n., 301-303
Prayers or Meditations (Parr), 250
Precationes aliquot novae (Erasmus), 269, 270
Precationes Biblicae (Brunfels):
  (1528), 37, 38, 79, 231
  (1531), 79, 80, 82, 83, 86, 280, 282-285
Precationes Christiani (Capito), 195
Preces et Meditationes generales (Vives), 269
Prefaces in the Primers, 61, 62, 74, 90, 106, 134, 144, 145, 155, 170, 173, 174, 185, 234, 258, 259, 281-283
Prime, 2, 3, 77, 121, 205, 264
Primers *(see also* Book of Hours, *Hortulus,* and *Manual):*
  Manuscript (English), 4, 5, 9, 82, 87, 93, 100, 101
  Marshall, 56, 116, 135, 139, 149, 164, 206, 209, 216, 234, 263, 279, 288, 289
  Rouen, 165, 169-171, 173, 180, 215, 216, 218, 231, 265, 267
  Sarum *(see also* Use of,), 28, 39, 45, 88, 92, 95, 104, 109, 135, 154, 186, 187, 200, 204, 209, 260-264, 269, 272, 288, 289
  Editions (English): Lost ed., (c. 1529), 11-17, 21-24, 26, 27, 37-39
    Marshall (1534), 28n., 50-55, 59-66, 70, 71, 73-75, 77, 82, 83, 90, 91, 94-100, 104, 106, 107, 111, 113-115, 128, 133, 136, 217, 279, 280, 282-285, 288n., 292, 300n., 302, 303
    Godfray (c. 1535), 73-78, 82, 95, 105, 122-124, 215, 217, 284, 285, 292, 303n.
    "Goodly" (1535), 104-116, 122-124, 133, 136, 138, 140n., 141, 145, 155, 157, 163, 208-211, 216, 217, 234, 247,

Primers *(Continued)*
  Editions (Continued)
    271, 279, 284, 288n., 289; (1538), 105n., 162, 163, 280
    Rouen (1538), 170, 171
    Bourman (1540), 212-214
    Hoskins No. 150 (c. 1540), 215-219
    Kele (1543), 216, 217, 218n., 240, 254, 292, 295, 296, 298n.
    Grafton (fragment, c. 1544), 254
    Henry VIII *(see also* Authorized), 247, 253, 256-274, 288, 289, 292-300
    Edward VI (1547), 274; Mary (1555), 274; Elizabeth (1559), 274
    For children (c. 1557), 178n.
    (English-Latin): Redman (1535), 86-103, 108, 110-116, 119, 122-125, 127, 131-139, 144, 148, 209, 219, 247, 273, 289, 292, 293, 296, 299n., 300, 301
    Gough (1536), 119, 121-129, 131, 144, 172, 179, 208-210, 217, 218, 254, 284, 289n., 292, 293n., 297n., 299, 300
    Hoskins No. 117* (c. 1536), 119n.
    Rouen (1536), 131-139, 141, 144-149, 170, 173, 219, 235, 261, 273, 286, 292-300
    Byddell (1537), 105n., 141, 150, 154-157, 160-163, 192
    Redman (1537), 141, 142, 144-153, 159, 162, 170-172, 174, 175, 177, 185, 215, 217, 218, 234, 250, 261, 263, 265, 268, 273, 287, 292, 294-296, 297n., 298, 300-303; (1538), 162, 174, 175, 186-188, 193, 212, 226, 230, 287, 289, 292, 300n., 301-303
    Rouen (1538), 169-173, 205, 286, 287
    Grafton (1540), 207-211, 229, 254, 292, 300n.
    Mayler (1540), 203-208, 210, 286, 287
    Hoskins No. 153 (c. 1540), 213, 214
    Toye (c. 1541), 230, 231; (1542), 234
    Hoskins No. 156 (c. 1541), 230, 231
    Petyt (1541), 225, 226; (1542), 234; (1543), 240; (1544), 250
    Henry VIII, 257, 261, 269
  (Latin editions; *see* Book of Hours)
"Printers of the Coverdale Bible," 117n.
Printers . . . of Westminster and London (Duff), 120n., 172n.
Privilege, royal *(see also* Patent), 53, 54, 71, 73, 80, 82, 84, 88, 104, 105, 121,

141, 163, 167, 177, 189, 190, 195, 207, 225n., 239, 246, 254, 256, 257
Privy Council, 167, 221-225, 242, 243
Proclamations, royal: (1529), 15; (1530), 14, 282; (1535?), 145; (1538), 167-169, 173, 177, 181, 190; (1541), 224, 232-234; (1543), 245
Profitable Treatise of Reckoning (Gough) 120n.
Prologues in Primers (*see also* Prefaces), 155, 156, 184, 185, 191, 195, 196
Prophet Isaiah (Joye), 25-27, 46, 99, 100, 113, 114, 137, 160
Prophet Jonas (Tyndale), 37, 75n.
Protestant Princes of Germany, 164, 200
Proverbs of Solomon (Joye), 73n.
"Prymer in English" (Birchenough), 87n., 148
Prymer or Lay Folks Prayer Book (1895), 4n., 100n.
Prymer or Prayer-Book of Lay People (1891), 4n., 5, 93n., 100-102
Psalms of the Passion, 22, 45, 59, 60, 64, 77, 88n., 97, 103, 121, 146, 186, 216, 218, 259, 260, 262, 268, 289
Psalms or Prayers Taken out of Holy Scripture (1544), 249
Psalter, English: "Psalter of David" (Joye, 1530), 14-16, 18-21, 23, 30, 31, 33, 34, 38-41, 45, 59, 64, 67, 77, 91, 94, 96n., 97, 98, 100, 103, 112, 113, 125, 135, 136, 210, 227, 234n., 292-300; (c. 1534), 73n., 112, 227; (c. 1541), 227, 228
    "David's Psalter" (Joye, 1534), 49, 53, 81, 84, 91, 96-98, 103, 112, 133-136, 138, 148, 210, 261, 292-300
    English-Latin (1540), 220, 261-263, 292-300
    Latin (Bucer, 1529), 19, 39, 67
Public Record Office, 53n., 55
"Publick Instrument" (1530), 13, 22
Purser, Dick, 34, 179
Pynson, Richard, 6, 15, 79, 84, 120n.

"Queens Prayers" (see *Prayers or Meditations*), 250
Quentin, John, 171, 218

Rastell, John, 120
Records of the English Bible, 166n., 202n.
Redman, John, 214, 222
Redman, Robert (*see also under* Primers), 73, 79-88, 90-101, 105, 107, 108, 110,

112-116, 120, 127, 133, 135-138, 141, 142, 143n., 145, 148, 149, 154, 157-160, 162, 165, 167, 174-176, 181, 183, 186-188, 196, 198, 204, 209, 214, 218-220, 222, 223, 225, 230, 231, 238-240, 247, 250, 273, 282, 285
Reed, A. W., 53n., 120n.
Reformation, The, 10, 49, 56, 104, 128, 210, 280
Regensburg, 221, 232
Regius, Urbanus, 282
Regnault, François, 9, 71, 131, 165-171, 173, 182, 272
"Regulation of the Book Trade Before 1538," 53n.
Relic Sunday, 29, 150n., 151
Repertorium Bibliographicum (Hain), 20n.
Repse, William, bishop, 225n.
Reu, M., 7n.
"Revelation of Antichrist" (Frith), 13n.
Reversed '4', 77, 78, 181n.
Revival of Learning, 105
Richard Grafton, Citizen and Grocer, 207n., 254n.
Richmond (Eng.), 54, 55
Ridley, Lancelot, 176
Right Way to the Kingdom of Heaven, 282, 283
"Robert Redman's *Prayers of the Byble*," (Butterworth), 80n., 85n.
Robin Hood, 75, 112
Rogers, John, 140
Rome, Bishop of (*see also* Popes), 48, 107, 132, 143, 155, 171, 186, 196, 248
Rouen (*see also* Primers), 131, 165, 171, 172
Roy, William, 13n., 16, 112n.
Rupp, E. G., 112n., 244n.
Ruremond, Hans van, 152n., 177n.
Rylands Library, Manchester, 235n., 282
Rymer, Thomas, 233n.

St. Albans, 213
St. Andrew's Day, 212
St. Anne, 60, 217
St. Augustine, 187, 267
St. Bartholomew's Day, 229
St. Bernardine, 271
St. Bridget, 6, 62, 106, 127
St. Chrysostom, 266
St. Cuthburga, 88
St. Jerome, 185; Psalter of, 88n., 98, 103, 121, 135, 146, 148, 186, 289n., 292

St. John the Baptist, 29, 50-52, 61, 88, 153
St. John's College, Cambridge, 93, 100n.
St. Katherine, 151, 208, 209, 217
St. Margaret, 151, 217
St. Martin's Day, 158, 159
St. Matthias, 23, 28
St. Nicholas' Day, 158, 159
St. Paul's Cathedral, 7, 215, 219
St. Paul's School, 7
St. Thomas of Canterbury (see also Becket), 29, 168, 169, 173-175
St. Ursula's Day, 152
Saints, Veneration of, 29, 90, 144, 210, 217, 264
Salisbury, Countess of, 225; Use of (see also Sarum), 39, 87, 103, 104, 121, 171, 230, 272
Salve Regina, 44, 45n., 88n., 92, 106, 177, 205, 206, 210, 230, 286
Salve Rex, 22, 45, 177, 205, 218, 230
Sarcerius, Erasmus, 196
Sarum, Use of (see also under Primers), 3-6, 39, 94, 109, 131, 139, 151, 154, 155, 166, 170, 171, 186, 204-206, 210, 216, 217, 225, 230, 234, 240, 246, 247, 256n., 259, 264, 266, 268, 286, 287
Savonarola, Girolamo, 53, 66, 67, 69, 80, 84, 121, 130; Expositions of (see also Exposition), 131, 132, 149, 172, 173, 204, 205, 225, 230, 285, 286
"Savonarola's Expositions" (Butterworth), 74n., 149n., 163n.
Sawtry, James (pseud.), 225n.
Sayle, C. E., 116n.
Seelenwurzgarten, 20
Selah, 136
Selden collection, 204-206, 286, 287
Sergeant, P. W., 55n.
Sermons, Luther's, 63, 64, 279, 280, 283
Seven Deadly Sins, 82, 83, 100, 123, 180
Seven Penitential Psalms, 3, 9, 14, 20, 22, 23, 45, 60, 64, 77, 88n., 97, 98, 110, 113, 121, 124, 135, 147, 185-188, 211, 216, 253, 259, 260, 265, 272, 288
Seymour, Jane, Queen, 118, 141
Shakespeare Jahrbuch, 8n., 251n.
Shaxton, Nicholas, bishop, 162
Sheppard, L. A., 20n., 117n.
Short-title Catalogue (cited also as S.T.C.), 6n., 9, 15, 20, 116, 178, 282
Signs, Printers' shop:
  Bible, 211
  Blue Garland, 184, 190

Signs (Continued)
  Maiden's Head, 178, 225, 240
  Mermaid, 120
  Our Lady of Pity, 53, 59, 60n., 66
  Rose Garland, 219
  St. George, 84, 88, 149, 176, 240
  St. Michael, 190-192
  Sun, 53, 59, 104, 155, 182, 195
  White Bear, 191, 192, 205
  White Hart, 195
  White Horse, 190-192
Sion Middlesex, 54
Six Articles, 183, 185, 201, 222-224, 241
Smith, H. M., 244n.
Smith, Thomas, 222
Smithfield, 128
Solomon, Books of, 219, 220, 228n.
Sotheby & Co., 119n.
"Statuta" (Colet), 7
Steele, Robert, 15, 112n., 168n.
Sternhold and Hopkins (Psalms), 275
Stokesley, John, bishop, 14, 15n., 16, 17, 19-21, 25, 189, 190, 234, 282
Stories and Prophecies of Holy Scripture (1536), 292, 293, 295, 296, 298-300
"Story of the Passion and Resurrection," (Hope), 30n.
Strassburg, 18-20, 25, 57, 79, 112n., 196
Strype, John, 50n.
Studies in Making of English Protestant Tradition (Rupp), 112n., 244n.
Subversion of More's Foundation (Joye), 35
Sum of the Holy Scripture, 13n., 14, 15
Sum or Pith of the 150 Psalms (Taverner), 195, 196, 235n.
Supplication for the Beggars, 13n.
Swinnerton, Thomas, 66

Taverner, Richard, 145, 181, 194-199, 215, 223, 228, 231, 235, 238, 239, 262, 268, 270, 272
Ten Articles, 119, 241
Ten Commandments, 3, 6, 32, 35, 36, 62, 63, 68, 74, 75, 79n., 82, 87n., 89, 122, 123, 132, 142-144, 174, 177, 179, 184, 187, 188, 218, 226, 252, 253, 257, 260, 281, 283, 289
"The Term 'Lord's Prayer' Instead of 'Pater Noster'," 144n.
Tessaradecas Consolatoria (Luther), 83n.
"Testament of Moses," 81, 239
Thirlby, Thomas, bishop, 241

Three Primers Put Forth in the Reign of Henry VIII, 28n., 106n., 111, 140n., 191n.

"Three Verities" (Gerson), 171

Tillotson, William, 239

Title-page Borders in England and Scotland (McKerrow and Ferguson), 127n., 176n.

Toye, Robert, 230, 235, 273

Transactions of the Bibliographical Society, 15n., 53n., 112n.

Treatise of Pictures and Images (Marshall), 57, 58, 78n.

Tudor and Stuart Proclamations (ed. Steele), 15, 168n.

Tudor Books of Private Devotion (White), 245n., 249n., 261n., 269n.

Tunstall, Cuthbert, bishop, 13, 16, 50-52, 74, 120, 168, 221, 281

Turk, The Great, 245

Turner, William, 66

Tyndale, William, 5, 8, 11, 12, 16, 18, 19, 23, 24, 26, 37, 42, 47, 49, 72, 75n., 105, 108, 116, 119, 128, 140, 150, 158, 161, 241, 242, 272, 273, 284

His work as translator (*see also* New Testament), 30-32, 34, 36, 37, 42-44, 64, 72, 78, 82, 89, 90, 99, 108, 109, 115, 118, 140, 141, 150, 151, 153, 156-160, 176, 186, 193, 198, 212n., 226n., 265

Typographical Antiquities (Dibdin), 55n., 120n.

University Microfilms, Inc., 60n.

Urbana, Ill., 7n., 251n.

Venice, 66n.

Very Godly Defense of Marriage of Priests (Joye), 225n.

Vienna, 112n.

Vigorous, John, 53, 54

Vilvorde, 118

Virgin Mary, "Our Lady" (*see also* Ave Maria), 2, 4, 5, 9, 20, 39, 44, 60, 63, 71, 88n., 93, 107, 108, 133, 174, 177, 210, 230, 262-265, 271

Visitation Articles and Injunctions, 143n., 162

Vives, Juan Luis, 269, 271, 272

Voysey, John, bishop, 162

Vulgate (*see* Bible, Latin)

Warham, William, archbishop, 11, 12n., 13, 48

Wayland, John, 184, 189-192, 203-205, 207, 214

"Weekdays Moralized," 141, 174, 215

Werke (Luther), Weimar ed., 67n., 83n., 279, 280, 283-285

Westminster, 246

Whitchurch, Edward, 156, 165, 182, 202, 207, 211, 220, 221, 223, 224, 227, 228n., 229, 231, 234n., 237, 239, 243, 246, 250, 255, 257, 274

White, Helen C., 245n., 249n., 261n., 269n., 274n.

White, John, 220n.

Wilkins, David, 13n., 15, 70n., 143

William Shakspere's Petty School, 7n., 251n., 274n.

William Tyndale (Mozley), 26n., 117n.

Williams College, Mass., 80n.

Wilson, Lea, 176n.

Windsor, 245

Wittenberg, 67, 279, 280, 285

Wolf, Adolf, 112n.

Wolsey, Thomas, cardinal, 13, 19, 47, 56, 120, 196, 281

Wood, Anthony à, 268n.

Worde, Wynkyn de, 1, 6, 8, 59, 89, 120, 219, 251n., 272

Wyatt, Sir Thomas, 243

Wycliffe, John, 4, 5, 9, 126, 153, 175

Wyer, Robert, 120n., 122

Wyly, John, 15

Zwingli, Huldreich, 96n.

Date Due